The Animal Estate

The Animal Estate

THE ENGLISH AND OTHER CREATURES IN THE VICTORIAN AGE

Harriet Ritvo

HARVARD UNIVERSITY PRESS
CAMBRIDGE, MASSACHUSETTS

Publication of this book has been aided by a grant from the
Andrew W. Mellon Foundation.

Library of Congress Cataloging-in-Publication Data

Ritvo, Harriet, 1946-
The animal estate.

Bibliography: p.
Includes index.
1. Domestic animals—England—History—19th century.
2. Domestic animals—Social aspects—England—
History—19th century. 3. Human-animal relationships—
England—History—19th century. 4. Animals, Treatment of—
England—History—19th century. 5. England—Social life and customs—19th century. I. Title.
SF53. R58   1987   636'.00941   87-11848
ISBN 0-674-03706-5 (cloth)
ISBN 0-674-03707-3 (paper)

For my mother and my father

Acknowledgments

While writing this book, I have incurred many debts. I am especially grateful to the colleagues who read the manuscript at various points, offering valuable correction and encouragement. Jonathan Arac, William I. Bennett, Rosemarie Bodenheimer, Harold J. Hanham, Ruth Arnon Hanham, Sarah Blaffer Hrdy, Katherine Keenum, James G. Paradis, and David Roberts helped me in this way. My research assistant Michele Lee sifted energetically through many volumes of popular Victorian periodicals and occasionally urged me to hurry up and finish. Many other people have been willing to listen to my concerns about the animal estate. I have benefited greatly from the informal suggestions of members of the Stanford Humanities Center, the Humanities Department of the Massachusetts Institute of Technology, and the Northeast Victorian Studies Association. Finally, I would like to thank my friends Karen and Eric Caines and Andrew and Jennifer Warren for their warm and generous hospitality, which made several protracted research trips to England very pleasant.

I appreciate the assistance offered by the librarians and archivists at the following institutions: Widener Library, the Museum of Comparative Zoology, Countway Library, and Houghton Library, of Harvard University; the British Library; the British Art Center, Beinecke Library, and Sterling Library, of Yale University; the Massachusetts Institute of Technology; Stanford University; the Library of Congress; the Boston

Athenaeum; the Rothamsted Experimental Station; the Bodleian Library; the Zoological Society of London; the Bristol Zoo; Chetham's Library; the Kennel Club; the Tyne and Wear Archives Department; the County Record Offices of Bedfordshire, Devon, Lancashire, and Merseyside; the British Museum (Natural History); the Victoria and Albert Museum; the Liverpool Record Office; the Manchester Central Library; and the Institute of Agricultural History and Museum of English Rural Life. To June Blackburn and Olive Martyn of the Royal Society for the Prevention of Cruelty to Animals I owe special thanks for their interest in my project and their willingness to help at long distance as well as when I was on the spot. I am grateful to the Institute of Agricultural History and Museum of English Rural Life, the Bedfordshire County Record Office, the Rt Hon. the Lady Lucas, the Zoological Society of London, the Rt Hon. the Earl of Derby, the Royal Society for the Prevention of Cruelty to Animals, the British Library Board, and the City of Manchester Leisure Services Committee for permission to quote from manuscript material in their possession.

My research and writing was expedited by several grants that provided funds for travel and for time off. A fellowship from the Stanford Humanities Center enabled me to devote 1985–86 to completing and revising the manuscript; one from the Massachusetts Institute of Technology's Old Dominion Fund supported research in England in 1982; and one from the Yale Center for British Art allowed me to spend a month using its Rare Book Collection and Photographic Archive.

My greatest debt is to Stephen Botein, who died unexpectedly last summer. We discussed this project at every stage, and without his wisdom and his love it would have been a poorer work.

Contents

I know people often wonder whether it is worth while to spend so much time and energy in watching the ways of wild birds while there are so many urgent problems of human sociology to be solved. I am convinced it is . . . But even if this were not so, and if I myself could not see any use in watching gulls, I am afraid I would not leave them alone. Blood is thicker than water.

Niko Tinbergen, *The Herring Gull's World*

INTRODUCTION

The Nature of the Beast

When in 1679 a London woman swung at Tyburn for bestiality, her canine partner in crime suffered the same punishment on the same grounds. King James I ordered a bear that had killed a child to be baited to death, and rural shepherds frequently hanged dogs caught worrying their flocks. *The Merchant of Venice* included a reference to "a wolf, hanged for human slaughter" sufficiently cursory to suggest that Shakespeare's audience recognized animals as appropriate participants in formal judicial proceedings. The idea that they might also respond to persuasion or threats underlay the efforts of rat-rhymers who adjured rodents, sometimes aloud and sometimes in writing, to leave premises in which they had become too numerous. And the earliest recorded laws in Britain implicitly invested animals with human rights and responsibilities. The wergild of Germanic jurisprudence extended to all members of the household, which included domestic animals as well as women and serfs. In the absence of human witnesses to a burglary, dogs, cats, and cocks were permitted, under the same code, to testify in court—or at least their presence in court was considered to strengthen the aggrieved householder's complaint.[1]

By the nineteenth century British authorities had stopped sentencing animals[2] to suffer and die for their crimes, and the practice of rat-rhyming had retreated to the Celtic fringes. Near the end of the Victorian period Edward Payson Evans celebrated this change as evidence of the incipient triumph of "refined and humanitarian modern conceptions of justice" over "gross and brutal medieval conceptions," which were illustrated by the numerous executions and excommunications he described in *The Criminal Prosecution and Capital Punishment of Animals*. Half a century later Arthur Koestler used this point of view as the foundation of his argument against the capital punishment of humans. He characterized the execution of a sow in medieval France as self-evidently barbaric and ludicrous, and asked, "Why do we find the hanging of an animal even more revolting and disgusting than the hanging of a human being?"[3] Much as the abolition of such spectacles might have indicated a general improvement in moral sensibility, however, the advent of self-consciously enlightened humanitarianism also had a reverse side. As animals were released from the burden of guilt for witchcraft, homicide, sodomy, and other crimes, a sense of independence and power that had been implicit in the ability to intentionally transgress was also withdrawn.

Nineteenth-century English law viewed animals simply as the property of human owners, only trivially different from less mobile goods. It followed that they were no longer held morally accountable for their actions; instead, the people who encountered or owned them were responsible for assessing the danger they might pose to person or property, and acting accordingly. Thus, a plaintiff who attempted to recover damages after a nursing cat bit first her dog and then her hand was told that she should have been aware "that cats rearing kittens are inclined to be savage and in a vicious state, even if gentle otherwise" and therefore have maintained her distance; conversely, a farmer who kept an unusually aggressive ram "well knowing that it was prone and accustomed to attack, butt and injure mankind," was held liable for injuries suffered by a plaintiff who had assumed that the animal possessed an ordinary ovine temperament. In the latter case it was the farmer who had to make compensation with his money, rather than the ram with his blood.[4]

The circumscription of the legal role of animals reflected a fundamental shift in the relationship between humans and their fellow creatures, as a result of which people systematically appropriated power they had previously attributed to animals, and animals became significant primarily as the objects of human manipulation. This change occurred between the early eighteenth century and the late nineteenth century (although, as Keith Thomas has demonstrated in *Man and the Natural World*, some of its manifestations had medieval roots), and it was in large part the consequence of the new methods of acquiring and applying knowledge associated with the Enlightenment. At the beginning of this period people perceived themselves to be at the mercy of natural forces; at the end, science and engineering had begun to make much of nature more vulnerable to human control. By means of either synecdoche or metaphor animals could represent the power of nature, and thus as it became less threatening, so did they. On the pragmatic level advances in such fields as stockbreeding, veterinary science, and weapons technology made actual animals easier to manage. Nowhere were these developments more striking than in England.

Once nature ceased to be a constant antagonist, it could be viewed with affection and even, as the scales tipped to the human side, with nostalgia. Thus sentimental attachment to both individual pets and the lower creation in general—a stock attribute of the Victorians—became widespread in the first half of the nineteenth century. These developments were echoed in literature and art, where a highly ordered aesthetic was replaced by one that valued irregularity and lack of restraint. Wildness became attractive rather than ugly; wild animals, like the peasants and exotic foreigners with whom they were increasingly classed, might evoke sympathy rather than scorn.

Because both emotional and analytic associations tended to blur the distinction between at least some people and the rest of the animate creation, discourse about animals in eighteenth- and nineteenth-century England also expressed many human concerns linked only tenuously to the natural world. Such associations represent a widespread rhetorical practice, which the Victorians exploited with special vigor. Animals had been integrated into many facets of English life, and as a result interactions with animals often reflected traditional understandings and deeply held convictions. Examining these interactions can clarify underlying and seldom-stated assumptions of English society, or it can identify areas of unexpressed tension. For example, when nineteenth-century dog breeders commented, as they did at great length, on the difficulty of persuading a prized bitch to mate with the male they had selected and only that male, their remarks were loaded with assumptions about the sexual proclivities of human females. By implication, they linked a problem of management in the kennel to one of management in the home. The very categories into which animals were divided often signaled important distinctions and oppositions. Why, for example, were the whippets raced by miners perceived as different from the greyhounds raced by more genteel sportsmen in nineteenth-century England? How was it that a stray cat, worth almost nothing, could be instantly transformed into a valuable show animal in the early days of cat fancying? Why did the English congratulate themselves upon the extermination of ferocious wild beasts within their island, but flock to see imported specimens? The answers to such questions illuminate the history not only of the relations between people and other species, but also of relations among human groups.

The following chapters explore the role of animals (more precisely, of the mammals with which people interacted most frequently and identified most readily) in nineteenth-century English culture, with excursions backward where appropriate. They present interpretations based primarily on texts produced by people who dealt with real animals—the records of organizations concerned with breeding, veterinary medicine, agriculture, natural history, and the like; the papers of individuals active in such pursuits; and the books, pamphlets, and periodicals produced for these specialized audiences. Canonical art and literature have provided only occasional corroborative examples; the large literature of animal fable and fantasy, which has little connection to real creatures, none at all. Even thus restricted, however, the animal-related discourse of nineteenth-century England was both enormous and diverse. It described a wide range of interactions, which might be inspired by primary motives as disparate as sentiment (petkeeping), economics (animal husbandry), and curiosity (natural history). Within a single animal species these disparate relationships often engaged both animals and people of many different sorts. There were, for example, few apparent overlaps between the interest of a fox hunter in a hound pack and that of a humane society constable in illicit fighting dogs or that of a show breeder in champion pugs.

This diversity was structured in several ways. Although no single pattern determined all human-animal relationships in nineteenth-century England, neither were they random or chaotic. They were, to begin with, limited by physical determinants: the zoological givens and the pragmatic ends imposed by people. In addition, they were conditioned by a limited set of metaphors or images. Each of the four major sections of this study illustrates one such trope. The discourse of popular zoology discussed in this introduction presented a moral hierarchy in the animal kingdom based on the hierarchy of orders in human society; the discourses of cattle breeding and dog showing analyzed in Part I corroborated human claims to superior status; the discourses of humanitarianism and disease control reviewed in Part II expressed anxiety about the maintenance of social discipline; and the discourses of zoo keeping and hunting examined in Part III justified and celebrated Britain's imperial enterprise.

Thus schematized, these discussions of quite different human-animal interactions seem to share at least a general concern about human society. They were more profoundly linked by the way they dealt with their ostensible subjects. The constraints imposed by the animals' biological nature and the practical purposes to which their owners dedicated them turned out to be not very restrictive of human understanding or interpretation. Even the interactions apparently most tightly structured by economics or anatomy, such as the treatment of disease or the production of meat for market, were often influenced by apparently unrelated social concerns. As material animals were at the complete disposal of human beings, so rhetorical animals offered unusual opportunities for manipulation; their positions in the physical world and in the universe of discourse were mutually reinforcing. Their ubiquity made animals particularly available to the Victorians, either in the flesh or as something to talk about. They figured prominently in the experience even of city dwellers. The streets were full of cabhorses and carthorses; flocks of sheep and herds of cattle were driven to market once or twice a week; many urbanites raised pigs and chickens in crowded tenements, or bred a variety of pets, from pigeons to rabbits to fighting dogs. Although these creatures might be strong in the muscular sense, they were also manifestly powerless, as were bulls in rural fields, lions in menageries, and even the dangerous game stalked by hunters on the African plains or in the Indian hills. And in the rhetorical sphere they were less potent still. If the power of discourse lies in its inevitable restructuring and re-creation of reality, the ability of human beings to offer counterinterpretations places inevitable limits on the exercise of that power. Animals, however, never talk back.

The many separate animal-related discourses[5] of nineteenth-century England constituted a single larger unit, which both discussed and exemplified a central theme of domination and exploitation. Animals were uniquely suitable subjects for a rhetoric that both celebrated human power and extended its sway, especially because they concealed this theme at the same time that they expressed it. The animal concerns discussed in the following chapters were by no means trivial or merely metaphorical; people were extremely interested in prize shorthorns and captive hippopotamuses and rabid dogs. Talking about them offered people who would have been reluctant or unable to avow a project of domination directly a way to enact it obliquely. This double function strongly suggests why animals figured so frequently and so prominently in the imaginative life of the most enthusiastically exploitative culture of the nineteenth century; perhaps it also suggests why they and the activities and institutions generated around them have been consistently neglected by subsequent scholars.

Animal Avocations

If animals symbolized a range of primarily human concerns, they also inspired a great deal of discourse about their physical and behavioral characteristics, their place in the natural order, and their relationship to people. Among the most influential mediators of such information and analysis was Thomas Bewick, who had become a renowned engraver of animals by the beginning of the nineteenth century. He grew up near the Tyneside village of Eltringham, where his father was the tenant of both a farm and a small coal mine. Bewick received about four years of formal education from a local clergyman; in addition, his curiosity about the surrounding countryside led him to read as much as he could about natural history. Most of the literature available to him, however, seemed lacking in one way or another. The illustrations in what was already in the 1760s a hardy perennial, Thomas Boreman's *Description of Three Hundred Animals*, particularly displeased him. He later asserted that "even at that time" he thought he could depict animals "much better than those in that Book." When Bewick was fourteen, his artistic bent prompted his father to apprentice him to Ralph Beilby, an engraver in nearby Newcastle. Although most of the work at Beilby's shop (as later at Bewick's, when he was his own master) consisted of advertisements, business cards, and similar routine commissions, during his apprenticeship Bewick also began to illustrate books written by others.[6] Finally, in

1790, he ventured an independent literary project, one grounded in the reading and observations of his rural childhood.

A General History of Quadrupeds, a popular illustrated encyclopedia of the furred creation, was an immediate success. Bewick was surprised by what he delightedly called the "glut of praises" that greeted his volume; in addition to more conventional appreciations, one enthusiast published a celebratory poem. The initial edition of sixteen hundred copies sold out rapidly, leaving an unsatisfied demand, attested by Bewick's letters to importunate would-be purchasers, that necessitated a second edition of eighteen hundred in 1791. Nor did this impression glut the market; the growing demand for popular natural history prompted Bewick to issue eight editions of *A General History* during his lifetime, as well as several separate editions of the illustrations without the text.[7] Although naturalists eventually turned to other popularizers for more up-to-date information, Bewick's works on quadrupeds and birds continued to attract book and art collectors. Bewick catalogs were published in 1830, 1851, and 1866; the durability of his appeal was evidenced in the latest of these, which described an 1865 auction at which "prices were given . . . which would have astounded collectors a short time before."[8]

The volume that triggered such intense and enduring appreciation was rather modest. Within approximately five hundred pages it offered entries ranging in length from a few sentences to many pages on what purported to be the entire range of known quadrupeds (a term frequently used in the eighteenth and nineteenth centuries by or for those who found that the term "mammals," as another zoological popularizer put it, "sounds too pedantically to be agreeable to good taste").[9] Almost every entry was illustrated by one of Bewick's appealing woodcuts. The kind of information included varied widely from creature to creature; among the possibilities were appearance, geographical range, habitat, diet, tastiness, temperament, utility, and history of contact with human beings. Thus the entry on the American elk or moose stressed its size and, secondarily, other features that made it attractive to hunters, such as its energy and strength; while that on the African wild boar concentrated on its evil disposition, calling it "vicious," "dangerous," and inclined to "vengeance."[10]

Although the distinguished geologist William Buckland flattered the hometown crowd when, during a speech delivered to a Newcastle audience in 1838, he credited Bewick with a major contribution to "the progress of natural history," made at a time when it was "unknown as a popular science but only to a few profound individuals," much of Bewick's success can be attributed to his successful exploitation of a well-established genre.[11] As he acknowledged in the prospectus for *A General History*, which was circulated in 1788 by more than a dozen booksellers in Newcastle and other northern towns, not only natural history in general, but the particular branch he proposed to address (mammalian zoology), had already inspired so many popular texts that to add to their number "may seem at first View both presumptuous and unnecessary." But Bewick went on to decry a gap in this literature between "voluminous Works," the expense of which confined them "chiefly to the Libraries of the Wealthy," and "smaller Publications" (like Boreman's *Three Hundred Animals*) so "mean and pitiful" as to "disgust every Reader of Common Observation."[12] He asserted that *A General History of Quadrupeds* would fill this gap by making information previously restricted to the privileged available to anyone with the will to read it.

By the middle of the eighteenth century, as a result of both European exploration of remote parts of the world and the patient efforts of investigators at home, knowledge about nature was accumulating rapidly. Not only had natural history emerged as a prestigious Enlightenment scientific discipline, it was also quickly becoming a fashionable amateur avocation.[13] In 1749 Louis LeClerc (later the Comte de Buffon) published the first volume of his massive *Histoire naturelle*, and natural history was for a time the rage of Paris. English translations of his work were soon produced, and their mere numbers suggest that they found a ready market. (There were at least six explicitly attributed to Buffon, mostly multivolume editions during the eighteenth century, as well as an indeterminable number of tacit derivations, of which Oliver Goldsmith's eight-volume *History of the Earth and Animated Nature*, 1774, was probably the most successful; this kind of extended unacknowledged borrowing was to remain characteristic of the literature of popular natural history.) The expansion in the number of natural history titles published annually gives some index of the growth in popular demand: from 1730 to 1749 all English publishers combined issued an average of two natural history books per year, a figure which quadrupled for the last two decades of the eighteenth century and multiplied many times afterward.[14] A more impressionistic indicator was offered in 1800 by George

Shaw, who prefaced a multivolume effort with the lament that "the general history of Quadrupeds has been so often detailed ... that a fresh publication on the subject must of necessity labour under peculiar disadvantages."[15]

The consumers of this literature made a diverse group, reflecting the eighteenth-century expansion of the audience for recreational reading throughout the middle classes and beyond their borders. Although book buying was restricted to the relatively prosperous, many more readers had access to books through the clubs and noncirculating libraries that spread throughout Britain toward the end of the eighteenth century. By 1821 it was estimated that there were sixty-five hundred such institutions, serving over thirty thousand families at annual fees between half a guinea and two guineas.[16] This audience included the wealthy and the humble, men and women, adults and children, the formally educated and autodidacts. Its miscellaneous composition made it both tempting and difficult to exploit with precision. Occasionally publishers effectively targeted a portion of the natural history market—luxuriously produced and illustrated works like Mark Catesby's *Natural History of Carolina* (1731–1743) could be purchased only by persons of means—but more often they hit or missed randomly. The distinction between works for juvenile and mature readers was particularly unclear. Frequently the size of the volume offered the only clue: although their contents might be nearly identical, books intended for children were usually smaller than those produced for adults. Bewick's *General History of Quadrupeds* exemplified this ambiguity; he conceived it for a youthful readership and was surprised to find it "so singularly noticed by such numbers of people grown up to maturity."[17]

Difficult as it might have been to define and subdivide, the popular market so effectively exploited by Bewick continued to expand. By the 1820s it was large enough to support the first booksellers specializing in natural history and to encourage several publishers to risk elaborate and sustained projects.[18] William Jardine launched the forty-volume *Naturalist's Library* in 1833; before the series concluded a decade later the standard edition size had been fixed at an impressive four thousand copies. Particularly successful volumes could sell twice as many, despite competition from imitators, such as the *Miscellany of Natural History*, which siphoned off a share of the market.[19] Equally optimistic were the publishers who founded monthly or bimonthly magazines of popular natural history, which transmitted the discoveries announced in the ponderous technical journals of learned societies to the audience of enthusiastic amateurs. At least seven such periodicals appeared between 1828 and 1834.[20] In 1844 Edward Newman celebrated the "unequivocal success" enjoyed by his yearling magazine, *The Zoologist: A Popular Miscellany of Natural History;* he continued to give his readers triumphant reports on circulation, noting several years later that "the average monthly sale of 1846 has exceeded, by more than one hundred, the average monthly sale of 1845," with a fourfold increase in Manchester alone.[21]

The enthusiastic patronage of a variety of natural history exhibitions from the middle of the eighteenth century onward confirmed contemporary publishers' and authors' sense of the size of their potential market. When in the 1760s Sir Hans Sloane's private collection became the nucleus of the British Museum, open to the public without admission fees, it attracted ten thousand visitors annually, many of whom, the museum officers complained, were "the lower kind of people." As the East India Company extended its influence through the subcontinent, the London headquarters accumulated samples of the natural productions of the territories under its sway. The collection drew the curious even before it was officially constituted as the India Museum in 1801; thereafter attendance grew steadily, averaging fifteen thousand to twenty thousand visitors per year by the middle of the nineteenth century.[22] In addition, the citizens of most substantial towns flocked to a constantly changing selection of live animal exhibits, from freaks like the "double cow" shown in London in 1748—a monstrosity with the leg, udder, and partial digestive system of a second cow growing from its back—to exotic imports. Thus in 1788, while working on the woodcuts for *A General History,* Thomas Bewick was able to view living models of the porcupine, the polar bear, the tiger, the lion, and a variety of monkeys without leaving Newcastle.[23]

An Ordered Creation

The audiences for zoological displays and popular zoological literature shared a fascination that was based on the intrinsic appeal of the creatures themselves. The richly miscellaneous detail with which works of popular zoology were crammed testified to what writers apparently perceived as their readers' rather indiscriminate curiosity about animals. In addition to offering such engaging general information as that the flesh of the capybara (a large South American rodent), though "fat and tender . . . has an oily and fishy taste," zoological popularizers occasionally went so far as to describe individual animals. Thus William Wood discussed not only the behavior and appearance of the hyena as a species, but also those of two tame captives that he had observed at London's Tower Menagerie in 1792.[24] The inherent attractions of zoology were considered sufficiently powerful to seduce both children and adults away from bad habits and to confirm them in good ones. In 1730 the author of the first children's natural history book published in English claimed that his volume would automatically "introduce Children into a Habit of Reading" because its contents would "Entertain" them and "engage their Attention"; more than a century later the naturalist Philip Gosse commended his subject for "inculcating many virtues and graces in a very pleasing manner."[25]

Animals appealed as subjects of human activity as well as objects of human curiosity. Many naturalists were attracted by the simple desire to participate, personally or vicariously, in an exciting exercise of human prowess. Natural history was often described as a human struggle against the chaotic and unfathomable variety of nature. Pioneering naturalists were frequently genuine adventurers, braving the unknown dangers of uncharted territories in order to emerge with hard-won bits of new information. According to one early British resident at the Cape of Good Hope, "the majority of the travellers who penetrated the interior . . . were . . . enthusiastically . . . devoted to scientific pursuits."[26] And the rhetoric of challenge might also appeal to those whose encounters with nature were less risky. In 1862 the Literary and Philosophical Society of Liverpool described zoological field work as a contest in order to persuade merchant marine officers to contribute to the "furtherance of Zoology" on their voyages. The society stressed the excitement of matching wits with nature—"the field . . . naturalist . . . revels in the contemplation of the habits, manners, and instincts of created beings"—and the gratification of "captures," which might be useful observations or even evidence of whole new species.[27]

This physical struggle and appropriation emblemized a more abstract process of domination implicit in both popular zoology and the scientific work it reflected and distilled. Naturalists of the eighteenth and

nineteenth centuries did not simply collect facts; with at least equal
energy, they classified them. The central importance of taxonomy was
implicit in the language serious naturalists used to describe their endeavor. In the first *Encyclopedia Britannica*, published in 1771, the entire
entry on natural history was structured by an intricately embedded series of (sometimes newly) technical terms for taxonomical categories,
of which the most inclusive was "animal" itself, defined as any "organized body endowed with sensation."[28] What made a system good—its
inclusiveness and flexibility—was an index of the significance of the
taxonomic enterprise. As well as providing a means of retrieving information, classification systems offered increasingly powerful explanations or interpretations of the material they structured. And, at least in
principle, they had to accommodate unpredictable new information
with the same elegance that they accounted for everything known
when they were devised. Thus they embodied a sweeping human claim
to intellectual mastery of the natural world.

The power and novelty of this assertion of intellectual control contrasted strongly with the assumptions underlying traditional zoological
texts. The bestiaries that were the main written sources of information
about animals from the late classical period through the Renaissance
implicitly presented a world in which, far from having control over the
order of nature, people were at its mercy. At the beginning of the seventeenth century Edward Topsell repackaged this tradition for English
readers in his massive *History of Four-Footed Beastes*.[29] Its often implausible
content—inconsistent alike with common sense and common experience—underscored the difficulty of discriminating in principle between the likely and the impossible in the absence of a systematic
understanding of nature. Thus Topsell confidently described, on the
authority of ancient sages, the medicinal value of powdered unicorn
horns and the poisonous qualities of domestic cats' flesh.[30] The order in
which animals appeared in bestiaries also implicitly defined people as
passive receivers of random information, dependent on chance for their
knowledge of the natural world. Bestiaries often started with the lion,
which medieval iconography put at the head of animal creation (followed by the lioness, who usually got a separate entry, although the
males and females of most other species were described together), but
the rest of the animals followed according to no predictable rule. Bestiaries made no attempt to group animals that were physically similar,

such as the dog and the wolf, or the lion and the tiger; nor in arranging their contents did they employ the anthropocentric binary distinctions, such as edible-inedible, useful-useless, wild-tame, and beautiful-ugly, which they frequently invoked to organize discussions of specific kinds of animals.[31]

The perception that the natural world lacked a rational pattern was not confined to the pages of bestiaries. If Topsell's readers categorized animals at all, they did so only on the basis of their immediate impact on human experience. A seventeenth-century drawing manual divided beasts into "those more harde to bee drawne for their shape, and action," including the lion, horse, rhinoceros, unicorn, and stag, and those which, like the elephant, camel, bear, sheep and "all manner of rough and shagge haire Dogs," were "more easie."[32] Game animals were often grouped according to how they were hunted. In one venerable system beasts of the chase included the buck, doe, fox, roe, and marten; beasts for hunting included the hare, hart, wolf, and wild boar; and beasts that afforded "great dysporte" included the badger, wild cat, and otter. Game laws reflected these categories. For example, badgers, otters, and foxes were not protected under the Game Act of 1671, because their alleged predilection for chickens made them "vermin."[33]

In the course of the seventeenth century the need for a more analytic mode of classification became obvious to the empirically oriented investigators who were beginning to collect zoological information based on the evidence of their senses, rather than the accumulated wisdom of previous authorities. Their method of acquiring information reflected a new human assertiveness with regard to the natural world, and it required an equally self-confident taxonomy.[34] One was forthcoming from John Ray, the most distinguished English naturalist of the seventeenth century, whose works on plants, birds, and fish laid the foundations for a system of classification based on structural affinities; in the eighteenth century the taxonomic project was carried still further by such systematizers as Buffon and, preeminently, Linnaeus. The alternative proposals differed about particulars, but as far as popular natural history was concerned, the claim of human authority implicit in the notion of scientific taxonomy was more significant than the specific content of competing systems. Indeed, popular authors might feel free to choose their system on aesthetic or moral, rather than scientific, grounds. Writing early in the nineteenth century, William Wood admitted that his decision to be guided by Ray rather than Linnaeus in ordering his work would be scorned by "rigid naturalists"; but he hoped the nonspecialist reader would pardon him for "the repugnance we feel to place the monkey at the head of the brute creation, and thus to associate him with man."[35]

Bewick's *General History of Quadrupeds* illustrated the unstated argument embodied in systematic classification. The animals were not arranged at random, as in a bestiary, or according to such superficial criteria as alphabetical order, geographical distribution, or the ways people used them. Although Bewick, like most zoological popularizers of his time, did not go so far as to use technical Linnaean terminology, he followed Buffon in arranging the animals by "kinds," or groups united by apparent structural affinity. Thus the "ox kind" included the zebu and the buffalo as well as familiar domestic cattle, and the "hog kind," the peccary and the tapir. The ordering of kinds was similarly systematic, with the grazing and hoofed kinds (horses, oxen, sheep, goats, antelopes, deer, camels, pigs, and elephants) first, followed by the carnivores (cats, weasels, bears, hyenas, and dogs), then rabbits and rodents, and finally monkeys and other hard-to-classify creatures like seals, bats, and armadillos. With the possible exception of these final bits and pieces, Bewick presented the animal kingdom as rationally ordered and easily comprehensible, a perception that was itself strong evidence of the power of human intelligence.

Developed as an expression of human dominion over the natural world, systematic natural history could also express other hegemonic relationships. For some naturalists, the religious significance of their work outweighed its scientific value. To William Swainson, a prolific popularizer, the "great characteristic" of natural history was "its tendency to impress the mind with the truths of religion"; in the words of the compilers of one children's zoology book, no other subject "excites such proper sentiments of the being and attributes of God."[36] Religious insights were always connected with human preeminence and mastery. Natural history elaborated a hierarchical vision of creation, with humanity at the apex. The more naturalists discovered about exotic animals in distant places, the less they doubted that human dominance was divinely ordained. According to William Burchell, who traveled extensively in southern Africa during the early years of the nineteenth century, this point was best appreciated in "a country in a state of nature, where men and multitudes of wild beasts of every class, roam unrestrained . . . Can we view animals of immense bulk and strength, either flying from man, or submitting to his domination, without acknowledging at once that their timidity or submission forms a part of that wise plan, predetermined by the deity, for giving supreme power to him who is physically the weakest of all?"[37]

The creatures closest to humanity in the order of nature made these points most satisfactorily. From a simply practical perspective, quadrupeds were relatively easy to observe and to interact with. Unlike birds, fish, reptiles, and insects, they occupied more or less the same space as did people, and, as one pragmatic author pointed out, they "cannot easily avoid us." Furthermore, according to another popularizer, "the similitude between their structure and our own" made them both more interesting than and intrinsically superior to other animals.[38] This closeness could, however, also be disturbing. As Charles Hamilton Smith, the president of the Devon and Cornwall Natural History Society, frankly put it, "we find some startling us by forms and actions so much resembling our own, as to excite unpleasant comparisons; others, causing just apprehensions, from their evident powers of mischief." Swainson worried "that man . . . should . . . be exposed to innumerable injuries, and even certain death, from those beings which he was appointed to govern, would appear, at first sight, anomalous, and inconsistent with the fitness of things."[39] Its power to resolve such apparent anomalies gave zoology much of its appeal. One attribute guaranteed human ascendancy. As Smith explained, "endowed with the prerogative of reason, [the human being] is enabled to render all subservient to his wants, and is distinguished as a being intended for higher duties, and a more exalted destiny."[40]

Good Creatures

Like Bewick's *General History of Quadrupeds*, most works of popular zoology consisted of independent descriptions of one species after another. If their taxonomical structure confirmed the hegemonic relation of people to the rest of animate nature, a metaphor powerfully embedded in the language and content of the individual entries made a parallel point about the relations between human groups. The animal kingdom, with humanity in a divinely ordained position at its apex, represented, explained, and justified the hierarchical human social order. Because of the gap that separated people from animals, the metaphorical hierarchy remained incomplete; animals never exemplified the best human types. But the sense of human dignity that barred animals from realizing, even figuratively, the highest human possibilities made them particularly appropriate representatives of the less admired ranks and propensities. Embodying the lower classes as sheep and cattle validated the authority and responsibility exercised by their social superiors. Embodying the lower classes or alien groups as dangerous wild animals emphasized the need for their masters to exercise strict discipline and to defend against depredations. These identifications constantly informed the language used to describe the various animals, and they were implicit in the system of values that determined the moral judgment pronounced upon each beast.

Sometimes, especially when the comparison involved alien races, the identifications were made explicit. The dichotomy between domesticated animals and wild animals was frequently compared to that between civilized and savage human societies. Darwin speculated that the wildness often shown by hybrids of domestic species had the same cause as the wickedness that characterized human half-breeds.[41] According to Abraham Bartlett, the superintendent of the London Zoo for almost half a century, domestic animals exhibited superior social skills and self-control: "They live, as a rule, in harmony with each other, they can be trusted together, and may be regarded as a happy family."[42] (Although most Victorians would have agreed on the desirability of such qualities, there were a few dissenters, such as Darwin's cousin, the eugenicist Francis Galton, who connected the mediocrity of most people with the mindless gregariousness of herd animals.)[43]

Such comparisons could be more precise. Darwin cited a report that two Scotch collies who visited Siberia "soon took the same superior standing" with regard to the native dogs "as the European claims for himself in relation to the savage."[44] The statement that "the Old World contains . . . the animals which are distinguished as the most powerful and most perfect in their structure, those of the New having for the most part a character of organization which assigns them a lower rank in the scale of animated beings," could easily be applied to the American Indians.[45] In case the reader were too cautious to make such a leap himself, Bartlett completed a comparison of the bold and vigorous animals of Africa with their less impressive Asian equivalents by claiming that few Asiatic peoples "bear comparison with your restless, wandering determined Arab race."[46]

When animals stood for foreigners, the hierarchy of nature was apt to be presented in the stark, violent terms of conquest. It was, concluded Burchell after his explorations in southern Africa, "a succession of destruction" with "each animated object submitting to its superior, and all to man. In him terminates . . . this graduated tyranny."[47] But the standard metaphor underlying popular zoology was more restricted. Neither the authors of such works nor the members of their audience understood contemporary English society as a tyranny. It was, on the contrary, a carefully modulated and delicately balanced hierarchy, which might be threatened with social chaos and economic collapse if its members, especially its subordinate members, failed to recognize their places and do their jobs. Thus the animal kingdom (that standard phrase was itself part of the metaphor) was generally compared to the lesser ranks of a domestic commonwealth. Descriptions of individual animals routinely expressed subordination in terms of service. The best animals were those that displayed the qualities of an industrious, docile, and willing human servant; the worst not only declined to serve, but dared to challenge human supremacy.

The divine justification of domestication made it particularly attractive as a representation of human social relationships. It was generally agreed that animals had been created for humanity to use, whether or not any function had been discovered for them. As one sporting writer put it, "there are certainly an immense number of animals upon the face of the globe, whose uses are at present unknown to us; and to presume that they are useless would be a kind of blasphemy."[48] In fact, subordination to human purposes transfigured and elevated the animal itself. The very propensity to be domesticated was, according to one nineteenth-century naturalist, evidence that some animals were not "entirely devoid of reason"; another asserted that domestic animals could be considered "reclaimed from wildness."[49] Animals could also serve people in other ways, as sources of hides, horns, and other commercial products, or as playthings. But fully domesticated animals were the most useful, and their condition expressed the clearest acceptance of the hierarchy of nature. As one humanitarian cleric observed, "those whose services are most required, as if conscious that they were ordained to be subject to man's dominion, yield to it without reluctance."[50]

Therefore putting animals to work was at once doing God's will and demonstrating the highest human capacities.

For this reason, popular zoology books devoted a great deal of attention to the familiar domestic beasts that most persuasively represented an orderly social hierarchy, even though it might have been assumed that readers who chose to investigate natural history, rather than agricultural improvement or horse racing or the dog fancy, were most interested in more exotic creatures. In crude quantitative terms, Bewick allotted thirteen pages to the horse, fourteen to the ox, seventeen to the sheep, eleven to the goat, eleven to the hog, and thirty-nine to the dog. The only other animals to receive equivalent attention were the elephant, a beast of burden in India, and the squirrel, which, although not exactly domesticated, was often tamed and kept as a pet.[51] A generation later, The Naturalist's Library made a similar allotment of space in the thirteen volumes it devoted to quadrupeds. Only the synoptic volume attempted to give equal attention to each mammalian order. The remaining twelve volumes included two on dogs; one on horses; one on goats, sheep, and cattle; and one on British quadrupeds, which repeated much of the ground covered by the other four. (Additional volumes were devoted to monkeys, felines, deer and antelopes, elephants, whales, seals, and marsupials.) Reciprocally, popular natural history also neglected the British wild animals that had stubbornly refused to adapt to human desires. They constituted a relatively meager group by the late eighteenth century, including only the fox, the weasel and its relatives, the wild cat, the badger, the deer, the hedgehog, the bat, and a variety of small rodents—wolves, bears, beavers, and boars had been exterminated long since.

Described in terms that suggested human servants, domestic animals provided the standard by which other animals were to be judged. But some domestic animals offered better models of the relations between human superiors and inferiors than others. For this reason, the most appreciated domestic animals were not the sheep, "the most useful of the smaller quadrupeds," or even the ox (the term used generically for cattle) "whose services to mankind are greater than those of sheep, for . . . they are employed as beasts of draught and burden."[52] Occasionally these creatures might show some understanding of their special bond with people—for example, a sheep that sought human help when her lamb was in trouble, or a bull that showed gratitude to a man who saved him from lightning.[53] And it was pleasant (especially in contrast to "the savage monsters of the desert") "to contemplate an animal designed by providence for the peculiar benefit and advantage of mankind."[54] Nevertheless, sheep were simply "inoffensive and harmless" (if not practically inanimate, as Buffon had contended), and a professor of zoology at the University of London felt compelled to defend the ox from "the common charge of stupidity."[55] Both kinds were the equivalents of mindless drudges.

Livelier animals that nonetheless acknowledged human superiority provided better models for human subordinates. Britons of all ranks were known for their love of horses. The affluent kept high-spirited thoroughbreds; those who followed the plow preferred horses to other draft animals, no matter how strong or cheap to maintain.[56] Popular natural history writers routinely characterized the horse as "noble," and sometimes as nobler than the class of humans generally charged with its care. In part this epithet, embodied in a flood of paintings and prints beginning in the early eighteenth century, reflected the traditional as-

A noble horse. From Thomas Pennant,
British Zoology . . . A New Edition, 1812.

sociation of horseflesh with aristocratic sport.[57] In part it reflected admiration for the horse's appearance; Bewick celebrated "the grandeur of his stature, the elegance and proportion of his parts, the beautiful smoothness of his skin, the variety and gracefulness of his motions."[58] And in part it reflected the horse's spirit. "In his carriage," according to another naturalist, "he seems desirous of raising himself above the humble station assigned him in the creation."[59]

It was, therefore, particularly gratifying to find that this splendid animal was made for servitude. "If there is any thing in the world of nature that seems clear, morally," asserted Philip Hamerton in 1874 (and he was a cautious thinker who knew that it was "foolish to carry speculation about Divine intentions far"), "it is that man has an authentic right to require reasonable service from the horse."[60] A century earlier, the zoologist Thomas Pennant had explained that the horse was "endowed with every quality that can make it subservient to the uses of mankind," including courage, docility, patience, perseverance, strength, benevolent disposition, and "a certain consciousness of the services we can render them."[61] Its obedience was the more valuable for being ungrudgingly offered by a proud, powerful creature capable not only of "strong attachment" but of righteous "resentment of injuries."[62]

Even more eager and aware in accepting the bonds of servitude was the dog, the favorite species of most naturalists as well as of their popular audience. The relation between humanity and its dogs was special—"as much foreseen and intended," in the view of one writer, "as that between sun and planet."[63] It epitomized the appropriate relationship between masters and subordinates. So natural was it for the dog to serve humankind that, unlike other long-domesticated animals, dogs did not need to be trained or broken to their primary allegiance. Each puppy instinctively repeated the choice made by its remote ancestors and attached itself to a human master by "spontaneous impulse."[64] And this subordination defined the master as well as the dog. As an inferior should know its station, so a superior should forthrightly exercise control. Peoples that had not yet domesticated the dog might not be fully human; the extent of canine servitude was an index of the advance of civilization. Bewick claimed that in "nations not yet emerged from a state of barbarism . . . the uses of the dog are but little known," and William Broderip, who was distinguished as a judge as well as a naturalist, noted that "their lot seems to be the worst, if it is cast among savage or imperfectly-civilized nations."[65] Dogs were often raised for food in such societies, which might account for the fact, recorded by Darwin, that English dogs were intelligent and lively, while those of Polynesia and China were "extremely stupid."[66]

Like horses, dogs were frequently characterized as "noble." Unlike horses, however, they lacked the standard external attributes of nobility: they were neither physically majestic nor particularly aristocratic in their associations.[67] So the epithet implicitly offered an alternative definition of "nobility," one appropriate to animals and other inferiors. It was the dog's "ungrudging love" for man that made it "delight to serve" him.[68] Again and again naturalists expressed their admiration for this "humble and laborious servant," whose single-minded devotion inspired its "conqueror" with feelings close to the "esteem," normally reserved for human beings.[69] Its "power of loving" was so great that "to kill a dog was always felt to be a sort of murder."[70] The dog understood and accepted its position so thoroughly that it did not resist punishment if it failed in its duty; it might even lick its master's hand as he delivered the corrective blows.[71] Even the dog's body proclaimed its profound subservience to human will. It was the most physically malleable of animals, the one whose shape and size changed most readily in response to the whims of breeders.

Bad Creatures

The concomitant of the praise heaped on animals that knew their places and kept happily to them was the opprobrium endured by less complaisant creatures. Some domestic animals had trouble meeting even the minimal standards of obedience set by sheep and cattle, let alone the high standards of cooperation set by the dog and the horse. Like disrespectful underlings, they did not adequately acknowledge the dominion of their superiors. The pig, for example, despite its incontestable value as a food animal, was routinely castigated as "selfish," "sordid," "brutal," and "gluttonous."[72] Sows were accused of devouring their own young, which in turn scarcely recognized their mothers; naturally, they did not recognize their human caretakers.[73] The torpid and insignificant guinea pig, often kept as a fancy animal in the nineteenth century, not least because it was a prolific breeder and relatively indifferent to the quality of its surroundings, was accused of being "disgusting," "devoid of sense," and "incapable of good."[74]

The most frequently and energetically vilified domestic animal was

A disgusting pig. From Thomas Bewick,
A General History of Quadrupeds, 1824.

the cat. It did not seem disposed to acknowledge human dominion and could hardly be said to have subordinated its will to that of its human masters. It served people by hunting mice and other vermin, and thus did not depend on people for sustenance. It might not even acknowledge that it had a master. Country cats frequently ran away and became half-wild; it was rumored that in the woods they mated with genuine wild cats. Often they did not distinguish between animals they were desired to kill and those they were not to touch on any account. Cats figured prominently in gamekeepers' museums—the collections of the remains of hawks, owls, weasels, stoats, and other nonhuman poachers that appeared frequently on barn walls and doors. One Victorian display was reported to include the heads of fifty-three cats; a Dorset gamekeeper boasted of killing three hundred cats in a single year.[75] There was no less drastic way to break a poaching cat of its bad habit. It was widely agreed that cats were both deceitful and difficult to train.[76] And as the dog's plastic body symbolized its desire to serve, so the cat's body symbolized its stubborn refusal. Unnervingly similar, in miniature, to its most ferocious wild relatives, the cat resisted breeders' attempts to modify its appearance.

The attitude of domestic cats provoked harsher criticism than did their behavior. It was not even clear that cats liked people, although they often lived with them more intimately than dogs. The cat was suspected of having "only the appearance of attachment to its master," and really either "dreading" him or "distrusting his kindness"; people feared that "their affection is more to the house, than to the persons who inhabit it."[77] Those who valued the eager obedience and camaraderie of the dog considered the cat a strikingly inferior domestic, "refined and very voluptuous . . . so wanting in the nobler qualities as to fail in winning the sympathies of noble and generous-hearted men." This explained why distinguished artists seldom used cats as subjects; they only appealed to "artists of a very low grade indeed." Derogated by the men responsible for maintaining household order and public discipline, cats might be favored by those who sneakingly sympathized with their desire for independence: they were sometimes considered "the chosen allies of womankind."[78]

If domestic animals symbolized appropriate and inappropriate relations between human masters and servants, the lessons to be drawn from wild animals were much more limited. Natural history writers dutifully recorded the many useful products that wild animals supplied to commerce, but they were unable to muster much enthusiasm about the fact that many of them, from kangaroos to hippopotamuses, could be eaten. (Occasionally they recorded the taste of various animals with the discrimination of gourmets. From Cape Colony came the report that the vaal rhebok "has the fault common to much South African game, of being somewhat dry." The lard of the great seal, by contrast, was deemed "most delicious." Lion meat was variously considered to "taste like veal"—a high compliment—and to "have a strong disagreeable flavor.")[79] Some speculations showed a limited sympathy for strange creatures; the author of one popular zoological handbook remarked that, though the sloth was "one of the most unsightly of animals, it is, perhaps, far from being miserable."[80] For the most part, however, wild animals were not even important enough to merit a moral judgment unless they somehow reflected human experience. Thus such varied creatures as the rhinoceros, the giraffe, the hippopotamus, the badger, and the camel might be dismissed as simply inoffensive.

The only wild animals to receive the unqualified praise of natural history writers were those that could be persuaded at least partly to abandon their unregenerate state. Elephants were the major recipients of such appreciation. They could not be considered domestic animals,

A docile elephant. From John Church,
A Cabinet of Quadrupeds, 1805.

because only the Indian elephant was routinely tamed, and even those
did not breed in captivity. Nevertheless they could be trained to be
extremely useful as beasts of burden and as mounts for hunters (unlike
horses, they were not afraid of tigers). Anecdotal evidence, the mainstay of eighteenth- and nineteenth-century natural history, suggested
that the elephant had not only acknowledged human mastery, but
grown to love it. There were occasional reports that once-tame elephants who had escaped would submit immediately to their former
yoke if they chanced to encounter their old keepers. One elephant in
an English menagerie refused to sleep unless its keeper was nearby. Another, in Indian service, became unhappy when deprived of the company of a certain child, who had to be placed, in his cradle, between

the elephant's feet.[81] The temper of tamed animals was consistently praised as "docile" and "mild," even "magnanimous."[82]

The only blot on the elephant's character was its reputation for vindictiveness and holding grudges. But naturalists were inclined to excuse this, insisting that elephants only avenged genuine injuries.[83] And in any case these small reminders of its formidable wrath emphasized the impressiveness of its submission. As one writer put it, "we cannot help being surprised that he, who is so well able to remain his own master, should so readily become the servant of another"; a fellow popularizer rhymed the same message for a juvenile audience: "The elephant is tame and wise, / And grows to a majestic size, / He carries Princes, in the east, / And is esteem'd a noble beast."[84] The "perfect subjugation" of the elephant by "a creature so inferior in bodily strength as man" was a powerful confirmation of the natural hierarchy, in which the human "head and hand subdue all living things, however enormous, to his will."[85] These observations were made with relief as well as complacency, for wild animals, like unruly human subordinates, could be threatening. As Bewick noted, "What ravages might we not expect from the prodigious strength of the elephant combined with the fierceness and rapacity of the Tiger!"[86]

Beasts of prey were as disturbing to contemplate as the elephant, horse, and dog were gratifying. Their carnivorous way of life disposed them to challenge people rather than to serve or flee them; they were rebels who refused to accept the divinely ordained dominance of humankind. Popular zoology books therefore tended to present them as both dangerous and depraved, like alien or socially excluded human groups who would not acknowledge the authority of their superiors. (Sometimes this analogy was made explicit, as in the statement that "in all countries where men are most barbarous, the animals are most cruel and fierce," meaning Africa.)[87] Because any tendency to disobedience was troublesome, even small creatures that could not directly defy human authority were castigated for their predatory propensities. According to Bewick, the weasel was "wild and untractable," dedicated to "rapine and cruelty," and displayed "a natural attachment to every thing that is corrupt"; Thomas Williamson, an early aficionado of subcontinental big game hunting, called the civet "perhaps the most obnoxious of all the wild tribes known in India ... sparing nothing which it can overcome ... and frequently killing, as it were, merely for sport."[88] If such animals could not be controlled, they might have to be exterminated.

"However much we detest all cruelty to the brute creation," intoned the author of *The Animal Museum*, the fox "is so destructive to the property of the farmer . . . that his destruction is absolutely necessary."[89]

Large, powerful animals were, naturally enough, even more threatening, and with one exception, they were described as unmitigatedly wicked. The exception was the lion, whose prestige as the king of beasts, lingering from the medieval bestiaries, was enhanced by its contemporary function as the emblem of British might. Although it was acknowledged to be dangerous and powerful, it was admired for its stately bearing and imposing mane, as well as for a relatively generous temper. Unlike other cats, it was believed, the lion did not kill more than it needed to eat or torture its prey for amusement. It might ignore "weak and contemptible enemies" rather than destroy them.[90] And it might be susceptible to the "moral dominion" of humankind. In the wild lions tended to avoid people once they observed the power of firearms, and lion tamers like Isaac Van Amburgh, an American who enjoyed an enormous English vogue in the first part of Victoria's reign, proved that

The triumph of virtue.
George Stubbs, *Lion and Dead Tiger*.

Nero being baited by dogs.
From William Hone, *Every-Day Book*, 1835.

the king of beasts was "by no means destitute of intelligent docility."
Menagerie lions were prone to complaisance if well treated; one was
observed to retreat before an aggressive goat.[91] In 1825 George Wombwell, the proprietor of the largest traveling menagerie in England, provoked a public outcry when he arranged for a large but gentle lion
named Nero to be baited by dogs trained for fighting.[92]

Nevertheless, many naturalists offered a less flattering image of these
creatures whose interests were so inimical to those of mankind. Edward
Turner Bennett placed the lion at the beginning of his elaborate guide
to the animals in London's Tower Menagerie in deference to its popular
reputation. But he advised his readers to guard against "the general prejudice" in the lion's favor by remembering that "physically and morally,
he is neither more nor less than a cat . . . with all the guileful and vindictive passions of that faithless tribe."[93] Its magnanimity—that is, its
reluctance to kill unnecessarily—was reinterpreted as "an insidious and
cowardly disposition, mixed with a certain degree of pride."[94] African
travelers went so far as to debunk the lion's majestic and commanding

presence. Encountered in the daytime, according to Dr. Livingstone, they appeared much like enormous dogs.[95]

About the tiger there were no two ways of thinking. It epitomized what man had to fear from the animal kingdom and from restive human subordinates. The tiger's beauty thoroughly misrepresented its character; some naturalists claimed it had been bestowed by providence "upon so despicable an animal to prove, that when it is not attached to merit, it neither deserves to be estimated or prized."[96] It was an "emblem of savageness and butchery," undoubtedly "the most cruel, rapacious, and destructive animal in creation."[97] It was greedy, reputed to stop feeding on one carcass in order to kill another animal and to slaughter an entire flock of sheep, leaving them dead in the field.[98] Like the wolf, the hyena, and some other big cats, it was often called "cowardly," which apparently meant unwilling to face men with guns.[99] The authors of *The British Museum* used the language of redemption to lament that "no discipline can correct the savage nature of the tiger, nor any degree of kind treatment reclaim him."[100]

The ultimate measure of the tiger's unregeneracy was its fondness for human flesh. Many tigers living in the populated parts of India and Ceylon routinely preyed on domestic animals and occasionally became man-eaters. Some turned to human prey because they were too sick or old to catch faster and less dangerous quarries. Most, however, were thought to be "cattle-lifting tigers" who had once "summoned up courage to attack the herdsman," and thereby added a tasty new item to their diet. The British public was both horrified and fascinated by such assaults. In 1800 the East India Company put a mechanical model of a tiger eating an Englishman, which had been captured in 1799 from a rebellious Indian potentate, on display at its London offices, where it drew crowds for several generations. Within the body of the tiger was a kind of organ, which caused particular delight when the handle was cranked, reproducing both the cries of a person in distress and the roar of a tiger.[101] The tiger was not alone in this predilection. All the major predators—other big cats, wolves, and bears—shared it, and even less formidable and more familiar creatures might transgress if offered the opportunity. Pierce Egan's *Sporting Anecdotes* included an account of a farm laborer who was suddenly attacked by six weasels, and renegade pigs occasionally attacked their masters' infants. The *Field* reported that a domestic rabbit previously fed entirely on vegetables had devoured

Tipu's tiger, a mechanical model of
a tiger eating an Englishman.

"two fingers of one hand and a finger and the thumb of the other" of a ten-month-old infant in Hull.[102]

Eating human flesh symbolized the ultimate rebellion, the radical reversal of roles between master and servant. The animals themselves seemed to appreciate this symbolism, for "it is said, that when a lion has once tasted human flesh he thenceforth entirely loses his awe of human superiority."[103] Natural history writers emphasized how attractive rebellion was to these despicable animals. Man-eating lions were reported to relish torturing their human victims; they "immediately dispatched" most animals, but in the case of people, they would "merely wound," then wait before delivering the final blow.[104] According to Swainson, it was "universally remarked, that when a carnivorous animal is acquainted with the taste of human blood, it shows a decided preference for that food."[105] Corrupt human flesh was as attractive as fresh meat. Hyenas were said to frequent cemeteries in order to dig up corpses, and jackals, "real cowards," shared the same ghastly taste.[106] Such scavengers might become predators, like the wolves of Caunpore in India, which had been first attracted by the plentiful bodies of "poor wretches" who had died in a famine, but having become "accustomed to human food . . .

frequently carried off children" and "actually attacked the sentries on their posts."[107]

Even if scavengers never threatened a living human being, their diet was intolerably presumptuous. Dead or alive, human flesh was forbidden fruit. Animals were supposed to serve the purposes of humanity, not appropriate it to theirs. To reverse this relationship was to rebel against the divine order, to commit sacrilege. The punishment for animals who dared to challenge the principles of hierarchy and subordination was drastic. Edward Lockwood, a retired official of the Bengal Civil Service, called "the extermination of wild beasts in the great food-producing districts . . . one of the undoubted benefits of British rule." He was proud of the part he had played in that process; although his publisher had warned him not to prose on, he allowed himself to boast, "I have allowed very few of the large wild animals which I have seen in India to escape."[108]

Nor were carnivores the only creatures who might attack men. Explorers in Africa reported that baboons and monkeys stole native children and attacked women carrying supplies. In his classic monograph on the gorilla the zoologist Richard Owen somewhat skeptically retailed the African belief that gorillas hoisted men into trees in order to strangle them; without qualification, the *Illustrated London News* offered its readers the same story, embellished with vivid details—the "terrible hind foot," the "enormous thumb"—and followed by the explanation that, "sheer malignity prompts the animal to this course, for it does not eat the dead man's flesh, but finds a fiendish gratification in the mere act of killing."[109] These reversals of the prescribed hierarchy could not be allowed to pass without comment. Although it was a vegetarian that lived quietly in impenetrable bush far from human settlements, the cape buffalo was accused by natural history writers of being "fierce" and "vindictive," because if wounded by a hunter it was liable to charge him and tear him apart.[110] Malice and insubordination were widely suspected among humankind's animal subjects.

A Different Order

One group of animals that received a great deal of attention from natural history writers represented neither useful servants nor threats to established authority: compared with other animals, monkeys and apes had little to do with people. They did not, with a few exceptions, live close to human settlements, nor were they particularly useful, although it was possible to eat some and tame others. (Monkey-eating was a problematic pastime, however. Many travelers reported that monkeys made excellent roasts, but some found "something extremely disgusting in the idea of eating, what appears, when skinned and dressed, so like a child.")[111] On the scale of values that determined the characterization of most quadrupeds, they should have registered as only moderately interesting, yet they fascinated writers of popular zoology and their audiences.

The source of this fascination was, of course, the similarity of wild primates to human beings. It was most striking in the great apes, who, long before Darwin, were suspected to link people and animals. In 1699 Edward Tyson published an anatomical comparison of a human being and a chimpanzee, to which he gave the Latin name *Homo sylvestris*, thus including it in the human genus. Probably as a result, the orangutan (with which the chimpanzee was frequently confused, not least by Tyson himself) was sometimes called by the English translation, "wild man of the woods," and this name may have been understood literally as well as figuratively in an age when there was no consensus that all human beings belonged to the same species.[112] One early eighteenth-century animal book included "a natural history of the Male Pygmy or Chimpanzee."[113] (For naturalists, as for taxonomists in the tradition of Linnaeus, the notion of family was not welded to the notion of descent or evolution.) During the nineteenth century a steady trickle of captive orangutans and chimpanzees made their way to England, where they enjoyed a few months or years as popular attractions before they succumbed to the cold, damp climate. Invariably, they were exhibited in ways that emphasized their likeness to people. They ate with table utensils, sipped tea from cups, and slept under blankets. One orangutan displayed in London's Exeter Change Menagerie amused itself by carefully turning the pages of an illustrated book. At the Regent's Park Zoo a chimpanzee named Jenny regularly appeared in a flannel nightgown and robe. Apes often boasted Christian names, which heightened the suggestiveness of clothes, forks, and books. Tommy, a chimp who lived at the Regent's Park Zoo in 1835 and 1836, was pronounced by one admirer to be greatly superior in "shrewdness and sagacity . . . [to the] human infant, and . . . for that matter, many grown individuals." A chim-

Wild orangutans drawn to look human.
From E. Donovan, *Naturalist's Repository*, 1822–1824.

Captive chimpanzee dressed to look human. From Charles Knight,
Knight's Pictorial Museum of Animated Nature, 1856–1858.

panzee acquired by the Earl Fitzwilliam in 1849 was reported to walk "perfectly erect" and handle "everything like a human being"; its food was "choice, and wine a favorite beverage."[114]

Reports of apes' behavior in the wild, however implausible and ill-documented, also emphasized their closeness to humanity. They were credited with the ability to use primitive tools. Orangutans, for example, were alleged to attack elephants with clubs and to cover their dead with leaves and branches.[115] And they appeared to feel an emotional connection with human beings. It was rumored that orangutans were "passionately fond of women" and would carry them off by force. When a young African boy abducted by chimps returned safely after a season's captivity, he claimed to have been well treated, especially by the females, who had fed him and protected him from snakes and beasts of prey.[116]

There was also no mistaking the connection of humankind with less advanced primates, or quadrumanes, as members of the order were often called in the nineteenth century, in order implicitly to exclude humans.[117] Although captive monkeys were not as quick as apes to adopt human manners, wild monkeys might claim kin in extreme circumstances. Not only did they look like babies when cooked, they often seemed to reproach human enemies for their thoughtless predation. According to one sporting officer who shot a monkey in Ceylon—and vowed never to shoot another—"nothing can be more distressing than to see how like human beings these poor creatures apply their handlike paws to the wound, and look at their assailant with so much sorrowful intelligence and great suffering."[118] Another hunter reported that after one of his companions had shot a female monkey, the entire troop followed them back to their camp, where the leader first threatened, then "by every token of grief and supplication, seemed to beg the body of the deceased . . . it was given to him: with tender sorrow he took it up in his arms, embraced it with conjugal affection, and carried it off . . . The artless behavior of this poor animal wrought so powerfully on the sportsmen, that they resolved never more to level a gun at one of the monkey race."[119] The only monkeys that did not inspire this kind of sympathy and interest were those perceived to be least like people in appearance and behavior. The doglike baboons were repeatedly described as disgusting and stupid, "simply hideous and repulsive."[120] Not only were they a travesty of humanity—they were compared to "the most God-forsaken of the human race"—but some naturalists speculated that they represented not "a primitive form of monkey life," but one that had degenerated.[121]

These resemblances did not raise monkeys and apes to the level of humanity, which stood majestically above the animal creation. As William Jardine pointed out in the introduction to *Monkeys*, the first volume to appear in *The Naturalist's Library*, "a strict comparison between the monkey and human organization" was "quite unnecessary"; indeed, human beings, "infinitely pre-eminent" and "stamped with a bearing lofty and dignified," should not even be included within the same "system" as the other primates.[122] But apes did inevitably challenge the conventional nineteenth-century animal hierarchy, headed by either the dog or the horse, humankind's best servants.[123] (Besides that of the bestiary tradition, which elevated the lion and other emblems of desirable human qualities, there were other possible hierarchies, such as that suggested by St. George Mivart, who wished to rank animals according to how well they were adapted to their function. This criterion prompted

Mivart to celebrate the efficient carnivores of the cat family as "the very flower and culmination of the mammalian tree.")[124] The claims of apes to preeminence rested on quite a different basis. One of the ways in which they resembled human beings was their intelligence. If reason elevated humanity above the beasts, argued some zoologists, then its closest equivalent should place chimpanzees and orangutans at the head of the animal kingdom.

Throughout the nineteenth century naturalists debated the rival claims of dogs and apes to be top animal in terms that made it clear that the issue was not simply taxonomical. In question was the more fundamental principle of whether animals should be ranked according to their utility to humankind, as literal servants or as instructive analogues, or according to some other standard. Intelligence, at least of the imitative and problem-solving kind displayed by apes, was of use only to the creature that possessed it. The intensity and duration of the debate showed that once it had been suggested, mental ability seemed a compelling criterion for ranking animals. But it did not, in the view of many combatants, mean that the apes were inevitably superior to other beasts. Naturalists who wished to promote the rival claims of domestic animals could emphasize what they considered to be the equally impressive mental qualities that such creatures possessed in greater measure than primates.

Although almost everyone who wrote about animals took a stand on this issue, it was hard to predict who would turn up on which side. Ape advocates did not obviously outnumber dog advocates as time passed and zoological progress accelerated, nor were scientific naturalists more likely than amateurs and popularizers to make the case for primates. For example, by the beginning of the nineteenth century Bewick and William Bingley, a writer whose most frequent subjects were travel and biography, had acknowledged the ascendancy of orangutans.[125] Yet as late as 1881 George J. Romanes, a close friend of Darwin's and a professional zoologist with a special interest in animal behavior, celebrated the "high intelligence" and "gregarious instincts" of the dog, which gave it a more "massive as well as more complex" psychology than the monkey family. Two years later Romanes revised his ranking slightly, including both dogs and anthropoid apes on level twenty-eight of a fifty-step ladder of intellectual development. Level twenty-eight was characterized by "indefinite morality" along with the capacity to experience shame, remorse, deceit, and the ludicrous. (Steps twenty-nine through fifty were reserved for human beings; worms and insect larva occupied step eighteen because they possessed primary instincts and could feel the emotions of surprise and fear.) Although this schema gave apes and dogs equivalent rank, Romanes was far from thinking that they possessed identical mental attributes. Rather, the ape had achieved its high status through intellect, the dog, on account of highly developed emotions.[126]

At issue was how to define animal intelligence—if, indeed, animals could be said to possess intelligence at all. Some naturalists denied that animals possessed any mental qualities besides instincts. A correspondent of the *Zoological Journal* asserted that although dogs and other animals exhibited behavior that closely mimicked such qualities as foresight, industry, and justice, in fact they were merely performing reflex actions, like Descartes's animal machines.[127] William Swainson considered animal intelligence to consist in the ability to work together with others of the same species, which made it more characteristic of insects than of quadrupeds, whose chief glory was, in his view, their large size.[128] Most naturalists were more generous, however, allowing the higher animals a grab bag of intellectual and emotional attributes. One representative inventory included imagination, memory, homesickness, self-consciousness, joy, rage, terror, compassion, envy, cruelty, fidelity, and attachment.[129] A few naturalists adapted for animal heads the complex methods of phrenologists, who divined qualities of human mind and character from the external conformation of the skull. According to one elaborate version, the qualities of amativeness, philoprogenitiveness, inhabitiveness, adhesiveness, combativeness, destructiveness, secretiveness, acquisitiveness, and constructiveness, as well as the external senses, were as common in animals as in people. Animals had a lesser share of such sentiments as self-esteem, love of approbation, cautiousness, benevolence, veneration, firmness, conscientiousness, hope, marvelousness, ideality, gaiety, and imitation, and of the ability to perceive individuality, configuration, size, weight, coloring, locality, calculation, order, eventuality, time, melody, and artificial language. Only the "reflective faculties" of comparison and causality were confined "principally, if not wholly" to human beings.[130]

Such systems inextricably confounded emotional and intellectual capacities. Phrenological analysis revealed, for example, that large foreheads, which indicated intelligence and ability to be tamed, were more common in domestic than in wild animals, although by this standard the seal, too, possessed "uncommon intelligence"; it also showed that the organ of adhesiveness was extremely pronounced in the dog, and that the organ of amativeness was better developed in the males of all species than in the females.[131] Analyses based on anecdotal accounts of animal behavior were equally imprecise. Casual observers might recognize intelligence in the way a dog hid on Sundays to avoid being chained while his master went to church, or the way pigs "if they hear one of their companions in distress . . . endeavour to assist him to the utmost of their power."[132] Even serious and self-conscious investigators were apt to define intelligence as the most impressive and appealing behavior of their pets. Although Romanes was well aware of the pitfalls of anecdotal observation, he used his favorite terrier, Mathal, to illustrate the "exalted level to which sympathy has attained" and the "intelligent affection from which it springs" in the dog.[133]

An index of the mix of mental qualities that naturalists valued in animals—and perhaps also of their desire to distinguish clearly between animal and human mental capacities—was the fact that well into the last part of the nineteenth century "sagacity" was the standard term for intelligence demonstrated by animals. An individual animal or species might be described as "intelligent," but the term "intelligence" itself was generally reserved for strictly human capacities. Conversely, if "sagacity" were attributed to human beings, it often had an ironic or less than flattering connotation. Sagacity could comfortably be stretched to describe a variety of mental phenomena. The phrase "animal sagacity" in the title of a book or article often signaled an abstract discussion of instinct or intellect, the kind of discussion that might conclude by appreciating the intelligence of apes. But in the common usage of naturalists, sagacity indicated not the ability to manipulate mechanical contraptions or solve logical problems, but a more diffuse kind of mental power: the ability to adapt to human surroundings and to please people. A somewhat circular calculation made the most sagacious animals the best servants.

If there was doubt about which was the most intelligent animal, the dog was clearly the most sagacious. The literature of natural history (and of dog appreciation) abounded with evidence of ingenious loyalty. One canine hero barked at an approaching coach until it stopped, thus saving the life of its master, who lay drunk in the road; another awakened its more admirable master, who had fallen asleep over a book, to warn him that an unsnuffed candle had set the bed curtains afire. The noble terrier Greyfriars Bobby watched over his master's grave in an Edinburgh churchyard for fourteen years, and other dogs refused food after their masters died until they expired themselves of hunger and grief.[134] The dog was viewed as "the only animal who always knows his master, and the friends of the family."[135] Its only possible rival on these grounds was the horse, whose "understanding," in the view of its most fervent admirers, was "superior to that of any other animal." (The mental aptitudes of the "docile and gentle" horse were particularly well suited to assist man and not to annoy him; though sagacious, the horse was "totally devoid of the cunning" of some troublesome creatures.)[136] The Indian elephant, another loyal servant, was also acclaimed for its "almost human wisdom," whereas the unsubmissive cat was pointedly denied "the sagacity, approaching almost to human reason, of the Dog."[137]

Appreciation of animal intelligence, especially as displayed by apes, might have undermined the structure that humanity had imposed on the natural world or challenged the animal hierarchy that valued obedient servants. But the concept of sagacity actually reinforced human dominion. It could be defined so that the animals that exemplified obedient subordination had the largest measure. In addition, the position of primates in the animal hierarchy could be made to seem less anomalous. Apes too were useful to humanity, although in a more abstract way than domestic animals. The strongest similarity between people and apes was in "external appearance"; they resembled humans closely in the face, nostrils, ears, teeth, eyelashes, nipples, arms, hands, fingers, and fingernails.[138] But even though "the form and organs . . . so nearly resemble those of mankind," according to one writer, "we are surprised to find them productive of so few advantages."[139] Apes could not talk or reason, and it was frequently remarked that young animals seemed the most like humans (perhaps, in phrenological terms, because their foreheads were higher), while "untameable ferocity and brutality . . . have been uniformly the concomitants of age."[140] A few vocal people were simply repelled by the physical resemblance between wild primates and people. But most apparently found it engaging. Not only did they flock to see live apes on display, they also enjoyed the illustrations of apes in natural history books, which often exaggerated the humanness of the primates' proportions and visages.[141] In a way, apes presented a living gloss on human ascendancy. As Frank Buckland pointed out, although "it is in the country of the gorilla that we find the very lowest specimens of the human race . . . we at once see how man, even though in a most degraded state, begins to show . . . his superiority of brain and mind." Swainson justified the attention he had devoted to the higher primates on similar grounds: "We have been particularly interested in *Quadrumana*, as their arrangement involved a question of much higher importance—the station of *Man* in the scale of being."[142]

A New Foundation

The publication of Charles Darwin's *On the Origin of Species* in 1859 is usually considered to mark the beginning of a new era in the study of life, superseding the static, human-dominated hierarchy elaborated by generations of naturalists. The very terms "naturalist" and "natural history" were soon to acquire an old-fashioned ring, as they were replaced by the more technical-sounding "zoologist" and "biology." Certainly, for those who were persuaded by it, Darwin's theory of evolution by natural selection eliminated the deity who had created the world for human convenience; it also eliminated the unbridgeable gulf that divided reasoning human being from irrational brute. *On the Origin of Species* itself dethroned both God and humankind almost implicitly. Rather than focusing directly on humanity, Darwin outlined an elaborate schema in which people occupied no especially prominent position. His subsequent works addressed the place of human beings in the natural order directly. In *The Descent of Man, and Selection in Relation to Sex* (1871) he discussed human evolution, arguing that the human mind as well as the human body had developed directly from animal forebears. Although Darwin acknowledged that the divergence in degree of intellectual power between people and animals was "immense," he nevertheless asserted that "there is no fundamental difference between man and the higher mammals in their mental faculties."[143] In *The Expression of the Emotions in Man and Animals* (1872) he continued this argument, using a series of illustrations to prove that humans and animals shared not only feelings, but also the physical means of expressing them.

However revolutionary it was from many points of view, Darwin's theory of evolution did not prescribe any real break in the system of traditional metaphors underlying descriptive natural history. Naturalists, after all, had always recognized an analogy between the human and the animal spheres. Even the most provocative feature of *The Expression of the Emotions*—the illustrations that implicitly compared cats and dogs and apes to people—had Enlightenment roots. Charles LeBrun, a seventeenth-century French artist whose manuals were widely used in eighteenth-century England, had suggested that painters could learn to depict certain human character traits by studying animals. After identifying an animal's temper, they were to "search in their Physiognomy the Parts which, particularly mark certain predominating Affections." For example, since "swine . . . are nasty, lascivious, gluttonous, and lazy," scrutiny of their countenances would help artists represent similar qualities in humans.[144]

Nor did Darwin's theory necessitate regrouping on a systematic level. Although the taxonomy established by Linnaeus and his predecessors had not implied a dynamic of development and progression, it did not insist on stasis. In some ways, the theory of evolution was a natural extension of the work of mastering the natural world earnestly begun by John Ray and his seventeenth-century contemporaries. And it was a still more forceful assertion of human intellectual domination—the power to perceive or impose patterns—than the systems of classification on which it was based. Although it eliminated both the divine sanction for human domination and the separation between man and beast, it did not diminish human superiority. On the contrary, it described the very process by which that superiority had been established. Clearly, if people were animals, they were the top animals; and with God out of the picture, the source of human preeminence lay within. Ironically, by becoming animals, humans appropriated some attributes formerly reserved for the deity. And in "the struggle for life," as the subtitle of *On the Origin of Species* put it, the other animals were still ranked according to their relation to humanity. This ranking was expressed more starkly than in most popular natural histories—the stakes were survival rather than approval or attention. To the extent that people dominated the environments in which animals lived, dogs and horses would multiply, while populations of tigers and wolves dwindled.

The emerging continuity between animals and people made it even easier to represent human competition, and the social hierarchies created by those who prevailed, in terms of animals. On the *Beagle* voyage the sight of the Tasmanian tribesmen, whose numbers were diminishing as the English population increased, had led the young Darwin to reflect that "the varieties of man seem to act on each other in the same way as the different species of animals—the stronger always extirpating the weaker."[145] Animals became the types not just of domestic servants and other laborers, but of the exotic peoples that Europeans subjugated in the course of the nineteenth century.

Indeed, it was not difficult to incorporate evolutionary theory within the conventional format of popular zoology. In 1883 Arabella B. Buckley, a friend of Alfred Russel Wallace, whose convergence on evolutionary theory spurred Darwin to compose *On the Origin of Species*, published an up-to-date children's book entitled *The Winners in Life's Race; or The Great Backboned Family*. Although she announced her intention "rather to follow the tide of life, and sketch in broad outline, how structure and habit have gone hand-in-hand in filling every available space with living beings, than to multiply descriptions of the various species," Bewick would have recognized most of her major categories. He would not have been surprised to find monkeys and apes described next to insectivores and rodents, the orders they most closely resembled, rather than "standing at the head of the animal kingdom"; that is where he had placed them himself. Many of Buckley's characterizations of specific animals would also have seemed familiar: for example, the "cowardly" jackal or the "degenerate" gorilla, "equal neither in beauty, strength, discernment, nor in any of the nobler qualities, to the faithful dog, the courageous lion, or the half-reasoning elephant."[146] Darwin may have transformed the relation between human beings and other animals in principle, but the egalitarianism he had suggested by including humankind among the beasts had little practical effect, even on the thinking of naturalists.[147] More influential was the notion of the survival of "the vigorous, the healthy and the happy," which seemed to justify and even celebrate human ascendancy.[148] Animals remained the symbols of various orders within human hierarchies, as well as the victims of human control.

Both the manifest content and the metaphorical structure of the literature of popular zoology conditioned all other discourse about animals in the eighteenth and nineteenth centuries. Its wide audience ranged from learned biologists—Darwin's footnotes, for example, frequently mingled citations to learned journals with references to much homelier sources[149]—to young children and the idly curious. By promulgating a coherent and hierarchical interpretation of the animal kingdom, this literature provided its readers with a shared set of assumptions, values, and associations that simultaneously confirmed human ascendancy and supported the established social order. The specific discourses that form the subjects of the following chapters show how this rhetorical structure could be adapted to express the concerns of such diverse groups as elite stock breeders, bourgeois pet owners, reformist public officials, and imperial administrators.

PART I

Prestige and Pedigree

CHAPTER ONE

Barons of Beef

The Durham ox had no special skills, and it closely resembled other shorthorned cattle in appearance. Yet for six years, beginning in 1801, it toured England and Scotland in a specially designed carriage, drawing crowds of admirers. On a single day in London, where the ox spent most of 1802, admission fees totaled £97. The animal's charisma was also projected through the media. During the same year more than two thousand people paid half a guinea for an engraving of the squarish, roan-colored beast.[1] Its initial exhibitor, one Mr. Bulmer of Harmby, Yorkshire, had shrewdly recognized the stolid ox's star quality when he paid the stiff price of £140; he sold it for £250 during its first year on tour, and John Day, the new owner, soon received offers of nearly ten times that amount. The charm that these astute businessmen had recognized in the Durham ox was, quite simply, its size. At the age of five, it was loaded with fat and weighed approximately three thousand pounds; a year later, according to the legend on the popular engraving, this "wonderful animal" was still "in a growing and improving state."[2] In addition to its imposing bulk, the Durham ox boasted impressive genealogical connections. As a shorthorn, it belonged to the most prestigious breed of its time, which was praised in prose by many sober agriculturists and in verse by the poet Wordsworth's brother-in-law (a banker). Its sire, Favourite, was also the sire of Comet, a renowned stud bull, and further up its family tree stood the patriarch Hubback, whose

45

blood ran in the veins of all the best shorthorns.[3] Combining massive presence and distinguished pedigree, the Durham ox exemplified the end toward which late eighteenth-century prize cattle breeding was directed; it was the type of bovine excellence.

Elite Cattle

In their magnificence as well as in their metonymic association with agricultural improvement, the Durham ox and its portly kindred embodied the values of the wealthy, often aristocratic landowners who produced exemplary livestock. They were elegant as well as ample; they were expensive to produce and to maintain; they often did not seem to be judged according to the same standards as the lesser beasts that were the mainstay of the livestock industry. The rhetoric of connoisseurship that accompanied their production and display emphasized these distinctive characteristics, not only within the community of elite stock breeders, but also to the multitudes who paid to admire either individual animals on tour or the prize stock assembled at shows. In yielding this tribute of money and appreciation, ordinary farmers and citizens were expressing patriotic pride in a period when John Bull and roast beef had become popular national symbols; they were also admiring the power and extravagance of the magnates who bred prize cattle and, implicitly, accepting the legitimacy of that group's identification of its own ascendancy with the national interest. Critics of these noble animals—who were present from the beginning, although less vocal then they subsequently became—also identified livestock with English prestige and prosperity, but they proposed alternative versions of both the ideal bovine and the social structure that it symbolically affirmed.

The association of meat production with the governing classes lent British livestock—primarily cattle, the most imposing and expensive, but also sheep and to a lesser extent pigs—a glamour they had not always enjoyed in their millennia of service to the farmers of Britain. The longhorned breeds that dominated the western seaboard of Britain until the early nineteenth century may have been descended from cattle that arrived with the people who built Stonehenge; the white markings that characterized many southern and midland herds were probably an inheritance from a different group of pre-Roman ancestors, the semi-wild cattle that patriotic breeders and fanciers liked to call "native."[4]

Drovers brought animals to market from the remotest corners of the island along routes that were well established by the seventeenth century; some of the oldest tracks in Britain, such as the Icknield Way that stretched from Norfolk to Southampton, may have been ancient cattle paths. A national trade in stock fattened for the butcher, centering on London's Smithfield Market, dated back to the Middle Ages.[5] Despite its economic importance, however, most of this long service had inspired little excitement. The enthusiastic attention commanded by certain animals beginning in the late eighteenth century, coincident with the emergence of prize stock breeding, signaled a shift in at least the rhetorical function of animal husbandry.

This shift was not explicitly acknowledged by the elite breeders who produced the celebrated animals. They claimed to be simply doing their patriotic duty, responding to a national need. As Sir John Saunders Sebright, both a practitioner and a proponent of high stock breeding, summarized several decades of effort in 1809, "The attention which gentlemen of landed property have . . . paid to this subject, has been extremely beneficial to the country."[6] The stated purpose of innovative animal husbandry was to breed stock that would grow larger and faster and thus produce more meat. The superior strains developed by experimental agriculturists would, according to this plan, be adopted by ordinary farmers. As a result, the avocation of elite amateurs would improve the finances of the rest of the agricultural community; it would also underpin national security. Increased food production was necessary to feed the rapidly expanding English population, which had nearly doubled in the course of the eighteenth century. In addition, as an island nation frequently at war with its closest neighbors during this period and potentially vulnerable to blockade, Britain needed to be able to provision itself. Meat was a particularly valuable commodity in international competition, because the ability of especially urban industrial workers to buy it was an index of British commercial prowess, and because, according to popular belief, it was the consumption of red meat that distinguished brave and brawny English soldiers from puny, sniveling Frenchmen.[7]

Viewed simply as accelerated meat production, experimental stock breeding could be understood as one component of the agricultural revolution, which inspired many eighteenth-century landowners with a new interest in the actual working of their estates. Enthusiastic "improvers," as these serious amateurs were called, introduced new crops, experimented with new techniques of drainage and cultivation, and tested the chemistry of the soil. As a result, it became possible to produce larger animals even without special attention to breeding: the enclosure of open fields in much of the Midlands released a lot of rich pastureland for sheep and cattle; and the introduction of all-year fodder like turnips and, later, oil cake (a by-product of linseed oil manufacture) allowed beasts to reach their maximum weight more quickly and to maintain their weight through the winter, when they could be sold at high "off-season" prices. Artificial selection for size made the final products still more spectacular. Gentry and aristocratic livestock fanciers tested these innovations at their own expense; the results were disseminated at meetings of the newly founded national and local agricultural societies and celebrated in the nascent agricultural press.[8] This publicity was ostensibly for the benefit of more modest farmers, such as the tenants of the elite improvers, who lacked the resources to experiment with new agricultural technology. They also, it turned out, lacked both the inclination to adopt new methods of which the efficacy had been clearly demonstrated and the curiosity even to read about them. Well into the nineteenth century the editorial columns of agricultural periodicals lamented the paucity of ordinary husbandmen among their readers.[9]

Elite breeders moderated neither their rhetoric nor their enthusiasm for their self-appointed task in response to the inattention of their designated target. This happy perseverance suggests that they may have actually been pursuing a rather different project. Such a reinterpretation would also help explain a series of disjunctions between the actual accomplishments of the improvers and the tone of the discourse in which they were commemorated. For example, their record of solid, if not widely adopted, technical advances might have justified quiet pride, but not necessarily the excitement that surrounded extravagantly formed prize animals and the meetings where they were displayed and admired. It did not explain why the sheepshearings sponsored by agriculturally oriented magnates—private versions of the shows sponsored by agricultural societies—were such dazzling social events. Nor did it explain why so many of the great men of the land, including the greatest, "Farmer George" himself, were eager to identify themselves with the new husbandry, and to lavish time and money on agricultural improve-

Sir Charles Morgan, Bt., presenting his prize bull to
King William IV; painting by J. H. Carter.

ment. It did not evoke the heady atmosphere of exalted purpose that
stirred patrons and exhibitors at the convivial dinners that always accompanied shows. The toasts offered at the banquet of the Holkham
sheepshearing (an annual show held by Thomas Coke, one of the best-
known improvers, on his Norfolk estate) in 1810 expressed this high
spirit. They have almost a martial vigor: "Constitution and King," "The
best use of the Plough," "Prosperity to Agriculture," "Breeding in all its
Branches," "A fine fleece and a fat carcass," and many salutes to worthy
individuals. Each toast was drunk separately, and the company, which
numbered in the hundreds, quickly became uproarious.[10] The animals
bred in this spirit were shaped for higher destinies than the knives of
ordinary butchers and the palates of ordinary consumers. In toasting
their noble animals, the elite livestock fanciers were celebrating themselves.

The dichotomy between the rhetoric of service and the less explicit
but more persuasive rhetoric of self-assertion and display was embodied

in the contrasting fates of the first two national organizations of agriculturists. The Board of Agriculture was established in 1793, after sustained lobbying by Sir John Sinclair, an earnest Scottish improver who
became its first president. It was an odd cross between a government
agency and a private corporation. Its members were recruited from the
most exclusive echelons of the agricultural world to perform a mission
of elaborate technical service; the board's early objectives included publishing agricultural surveys of Britain (the only objective actually accomplished), organizing research in farming and chemistry, training
students, and sponsoring essay competitions. The minutes of board
meetings, which were held more or less weekly, recorded an unsystem-
atic but inveterate attention to these objectives—a typical entry was
"Read Mr. Powell on Ryland sheep. To be kept."—and attendance soon
dwindled. Sinclair made brave public pronouncements from time to
time about the efficacy of his board, and as late as 1831, nearly a decade
after its demise, he claimed that "the country is in a great measure indebted [to it], for its rapid advancement in rural and agricultural affairs."
But in fact the board was never as vigorous as such contemporary provincial agricultural societies as the Bath and West; its relentlessly pragmatic mission did not engage its elite national constituency.[11]

The Smithfield Society (the name was changed to Smithfield Club
in 1802), by contrast, institutionalized the sense of good fellowship and
happy self-assertion expressed in the heartfelt Holkham pledges. It first
met on December 17, 1798, under the chairmanship of Francis Russell,
the fifth duke of Bedford, with most of the aristocratic stars of livestock
husbandry in attendance; Arthur Young, the indefatigable popularizer
of improvement, became the first secretary.[12] All these gentlemen were
on the spot because the pre-Christmas season at Smithfield was a busy
time; club legend credited the crowds that flocked to see "some extraordinary fat beasts" sent by the duke of Bedford to a butcher named Gib-
lett with providing the immediate inspiration for the annual livestock
exhibitions that were to be its major activity.[13] The first show, held a
year later, was accounted a complete success. According to one admiring chronicler, it "did great credit to the exhibiting graziers, and great
honour to the largest market in the world." He characterized the sponsoring society, with its membership composed of "a considerable number of noblemen and gentlemen," as "that admirable, that practical, and
truly patriotic institution." Even the middlemen and small consumers

who supported the extraordinary achievements of club members with solid tokens of appreciation were included in the swelling emotion: "The prize ox was sold, together with his companion, for 200 l. to one butcher . . . who appears to possess a spirit formed to meet and invigorate that of the first of graziers; and the liberality of the public has been such as is well-calculated to support and continue the honourable exertions of both these patriots, as will appear from the very extraordinary prices given for various parts of the . . . prize bullock."[14]

Like the Board of Agriculture, the club was ostensibly dedicated to blazing trails for small farmers to follow, but neither the animals they showed nor their economic philosophy suggested much commonality of purpose with such cultivators. Both in speech and action, the members of the Smithfield Club consistently indicated that the main recompense for breeding show animals was intangible. In 1800 the duke of Bedford explicitly dissociated the club from the policy of raising prices to increase profits, observing somewhat cryptically that "the only true object of the farmer is to profit, not by high prices, but by *great products*." And the club followed this advice in the conduct of its own affairs; that is, it was resolutely indifferent to its balance sheet. Although breeders competed eagerly at the first Christmas cattle show to see whose beasts were "the fattest and best," and the public paid to view the results, the Club lost money on it. Prizes alone—£52 10s. in plate, a form of award that, though expensive, offered recognition rather than liquidity—cost more than the £40 3s. received from paid admissions.[15] The club's fiscal troubles deepened as show expenses continued to outstrip proceeds. In 1814 the president (then John Russell, the sixth duke of Bedford, who had inherited the presidency, along with the dukedom, from his brother) had to subsidize the prizes, and a few years later finances had become so precarious that he proposed no prizes be offered. But the membership rebelled at the idea of eliminating these powerful symbols. And wealthy breeders were not the only ones who valued the magnificent displays of enormous animals. During the agricultural depression of 1815, one farming periodical thought that suffering cultivators would be pleased "to learn that no abatement of zeal or exertions seems visible with the graziers and cattle-feeders, who exhibit their fat stock for the premiums annually offered" by the Smithfield Club.[16]

Profit was not the only concern of ordinary farmers disdained by the aristocratic and gentry breeders who belonged to the Smithfield Club. In 1821 the duke of Bedford provoked an explicit declaration of purpose by proposing that the club itself be discontinued. It had, he claimed, achieved its proclaimed goals; British markets were now "abundantly supplied" with "the best and most profitable breeds of sheep and cattle."[17] But club members refused to be held to such a literal interpretation of their purpose. Once again they rebelled, unanimously resolving on the contrary that "the Club ought to continue and receive the utmost support from its members."[18] The Smithfield Club sailed strongly into the Victorian period. Under the vigorous leadership of Viscount Althorp (later Earl Spencer), the Christmas cattle shows increased in size and popularity, ultimately requiring removal to more commodious quarters, and the competition among exhibitors remained keen. "After an existence of half a century," noted the *Illustrated London News* in 1853, the Smithfield Club Fat Cattle Show "still flourishes, and receives undiminished support from contributors of stock," who basked both in their reciprocally reflected esteem and in the only moderately tempered approbation of the multitudes, who also equated the preeminence of the imposing prize beasts with that of their elite masters. They willingly paid to indulge what the journalist called "the aristocratical admiration which forms so striking a feature in the British character, by closely inspecting, admiring, and tormenting the bullocks sent by Dukes and Earls."[19]

Rank and Ancestry

The annual Smithfield shows functioned as ceremonial reenactments of the traditional rural order. They celebrated and reaffirmed the position of the wealthy and powerful magnates who headed it, by parading the symbols of their magnificence in the form of extraordinarily large beasts. Their rhetoric of service reminded ordinary farmers that the men who could afford to raise prize animals were their natural leaders, at the same time that the opulence of the display underlined the exclusiveness of high stock breeding. This had been an important part of its appeal from the beginning, both to the breeders themselves and to their public audience. Even the entrepreneurial Robert Bakewell, who did not belong to the gentry and who was one of the few to make a fortune as a breeder, understood the need to cultivate the aristocratic amateurs who patronized stock breeding and to maintain its status as an elite pastime. In 1788 he reported proudly that "I had an hours conversation with the King on the subject of breeding which he seemed much pleased with and listened to what I said with great attention"; the next year he extended a visit to London in order to lobby "some of the great Folks," including the King, to set aside some Crown lands as experimental farms.[20] The first four presidents of the Smithfield Club, whose combined tenure spanned sixty years, included three dukes and an earl, and the nobility and gentry were heavily represented among the membership. By the nineteenth century it was assumed that the proprietors of landed estates would try their hands at livestock fancying; thus periodicals like *Land and Water* and the *Annals of Sporting and Fancy Gazette*, which were devoted to masculine country pursuits, regularly featured breeding advice and cattle show reports.

The public presentation of prize stock breeding strongly suggested that its function was more metaphoric than practical. The elaborate structures that some breeders built to accommodate their livestock and their products, such as the eleventh duke of Norfolk's fortress-like cowhouse and the fifth duke of Bedford's Chinese dairy, proclaimed the special status of both animals and owners precisely by dissociating them from ordinary farmyard activities.[21] Similarly, reports of livestock shows routinely emphasized their glittering patronage, presenting them primarily as occasions for social display rather than technical enlightenment. In describing the annual show of the Sussex Agricultural Society, held at Lewes in 1801, the *Commercial and Agricultural Magazine* featured a list of attendees including "the Prince of Wales, the Stadtholder, the Dukes of Richmond and Bedford; the Earl of Egremont, Lord Pelham and the President of the Board of Agriculture (Lord Carrington), with a long train of the Nobility and Gentry." (The interest shown by foreign aristocrats in English stock breeding and the ceremonial role they often played at shows also underlined the difference between the production of prize cattle and ordinary agricultural activities.) The Smithfield Club minutes proudly noted visits to its annual show by Prince Albert and the duke of Cambridge in 1840 and by Prince Albert and Queen Victoria in 1844.[22]

The expense of high stock breeding guaranteed its continuing cachet. The agricultural press repeatedly warned ordinary farmers not to compete in inappropriate arenas, where, even in the unlikely event that they were successful, they would be rewarded mainly in prestige, a coin that few could afford to accept. Of a social-climbing breeder who unwisely disregarded this admonition, one journal reported in 1830 that he "had decreased in property . . . til his finances are exhausted, when he has to console himself on the good he has done to the community at large [and] the great acquaintance he had once made." In 1845 the *Journal of the Royal Agricultural Society of England* sternly warned ambitious young farmers who might be inclined to test their skill and judgment by fattening an animal or two to show that this was "generally a most unprofitable affair," best left "in the hands of those gentry who can afford the loss." It was unprofitable because winning was unlikely, because most shows provided no compensatory recognition for excellent animals that did not place, and because it was unwise to invest so much in the life of a single animal. As late as 1867 the breeding of "the purest tribes" of shorthorns was still "in the hands of gentlemen and wealthy agriculturalists." Underlying this prudent advice was the suggestion that the sensible farmer would leave such ostentatious displays to his betters, to whose purses and positions they were more suitable; that in entering the stock breeding lists he would be forgetting his place.[23]

Prince Albert's career as a livestock exhibitor persuasively demonstrated the reciprocal relationship between generous financing and success as a breeder of prize animals. His triumphs were the more impressive because before he married Queen Victoria in 1840, royal interest in agriculture had languished for several decades, giving him no foundation on which to build. Nevertheless, his lavish improvements began to bear fruit almost immediately. He first exhibited in the Smithfield show of 1843, where a pen of his pigs was highly commended, although his two oxen received no notice. From then on he showed regularly at Smithfield, and his cattle and pigs figured as often in the prize lists. He exhibited less frequently but with equal success at the shows of the Royal Dublin Society and the Royal Agricultural Society of England (RASE), as well as those of the Midland Counties' Association and several other regional societies. Between 1843 and his death in 1861, the prince consort's animals won almost £1,000 in medals, as well as two bronze medals, thirteen high commendations, and twenty-one simple commendations. (He also won one gold medal on his own account, for being a generally good fellow and supporting the Royal Agricultural Society of Ireland.) Impressive as the Prince's haul of prizes was, it did not approach the cost of stocking and maintaining the royal farms.[24]

The money spent by Prince Albert and his wealthy fellow breeders did not, however, vanish entirely; it became part of the hegemonic discourse concealed beneath the rhetoric of public service. The value of prize cattle was regularly reconfirmed when they, or their breeding services, or their offspring were sold. Prices were high in this market, although still not high enough to balance the accounts of the relatively small circle of elite breeders who participated in it, and they bore little relation to the animals' practical utility. Their magnitude symbolized the significance of the enterprise as a whole, as well as the financial power of those who could afford to participate. Breathtaking price tags reflected the amount of prestige that the buyer acquired along with the animal. One reason that shorthorn enthusiasts endlessly reprinted the details of the auction of Charles Colling's stock in 1810 was that the prices were enormous for the time. Comet, the best bull, fetched 1,000 guineas and Lily, the best cow, 410; even relatively ordinary animals sold for between 100 and 200 guineas.[25] They definitively established the preeminence of the breed, and, within the breed, of animals descended from Colling's stock. Such cattle became, in a sense, collector's items, and sales of genealogically distinguished animals began to resemble the sales of other precious objects. In 1865 a leading article in the *Times* made the comparison explicit: "There was sold at Willis's Rooms a collection of articles, first-rate productions in their way, and the result of extreme industry and skill. Twelve sold for £6,510—i.e., for an average of £542 10s. each. Five sold for £1,699 10s.—i.e., for an average of £339 18s. each . . . They were shorthorned cattle . . ."[26] The writer's tone signaled his astonishment at the prices; his language implied that the auctioned cattle had become works of art. They could not have been more strongly differentiated from working livestock. Possession of such animals required no pragmatic explanation. They were intrinsically desirable objects of conspicuous consumption.

Published praise of elite cattle often characterized their distinctive qualities in vaguely aesthetic or emotional or even moral terms, which primarily communicated the intensity of the admirer's response. Io, a shorthorned cow exhibited by Lord Althorp and "literally loaded" with flesh, was a creature of "great substance"; Mr. Gibbs's longhorned cow displayed "great . . . character." George IV was so struck by reports of the "beauty and symmetry" of a Southdown wether that its owner brought the sheep to Brighton, so that the King could see it before it was slaughtered. His Majesty declared himself highly gratified by his inspection. A Devon ox of the earl of Leicester's "was considered as beautiful and perfect as any ever seen, and does great credit to the Noble Earl's skill and judgment."[27] Whole breeds could also inspire intense appreciation. An anonymous admirer of shorthorns described Charles Colling's strain as a "numerous race of beautiful animals." Their charm was an index of their virtue, according to another expert. A writer for the *Quarterly Review of Agriculture* found shorthorns "irresistibly attractive." He rose to heady lyrical heights, extolling "the exquisitely symmetrical form of the body . . . bedecked with a skin of the richest hues . . . ornamented with a small . . . head [and] prominent mildly beaming eyes." Transfigured from workaday creatures of farmyard and slaughterhouse, prize cattle became embodiments of beauty and elegance.[28]

In order to distinguish among these excellent creatures, however, more precise standards were required. Most elite breeders and the judges who were drawn from their ranks seemed to agree that the most impressive animals were those that pushed natural limits or approached unattainable ideals. The most obvious limit was size. All the prize animals regularly featured in agricultural periodicals were generously proportioned, and some were notable only for their grossness—for example "a very remarkable Devonshire heifer" who weighed over 1300 pounds although only 13½ hands high, or a Leicestershire hog which, at 960 pounds, "is supposed to be the largest in the kingdom."[29] The numbers projected the same crude magnificence that attracted crowds to admire the Durham ox. Similarly, when the excellences of different breeds were compared—a tricky matter, since, as one early nineteenth-century agricultural writer explained, "what would be an imperfection in one sort, may be none in another,"—the bottom line tended to be size. Thus Henry Berry, an earnest defender of shorthorns against the rival claims of Herefords, based his argument on their superiority in the "valuable properties of obtaining early maturity, and great weights."[30]

Size was also the usual criterion for deciding impromptu breed-to-breed competitions, which might be triggered when some warm advocate offered a general challenge on behalf of his favorite strain. In this respect, as in others, the contests offered an exaggerated version of the flamboyant display institutionalized in show competition among indi-

The gala banquet that climaxed the RASE show of 1843.
From the *Illustrated London News.*

vidual animals. They usually involved great fanfare, specially appointed judges, prizes for the winner, and lots of betting, all of which inspired extra enthusiasm and bravado among the principals and their supporters. One such gauntlet was thrown down in 1839, at a public dinner on the eve of the first annual show of the Royal Agricultural Society of England (still called the English Agricultural Society at that point). In order to publicize the virtues of Sussex cattle, Mr. Selmes, of Beckley, Sussex, offered to match one hundred of his animals against one hundred belonging to any one else in England. The challenge was accepted by the chairman, no less a person than the Earl Spencer, the president of the Smithfield Club. Although the challenges were couched in the standard rhetoric of patriotic service—helping farmers to select the best breed for their herds—the disjunction between these assertions and the actual results of the contests was so obvious that not even fellow breeders could be persuaded to take them seriously as measures of the comparative merit of different breeds. Indeed, the very next year the council of the fledgling RASE, which had been founded to mediate between the goals of the Smithfield Club and those of the defunct Board of Agriculture, moved to eliminate this freewheeling approach, resolving "that the Society cannot sanction challenges of any kind."[31]

Prize cattle were celebrated in pictures as well as in words. Livestock portraiture became popular in England in the middle of the eighteenth century, and cattle were much the most frequent subjects of the genre. Owners commissioned artists to paint their favorite beasts, while humbler enthusiasts contented themselves with mass-produced engravings.[32] Many agricultural periodicals catered to the apparently insatiable appetite of their readers by providing each month an engraved animal portrait suitable for framing. Even after illustrations of this kind had been available for half a century, they were considered effective in attracting an audience to a new publication. In the preface to its first issue, which appeared in March 1845, the *Agricultural Magazine, and Journal of Scientific Farming* promised "in every Number we shall present our readers with splendid Engravings of Prize Cattle . . . and such like objects." The journal's editors apparently considered this promise so compelling that they repeated it in the subtitle, which also proclaimed "Illustrated with Engravings."[33]

The Castle Howard Oxen, lithograph by J. W. Giles,
after H. Strafford, c. 1840.

A massive ox. George Stubbs, *Lincolnshire Ox,* 1790–91.

Like the verbal descriptions they often accompanied, portraits of prize oxen indicated profound admiration for their subjects; they were more direct, however, in identifying the grounds for this appreciation. In contrast to the rhetoric of delicacy and refinement, the portraits often displayed an almost brutal mass, mitigated only by the animal's composed posture and benign expression. Cattle were always depicted from a full side view that emphasized their solid, square bodies, which appeared yet solider between slim, short legs and relatively diminutive heads. Often they were depicted alone, looming against the background of a distant landscape. If a composition included human figures, the noble animal was apt to dwarf them. Breeders encouraged artists to stress grandeur, an emphasis which symbolically enhanced the stature of the animal's owner. To appeal to this interest in sheer size, Thomas Bates made sure that both mass-produced engravings of his carefully bred shorthorns and the paintings on which they were based were "drawn . . . so that the dimensions of each part of an animal might be at once ascertained." Some breeders were more concerned with dimensions than with accuracy. Thomas Bewick once lost a commission for refusing to enhance the amplitude of the animals he was painting. He objected to sticking on "lumps of fat here and there," after the manner of fashionable livestock portraits, when he could see no such protrusions on the beasts in front of him. Thomas Sidney Cooper (also known as "Cow" Cooper), who had a long and prolific Victorian career as a livestock painter, may have owed his durable appeal to his willingness to endow his subjects with monumental forms and noble expressions.[34]

If prize animals figured their wealthy owners, it was not surprising that they were valued for the qualities that distinguished the human elite: dignity, social position, and breeding. Especially a stately prize bull, from which vast herds might spring, seemed a fitting representation of the lord of the manor, in traditional agrarian ideology the quasi-patriarch of an extended rural family. (That such a family might transcend species as well as class barriers was implied by the congratulations extended by the *Annals of Sporting and Fancy Gazette* to a Yorkshire gentleman, who, on a single August morning, was presented with twin baby daughters, eight piglets, and seven kittens.) A collection of cattle portraits, the record of generations of celebrated stock, resembled a gallery of distinguished ancestors, and a collection of cattle pedigrees was like a family tree. These records might offer a model for human practice as well as an emblem of it; Lawrence Stone has suggested that the example of eighteenth-century livestock breeding "inevitably led men to choose their wives as they would a brood mare, with a great care for their personal genetic inheritance."[35]

The appearance of the first volume of the *General Short-Horned Herd Book* in 1822 emphasized the analogy between human and bovine genealogy. It was a rather luxurious volume, printed in large type on heavy paper with wide margins, and it had long been awaited by breeders and fanciers. The idea for the compilation was initially broached at an agricultural meeting in 1810, and George Coates, who compiled the *Herd Book*, alluded in its preface to "the universally *admitted want of a work of this sort.*"[36] Modeled on the *Stud Book*, established three decades earlier to catalog thoroughbred horses, the first animals to be selectively bred in Britain, it identified each cow and bull by name.[37] This was necessary for detailed record keeping, but it also increased the personal dignity and individuality of the animals, making it easier for people to identify with them. Coates then noted the animal's color, birthdate, owner, breeder, and ancestors for as many generations as they could be traced. (This was often as many as five or six, even at the beginning, since some breeders had begun to record genealogies much earlier; at the end of the nineteenth century the oldest shorthorn pedigree could be traced back to 1760.)[38] The entries for cows also included a table of information about their offspring. In 1825 the author of an agricultural encyclopedia found the fact that the "pedigrees of the best cattle have been preserved with no less care . . . then those of race horses" sufficiently surprising to remark.[39] But he did not go on to contemplate the equally compelling and more astonishing resemblance between the *Herd Book* and the tome in which many of the owners and breeders listed by Coates had their own entries: Debrett's catalog of the peerage and baronetage of Great Britain.[40] Many genealogically distinguished humans tended their own and their animals' bloodlines with equal assiduity; Lord Althorp, who was well known to sit down every Monday morning, even when he was in London, to update his pedigree records, may have been only unusually methodical in his application.[41]

For both animals and people a distinguished lineage divided those with hereditary claims to high status from arrivistes. Thus, those who cared the most about maintaining the purity of bloodlines needed to exercise constant vigilance in order to ensure not only that they were not contaminated or falsified, but also that they continued to represent an absolute distinction between prize cattle and those dedicated to workaday purposes. For some breeders even the *Herd Book* was not exclusive enough. Although he had supported its original publication, Thomas Bates, who belonged to an old gentry family, stopped listing the members of his famous Kirklevington herd after Coates, who had been his friend, died. His disdain had several grounds. Because the editor did not systematically check information submitted by breeders, they could use their entries to "puff off" their stock deceptively; it functioned as advertising as well as a historical record. Equally distressing, in Bates's view, was the fact that the *Herd Book* included all registered pedigreed shorthorns, even those destined for ordinary uses. He thought it should list only animals likely to figure in the best future pedigrees, not "mere fat and dairy stock."[42] He cast aspersions on other strains in terms that emphasized his demanding standards, characterizing Charles Colling's legendary beasts as "mongrels." The very names of his animals suggested that if other pedigreed shorthorns were aristocrats, his were something better still. Instead of devising a new name for each cow or bull, he recycled the old ones, numbering them "like a

royal succession." When his herd was sold at auction in 1851, it included the third, fourth, fifth, and sixth dukes of York among the bulls
and duchess the fifty-fourth through sixty-fourth (with a few gaps)
among the cows.[43]

Bates's views on pedigree were simply an extreme version of those
held by other breeders of prize cattle. He valued not merely the length
of a pedigree, but *"the length of time there had been a succession of the best blood,
without any inferior blood intervening."*[44] As a result, he was an uncompromising advocate of in-and-in breeding from stock of certified excellence, that is, of mating closely related animals. He dismissed with contempt suggestions that occasional crosses produced real benefits—the
restoration of vitality and the correction of innate weaknesses intensified by inbreeding. His values transcended such everyday pragmatism;
distinguished lineage should not, he felt, be compromised for mere
mongrel vigor. After all, as a correspondent of the *Agricultural Magazine*
pointed out in 1845, "there are two distinct . . . classes as relates to the
breeding of animals." Stock destined merely "for use" had no need of
pure bloodlines. But as regarded stock reserved for the higher task of
"improving the qualities . . . of the species generally," most fanciers
would agree with the author of a breeding manual published in the
1820s that "the descent or lineage of animals is . . . a matter of the
utmost importance."[45]

Like the predilection for fatness, exaggerated esteem for racial purity
divided elite breeders from people more pragmatically concerned with
meat production. Livestock fanciers disregarded warnings from experts
that the leading breeds were deteriorating, not simply because of inbreeding, but because certain pedigrees were regarded as desirable no
matter how unimpressive the animals they adorned. In the hands of
ignorant or unscrupulous breeders, inferior members of celebrated bovine lineages were allowed to procreate, thus simultaneously diluting
the bloodlines and undermining their value. The testimony of butchers,
who would pay £2 or £3 more for crossbred than for pedigreed oxen,
and others representing the public market for livestock, had, predictably, even less effect. Judges in the duke of Richmond's cattle show of
1853 were praised for "having been guided chiefly by a regard to the
purity of the breed," rather than to qualities that would have appealed
to the "uninitiated." Five years later an article in the *Journal of the Royal
Agricultural Society of England*, with somewhat circular logic, cited the fact

The Duke of Northumberland, one of Thomas Bates's aristocratic shorthorns.
From Cadwallader John Bates, *Thomas Bates and the Kirklevington Shorthorns*, 1897.

that purebred animals won most of the prizes at national shows as incontrovertible evidence that crossing was "a speculative, if not a dangerous proceeding."[46]

Technical Considerations

The wealthy agriculturists who owned extravagantly formed prize cattle and presided over elite organizations, shows, and sheepshearings were not the only ones interested in the rhetoric of stock breeding. Parallel to their discourse of exclusiveness and self-display developed an alternative grounded in technical values. It celebrated not the power and position of the proprietors of landed estates, but the intelligence and manipulative skill of the men who actually produced the emblematic animals. Although aristocratic and gentry fanciers usually provided the money for the development of highly pedigreed strains, they seldom provided the knowledge or brains.[47] Even the most committed and enthusiastic amateurs were apt to get into trouble when they tried to make their own decisions about selecting and managing their livestock. Despite his meticulous record keeping and his dedicated service to the Smithfield Club and the RASE, Lord Althorp's breeding decisions resulted in "deformed and unhealthy" cattle with "thin quarters and no breasts"; he made matters worse by constantly "doctoring and dosing them."[48] On the whole his peers preferred to act as patrons, leaving the practical decisions to the technical innovators who interpreted the fruits of their labors not as reaffirming the traditional rural order, but as legitimizing the aspirations of skilled, hard-working professionals. As most of these experts were employed by elite fanciers, so their discourses were not sharply distinguished; a single splendid animal could represent the goals of both groups, and a single text often contained elements of both points of view. Nevertheless, the rhetoric of the animal husbandry specialists was ultimately antitraditional, and thus inevitably at odds with that of the landed proprietors.

It was in the interest of both groups to emphasize the progress that had been made since the middle of the eighteenth century; they agreed in their low estimate of the livestock which had previously populated Britain. It consisted of a mishmash of local strains, developed as a result of the interplay between mostly random matings and environmental conditions.[49] Most breeds were all-purpose—that is, sheep produced both wool and meat, and cattle produced both milk and meat—although some had individual strengths on which shrewd breeders could capitalize. For example, since Lancashire farmers preferred to breed from yearling bulls, their longhorned cattle tended to mature earlier than other kinds; in addition, their milk was considered particularly good for cheese making.[50] The "general views" of the agriculture of the counties of England and Wales that the Board of Agriculture commissioned soon after its establishment attempted to identify such qualities in order to expedite improvement. Thus it was revealed that in Chester "the size, form, and production of the udder is more attended to than the figure and bulk of the beast," and that Monmouth produced large oxen "much in demand among English graziers." Perhaps more important, however, was the denigration of most old-fashioned strains—the black cattle of Carmarthen that were "ill-shaped and unprofitable to the pail" and the Cumberland longhorns that lacked "any peculiar good qualities"—in implicit comparison to those being developed by the new animal husbandry technology.[51]

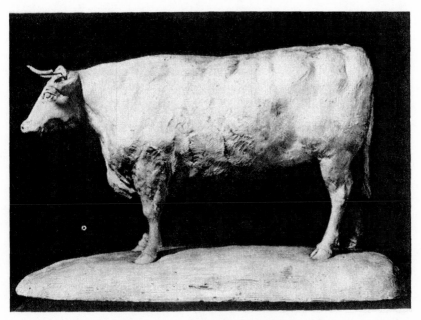

One of Garrard's models, *The Wonderful Ox* (*Holderness Shorthorn*).

One reason for the inferiority of the preexisting stock was conceptual. Even when they were not simply geographical, traditional schemes of discrimination did not offer much direction for the exercise of the improver's expertise. By way of differentiating regional strains of cattle, one mid-eighteenth-century husbandry manual noted that "in Staffordshire they are commonly black, and in Gloucestershire red," another that "in some parts of Surrey we meet with the White Sort." The standards of excellence were also quite different from those generally accepted by the end of the century. Where Sir John Sinclair listed the "most desirable properties of livestock" as size, form, early maturity, hardiness of constitution, and prolific quality, one of his predecessors recommended choosing cows that were "high of Stature, long-bodied, having great Udders."[52] Neither question—how to distinguish breeds from each other and what standard to apply to individuals of given breeds—had been completely settled by the end of the eighteenth century. For this reason, the Board of Agriculture commissioned the artist George Garrard to create a series of rather large scale models (two and a quarter inches to one foot) of livestock breeds (mostly cattle, with a few sheep and pigs); and when he put them on public display at his house in Hanover Square, the board appropriated 5 guineas for tickets so that its members could examine them. In an enormous folio volume based on the exhibition, Garrard stressed the impressive technical expertise embodied in the animals he had portrayed. His readers would have access, he asserted in the introduction, to "ideas which have seldom been obtained without great expence and the practice of many years."[53]

Garrard thus implicitly distinguished such elite fanciers as the members of the Board of Agriculture from the breeders who had developed the exemplary strains. Robert Bakewell, the most famous stock breeder in England when he died in 1795, epitomized the new agricultural technologists. Although his legendary skill as a breeder made him rich and attracted the admiration of wealthy amateur agriculturists, he did not belong to the upper classes. Like his father and grandfather, he was the tenant of the Leicestershire farm known as Dishley Grange; in his youth he laid the foundation of his future eminence by careful observation of the practices of other farmers. The chronology of the first part of his career is not well established, but he may have experimented with cattle and sheep breeding for fifteen years before he achieved a reputation among specialists, and for twenty-five before he was discovered by Arthur Young in 1770. In his later years, corpulent and hospitable, he often received aristocratic visitors who came to examine the evidence of his technical prowess: the fleshy, symmetrical and fine-boned strain of sheep, called New Leicesters or the Dishley breed, that he had developed out of the heavy-boned, awkwardly built, and slow-feeding old Leicesters indigenous to his neighborhood, and the similarly proportioned cattle derived from earlier longhorns.[54]

Bakewell's characterizations of his animals made clear that their impressive bulk meant something quite different to him than it did to his aristocratic patrons. It symbolized not social power or preeminence, but the ability to manipulate natural raw material; the reward for success was not status but money. Although he had a reputation for kindness to his animals—it was reported that as a result of his patient treatment of them, even "his largest bulls would suffer themselves to be led by a child, with a twine thread"—his rhetoric transformed them from living creatures into inanimate objects. On the theoretical level, he held that an excellent cow or sheep was "the best machine for converting herbage into money." Using a homelier metaphor, he likened the ideal animal to a "hogshead . . . truly circular, with small and as short legs as possible: upon the plain principle, that the value lies in the barrel."[55] To achieve this goal, he selected individuals inclined to fatten and to mature early—the less time between birth and butcher the better. Thus absolute size was a by-product of more important commercial qualities— the external characteristics that promised the smallest possible proportion of unsalable bones and offal in the final carcass. Bakewell's disciple George Culley emphasized the inconsistency thus implied between Bakewell's pragmatic objectives and the less tangible goals of amateur fanciers: "It perhaps has been . . . the idea of largeness, or the wish to breed the biggest . . . that has so long prevented our breeders from . . . distinguishing the most valuable kinds." Another index of this disjunction was Bakewell's tendency to view even his living animals as a collection of parts. His most elaborately engineered creatures were relatively large in the expensive rump cuts and small in the cheaper shoulder ones; he once boasted to an astonished French visitor that he could produce "beasts which would put on fat in the tail."[56]

Bakewell's results were achieved primarily by means of in-and-in breeding, a technique which he championed as earnestly as the most elaborately pedigreed agriculturist. Arthur Young recounted with admiration that "he sets entirely at naught the old ideas of the necessity of variation from crosses; on the contrary, the sons cover the dams, and the sires their daughters with no attention whatever to vary the race." But once again Bakewell imbued an apparently shared discourse with an alternative meaning. He did not see his own lineage reflected in the racial purity of his animals any more than he sympathized with the occasional religious objections to in-and-in breeding on grounds of incest. As Culley reiterated the master's teaching, "there can be *no danger* in breeding by the nearest affinities, provided they are possessed in a *superior degree* of the qualities we wish to acquire."[57] From this point of view, in-and-in breeding lacked either a political or a religious charge; instead, crossing within a restricted lineage of animals selected for desirable characteristics was simply an effective technique for increasing control over the quality of the next generation.

If Bakewell was widely praised for his animal husbandry, the reverse was true of his commercial practices, which clearly signaled his indifference to the rhetoric of patriotism and public service enunciated by elite fanciers. Bakewell was a businessman eager, as far as was possible, to reserve the profits of his ingenuity to himself. He went to unusual lengths to maintain control of the stock he had developed. He refused to sell his bulls and rams. Instead, he hired them out, a practice greatly resented by some potential clients, but one that enhanced the value of his animals' services as it slowed the spread of competition. In 1791 Young reported that one of Bakewell's tups rented for 1,000 guineas per season (during which time it would be expected to cover one hundred ewes) and one of his bulls was let out at not less than 25 guineas per cow. Bakewell continued to protect his investment of time and expertise to the very end. It was rumored that when his best animals were past service, they were fattened and sent to the butcher—but not before being infected with sheep rot (a virulent parasitic disease) to make sure that no one else used them as studs.[58]

He was as stingy with advice as he was with his animals, again in contrast with the practice of landowning amateurs. Typical was the response which, as he wrote somewhat coyly to Culley, he had freely proffered to the Envoy Extraordinary from the Elector of Saxony: "The whole of [my] Art . . . was in choosing the best Males to the best Females and keeping them in a thriving state."[59] And although informed speculation identified Leicesters and longhorns as the sources of his improved sheep and cattle, Bakewell himself never revealed either his root stock or the more recent ancestry of his animals; he kept no breeding records and rumor had it that an old shepherd was his only confidant. Several generations of agriculturists grumbled about "the mystery with which he carried on every part of his business, and the means which he employed to mislead the public," often revealing their own allegiance when they attributed it to "the selfishness of a trader."[60]

These persistent complaints from high stock breeders emphasized the bifurcated nature of Bakewell's audience. Although he was celebrated by elite agriculturists in his later years, he retained his affiliations with farmers whose herds and flocks were designed for the commercial market, and according to a later grazier, his business methods were unsurprising when considered in this context. Bakewell was, after all, preeminent but not unique; his peers were not the wealthy fanciers who admired his most extravagant productions, but other commercial breeders, of whom, it was estimated in 1790, the Midlands contained fifteen or twenty of his caliber. Their achievements were measured not in show prizes or in the gushing appreciation of agricultural journalists but in the fact that the weight of ordinary English cattle and sheep at slaughter nearly doubled in the course of the eighteenth century.[61] And even the aristocratic and gentry amateurs whose elegant stock was dedicated to such different ends implicitly acknowledged the disjunction between their cattle, which were appropriately characterized as "enormous" and "magnificent," and those that populated most English pastures. Without moderating the assertion that breeding these creatures evidenced their selfless patriotism, they also encouraged parallel activities explicitly designed to meet the needs of market-oriented farmers.[62]

As usual, the dukes of Bedford were in the forefront. In addition to the high stock breeding that was their primary concern, they sponsored other enterprises specifically geared to the more prosaic animal husbandry of their tenants. Sometimes they used their vast resources to provide information that farmers whose profit margin was narrow might find useful. Young reported one experiment—an expensive proposition requiring spare animals, fodder, and time—on the fattening properties of four sheep breeds under different conditions. Woburn Abbey was also the site of a series of carefully recorded trials of the fattening properties of cattle, sheep, and pigs, the results of which were also intended to aid small-scale cultivators.[63] More permanent was the implicit institutional recognition that an alternative rhetoric required an alternative arena. Although the Woburn sheepshearings had been instituted by the fifth duke of Bedford to improve the practice of area farmers, they had quickly attracted distinguished agriculturists from all over England, who monopolized the prizes for cattle and sheep. Only the plowing competitions were left for the locals. Perhaps that is why the duke became the founding patron of the Bedfordshire Agricultural Society in 1801. Its prize list expanded gradually, with the support of the dukes of Bedford, until it duplicated for local contestants those offered at the more glamorous sheepshearings.[64]

The Critique of Fat Cattle

Segregation minimized the contrasts between the alternative discourses embodied in stock breeding, but it could not eliminate them. Occasionally, therefore, when discrepancies between the competing value systems became unavoidably obvious, direct confrontations took place—usually in a public arena which claimed to represent the entire

Elite breeders and elite animals at the Woburn Sheepshearing,
a private agricultural show; painting by George Garrard.

enterprise. Coates's *Herd Book,* which officially or quasi-officially set the extreme limits of elite status among shorthorned cattle, sparked many skirmishes about whether mere pedigree was a sufficient basis for inclusion, or whether, as Bates urged, a more stringent standard should be applied. Exclusionists won few victories in these struggles. The *Herd Book* remained open to all shorthorns, even without much verification of their alleged ancestry; perhaps predictably, farmers, who valued the book as much for its advertising potential as for its stockpile of pedigrees, outnumbered aristocratic and gentry fanciers among the listed owners.[65] The major battles were provoked by the more spectacular institutional displays that the amateurs definitively controlled: the prize cattle competitions sponsored by the Smithfield Club and a few other national organizations, at which the winners were announced with great fanfare on the spot and widely ballyhooed in both the general and the agricultural press.

Not everyone was equally pleased with the massive creatures that embodied the pride of their aristocratic owners, however. Among those who thronged to admire the highly bred livestock were some who did not understand the display of prize animals as a pageant, and, especially if they took the patriotic and utilitarian rhetoric of high stock breeders literally, were apt to worry about the practical consequences of the judges' preferences for impractical beasts. If these animals were singled out for praise, detractors feared, it was likely that their characteristics would be diffused through British herds, determining the shape of cattle to come.[66] A similar critique might also be mounted by those who recognized but rejected the symbolic function imposed on the shows by the elite breeders who staged them. These reservations could be expressed as denigrations of either the animals or their owners. Half a century after the first Smithfield show, an angry critic characterized most of the prizewinning animals as "mere fat, unwieldy, imbecile brutes." A less agitated but perhaps more trenchant analyst explained the prize animals as "a collection of agricultural luxuries," the playthings of "Dukes and Earls" who "can afford a fancy, whether it is the purchase of a Titian, or the production of a prize bullock." In his view it was probably harmless, but certainly did no good to farmers who had to "confine themselves to what is moderate and profitable."[67]

Such criticism had shadowed the public celebration of fat cattle from the beginning. The December 1800 issue of the *Commercial and Agricul-*

tural Magazine included both interpretations of the animals displayed at the second Smithfield show. It began with a portrait of the ox, "beautifully proportioned, and ... of enormous weight," that had won first prize; the accompanying report rejoiced that "this year's exhibition ... exceeded last year's both in the number of candidates, and in their general fatness and form." This editorial appreciation was, however, immediately followed by "The Humble Petition of 500,000 Frugally Disposed Housekeepers, Resident in the United Kingdoms of England, Scotland, and Ireland," who viewed the *"raree show"* of "overgrown cattle" with "no small degree of alarm." The petitioners implicitly set the breeders' image of magnificent whole animals against their own ideal picture of a useful bovine—one divided up into easily assimilable segments. If the self-indulgent "amateurs" whose productions were displayed at Smithfield had their way, according to these concerned citizens, "we should not have a pound of butcher's meat which either ourselves or our families could eat."[68]

In general, the attack on fat cattle was couched in terms of utility. The criticism worked on both the literal level, by denying the practical value of prizewinning animals, and on the level of metaphor, by undermining the imposing qualities of the beasts and implicitly challenging the equation between the interests of landed fanciers and those of the nation at large. Edibility provided an obvious criterion for counterjudgment; the hefty carcasses of highly fed show animals and their relatives were of no use if consumers had no appetite for them. It was easy to test the taste appeal of the flower of British husbandry. Some Smithfield prizewinners did not have long to enjoy the admiration of the multitudes. Until 1815 club regulations required that competing oxen—which would not, in any case, go on to produce a new generation—be slaughtered and weighed after the show, the results to be recorded by the club secretary as part of "an enlarged inquiry into the merits of different breeds." Their subsequent fate, however, suggested that the purpose of this exercise was more theatrical than scientific. Fashionable butchers bought the most celebrated carcasses and put them on display in their shambles, where the public could gaze on them one last time before they were purchased by great ladies who liked to serve roasts that could be identified by name. Or the animals might posthumously enjoy the judicious appreciation of elite connoisseurs. In 1808 a London correspondent wrote Bates that "a piece of your fat ox" had been announced and eaten at a dinner sponsored by Lord Somerville, a leading improver and an active member of the Smithfield Club.[69]

The critics dismissed this evidence, claiming that even if a few rich people wished to throw their money away on "famous meat . . . to be *admired* in the parlor, and wasted in the kitchen," there was no other market for the "high-priced and greasy ware." Although increased meat production was supposed to enhance the diet of the laboring classes, most working people rejected overfat meat in disgust, when they had any choice. A country clergyman, who included an elite butcher shop in his tour of metropolitan sights, "could hear nothing but the language of aversion and ridicule, in the surrounding and gaping crowd." And if laborers, whose muscular and digestive vigor was guaranteed by strenuous physical exercise, avoided such fare, who could happily or safely eat it? In 1827 one observer announced that "there is scarcely a human palate so vitiated as to relish such rancid and oleaginous food as the beef of the pampered prize oxen generally is."[70] These grave charges implied that, far from being patriotic, the efforts of high stock breeders might be treasonous, undermining the livestock industry and poisoning the citizens who depended upon it for their food.

Champion cattle were vulnerable to criticism on other pragmatic grounds as well. As the emphasis on pedigree made clear, the primary function of such creatures was to produce offspring that would transmit their desirable qualities to future generations. Yet the techniques used to ensure that they realized their hereditary potential often impaired the reproductive capacity of the animals alleged to possess the most valuable genetic endowment. Breeders identified cattle with show potential at an early age and put them on lavish feeding programs designed to load them with as much flesh as possible. In prize bulls the resulting fertility problem was often simple sluggishness, which could be remedied by a period on short commons. But excessive fattening frequently caused permanent reproductive damage to heifers, so that many outstanding females failed to become the mothers of the next generation.[71] Further, all prize animals were products of in-and-in breeding. Although this system was incomparably effective in establishing pure strains that would breed true, it was also, when continued for several generations, likely to impair the fertility of highly bred animals and make them more susceptible to disease. In both cases the sufferers would be not breeders of the prizewinners, but the owners of their several times removed descendants. Fanciers who had invested in Colling's cattle at the 1810 sale and subsequently maintained their herds exclusively by inbreeding, often found them slowly declining in vigor and value as a result, and similar problems accounted at least in part for the waning reputation of Bakewell's breeds in the nineteenth century.[72]

If the health of prize cattle could be vitiated by the very genealogical and physical qualities for which they were celebrated, the regimen under which they lived also impaired their day-to-day physical functioning. To those not attuned to the standards of magnificence that dominated livestock shows, fat beasts simply looked sick. *Punch* frequently remarked on the shortness of breath of the prizewinners and the difficulty they found in moving. Most competitors were delivered to their show pens in special wagons; some had to be carried where they could not be wheeled. (Pigs were even worse than cattle in this regard; some highly admired specimens were so obese that bulging flesh obscured both their legs and their foreheads.) One clergyman objected that it was inhumane to fatten beasts to such extremes. He felt that animals "unable to stand and scarcely able to move or breathe, from the state of overwhelming and torturing obesity to which they had been unnaturally forced," provided a "cruel and unchristian exhibition."[73]

To some extent, the Smithfield Club—that is, the pacesetting breeders who figured most prominently in its activities—retreated in the face of these sustained criticisms. Writing in 1805, an apologist blamed some of the early competitors for not understanding the club's purpose ("the selection of such breeds . . . as . . . yield the greatest quantity of good . . . from the produce of a given quantity of land . . . and the best . . . modes of fattening each kind of animal for market") and producing animals of "monstrous fatness." As a result, he asserted, "much obloquy unjustly fell on the Club, and its patriotic members." Without explaining why the show judges had decided to reward such misconceived efforts, he assured his readers that the description of the prizes had been altered, "so as . . . to exclude competitors who, from vanity or other motives, might entertain views different from the very laudable ones which actuate the Club." One Joseph Pawsey, writing to Lady Lucas in the same year, announced that "*fat* cattle are declining in price, [and] I presume the Duke of Bedford's plan of very fat Cattle & Sheep in particular will be given up by prudent *men*."[74]

Attentive readers of the agricultural press might, therefore, have been surprised to learn, ten years later, that the great majority of the animals exhibited in the Christmas cattle show were "gross, coarse-boned and excessively fattened." At the 1821 show, the judges were "guided in their decisions by the quantity of flesh." In 1832 the judges received special written instructions requesting them "to keep strictly in view the object for which the Smithfield Club was originally instituted," presumably to counteract their inclination to award the prizes to the fattest beasts.[75] Lapses and recoveries continued. The 1847 Smithfield show was "much less objectionable on the score of excessive obesity than any preceding one for a long time past"; one reporter remarked with relief that "the great fat question is now subsiding into reasonable limits." The same, oddly, was noted of the 1852 show, and again in 1853 "a most decided advance was observable . . . in the absence of those huge masses of fat that formerly were so characteristic." At the 1857 show once more the animals did not seem "so outrageously fat as formerly."[76]

The continuing and hard-to-suppress predilection for fat animals was not confined to Smithfield exhibitors and judges. In 1821, just before it went out of business, the Board of Agriculture sponsored its only agricultural exhibition. Protesters interrupted the prize ceremony, complaining that although the purpose of the show was to encourage the production of good breeding stock, the premium had been awarded to a bull "which was too fat to serve."[77] Soon after its foundation, the RASE began to sponsor a national agricultural show each summer. Stock judges at the first one, held at Oxford in 1839, were sternly instructed to assess animals on the basis of their breeding potential, not their weight. Despite this precaution, the new organization nevertheless followed in the footsteps of the Smithfield Club. Stringent new rules for evaluating entries in the livestock competition had to be promulgated before the society's show of 1853, held at Gloucester; as a result, "many of our first breeders refused to exhibit, not choosing to run the risk of their animals being disqualified for over fatness." Nevertheless, by foreign standards, the society was soft on excess weight. In 1856 its journal regretfully reported that some of the English cows and heifers sent to an agricultural exposition in Paris had been "excluded from the competition on the score of being too fat and . . . not likely to breed." More than half a century of serious criticism from clients and consumers had failed to erode the English high stock breeder's affinity for portly beasts.[78]

In part this was because elite breeders clung to their utilitarian rhetoric, which, along with the generalized language in which it was often expressed, suggested that they shared their critics' goals. George Culley characterized the object of his breeding efforts as *"well-proportioned handsome animals,"* which would display "beauty or symmetry of shape," meaning a firm, compact carcass, deep and broad; "utility of form," or a body proportioned so that the less valuable parts were as small as possible; finely marbled flesh, which was indicated in the living animal by "the firm and mellow feel" of the skin; and "early maturity," or the power to begin producing fat as soon as possible. The splendid animals would be likely to have been bred from parents who were "small-boned, straight backed ... kindly-skinned, round-bodied, and barrel-shaped."[79] Size was nowhere stipulated as a component of this elegant ideal; it was even denigrated when, as often happened among Yorkshire shorthorn breeders in the pre-Colling era, the desire to produce the largest possible animals threatened to overwhelm concern for "quality." Condemning such crude pursuit of weight as grotesque and vulgar, aficionados of show cattle seemed to agree with small farmers and consumers.[80] But this convergence of views was only apparent. What the critics of show animals wanted was cattle of modest overall proportions. Breeders, by contrast, wished to produce animals whose metabolism was geared to the production of flesh. They therefore tried to eliminate competing internal claims on the animals' energy. Large-boned, rangy cattle were inefficient feeders; a small compact skeleton guaranteed that as little food as possible would be wasted on general maintenance of the animal, and that as much as possible would stick to its ribs. Therefore, although aristocratic breeders sometimes claimed to share the distaste of farmers and consumers for mere size, they applauded every increment of desirable flesh.

The advocates of enormous prize cattle may have been franker about what they admired when they defended size for its own sake, although they still asserted that their motives were strictly practical. Even if prize cattle were "more fat than the ordinary market requirements," President Philip Pusey asserted in the first paper read to the RASE, "the power of reaching that excessive size is the only test by which the capacity for acquiring useful condition, at the cheapest expense and at the earliest age, can be tried under the encouragement of public emulation and competition."[81] By demonstrating the extreme possibilities of their breeds of cattle, at great expense to themselves and without the likelihood of reimbursement from the market, this argument continued, selfless and noble breeders allowed ordinary farmers to gauge the properties of more modestly endowed animals. Despite such protestations, it is far from clear that the major national shows were arranged to encourage ordinary farmers to draw useful conclusions, or that the major exhibitors understood their participation as so public-spirited. A memorandum written by a Bedfordshire farmer after he attended the 1827 Smithfield show, to remind himself how to prepare more effectively for future visits, suggested more confusion than enlightenment: "Get good opinions which are the best Cattle, Sheep & c. So as to be furnished with conversation . . . Attend the Committee to know what is going forward."[82]

Shows sponsored by regional societies, even those organized on a very large scale, more effectively embodied the concerns of professional farmers and breeders. Thus when T. C. Hincks, who criticized the RASE shows of the early 1840s as insufficiently relevant to the concerns of ordinary farmers, suggested those of the Yorkshire Agricultural Society as alternative models, he was proposing a revolution in discourse. By taking the rhetoric of improvement literally and seriously, Hincks showed how divergent were the alleged goals of prize cattle breeding and its actual results as determined and celebrated at prestigious national livestock shows. If show animals were intended to improve the herds and flocks of ordinary farmers, he argued, then farmers should be able to show the animals they had found most useful. Because wealthy amateurs inevitably crowded such competitors out of the ring, Hincks wanted to make gentlemen occupying their own land and even tenant farmers renting more than three hundred acres ineligible for money prizes. Even more important, he felt, was the question of collecting useful information, the raw data which was available in massive quantities at each national stock show, but which was inexplicably allowed to escape without being recorded while the organizers invested their energy in "mere pageants," characterized by "pomp and circumstance" inappropriate to a technical economic enterprise.[83] He thought that the judges' standards for merit in each class should be circulated before each show; that the name and pedigree of each animal, along with the breeder's name and address, should be included in the printed catalog (this policy was adopted by the RASE several years later);[84] that the judges should record the "facts" upon which they had based their opinions; and that these facts should be published for the benefit of agricultural scientists and others who could make use of them. According to this prescription, livestock exhibitions would no longer provide occasions for symbolic affirmation of the traditional rural order; instead, they would celebrate and enhance the alternative authority embodied in technical expertise.

The Widening Circle

In its most highly publicized and expensive form, livestock breeding represented and reinforced the power and position of elite fanciers, although it also appropriated the rhetoric of utility. Many English citizens had no objection to this. They respected wealthy landowners without begrudging them their privileges and were content to admire the pageantry without wondering whether they would suffer as a result. This appreciative public was inclined to accept the claims of aristocratic and gentry agriculturists to represent the nation at its best and to celebrate their excesses as evidence of shared distinction. The very soberest authorities were wont to congratulate the British on their aptitude for producing superior stock. Even Caesar had noticed the size of the British herds; according to Mela, "cattle constituted the true wealth of the Britons." An early president of the RASE discerned "in the people of this country a peculiar disposition and talent for encouraging the finest animal forms."[85] And it was fitting that such splendid native products be cultivated at the social pinnacle, from which, in the view of one agricultural journalist, "all honour and high bearing" flowed.[86]

The counter to this hegemonic rhetoric came from people who interpreted livestock breeding as the expression of less traditional values—who defined individual worth not by social position but by skill and enterprise. This point of view probably had more adherents than was obvious even to those who advocated it; just as the rhetoric of professional breeders was entangled with that of landowning amateurs, so the crowds who flocked to admire the overbearing animals displayed at national agricultural shows may have been paying tribute as much to the technical skill of the professionals as to the preeminence of their patrons. One practical-minded critic retroactively berated the multitudes who had paid to see the Durham ox and the first Smithfield

Christmas cattle show because these frivolous displays "have not such business depending on them as might be desired," but instead represented only "the eagerness of fancy agriculturalists to win prizes." In order to emphasize the magnitude of this popular folly, he noted that attendance had exceeded "anything except the Crystal Palace of 1851."[87] This comparison of spectacles may not have been completely fortuitous. The primary attraction of the Great Exhibition, its manifold illustration of the human ability to manipulate the physical world, was also implicit in the masterpieces of agricultural technology, monuments as much to the engineers who had designed them as to the wealthy agriculturists who had paid for them.

Even the identification of beef with "the character and propensities of the nation" could be incorporated into the rhetoric of innovation. After all, John Bull was a yeoman, not an improving landlord. The patriotic claims of elite stock breeders were based on domination, which was symbolically expressed in the vast size of prize specimens. This rhetoric either metaphorically equated enormous prize cattle with their similarly magnificent owners or, using a displacement based on the animals' simultaneous functions as representatives and chattels, metonymically presented them as ostentatious evidence of their owners' powers of consumption. *Punch* ironically underscored this point in describing an imaginary prize footman show, where the first prize went to "Sir G. Chokefull, Bart., for a hall porter, aged 68: weighs 20 stone, fatted on 15,000 lbs. of roast beef, cabbage, hot-rolls, and porter. Waddled to the show 100 yards, wheeled in his chair the rest."[88] The patriotism of agricultural engineers, on the contrary, emphasized superior English ability to manipulate and produce, buttressing its verbal assertions with statistical rather than visual imagery. Enormous numbers, as opposed to enormous animals, testified to the prowess of expert professional breeders. The English ate six times as much beef as did the French, who even so were pitifully unable to supply their own demand. "It was certainly gratifying to England," according to one analyst in 1840, that 22 million French agricultural laborers working 40 million hectares produced only 40,000 horses, 800,000 oxen, and 5,200,000 sheep annually, while 5 million British farm workers with only 13 million hectares produced 170,000 horses, 1,200,000 oxen, and 10,200,000 sheep.[89]

The alternative interpretation of livestock breeding offered by agricultural professionals, their admirers, and those who sympathized or identified with their goals may also have included a more abstract objection to the hegemonic rhetoric of elite landowners. If stock breeding—both the possession of enormous animals and the process of developing and extending pedigrees—symbolized leadership and social prestige, then prize cattle did more than enhance the position of their owners. They implicitly excluded those who could not afford them, drawing a single, significant social division between wealthy amateur agriculturists and all others. Consequently, some critics in relatively modest financial circumstances resented the metaphorical association of stock breeding and human preeminence because it seemed to deny them a kind of social distinction that they coveted. They were to find, however, that breeding a smaller and less expensive animal provided equal opportunity for careful discrimination of rank.

CHAPTER TWO

Prize Pets

In 1911 Judith Neville Lytton's *Toy Dogs and Their Ancestors* took on what was known as the doggy world of England.[1] Lytton was a knowledgeable and opinionated young dog breeder, tennis champion, and general animal fancier, who later wrote extensively about thoroughbred horses. Her aristocratic background—she was a baroness in her own right and the wife of an earl—distinguished her from most serious fanciers of pedigreed dogs. Similarly, *Toy Dogs* did not belong to the ordinary run of breed books, which cozily rehearsed the accepted standards for show dogs, spotlighted a few successful kennels, then dispensed received wisdom about feeding, treatment of minor illnesses, and similar quotidian concerns. Lytton relegated these routine items to the end of her richly illustrated volume. She devoted the initial chapters to a systematic assault on the contemporary toy dog fancy, mounting her attack in terms that could have been applied to any group of pedigreed dogs and their admirers.

In Lytton's view giving detailed practical advice to owners and breeders was putting the cart before the horse. Before fanciers devoted effort and expense to raising and showing dogs, they had to ensure that the animals merited the outlay. Although an elaborate structure for assessing and certifying dogs had developed over the previous half-century— a pyramid based on local and breed-specific clubs and shows, culminating in the national, multibreed Kennel Club—she felt that this structure was resting on sand, or worse. It was, she charged, designed to enforce standards that had no basis in nature or aesthetics but reflected the ignorant, self-interested caprices of fanciers who wished to boost the prestige of their own stock. Not even the accepted breed categories survived her scrutiny. She used strong language to emphasize the seriousness of the situation. To outsiders, she charged, "the present judging system appears ridiculous and contemptible."[2]

She based her criticism, in part, on obvious defects of animals with classy pedigrees: they were physically unsound, they had sparse coats and ugly expressions, and they were excessively timid, sluggish, and idiotic. These faults had only to be pointed out to be acknowledged. Any breeder with even a smattering of Darwin would have agreed that art should follow nature in preferring the strong and beautiful to the weak and grotesque. But this was only the beginning of Lytton's complaint. Much of what displeased her about Edwardian toy spaniels— square jaws, black and tan coats, and relatively stocky physiques— seemed rather neutral on that stern scale. Such characteristics revealed what Lytton considered the most unforgivable flaw of the toy spaniels of her day: that they had diverged from their historical prototypes. Although their ancestors could be certified for many generations, they did not, in her opinion, resemble the dogs that had established their ostensible breed. As a result, she insisted, their pedigrees were fundamentally fraudulent, however long and well documented.[3]

There was no question that the toy spaniel had a venerable history. The names of its two major sub-breeds took it back at least to the Restoration: the King Charles (named for Charles II) and the Blenheim (after the palace built by the first duke of Marlborough). The breed, or one closely related, may also have flourished under the name of "comforter" during the reign of Elizabeth I.[4] In Lytton's view the toy spaniels she saw around her had diverged from the original Stuart or Tudor pattern in color, size, and facial configuration. The scarcity of concrete information about the pre–nineteenth-century history of the breed made these assertions difficult to prove, but she marshaled an eclectic variety of evidence, including pictures as well as written documents, to demonstrate that "the present square-jawed, heavy, noseless type was introduced . . . no earlier than . . . 1840"; that it was, indeed, a "modern fake"; that "the whole red variety . . . cannot be traced back more than eighty years"; and that "the present standard and scale of points had apparently no foundation earlier than 1885 or 1887." In sum, she asserted, "there is a hopeless confusion in the naming of breeds and in the type desired."[5]

Lytton's criticism struck at the heart of the dog fancy, focused as it was on a series of finely graded differentiations, which functioned both to establish the unique character of each breed and to assess the relative excellence of dogs of the same breed. Firmly grounded in the animals' physical attributes, which were endlessly rehearsed in manuals and concretely exemplified in show after show, this elaborate system of categories metaphorically expressed the hopes and fears of fanciers about issues like social status and the need for distinctions between classes. Unlike Lytton, most late Victorian dog fanciers belonged to the urban business and professional classes. To many of them, the figurative dimension of dog fancying may have been the more important; it offered a vision of a stable, hierarchical society, where rank was secure and individual merit, rather than just inherited position, appreciated. The content of fancying categories thus became a by-product of the process of assigning ranks and orders, and one powerful criterion for a specification was whether it made this process easier. By analyzing the physical consequences of this policy, Lytton also undermined the rhetorical manipulations that masked it. Toy spaniels had lost their historical authenticity as well as their beauty and vigor at the hands of fanciers who had disingenuously proclaimed that they were protecting and improving the breed.

Class Barriers

Lytton assaulted the dog fancying establishment as both a radical and a conservative. Her method was that of a Young Turk, but her accusations implicitly labeled adherents of the entrenched bureaucracy as arrivistes. They cherished the letter of tradition, she claimed, with their punctilious recording of pedigrees, while disregarding its spirit. Although they might place themselves within the ancient British tradition of dog breeding, she insinuated, only aristocratic fanciers like herself, who strove to maintain old values and old stock, really belonged there. Although Lytton did not go so far as to say so, this very association of dog breeding with the social elite was one of the things that attracted the fanciers whose self-interested manipulations she deplored. Adopting an upper-class avocation was a way of reinforcing their own social position. And the dog fancy was perhaps uniquely open to people of moderate means—certainly much more so than high stock breeding. Although dog breeding was not apt to be a profitable hobby, it did not require either great wealth or broad acres. A beginner could invest a fortune—one Mr. Stephens of Acton spent £2,000 in setting up a fox terrier kennel—but it was generally agreed that £25, wisely laid out, should suffice.[6]

The British had owned dogs from the beginning of recorded history, but the relation of most Victorian fanciers to their animals, kept purely for companionship and amusement, was rather new, especially outside the highest social ranks. The invading Romans had described animals identified by nineteenth-century experts as mastiffs, and King Alfred's laws included fines to be levied on the owners of dogs that killed or maimed people. The subjects of these ancient references were doubtless working animals, however, as were the medieval ancestors of later hounds and gun dogs.[7] Unmistakable pets first appeared in the middle ages, as the playthings of courtiers and members of privileged religious orders. Episcopal authorities tried repeatedly to suppress petkeeping among monks and nuns, with little success, but the practice did not spread among ordinary citizens.[8] Although working dogs were ubiquitous in the Renaissance—they turned cooking spits, pulled carts, herded sheep, retrieved game, baited wild animals, and competed in sporting events—pet dogs remained the province of the upper classes, particularly of their female members. King Charles II may have been the first man to declare a public passion for them. When his pets were stolen, as seems to have happened with some frequency, he was inconsolable; once he advertised in a newspaper for a favorite's return. His brother, James II, shared this fondness, as, apparently, did his successors, William and Mary, during whose reign the pug, like William a native of the Netherlands, became established among the English aristocracy. At about the same time, dogs with elite connections, both pets and sporting animals, began to sit for formal portraits.[9]

Despite these exalted pacesetters, it was almost a century before petkeeping became respectable among ordinary citizens. To some extent, the change paralleled the increased public indulgence of the softer emotions during the last part of the eighteenth century and found literary expression in, for example, Christopher Smart's apostrophe to his cat Jeoffry.[10] Although the most extravagant avowals of attachment to pets were still reserved for the upper classes, by the early nineteenth century such effusions were more likely to be greeted with general sympathy than with disapprobation or derision. When, in 1808, Lord Byron (Lytton's great-grandfather) buried his Newfoundland dog Boatswain "within . . . the precincts of the sacred Abbey of Newstead," many of his less distinguished countrymen shared his sense that a dog offered greater loyalty and affection than any human friend or servant—or, as Byron put it on the monument, "all the Virtues of Man without his vices."[11] Increasingly, they felt the same way about their own animals. By the middle of the nineteenth century what has been called the Victorian cult of pets was firmly established. *Punch* frequently satirized the foolishness of dog lovers who fed their pets from the table, dressed them in elaborate outfits, and allowed them to inconvenience human members of the household.

Love was not, however, the whole story. The intensifying attachment of members of the middle classes to their animals could also be measured in cash. Entrepreneurs quickly exploited a range of new commercial opportunities. By mid-century there were approximately twenty thousand London street traders who dealt in live animals, and at least a dozen who specialized in the brass collars, priced from 6d. to 3s. apiece, sported by most respectable Victorian dogs. On the shady side, professional dog stealers would abscond with a cherished animal, then offer to restore it for a price. In 1844 individual Londoners paid from £2 to £50 to ransom favorite pets.[12] More formally marketed were such kennel care products as Spratts Patent Meat "Fibrine" Dog Cakes ("As supplied to the Royal Kennels"), Ashworth's Patent "Metallic Comb-Brush," and, at £10 10s., Boulton and Paul's Dog's House and Yard Combined. At the top of the line a few merchants indulged clients who wished to pay 30s. to have their monogram clipped into their dog's fur, or £5 for a satin wedding coat, or up to £60 for collars and other ornaments of gold and silver.[13]

The publishing industry also catered to the increasing audience of middle-class dog fanciers. Before the nineteenth century, books about dogs were few and far between, and most simply rehashed the curious information offered in Johannus Caius's *De Canibus Britannicus*, published in Latin in 1570 and in translation, as *Of Englishe Dogges*, in 1576. Caius's treatise was an annotated list of Tudor dog types, compiled as a favor to the Swiss bestiarist Konrad Gesner.[14] An expanded market inspired a sudden stream of dog books beginning with Sydenham Edwards's handsomely illustrated *Cynographia Britannica*, which was issued in parts between 1800 and 1805. These volumes reflected both the emotional and the material concerns of genteel pet owners. Whereas earlier dog literature seemed simply a specialized branch of natural history, the new books included not only descriptions of the dogs' physical and moral characteristics, but a selection of heartwarming and enlightening anecdotes. In addition, like the animals they described, most were luxury items, suitable for conspicuous display.[15]

The cherished animals themselves carried impressive price tags, which increased as the dog fancy flourished. Indeed, Charles Rotherham, the veterinarian who attended Queen Victoria's kennel, attributed an absolute rise in the canine population of London between approximately 1865 and 1887 to the snowballing value of purebred dogs. And in turn, according to one journal of the fancy, the "high prices paid nowadays" showed "the progress of the canine race." By 1891 champion collies and St. Bernards sold for £1,000, and hopeful buyers offered £375 for a prize fox terrier and £250 for a particularly distinguished King Charles spaniel.[16] Price was a sensitive indicator of differences among animals. Pedigreed but undistinguished specimens of popular breeds could be had for much less—about 3 guineas if they were merely of pet quality, and a minimum of £10 if "sufficiently perfect" to win in the least competitive shows.[17]

Such carefully chronicled expenditure referred ultimately to the status of the owner rather than that of the dog. Despite its genuinely sentimental roots, much middle-class petkeeping was shadowed by similar motivations. After all, the maintenance of idle animals was a custom borrowed from the upper echelons of society and constituted a metonymic attempt at assimilation; the elaborate certification and registration of pedigreed animals was hardly designed to guarantee their emotional qualities. The incorporation of dogs into the rhetoric of social aspiration did not go unnoticed by those whose practices were being appropriated. Lytton was not the first aristocratic fancier to draw a line between traditional fancying and that introduced in the course of the nineteenth century, although she was rather atypical in choosing to focus her concern on a pet breed. Members of the elite more frequently tried to draw a line between their companion animals—the sporting dogs traditionally associated with rural life—and the pet dogs, designed simply for human pleasure, that urban fanciers favored. As early as 1824, the anonymous but red-blooded author of *The Complete Dog Fancier; or, General History of Dogs* had announced that, his title notwithstanding, "those [dogs] which some fond ladies make their daily pastime, have no business in these pages."[18] His animosity was echoed more mildly in the content of many contemporary volumes of canine appreciation. Until about 1840, most of them were ostensibly addressed to sportsmen and paid primary attention to hounds and gun dogs; but afterward the burgeoning literature gave at least equal attention to the pet breeds typically kept by prosperous urban dog owners.

Rural fanciers were no better pleased when their favorite breeds began to appear as urban pets and in the show ring. It was common knowledge that "Masters of Fox Hounds abominate dog shows"; one sportsman suggested that they "have occasioned more mischief than years on years will serve to eradicate." They feared that animals bred as show dogs or pets would be useless in the field. To address these fears the Kennel Club instituted competitive field trials for sporting breeds like setters and pointers, the results of which supplemented show bench rankings by measures of actual performance. Even "Stonehenge," a crusty critic and perhaps the most highly respected sporting journalist of his time, admitted that this countermeasure had been effective. Yet the sporting interest continued to air its contempt for pet dog breeders. After almost half a century of formal dog shows, the author of a manual for dog owners noted that "the sportsman will as a rule have nothing to do with the fancier's production."[19] Correctly interpreting the aspirations figured in these indulged animals, gentry fanciers were defending their turf as well as the utility of their animals.

Middle-class fanciers did not reciprocate this hostility. On the contrary, they were pleased to be associated with their betters, even if at cross-purposes. The higher the rank of a breeder, the more enthusiastic the public reception was likely to be. Titles were thinly scattered among the ranks of fanciers, and any aristocrat who became serious about showing was guaranteed effusive appreciation. Readers of the *British Fancier Annual Review*, for example, were treated to profiles of elegant kennels like those of the Prince of Wales at Sandringham and the duchess of Newcastle at Clumber House; the *Kennel Review* featured the Queen's favorite pets (collies, terriers, and a dachshund). In 1896 the

Ladies' Kennel Journal published a photograph album entitled *Notable Dogs of the Year and Their Owners*. Some photographs included just the owner, some just the dog, and some both; but all were arranged according to the owner's rank. The opening section included the child Queen of the Netherlands and her charming but undistinguished Irish setters, as well as a large selection of Queen Victoria's dogs and many members of the royal family. A string of titled and honorable women followed and then, finally, the merely genteel fanciers and their pets. The less exalted the owner's social standing, the more likely was her pet to be a champion.[20]

When very high rank was at issue, some fanciers were willing to sacrifice even the meritocratic competition that structured their activities. The participation of royalty was especially coveted. Charles Lane (self-styled "breeder, exhibitor, judge") reported several occasions on which he was approached by members of show committees, who wished to ensure that the Queen's entries ended up in the prize list. But the stalwart judge stood for principle rather than excessive deference. He protested that "although I will not admit Her Majesty has a more loyal or devoted subject than myself, I am here in a public capacity as a judge"; the royal dogs had to be judged "on their merits," like all the others. The resulting impartial awards, according to Lane, "caused general satisfaction," and he remained certain that they would "have been approved by Her Majesty . . . if the circumstances came to be known at the palace."[21]

Elite patronage could boost the stock of a breed, as fanciers strove to identify their own tastes with those of their social superiors. Collies, Queen Victoria's favorite breed, were the most conspicuous beneficiaries of such preference; the sovereign's partiality also helped popularize Pomeranians. The pug, out of favor for much of the nineteenth century, was revived "thanks to the care of Lord Willoughby" and other aristocratic admirers. A foreign variant, the black pug, caught on quickly after its initial public appearance in 1886; its first English owners included Lord Londonderry, Lady Brassy, and the Queen.[22] The exalted rank of admirers might rub off on a breed, which could then pass it on to more ordinary fanciers. Pugs were often characterized as "aristocratic," as were collies, bloodhounds, borzois, and deerhounds, among others.[23] Once established as aristocrats, dogs received treatment commensurate with their rank. Fancy periodicals regularly featured profiles and portraits of distinguished champions. The *Fox-Terrier*

Chronicle, the only nineteenth-century periodical devoted to a single breed of dogs, covered the terrier elite the way that newspapers and other periodicals covered human high society. Issues might occasionally carry "Portraits of Fox Terrier Men," but the staple departments included "Portraits of Celebrated Terriers," "Biographies of Celebrated Dogs," "Gossip," "Visits" (a euphemism for matings), and "Debutantes" (dogs making their first dog show appearances).

Like people, however, dogs occupied the full range of social ranks; an English sportsman on safari described his canine retinue as including "dogs of high and low degree, from the purebred English greyhound to the Kaffir cur."[24] Most fanciers were as eager to dissociate themselves from the common people as to ally themselves with the aristocracy. Vulgar associations could preclude a breed's acceptance in genteel circles. Although the whippet, which had long been popular among laborers in Yorkshire and Lancashire, was recognized by the *Stud Book* in 1892, Rawdon Lee doubted that it would become popular. The pedigrees of even the listed specimens were not well documented, and "its surroundings have not, as a rule, been of the highest in the social scale."[25] In certain cases, nevertheless, genteel fanciers were willing to adopt animals from humble backgrounds, usually when they could view their previous owners as temporary custodians. Thus the fact that toy spaniels were bred in the East End of London as well as at Blenheim Palace did not impair their popularity. And, apparently, the readers of the *Sportsman's Journal and Fancier's Guide* did not scruple to accept the advice offered in January 1879: "The distress among the colliers in South Yorkshire . . . combined with their inability to pay the increased dog tax, is inducing large numbers of them to part with their pets. Dogs . . . of no small value, can be had for nothing."[26]

Ordinarily, class barriers were rigidly observed, even, in the view of some experts, by the animals themselves. Edward Jesse, author of the compendious *Anecdotes of Dogs*, claimed that what he called the Irish wolfdog could identify descendants of the ancient kings of Ireland, on which *Punch* commented, "reader, if you can swallow that you can of course bolt the whole Book of Jesse without wincing."[27] Although he was a zoologist specializing in animal behavior, George Romanes could be similarly credulous. He retailed the story of a retriever who, while wandering alone, struck up an acquaintance with a rat-catcher and his cur, but as soon as his master appeared abruptly "cut" his new friends.

According to Romanes, this proved that dogs understood "the idea of caste."[28] In general, however, fanciers did not rely on the perception of their animals to ensure that they would keep suitable company. Although there were knowledgeable dog breeders at every level of English society, the fancying establishment was carefully segregated by class. Many dog clubs sponsored auxiliaries for less genteel fanciers with lower membership fees and reduced privileges. Similarly, some shows levied cut-rate registration charges on dogs entered in special workingmen's classes, so that even dogs of the same breed competed only with their social equals.

If association with the lower orders compromised the standing of even pedigreed animals, dogs without breed standing were unquestionably beyond the pale. As the stock of well-descended animals rose during the nineteenth century, that of commoners fell. Most of the dogs that Caius had described in the sixteenth century would probably have been lumped together by Victorian fanciers in the catch-all class of mongrels or curs. It was a class about which they had little good to say. According to one expert, its members did "ninety per cent of all the mischief that the canine community is charged with committing"; another stated that "old dogs of a poor breed often become very dirty." They were "useless" and "miserable"—nothing but "rubbish." Any lapse from purity was enough to consign an animal to this category. Prospective dog owners were admonished that "your half-mongrel Pomeranian is a perfect little brute—a heel-biter and a coward" and that "there cannot be an uglier, more selfish little beast of a dog . . . than a mongrel or badly-bred pug." At best such half-castes (although probably not half-pugs) might be useful and loyal to "the farmer and the grazier."[29]

But it behooved more elevated members of society to avoid "vulgar" companionship. Manual after manual warned that a careless choice of pet could signal the owner's lack of distinction and discrimination. Everett Millais, a highly respected writer on canine subjects, generously speculated that such gaffes might merely reflect "want of knowledge"; the explanation could not be a mean financial one, he suggested, because "it is an old maxim that it costs no more to keep a purebred dog than to keep a mongrel." But most observers felt that ownership of mongrels revealed latent commonness, especially since, as the *Dog Owners' Annual* crowed in 1890, the general tone of pet dogs had greatly improved. "Those of the past," it reported, "were, by comparison, little

THE STREET DOG-SELLER.

The alternative to pedigreed dogs: a street vendor hawking mongrels.
From Henry Mayhew, *London Labour and the London Poor*, 1861–62.

better than mongrels; whilst at the present time we constantly see dogs of all kinds of the purest type." With such competition, the same periodical warned several years later, "nobody now who is anybody can afford to be followed about by a mongrel dog."[30]

The Institutionalization of the Dog Fancy

If keeping a well-bred dog metonymically allied its owner with the upper ranges of society, then the elaborate structure of pedigree registration and show judging metaphorically equated owner with elite pet. The institutions that defined the dog fancy projected an obsessively detailed vision of a stratified order which sorted animals and, by implication, people into snug and appropriate niches. Dog breeds were split and split again to produce categories in which competitive excellence could be determined. Aficionados of each breed developed a set of points prescribing the ideal toward which breeders should direct their efforts, and these ideals were publicly ratified and enforced in dog shows, which offered a dizzying range of classes and then abstracted from them a carefully calibrated hierarchy of animals, ranging from those who did not place even in their sub-breed category to the best of show.

Although this system appeared secure and stable, grounded in biological imperatives and validating centuries of English dog breeding, in fact it resulted from an impressive collective act of will and imagination. Even the basic categories of the dog fancy—the breeds—were relatively recent constructions. The human upper crust might have been fondling lap dogs and following hounds for centuries, but there was little evidence of the relationship between these ancient animals and the highly bred and well-documented pets of the late nineteenth century. Indeed, the very notion of breed as it was understood by Victorian dog fanciers—a subspecies or race with definable physical characteristics that would reliably reproduce itself if its members were crossed only with each other—may have been of relatively recent origin. Dr. Caius's list of Tudor dog types bore little resemblance to modern schemes of classification. He recognized only seventeen varieties, far fewer than existed in the nineteenth century: "Terrar, Harier, Bloudhound, Gasehunde, Grehound, Leuiner, Tumber, Stealer, Setter, Water

Spaniel or Fynder, Land Spaniel, Spaniel-gentle or Comforter, Shepherd's Dog, Mastive or Bande-Dog, Wappe, Turnspit, Dancer."[31] Some of these names anticipated those of nineteenth-century breeds, but it is unlikely that they referred to identical or even closely related animals. Caius's classification was based on function rather than physical appearance. He grouped his types under three larger categories, all unmistakably utilitarian: hunting dogs, pet dogs (this category included only the spaniel-gentle), and dogs that did menial work. Any large dog would have been called a mastiff; any lapdog a spaniel-gentle. An eighteenth-century sporting encyclopedia complicated these traditional functional categories with overlapping divisions based on coat color, which suggested that a dog with red spots was "fiery, and hard to be managed," while a yellow one was "of a giddy nature, and impatient."[32]

It was not until the eighteenth century that breeds in the modern sense began to emerge, starting with foxhounds, the most carefully bred dogs at the end of the century, although among the most "mongrelly" at its outset. Consensus about the desirability of the remodeled type emerged among Masters of Fox Hounds without institutional guidance or corroboration. By the early nineteenth century most hunts had adopted either the type embodied in the Quorn pack or the Brocklesby strain developed by the first Lord Yarborough.[33] When the 1795 records of the foxhound kennel at Beachborough classified individual dogs by breed, they identified the kennel from which the animals had been purchased. This informal reliance on a trusted strain persisted among some upper-class dog fanciers well into the nineteenth century, after the system of registered pedigrees had become firmly established. Thus in 1848 James Brierly of Mossley Hall, was able to determine that the earl of Derby's bloodhound bitch was that "rara avis," a real thoroughbred (hard to find because the few proprietors of such animals adhered to "principles of keeping the breed to themselves"), as a result of which he proposed mating her with one of his males of similarly exclusive descent. Aristocratic pug owners, in particular, preferred exclusive "private pedigrees" to those that had been publicly registered and were therefore available to anyone with sufficient money to buy them.[34]

These secluded and somewhat idiosyncratic records were not much use to the mid-Victorian regularizers of the dog fancy. And the only preexisting foundations for their taxonomical labors referred to sport-

Dogs classified by both breed and function. From R. W. Dickson,
A Complete System of Improved Live Stock and Cattle Management, 1824.

ing breeds that never gained popularity as show animals. Foxhound pedigrees were routinely if unofficially maintained by the end of the eighteenth century. The next breed to attract genealogical attention was the greyhound. Early in the nineteenth century Major Topham of the Guards, a celebrated wit and sportsman, began to publish a register of matings and births among his coursers. But for most breeds the first *Kennel Club Stud Book*, published in 1874, initiated formal pedigree keeping, and even the entries that included some ancestry did not reach far into the past. One cocker spaniel's descent was traced back to 1866; a mastiff listed forebears for eight generations.[35]

The paucity of historical roots may have made fanciers more eager to specify the grounds of contemporary distinction that separated their dogs from the run of the canine mill, especially since the conventional boundaries not only between breeds but between the dog and similar animals turned out to be rather uncertain. Before the family history and personal attributes of individual animals could be certified as impeccable, it was necessary to assign them to a clearly defined category. This way it could at least be determined that their relatively recent family history and their personal attributes were beyond reproach. Thus the number of recognized dog breeds expanded steadily through the nineteenth century. In 1800 Sydenham Edwards listed only fifteen, although he restricted his attention "to what are termed the permanent . . . races," excluding the mixtures, "which, by repeated crossing in various breeds become almost infinite." Near mid-century, veterinarian William Youatt described almost forty varieties of the domestic dog, in addition to several wild breeds, but one-quarter of them were sub-breeds of greyhounds; a contemporary sporting encyclopedia listed over sixty breeds, including, rather confusingly, the "Prairie Dog of North America." Another index of category problems was class 220 at the Cruft's show of 1890, which consisted of "stuffed dogs, or dogs made of wood, china, etc."[36]

The profusion of new varieties led to recurrent attempts to systematize, in order, at least, to allow fanciers to make sense of the welter of show classes. The sporting encyclopedia offered six general, if motley, categories—wild dogs, greyhounds, hounds, fowling dogs, pastoral or domestic dogs, and mastiffs and their kind; a zoologist who cataloged the dog collection at the British Museum (Natural History) suggested a more sensible but equally unwieldy set of affinity groups based on

wolves, greyhounds, spaniels, hounds, mastiffs, and terriers. The scheme
Rawdon Lee used for his compendious, three-volume *History and Description of the Modern Dogs of Great Britain and Ireland*, which also recognized
approximately sixty breeds, simply divided the animals into sporting
and nonsporting categories. It was published in 1894, and the Kennel
Club quickly adopted it as the official basis for classes in shows and in
the *Stud Book*.[37]

All these lists and categories and family trees came to life at the
shows that regulated and defined the dog fancy. Shows vividly illustrated the enormous range of available breeds as well as "the purest
type" within each of them. In addition, by imposing complex controls
on both animals and owners, they reenacted the elaborate structure of
the fancy. Each dog was precisely defined by the class it competed in,
which could reflect age, sex, color, and previously demonstrated merit,
as well as breed. Dogs that won prizes in so-called championship classes
were entitled to prefix their names with the coveted honorific "Champion."[38] When not in the ring, animals were (at least in principle) confined in assigned cages that were arranged in long rows and labeled to
correspond with the program listings. During the judging process, decorum was expected of both dog and owner. More broadly, the same
standards were extended to the crowds, and the transparent respectability of these highly regimented and ritualized occasions attracted
new fanciers and enhanced the prestige of fancying as an avocation.
The advent of modern dog shows purged dog fancying of an earlier, less
savory reputation as suitable only for country squires, who needed foxhounds and shooting dogs, and for the rough urban types who liked to
bet on bulldog matches and greyhound races. Show prizes were
awarded for elegance and breeding, rather than brute strength and
speed. The former were rubrics under which the self-consciously genteel—even ladies—did not hesitate to compete.

The rapidity with which the newly institutionalized dog fancy blos-
somed in the second half of the nineteenth century suggests that some
such outlet for competition and demonstration was urgently desired.
The first dog show was held in Newcastle on June 28, 1859. It was
sponsored by a local sporting-gun maker named Mr. Pape, and there
were only sixty entries in two classes (both for gun dogs: pointers and
setters). Mr. Pape provided the prizes from his inventory. This seemed
like such a good idea that a Mr. Brailsford organized a larger show of

sporting dogs in Birmingham a few months later, which was, in turn, so successful with both dog owners and the public that it was repeated the next year, with the addition of thirteen classes for nonsporting dogs.[39] The inclusion of pet animals significantly increased the shows' popularity. By 1865 they had prospered so much that the organizers formed a company and built the Curzon Hall, where they continued to flourish. The first really large show—with over one thousand entries—was held in Chelsea in March 1863, and the first international dog show took place, also in London, two months later. Shows on the grand scale spread to Scotland in 1871, the date of both the first Scottish national show (held in Glasgow) and the first Scottish metropolitan exhibition (held in Edinburgh). Little more than a decade after their birth, dog shows had arrived at vigorous maturity.[40]

In 1900 one expert estimated that "taking out Saturdays and Sundays, there is a Dog Show being held somewhere or other on every ordinary day of the year." Already by 1889 there were fears that "we have *too* many shows," but the numbers continued to increase. There were 217 shows in 1892, 257 in 1895, 307 in 1897, and 380 in 1899. Most of these were small-town or regional affairs, offering local fanciers the chance to show off their pets and perhaps prepare for the big time. There was also a well-established national circuit of major exhibitions. Its high points were the Kennel Club shows (usually two a year—one in the summer and one in the winter) and the Cruft's show, all in London, and the National Dog Show, which took place in Birmingham.[41] The size of the major shows was another indication of the appeal of dog breeding. In 1890 almost fifteen hundred dogs competed at the Kennel Club show, and over seventeen hundred were entered in a show at the Crystal Palace. Provincial shows could be nearly as attractive: shows at Manchester and Liverpool the same year displayed over fourteen hundred competitors, and one at Brighton drew over one thousand entries.[42]

The rhetoric surrounding dog shows indicated not only their popularity, but also the recurrent concern of owners and breeders about the reputation of the dog fancy. Thus the shows sorted people, as well as dogs. In 1900 Charles Lane looked back "many years since" to the shows held in Warwick under the active patronage of the late earl of Warwick. These "delightful gatherings" were "admirably managed by a . . . courteous committee of 'real workers,' whom it was always a pleasure to meet"; they attracted "the 'Flower of the Fancy,' both dogs and people."

The status of dog breeding was an issue, apparently, that could not simply be resolved and forgotten. Much closer to the time when Lane was reflecting complacently on the past, fanciers were proudly pointing to recent triumphs over even the shadow of vulgarity. In 1894 the *Ladies' Kennel Journal* announced that one of the objectives of the organization that sponsored it, the Ladies' Kennel Association, was "to prove that, though [its members] may be . . . what a certain class of critic is pleased to call 'doggy' women, they are, none the less, gentlewomen." No less averse to tooting its own horn in this connection, the Kennel Club announced several years later in its journal that "the efforts of the Kennel Club have resulted in elevating the general tone of canine exhibitions."[43]

This at least was the canonical picture, promoted by the Kennel Club and other guardians of the carefully constructed establishment. They recognized, of course, that Mr. Pape had not conceived his dog show in a flash of blinding inspiration. He was implementing a suggestion made repeatedly by thoughtful dog breeders and tried unsuccessfully at least three times before 1859.[44] In 1847 Robert Vyner, a one-time Master of Fox Hounds, suggested that "nothing would be more likely to improve the breed of fox-hounds than prizes, to be awarded by competent judges." In 1854 "Bow-wow," a correspondent of the *Courser's Annual Remembrancer, and Stud Book*, argued that, since "the greyhound is a purely national animal, brought to greater perfection in this country than any other, and it is unrivaled for its symmetry, beauty, and points of breeding . . . why should we not have an 'Exhibition of Dogs'"—an exhibition which, he hoped, would also include mastiffs, deerhounds, and bloodhounds.[45] Both these fanciers based their suggestions on the readily available example of livestock shows, which many of the gentry breeders of sporting dogs attended regularly; indeed, some of the dog shows that were subsequently established, including that held in Birmingham, owed much of their box office success to being scheduled at the same time as important agricultural exhibitions.

If the officially promulgated line of descent for dog shows derived them from well-established livestock shows, there was also a somewhat shadier collateral lineage. Dog shows of a sort had been going on long before 1859, although they lacked elaborate class divisions and certified judges. Public houses were their most frequent venue. Hugh Dalziel, an eloquent and distinguished breeder of collies under the new dispensation, remembered the "convivial meetings" of what he called "the pre-historic age of dog shows" (when his own main interest had been bulldogs) rather fondly. Every member of the company was exhibitor, spectator, and judge; they examined each other's animals, then arrived at a noisy consensus. The gatherings were often subsidized by landlords to attract customers with "doggy proclivities," who were apparently considered desirable additions to a tavern's clientele. In the 1840s Jemmy Shaw's establishment near the Haymarket and Charley Aistrop's in St. Giles were favorite London locations for these one-breed shows; they were held in rooms reserved for rat-killing competitions on other evenings.[46] Sporting and fighting breeds were featured most frequently, but even aristocratic pet breeds might be displayed in these inelegant surroundings. Lytton recorded a toy spaniel show as early as 1834 at the Elephant and Castle, and one in 1851 at the Eight Bells. In acknowledging such precedents, as in other ways, she outstripped most of her fellow fanciers in social candor. According to Dalziel, in "polite circles" the birth of dog shows in "sanded parlours" was "generally ignored"— one of many instances when "it is felt to be inconvenient . . . to trace the pedigree too curiously, lest the low origin might be found inconsistent with existing pride."[47]

The behind-the-scenes realities of dog shows often belied their superficial order and decorum, however; paradoxically, one index of how much fanciers valued the hierarchical ideal embodied in the judging process was the amount of divergence from it they were prepared, albeit unwillingly, to tolerate. If badly designed, the neat accommodations prepared for competitors could quickly become chaotic. At the 1863 Chelsea show, according to Stonehenge, the lavishly decorated hall seriously misrepresented conditions below. No water or water dishes had been provided for the animals; worse, the dogs were inadequately caged and on chains so short that "their owners were continually letting them out." One elderly lady was bitten in the arm by a retriever.[48]

These problems threatened the shows' participants as well as their image. In exchange for the chance of a prize, owners had to risk their cherished pets' lives. Even shows offering reasonably comfortable and sanitary accommodations frequently spread distemper, which was particularly dangerous to competitors in the puppy classes. And if an animal survived the show itself (where the behavior of spectators might present additional hazards—at a cat show held in Birmingham in 1875, one admirer held the lighted end of his cigar to the nose of a prize-winning tom), it had still to brave the journey home.[49] The railroads' treatment of animals was a constant subject of complaint by humane organizations, as well as dog fanciers. Dogs were allowed to suffer, and sometimes to perish, from cold and hunger; they were often lost; and at the best of times they were transported "in a dirty den called a boot—rank with accumulated filth of every kind."[50]

It was bad enough when the incompetence of show organizers endangered the health of the competitors. Much more outrageous, in the view of fanciers, were careless administrative arrangements that jeopardized the whole purpose of the show. In a second and severer assault on the 1863 show, Stonehenge detailed further horrors. Dogs were judged with the names of their owners attached to their collars, instead of the numbered tickets that would have preserved anonymity. The arrangement of the exhibits repeatedly violated the integrity of classes: retrievers were mixed up with setters; foreign dogs were lumped together indiscriminately; and a group of puppies occupied the bench allotted in the catalog to "Wolf, brought from the Crimea." In a show that featured confusion, rather than clarity, order, and rank, it was not surprising that some observers (although not Stonehenge) questioned the probity of the judges.[51]

From their initial appearance in 1859, public dog shows had been dedicated to the achievement of three related goals: to improve the various breeds of dogs, to display model specimens, and to discourage the breeding of mongrels. When they selected the prizewinner in each class, therefore, judges were not simply recognizing a particular outstanding animal. At the same time, they were identifying the strain to which the prizewinner belonged as promising breeding material, and they were endorsing a type toward which other breeders should aspire. Especially in awarding the prizes at important shows, which were widely reported and criticized in the press, judges wielded considerable power. If they were not perceived to exercise it reliably and responsibly, the elaborate structure of dog showing, which rested at bottom on public confidence in their honesty and discrimination, would collapse.

Yet, especially in the first two decades, it was hard for even the most competent and conscientious judge to do his or her job properly. There was, to begin with, too much to do. Large shows might have only ten judges for several hundred classes.[52] In addition to assessing the quality of the dogs on display, a judge had to be alert for "faking"—practices one dog-showing manual summarized as "plucking out white hairs . . . , dying the coat, cutting the cartilage of the ear to make it droop, shortening a tail that is too long . . . , cutting the coat with scissors." Nor did the exhibitors make the job easier. In the ring, fanciers frequently tried to maneuver their animals so as to cut off the judge's view of other competitors; they were also apt to offer distracting praise of their own dogs and criticism of rivals.[53] This was all in the spirit of good clean fun, the kind of thing the most refined breeder might try in order to gain coveted recognition for his or her pet.

Behind the scenes there was actual fraud. Animals were doctored; misleading or false descriptions were inserted in catalogs; buyers who had paid for the stud services of champions, or for the champions themselves, were swindled with inferior animals. Even the lesser animals ordinarily purchased by new fanciers might be similarly misrepresented; Gordon Stables recommended that inexpert purchasers avail themselves of the approval service offered by the editorial offices of several periodicals, which would hold their money until the animal and its pedigree had been certified genuine and acceptable.[54] The people who perpetrated such crimes were dangerous to the dog fancy on two counts. They cheated individuals, and their shady reputation might impugn the respectability of the fancy as a whole. For none of those who considered themselves disinterested dog lovers—whose motives in showing, that is, were untainted by the desire to make a profit—doubted for a moment that these criminals were "pure dealers . . . they show for the purpose of winning the money prizes, and to enable them to sell the dogs they breed." They were unsavory holdovers from the bad old days of tavern shows.[55]

To preserve the newly genteel reputation of dog shows, a group describing its members as "true sportsmen . . . who breed to win and to whom pecuniary questions are of no moment" formed the Kennel Club in 1873. Its main initial concern was to combat fraud by establishing the identity and descent of pedigreed dogs. At the same time it developed an interlocking system of shows and registration designed to limit competition to a carefully screened segment of the canine, and, implicitly, of the human population. The first volume of its *Stud Book*, which listed dogs exhibited since 1859, appeared in 1874. Geared to the show

Intense competition for prizes in the show ring.
From Judith Neville Lytton, *Toy Dogs,* 1911.

circuit, the *Stud Book* concentrated on dogs that had won prizes. Its editor acknowledged that some "excellent and well-bred dogs" might have been excluded as a result of this policy; but, he argued somewhat circularly, "the value of the blood and pedigree is demonstrated on every page, as nine-tenths of the later prize winners trace back to prize blood." Keyed to the *Stud Book* was a national registration system for pedigreed dogs. The *Stud Book* also included a code of rules for dog shows, one of which prohibited any unregistered dog from entering a show held under the auspices of the Kennel Club.[56]

The Kennel Club encountered resistance in implementing these reforms, sometimes from the disreputable operators whose business interests were threatened, sometimes from competing groups like the organizers of the Birmingham show, who resented what they viewed as a national power grab. But most fanciers strongly preferred dignity, discipline, and quality control to the *caveat emptor* ethos of the untrammeled market. So the Kennel Club triumphed relatively quickly. By 1892 its fighting days were far behind it, in the view of a rising generation of activists, who accused it of having degenerated into a social club for well-bred fanciers.[57] But in a way this evidenced the thoroughness of its achievement. Under its guidance dog showing had left its raffish origins behind. It had become a respectable and well-regulated pastime, a reflection of the carefully calibrated human social order.

Determining Breed Standards

The structures that evolved in the third quarter of the nineteenth century to regulate the breeding and showing of pedigreed dogs figuratively expressed the desire of predominantly middle-class fanciers for a relatively prestigious and readily identifiable position within a stable, hierarchical society. Most of the institutions of the fancy—shows, stud books, and breed societies—had been borrowed from high stock breeding, and their conservative symbolism survived the translation. Yet the Kennel Club was not simply a scaled-down imitation of the Smithfield Club. While recognizing the seductive charm of aristocracy, the Victorian dog fancy embodied a set of values that undermined the traditional social code that structured high stock breeding. The identification of elite animal with elite owner was not a confirmation of the owner's status but a way of redefining it. Thus a metaphor that signified stability in the world of prize cattle signified change in the world of prize dogs. And although pedigree was important, the rhetoric of distinguished descent was invariably strongly modified by a more individualistic ethos. Dog owners were more intimately involved in the web of competition than the owners of prize livestock; they even appeared in the ring along with their animals. Breeds might flourish as a result of elite associations, but inherited rank did not ensure a distinguished career for an individual animal. Although a respectable pedigree was essential as a "guarantee of purity of blood," it did not guarantee anything beyond that. Indeed, experts warned that the inflated pecuniary value of the offspring of celebrated champions could result in the preservation of inferior animals in the most distinguished pedigrees.[58] Becoming a champion was primarily an achievement of the individual dog and owner, and only secondarily a ratification of the animal's ancestry.

In fact, the dog fancying establishment was structured by two apparently complementary but ultimately inconsistent metaphorical systems. The uneasiness it inspired among aristocrats like Lytton and sporting country squires reflected more than a desire to defend their turf from interlopers. At the same time that the elaborate divisions of dogs into breeds and classes, and of individuals into precisely ranked hierarchies within those classes, seemed to imitate and thus endorse the stable, rigidly hierarchical social system represented by the human upper orders, the content of those discriminations—or rather, their lack of content—undermined it. As Lytton sensed, the problem was what was ranked. The hierarchy projected through the display of prize livestock consisted of ranks determined by concrete and stable differences among people. Similarly, the dog breeds most closely associated with gentry fanciers—greyhounds, foxhounds, and shooting dogs—were judged not in the artificial environment of shows but by their performance in the field. Among show pets, however, rank was divorced from any practical criterion; many breeds were judged according to standards set simply for the sake of making distinctions. In 1866 Stonehenge charged that "at present, exhibitors do not know what points will ensure a prize, and all is confusion." Several years later he complained that, although dog shows had multiplied and increased in popularity, there was still "no standard of merit by which to be guided in breeding and judging. In many cases the choice of points is wholly arbitrary, as in the toy dogs; for no one can contend that on any other principle a small eye shall be a merit in one breed (toy terrier) and a defect in another (King Charles Spaniel)." Sometimes qualities were valued only because they were unusual or difficult to produce. The prizewinning pedigreed dogs of the late nineteenth century seemed to symbolize simply the power to manipulate and the power to purchase—they were ultimately destablizing emblems of status and rank as pure commodities.[59]

Even if there was no reason to prefer one set of points over another, fanciers agreed that each breed required a model or standard so that the central business of classification and ranking could proceed. Most of the breeds judged at late nineteenth-century dog shows had therefore been created out of whole cloth, or something very close, in the not-too-distant past. The rather ferocious selection pressures that shaped the evolution of the foxhound did not provide equally clear direction even for all sporting dogs. The beagle, for example, had "a place among the very oldest English breeds," as one aficionado proudly claimed in 1898. Rumor identified it with the "brach" of past generations, and legend suggested that good Queen Bess had owned a pack of the animals small enough to fit in her glove. Yet no one was quite certain what a beagle was like. It was certainly a hound, and probably the smallest kind of hound. How small was one of many vexed questions. In 1879 Vero Shaw, a vigorous and intelligent observer, had suggested that the difference between contemporary beagle packs was "certainly chiefly one of size." The author of the *Kennel Gazette's* "Retrospect for 1898" reported happily that "we are gradually getting back to the little compact hound," and in the same year Shaw warned prospective beagle buyers not to "pay much attention to an animal over 14 in. high at the shoulder"—although a critic hoped that "so old-fashioned a breed" would not be "constitutionally ruined to satisfy a modern rage for undersized specimens." Beyond this there was even less agreement. One reporter complained, after the 1888 Kennel Club show, that "there are so many sizes and types of beagles that it must always be a very unsatisfactory task judging them when only one class is provided."[60]

Yet all the disputants assumed that a standard or ideal beagle existed, even though there was no historical evidence for a single, true, ancient beagle type. The heyday of the beagle had been in the slow, unfashionable days of hunting, before sportsmen became particular about the species of their quarry or the lineage of their dogs. Already in 1800 Edwards observed that beagles "are by no means in such repute as formerly, a complete pack of them being rarely seen." Dashing sportsmen preferred stronger, faster dogs, and were repelled by the beagle's fondness for chasing the lowly hare. A beagle enthusiast noted wishfully in 1823 that although beagles had been "almost abandoned, owing to the introduction of the fleeter and more fashionable harrier . . . more packs are now to be met with than . . . a few years since," which he attributed to the fact that their slow pace made them easy for timid riders, ladies, and unmounted rustics to follow.[61] He may have been premature in his celebrations, however. In 1861 there were still only a few beagle packs, and at the Kennel Club show of 1894, the beagle classes were canceled because of insufficient entries.[62]

This spotty record gave the Beagle Club little basis on which to begin its work when it was formed in 1895 to further "the true interests of the breed."[63] The founders of the Beagle Club admitted that "the true Beagle is in great danger of disappearing owing to cross and careless breeding," and they recognized that the difficulty of their task was compounded because "there is no standard to breed to, and . . . no two Beagle judges are of the same opinion." But the club took its mandate seriously. Where there was a name, there was a breed; and where there was a breed, there had to be a standard. The prestige of the club's members was at stake along with that of the animals with which they identified. They set themselves a double task: "to improve the make and look of the Beagle; and at the same time to render it more suitable for work." In a sense the club succeeded. Whether the breed was restored and improved, or newly imagined and created, enforceable standards were developed. And once ranking became predictable, beagles began to increase steadily in popularity and prestige.[64]

Like the beagle, the bulldog ostensibly sported a long history. Although Caius did not include it among his British dogs, the bulldog's advocates considered it coeval with and emblematic of Anglo-Saxon civilization. Pierce Egan, a chronicler of the early nineteenth-century sporting scene, had characterized it with the thoroughbred horse, the game cock, and the pugilist as one of "the peculiar productions of BRITAIN and IRELAND, unequalled for high courage, stoutness of heart, and patience under suffering."[65] And to an even greater extent than the beagle, it had survived its original function and been redesigned according to standards that seemed completely arbitrary. In 1900 it was "amongst the most popular breeds" of pedigreed dogs, pampered, according to one fancier, more than any other variety; another identified bulldog puppies as particularly "delicate." Bulldogs were said to be so indolent that they did not have much natural appetite, but "as a *thin* Bull Dog is an abomination," it was necessary to coax them to eat. Although fanciers always liked to see their special breed rise in public favor, the bulldog's wide acceptance caused a kind of identity crisis among its most faithful adherents. A show of old-fashioned bulldogs would not have attracted a more "fashionable crowd" than other dog shows; no one had ever referred to the traditional article as "a ladies' dog, as its kindliness of disposition admirably fits it."[66]

The good old days of bulldog fancying ended in 1835 when Parliament made bull baiting illegal. Before then bulldogs, like foxhounds, had been bred for function; indeed the category may have identified not a breed but a motley group of similarly talented animals. The requirements of bull-to-bulldog combat were exacting. Enraged bulls charged with their heads down. In order to avoid the lethal horns, the dogs had to be low to the ground and relatively nimble. Because a bull was most vulnerable on its tender nose, the bulldog needed strong jaws as well as the dumb courage to jump at the bull's face and the perseverance to hang on. The quality of the animals was tested regularly under fire, and prowess was more important than appearance in determining rank. Late eighteenth- and early nineteenth-century portraits of renowned bulldogs showed animals that varied widely in size and shape, even making allowance for the unequal skill of the artists. Some even lacked the characteristic bulldog countenance, retrospectively described as one in which "the broad, projecting underjaw ensures the terrible tenacity of grip; the wide nostrils, placed far back, enable the dog to draw unimpeded breath while keeping his teeth fixed on the yielding cartilage of the bull's nose."[67]

After the abolition of bull baiting, the bulldog went into a decline. Within twenty years it was announced that "this fine specimen . . . is at the present day almost dying out." When the Bulldog Club was launched to save the breed in 1874, the bulldog was "at a discount." The unsavory surroundings with which the bulldog had been associated may have had almost as much to do with its near extinction as the ban on bull baiting. Although it might occasionally have been the pet of ladies and gentlemen (Lady Castlereagh, the wife of the Regency foreign minister, was reputed to have driven in the park with a large bulldog on the

A MASTIFF .

A BULL-DOG .

A mastiff and a bulldog, breeds hard to distinguish
in the eighteenth century. From Thomas Boreman,
A Description of Three Hundred Animals, 1736.

A pomeranian with an early nineteenth-century bulldog,
shown lacking many of the characteristics later associated with the breed.
From John Church, *A Cabinet of Quadrupeds*, 1805.

seat beside her), its patrons were, as a rule, not among "the better class
of fanciers," and the places where specimens were generally to be found
earned the breed the name of "the pot-house dog."[68] William Youatt
asserted that although keeping such sporting dogs as spaniels, pointers,
and even greyhounds caused "no diminution in respectability," a young
man with a bulldog would "speedily become profligate and debased." In
addition, the "fondness of the lower orders in some districts for the

fighting and baiting propensities" of bulldogs continued after 1835, and there were doubtless still opportunities for the animals to show their stuff. Those dogs not kept for fighting were "principally bred by professional dog-fanciers," the lowest echelon of fancying society.[69]

So the fledgling Bulldog Club had its work cut out for it: to redefine a breed that had outlived its usefulness, that had no social cachet, and that appeared to ordinary dog lovers ugly, stupid, and brutal. It was, in the words of the club's official description, "much maligned and . . . very little understood."[70] The first step in the rehabilitation of the bulldog was rhetorical: to blame people for the unpleasant qualities that had been attributed to the dog. While Youatt had characterized the bulldog as "scarcely capable of any education, and . . . fitted for nothing but ferocity and combat," and the lion tamer Van Amburgh had considered it as brave as any wild beast but "rather deficient in its range of ideas," later writers pointed to extenuating circumstances. According to Dalziel, the bulldog's courage made it "the only dog with sufficient endurance to serve the cruel purposes of depraved owners." And the strategy worked; the newly imagined bulldog caught on among respectable fanciers. By 1885 it was second only to the collie in popularity, as measured by dog show entries. It began to be described as "peaceable" and "intelligent," even "benign-looking." An advertisement for the sale of a champion named Bully McKrankie noted that "he has always been kept in the house and is a great pet." Bulldog shows drew larger gates than any other one-breed show.[71]

As soon as the breed took its place in the show ring, however, it became clear that no generally accepted or rationally founded breeding standards had replaced the old law of survival of the fittest. A correspondent who had "only quite recently entered the Bulldog Fancy" implored the editors of the *Sportsman's Journal and Fancier's Guide* to favor "green fanciers" with a brief description of "the points, general make and shape . . . of the bulldog." His independent research had, he complained, only compounded his confusion: "At present . . . after trying to collect some information, we are worse off than when we commenced." Almost any feature of the animal was open to debate. Veteran aficionados offered contradictory opinions, and, true to the bravura spirit of the bulldog fancy, they offered them with ringing confidence.[72]

The Dudley nose question, for example, convulsed the Bulldog Club for over a decade. (Dudley or flesh-colored noses occurred in some

The new model bulldog of the Bulldog Club.
From the *Kennel Gazette*, 1899.

strains of fawn-colored bulldogs, usually in conjunction with light eyes and a yellowish countenance.) In 1884 the club voted to exclude dogs with Dudley noses from competition, defeating a counterproposal that they be considered *sine qua non* in fawn bulldogs. Dudley nose advocates lobbied energetically among club members; a spirited correspondence aired in the canine press. But the majority repeatedly reaffirmed its position, although in 1895 it conceded that dogs with part-Dudley noses (black and flesh-colored) could "compete and win if they were sufficiently good in other respects." Experts outside the polarized club membership viewed the issue with greater detachment. "Personally," confessed Rawdon Lee, "where a dog is otherwise good, I would not disqualify him for Dudley markings."[73] More functional features were also subject to the same kind of arbitrary assessment, sometimes in defiance of the animal's practical requirements. One *Kennel Gazette* reviewer claimed that to be "distingué" a bulldog should be "well out at the shoulder and with a good broken up face"; a dog lacking either was doomed to mediocrity. But Lee characterized this shoulder configuration as a crippling deformity. He cited the example of Dockleaf, a renowned champion of the early 1890s and the property of the eminent bulldog breeder Sam Woodiwiss, which collapsed after walking a mere two miles.[74]

Although experts agreed that the late Victorian bulldog differed noticeably from its fighting ancestors, they disagreed in their assessment
of the new model. Stonehenge thought that "the modern bulldog" was
"decidedly neater in shape" than its forebears, but a few traditionalists
regretted the change. Some characterized it as simple declension—
modern bulldogs were less active, and "want of character" was prevalent
among them. Others were harsher in their judgments. According to
George Jesse, a self-appointed defender of oppressed canines, "the disgusting abortions exhibited at the shows [were] deformities from foot
to muzzle . . . and totally incapable of coping with a veteran bull." There
were, however, no more bulls to cope with. The only influence on the
make of the bulldog was the pleasure of its admirers.[75]

The collie was the most popular pet dog in late Victorian England
and a prime example of a breed reconstructed to express the figurative
needs of fanciers. Collies were originally valued for the qualities they
had developed as hardworking Scottish sheepdogs—intelligence, loyalty, and a warm shaggy coat. Once they were firmly established in the
Stud Book, however, breeders began to introduce modifications and improvements, which were tested not against the rigors of the Highland
winter, but in the fashionable marketplace. By 1895 there were seven
independent clubs devoted to the breed's welfare, many of which sponsored all-collie shows, as well as strong collie representation in the Kennel Club and regional canine associations.[76] The large number of pedigreed collies seems to have exacerbated the tendency of fanciers to
fabricate subtle points of distinction between animals and artificial
models to measure them against. As a result, fashions changed swiftly
and collie standards were among the most volatile; breeders redesigned
their animals or restocked their kennels in accordance with the latest
show results. Plasticity could even take precedence over pedigree; in
order to instill some temporarily admired attribute, breeders were
sometimes willing to contaminate the strain. In the early days of showing, collies were frequently crossed with Gordon setters, to achieve
then-fashionable glossy, black-and-tan coats. For decades experts could
detect "traces of this bar sinister"—the telltale ears, head, and general
heaviness—in many show animals. Even without crossing (which became less common as the *Stud Book* gained sway), fashion could undermine the character of the breed. The 1890s saw a craze for exaggerated
heads with long, pointy noses. In 1891 a *Kennel Gazette* reviewer com-

DOG FASHIONS FOR 1889.

Extravagances of fancy dog breeding. From *Punch,* 1889.

plained that show judges had given all the prizes to "dogs of this greyhound type whose faces bore an inane, expressionless look." Critics alleged that such dogs could hardly display the intelligence characteristic
of their breed because there was no room in their heads for brains.[77]

Specialist clubs were supposed to defend their breeds against the vi-
cissitudes of fashion, but they had few other guides in their attempts to
establish standards for breeders and judges. Their eagerness to establish
the separate identity of their chosen breed inclined club activists to
focus on "arbitrary and conventional points" that were easy to define,
and to neglect the character and bearing of the whole animal. The Collie Club was no exception. It was even proposed, at a Collie Club meeting in 1884, that collie classes at shows be reorganized according to
color. This notion, however, went too far and was overwhelmingly rejected by the membership. Such distinctions were not sufficiently subtle
or difficult to produce credible rankings. In addition, adopting them
would implicitly have compromised the gentility of the collie fancy by
linking it to the color-coded displays of fancy mice, rabbits, and guinea
pigs that were recognized as the preserve of the vulgar.[78] From this
point of view the diminished utility of working breeds might seem at-

tractive to fanciers, as a barrier between the dogs' original breeders and their new patrons. There was little overlap between the rough shepherds who bred collies for work and the affluent amateurs who bred them for show, and fanciers were inclined to believe that the dogs had benefited from their transplantation. Although the original working collie was apt to be rude and hostile to strangers (and likely to savage the sheep in neighboring flocks when off duty), "constant association with his superiors has improved his disposition immensely." The dog had become worthy of its elegant new surroundings, "despite his lowly origin (for, after all, he is but a sheep dog)."[79]

On the whole, however, newly codified breed standards were designed to privilege rank by competition rather than rank by association. The juxtaposition of arbitrarily established criteria (the major purpose of which was to make judgment possible) with swiftly changing fashions not only in favorite breeds but in preferred types within those breeds symbolized a society where status could reflect individual accomplishments and was, as a result, evanescent, lacking in foundation, and in constant need of reaffirmation. As most dog fanciers were, in this sense, self-created, so their exploitation of the physical malleability of their animals was extremely self-referential. Its goal was to celebrate their desire and ability to manipulate, rather than to produce animals that could be measured by such extrinsic standards as utility, beauty, or vigor. Thus it was an index of their paradoxical willingness aggressively to reconceive and refashion the social order in which they coveted a stable place.

The Cat Fancy

If the elaborately distinguished and carefully graduated classes of the dog fancy mirrored breeders' desire to improve their own social positions, the subsequent development of a different animal fancy highlighted the inconsistency inherent in the rhetoric of pedigreed pet breeding. *Canis familiaris*, the domesticated dog, is among the most plastic of species. The enormous variation in size, shape, temperament, and athletic ability among individuals and breeds might have seemed to explain—and, indeed, to have required—the complex subdivisions that quickly came to characterize dog shows. The reverse is true of *Felis domesticus*, the domesticated cat. Members of this species differ from one another in little but their coats. Indeed, in the early years of dog show-ing, cats were not prestigious fancy animals. If they were shown at all, it was usually as an addendum to an exhibit of rabbits or guinea pigs, which were also distinguished by such superficial characteristics as fur length and color.[80] But in their relations to their owners, pet cats were much more like dogs than like the rabbits, rodents, and prize poultry that were widely bred for purely ornamental purposes, and their owners were almost as likely as dog owners to identify with them. As a result, cat advocates constructed an analogous series of institutions to classify and evaluate their pets.[81]

Like the pioneering dog fanciers of mid-century, the architects of the organized cat fancy decided that their first task was to construct a tax-onomy. But before they could establish a system of breeds and pedi-grees, they had to solve a problem that their predecessors had not had to confront. Cats' mating habits made it difficult for fanciers to influence the appearance of the next generation, or even to know its parentage. Unlike dog breeders (and livestock breeders, for that matter), whose animals were usually willing to mate with a designated partner, cat breeders had to cope with animals accustomed to making their own decisions and implementing them out of sight of their owners. As late as 1868 Darwin claimed that people had done "nothing by methodical selection; and probably very little by unintentional selection," to influ-ence the development of the domestic cat except saving the prettiest kittens in each litter and killing adults that poached game.[82] Thus the engagement of early cat fanciers in their animals' reproductive activities was more passive than that of dog breeders, and the physical evidence of their influence less compelling. Because of the difficulty of maintain-ing pure strains, there was no guarantee that a prize animal would pro-duce prize offspring; and a sharp-eyed fancier might well spot a cat with magnificent show potential prospecting among the garbage. Conse-quently, the prices commanded by late Victorian prize cats did not ap-proach those of dogs. As little as £1–£2 was regarded as a "long price" for kittens "good enough to win at a first-class exhibition."[83]

The inherent resistance of the species to subdivision and genetic ma-nipulation did not discourage cat fanciers, who assaulted these biolog-ical impediments by establishing breed categories, each with ascribed standards and a hierarchy of animals within it. The first cat show took place in the Crystal Palace on July 16, 1871. It was organized by Har-

An early feline champion,
which was not too different from an ordinary cat.
From Harrison Weir, *Our Cats*, 1889.

rison Weir, a well-known writer about and illustrator of animal subjects, who later became president of the National Cat Club. His objective in proposing the show was appropriately taxonomical, although he characterized the endeavor in terms of discovery rather than invention: to encourage greater attention to "the different breeds, colours, markings, etc.," and he projected an elaborate structure of classes for "the different varieties of colour, form, size, and sex." As at early dog shows, despite these finely drawn subdivisions, there was some confusion about the boundary between species. One of the prizewinners was a Scottish wild cat. Cat owners proved as eager as dog fanciers a decade and a half earlier for a chance to display and compare their animals. Weir's show was so successful that the Crystal Palace Company, which had allowed him to perform his duties as organizer as a "labour of love of the feline race," rewarded him with a large silver tankard. Large cities like Birmingham and Glasgow immediately followed the metropolitan example, and within a decade or so even the smaller provincial towns could "boast of an annual exhibition of feline favorites."[84]

That the class categories proposed for these shows relied on color differences, the only readily available index of "breed" distinctions, revealed their weakness, although fancy organizers tried to disguise the problem by associating color with less superficial characteristics. One early attempt was made by Gordon Stables, active in the cat fancy as well as the dog fancy, who suggested thirteen categories: tortoiseshell,

tortoiseshell-and-white, brown tabby, blue and silver tabby, red, red tabby, red-and-white tabby, spotted tabby, black-and-white, black, white, unusual color, and any other variety. Stables was careful to cover himself against objections, explaining at one time that his purpose was "to describe the classification of cats generally adopted at pussy-shows, instead of dividing them, as they otherwise ought to be, into the different species and breeds" (although he did not specify these breeds). On another occasion he asserted that, although there was "properly speaking" only one breed of domestic cat, "colour is often the key to [its] character . . . , to its temper . . . , to its qualities as a hunter . . . , and its power of endurance." He claimed, for example, that tortoiseshells were "good mothers [and] game as bull terriers," while tortoiseshell-and-whites were "very clever, docile, and tricky"; black cats were "noble and gentlemanly," whites "far from brave . . . fond of . . . society . . . gentle . . . often delicate"; the black-and-white "sometimes . . . did not trouble himself too much about his duties as a house-cat."[85]

Stables' categories soon went out of fashion, largely because most cats shown in the 1880s and 1890s would have fallen into his last two classes. But what replaced them was not very different. The scheme that Weir developed for the Crystal Palace shows was also color-based, although it specified a broader range of colors and divided animals into shorthair and longhair classes as well as by sex and age. (The 1889 Crystal Palace show, which attracted 511 entries in 54 classes, grouped 102 of them under a division that was not part of Weir's original plan but that reflected the concern of dog fanciers that animal hierarchies reproduce human ones: Cats Belonging to Working Men.) Subsequent schemes were simply refinements. Eye color, for example, gradually became a more important component of judging, and categories were added to accommodate newly imported strains like the Siamese and the Abyssinian. The specialist cat clubs, which began to spring up at the turn of the century, also followed color lines; among the first founded were the Silver and Smoke Persian Cat Club and the Orange, Cream, Fawn and Tortoiseshell Society.[86] As the National Cat Club, modeled on the Kennel Club with its interlocking system of pedigree registration and closed shows, assumed control of the organized fancy, breeders began to claim that "a much greater study was made in the science of Cat-breeding."[87] But this had no noticeable effect on the category divisions, which, despite constant effort on the part of fanciers, could not be made to imply much beyond color. Yet fanciers were never tempted to abandon a taxonomical enterprise that kept petering out in triviality; instead, they struggled the harder to justify complex class divisions by endowing them with greater significance.

The distinction between longhairs and shorthairs was more productive than those based on color, because the first represented exotic "oriental" imports (more or less interchangeably called Persians and angoras), while the second was the native English type. Stables identified shorthaired tabbies, in particular, as "the real old English cats—the playmates of our infant days and sharers of our oatmeal porridge." Nevertheless, he preferred "Asiatic cats" as pets. Though not so hardy as shorthairs, or so good as catching mice, they were "extremely affectionate and loving."[88] Subsequent fanciers agreed on the dichotomy while differing about its implications. One found longhairs "lazy and listless," though fashionable, and "not such pleasing companions" as the "sleek, agile, graceful, and intelligent animals with which we are more familiar"; another considered Persians "not so amiable" as shorthairs, but "more intelligent" and more inclined to "make themselves at home in their surroundings." Whatever their nature, fanciers clearly preferred foreign cats. Of 740 entries at the Crystal Palace show of 1896, 485 were longhairs, 64 foreign shorthairs, and 191 English shorthairs. "It almost looks," lamented a patriotic reporter, as though the native breed "were being dropped as a fancy animal."[89]

Many of the foreign shorthairs were Siamese cats, which became relatively popular in the mid-1890s. Previously they had been quite rare; barely twenty individuals were exhibited between 1871 and 1891, and as late as 1896, the *Ladies' Kennel Journal* could identify only four English breeders. Victorian legend held that the animals were the special property of the King of Siam; the few cats that made their way to Europe were considered either very special gifts or the booty of daring thieves. But "great changes in Siam" in the early 1890s (the result of pressure from British and French colonizers in neighboring territories) were believed to have produced a "comparative abundance of imported cats." The Siamese was praised for its beauty and temperament, and its romantic origin enhanced its appeal. But it is likely that among the Siamese's most powerful attractions was its very distinctness, which made it incontestably a breed apart.[90]

Even more than the dog fancy, the cat fancy celebrated the primacy of process over content. A typical turn-of-the-century claim about the progress of cat breeding distilled the circularity and self-reference of the enterprise: "Classes at shows on more extended lines have been established, and they are now judged by those who really understand the subject, therefore each variety is sure to improve; especially when it is clearly laid what has to be bred up to." The abstract idea of hierarchy was more important than the concrete basis of ranking. As standards were being developed, often the determining criterion was, as with dogs, simple rarity. Thus tortoiseshell toms were considered desirable because orange-colored cats are usually female—indeed, it was widely if incorrectly rumored that the Zoological Society of London had offered £250 for such an animal—and brown eyes were prescribed for black cats just because they seldom occurred. Yellow, the most common eye color, was analogously denigrated as an indication of low quality.[91] Breeding standards functioned to identify the animals best adapted for the purposes of the fancy; the most satisfactory criteria were those that allowed distinctions to be made and prizes awarded most efficiently.

Not all these distinctions were founded in biology; cat fanciers were relatively unsuccessful in reproducing among their animals the physical variety exemplified by dog breeds. This did not, however, compromise either the enthusiasm with which they prosecuted their objectives or the way in which they structured competition. Problems that resisted solution on the level of applied zoology could be attacked on the higher plane of rhetoric. The elaborate categories of the cat fancy were, among other things, an exercise in projection and fantasy; most feline breeds were verbal rather than biological constructions. Even among domestic animals, pets were especially available for such manipulation. They were utterly at their owners' disposal in more ways than one; they were chattels, and there was no significant human counterinterest to reinterpret fanciers' rhetoric or reconstruct their taxonomy. *Punch's* intermittent jibes at the sentimentality of pet owners, and the criticism of their extravagance that occasionally appeared in other periodicals, hardly constituted significant challenges to the figurative structure of fancying. Even aristocratic stock breeders confronted more substantial rhetorical resistance, both from the technical experts who reinterpreted a shared set of images to support a divergent social ideal, and from consumers and humbler participants in the meat industry, who rejected both their values and their metaphors. Unlike prize cattle, pets were widely acknowledged to be useless, except for emotional and rhetorical purposes. This was, however, a function of their status rather than their species. At about the same time that pedigreed pet dogs were being marginalized as mere objects of their owners' indulgence and symbols of their aspirations, other less fortunate dogs became the focus of a serious confrontation between human groups. In this case realities of power generated a more anxious and confused rhetoric.

PART II

Dangerous Classes

CHAPTER THREE

A Measure of Compassion

At the beginning of the nineteenth century the English would have been surprised to hear themselves praised for special kindness to animals. They were surrounded by evidence to the contrary in a society that exploited animals to provide not only food and clothing, but also transportation, the power to run machinery, and even entertainment. The streets of London were crowded with horses and dogs that served as draft animals and beasts of burden; in addition, passers-by often encountered herds of cattle and sheep being driven to the Smithfield livestock market.[1] Many of these animals were obviously exhausted or in pain, as were many of the horses and donkeys used for riding. Off the streets, but not hard to find, were slaughterhouses and the knackers' yards where horses no longer fit for work were butchered. Popular amusements included cock fighting, dog fighting, rat killing, bull running, and the baiting of wild animals. Few people registered distress at the animal suffering that surrounded them, and many took pride in the doughty national character revealed by its infliction. When, in 1800, the House of Commons considered the first animal protection bill ever presented to it, which sought to abolish the sport of bull baiting, few members bothered to attend the session, and some of those present made fun of the whole idea. According to the *Times*, which hailed the bill's defeat, the issue was beneath the dignity of Parliament. In the debate the future Prime Minister George Canning defended bull baiting

on the grounds that "the amusement inspired courage and produced a
nobleness of sentiment and elevation of mind."[2]

The Meaning of Kindness

Those who deplored the mistreatment of animals agreed that the English were especially inclined to inflict it. One patriotic journalist regretfully concluded in 1825 that, "attached as we are to our native land
. . . we are bound to confess, that the proverb is but too true, 'that England is the hell of dumb animals'"; a decade later the naturalist Edward
Jesse wrote that "of all the nations of Europe, our own countrymen are,
perhaps, the least inclined to treat the brute creation with tenderness."[3]
Abuse of animals was perceived to be widespread even among those
who had no occasion to beat oxen or overwork horses. A country correspondent of the *Zoologist* complained in 1853 of "the continual and
wanton persecution of birds [and animals] in England, as contrasted
with their kind treatment in Norway," especially by farmers and garden-
ers who mistakenly considered them pests.[4] The indifference of ordinary citizens could also be criticized as complicity. William Hamilton
Drummond, a clerical proponent of humane principles, regretted that
in a country where "the duties of morality and religion have such eloquent advocates" so little attention was devoted to the abuse of animals.
In 1832 a humanitarian periodical cited public apathy in the face of the
horrors of the Smithfield market as evidence that "Englishmen are really
guilty of that love of cruelty which Hazlitt used to say was inherent in
their character."[5] The theme of English brutality was sounded well into
the second half of the nineteenth century. In 1868, after referring the
home secretary to an article on the subject in the *Daily Telegraph*, Queen
Victoria opined that "the English are inclined to be more cruel to animals than some other civilized nations are."[6]

By the end of the century, however, a humanitarian crusader could
celebrate the fact that "to an increasing part of the race, especially in
Anglo-Saxon countries, this sentiment of tenderness for those of the
sentient lower creatures which are capable of recognising it . . . has become an element in the spiritual life so strong that the continual violation of social obligations to them is a cause of pain and revolt"; he was
strongly encouraged by the spectacle of squirrels begging confidently
for food in public parks, rather than fleeing from feared torture. And as

The Celebrated Dog Billy Killing 100 Rats at the Westminster Pit.
From Pierce Egan, Anecdotes of the Sporting World, 1827.

early as the 1830s, despite the circumambient evidence to the contrary, the English humane movement had begun to claim kindness to animals as a native trait and to associate cruelty to animals with foreigners, especially those from southern, Catholic countries.[7]

To some extent this shift in paradigm reflected real changes. Members of the humane establishment, who were the most frequent sources of such assertions, could point with pride to a series of administrative and legal breakthroughs and to steadily widening public support for their activities. When Richard Martin introduced his bill "to prevent cruel and improper treatment of Cattle" (interpreted broadly to include most farm and draft animals, but not bulls or pets) in 1821, it was endorsed by both the clergy and the London magistrates, and many ordinary citizens signed supporting petitions. It passed the Commons, but not the Lords that year, and gained easy approval in both houses in 1822.[8] In 1824 the founding members of the Society for the Prevention of Cruelty to Animals (SPCA) assembled for the first time in a London tavern. Their purpose was to extend what Martin referred to as the "revolution in morals" that had resulted from the passage of his act. (He gave as an example of this revolution that gentlemen no longer felt they could get rid "in any manner" of a racer or a hunter that had served them for years.)[9]

Within less than a decade, the society's membership rolls had prospered sufficiently to justify the production of elaborate printed annual reports. The first of these, published in 1832, documented a thriving organization, busy with prosecutorial and propagandistic activities, as well as lobbying efforts in favor of additional humane legislation.[10] In 1835 these efforts were rewarded by the passage of "An Act to Consolidate and Amend the Several Laws Relating to the Cruel and Improper Treatment of Animals," which extended the protection of Martin's act to domestic pets and prohibited animal combats like bull baiting and cock fighting. Capitalizing on this increased interest in humane issues, the society distributed twenty-five thousand abstracts of the new law during the next year. Parliament extended and reformulated the anti-cruelty legislation at intervals throughout the rest of the century, and the society documented this progress in a series of publications.[11]

The progress so commemorated had its limits, however. Martin's act had been a long time coming. A second bill to prohibit bull baiting had failed in 1802. In 1809 Lord Erskine, a former lord chancellor, introduced a much broader bill for "Preventing Wanton and Malicious Cruelty to Animals," which would have protected both farm animals and pets. Although it received favorable attention in the press—even in the *Times*—and was passed by the Lords, it was defeated in the Commons. The next year, when Erskine attempted to reintroduce the bill in the House of Lords, it was received with hostility, and he was forced to withdraw it.[12] No animal protection legislation was introduced for another decade. Every attempt to extend humane legislation encountered resistance and even ridicule, despite abundant evidence of continuing cruelty and the apparent success of previous laws. Both Martin's attempts to broaden the provisions of his act—a bill to abolish bull baiting and dog fighting in 1823 and one to protect dogs, cats, and monkeys in 1824—failed amid suggestions that they were "a petty, trumpery, and blundering kind of legislature" and that the next step would be to protect flies and beetles.[13]

Nor was the history of humane organizations an unbroken series of triumphs. The SPCA was not the first humanitarian attempt to organize in defense of suffering animals. The Reverend Arthur Broome, one of the founders of the society in 1824, had attempted to form an animal protection group immediately after the passage of Martin's act, but it had petered out after only a couple of meetings. A Society for the

Suppression of Wanton Cruelty to Animals, established in Liverpool in 1809, had been similarly evanescent.[14] And although the group established by "divers benevolent persons," as the organizers of the SPCA described themselves in their Act of Incorporation, proved more enduring, its future seemed shaky at the beginning.[15] Divergent views on how vigorously to seek out and prosecute offenders surfaced at the initial meeting and subsequently led to several schisms. On a less philosophical level, money quickly became a problem, and in 1826 the society had to suspend operations for two years. Lewis Gompertz, the secretary who successfully resolved these financial difficulties, was an able administrator but, as both a Jew and an eccentric, a public relations liability. He was eased out of his position in the early 1830s.[16]

The connection between Englishness and kindness to animals was forged during this difficult and uncertain period in the development of the humane movement. It was probably not so much a description or celebration of current reality—that would have smacked seriously of wishful thinking—as a rhetorical strategy with several purposes. One was to redefine the social location of concern for animals. Although the expression of anticruelty sentiments had become fairly widespread by the early nineteenth century—they could even be encountered in such general audience periodicals as the *Kentish Herald*, which in 1802 characterized a Lincolnshire bull baiting as "torture" and "a shocking spectacle"—acting on them was often perceived as the preserve of such eccentrics as one Mrs. Greggs of London, who bequeathed £150 per annum so that a trusted black servant could continue to care for her eighty-six cats.[17] The equation of kindness to animals with Englishness implicitly placed humane issues in the mainstream of reformist concerns.

A series of the most persuasive testimonials quickly converted what began as a brave assertion into fact. In 1835 the Society for the Prevention of Cruelty to Animals acquired the first of many royal patrons, the duchess of Kent and the then-Princess Victoria, and in 1840 Queen Victoria granted it permission to prefix "Royal" to its name. The *Annual Report* for 1841 announced that the yearly general meeting had been "very fashionably attended." Even the schismatic Association for Promoting Rational Humanity towards the Animal Creation, which flourished briefly in the 1830s, numbered a duchess, an earl, three countesses, three bishops, and assorted barons and baronets among its two hundred and forty members.[18] By 1900 the RSPCA epitomized respectable philanthropy; it had become "one of the standard charities remembered by British maiden ladies and others when making their wills."[19]

More controversially, the identification of animal protection with solid English virtue could also function as an instrument of marginalization. Those who violated the canons of what was often called "humanity" by its most eloquent advocates were not only sinful but also, in at least a rhetorical sense, excluded from the national community. This double condemnation was intensified by the strong positive connotation carried by the adjective "English" and the corresponding negative implied by "foreign," an opposition neatly expressed in the credo of a late Victorian bulldog breeder, who avoided crosses with alien stock on the grounds that it "must be inferior *because* it is foreign."[20] Once established, the equation seemed to empower—indeed, to obligate—the humane to restrain the cruel. But the very force of this rhetorical weapon made it difficult to apply. Those who might find themselves among the damned were often reluctant to accept the definitions proposed by the humane establishment. Thus public discussion of cruelty to animals became a rhetorical battlefield where combatants struggled over the moral constitution of English society as well as over the propriety of inflicting pain on lesser fellow creatures.

The Appeal of Animal Protection

The opposing armies in this rhetorical battle were not arrayed symmetrically. That is, only one side adopted an offensive strategy, accusing the other of brutality and working to impose the consequent penalties; the other side simply attempted to parry these thrusts, denying the cruelty of its practices and, by implication, rejecting the social map proposed by its accusers. This struggle had, by the nineteenth century, already accumulated a long history. Forerunners of the predominantly middle-class reformers who championed the cause of animals had been attempting to regulate the allegedly cruel behavior of groups they perceived as particularly disorderly for several centuries. Although orthodox Christian theology did not encourage concern for animal suffering, a few Elizabethan and Jacobean ministers of strong Protestant leanings had preached sermons on man's duty to the brute creation. Sixteenth- and seventeenth-century Puritans were also among the first to object to such sports as bear baiting, stressing both the associated gambling, noise, and disorder, and the suffering endured by the animals; cock fighting and cock throwing (a sport in which spectators threw stones at tethered birds) were prohibited by the Protectorate in 1654.[21] Critics viewed cruelty to animals as both an index of depravity and a predictor of further moral degeneration, and the goal of those seeking to suppress brutal practices was as much to protect potential human victims of these outlaws as to mitigate the suffering of beasts. The Victorian critique of "inhumanity" similarly confounded two missions: to rescue animal victims and to suppress dangerous elements of human society.

The complex relationship between sympathetic concern for animals and manipulation of people was clearly expressed in the only genre of eighteenth-century literature that focused repeatedly on humane issues. Books written specifically for children were new in the eighteenth century, and from the first they aimed to improve and instruct, not just to entertain. (This was required not only by the educational philosophy of John Locke, but also by the fond hopes of the middle-class parents whose children were the main audience for this new literature.)[22] Animals were quickly recognized as promising didactic instruments, and works of both juvenile natural history and moral fiction were loaded with uplifting messages about the need to treat them kindly. Eleanor Frere Fenn, author of *The Rational Dame; or, Hints towards Supplying Prattle for Children*, offered a representative justification of this practice when she asserted that "nothing could more effectually tend to infuse benevolence than the teaching of little ones early to consider every part of nature as endued with feeling."[23] It was necessary to infuse benevolence because it did not come naturally, especially to boys. The editor of one version of Samuel Jackson Pratt's popular *Pity's Gift* said it bluntly: "Every one must have noticed in most children, a tyrannical, sometimes a cruel, propensity to torment animals within their power, such as—persecuting flies, torturing birds, cats, dogs &c." Such children needed "lessons of compassion for the *dumb creation*, as a fellow feeling for their own species . . . because an early neglect of the duties of humanity, in regard to the *first*, leads but too naturally to an omission of those duties as to the *last*."[24]

Thus the need to be kind to animals provided continual occasions to exercise self-control, and children who refused to take advantage of these opportunities were seen as likely to grow up to be dangerous to themselves and other humans. Children's fiction provided many monitory examples, such as young Master Jenkins in Sarah Kirby Trimmer's *Fabulous Histories*, who first appeared having "laid hold of Miss Harriet's dog, and . . . searching his pocket for a piece of string, that he might tie him and the cat together."[25] As he grew up, he continued to bully both animals and, when possible, people; he met his unregretted end when a horse that he had been beating threw him. By contrast, Harriet and Frederick Benson, who had been well instructed by their humane and dutiful mother, became happy and benevolent adults. In stories of this genre kindness to animals was a code for full and responsible acceptance of the obligations of society, while cruelty was identified with deviance.[26] The need for compassion was intertwined with the need for discipline.

The connection between cruelty to animals and bad behavior to humans proved compelling and durable. Generations later John Ruskin needed to know little more about a boy than that he had dirty hands, a low forehead, and liked "a shy at the sparrows" to consign him to the bottom of the moral heap.[27] Crusaders against any particular kind of animal abuse were apt to use this as either their opening volley or their crowning argument. For example, one early Smithfield reformer feelingly described the cattle after a day in the market as "goaded and bruised in every part, with nothing to assuage their hunger or thirst, weary and foot-sore with their previous travel," but concluded that "it is the dreadful effects produced by the practices I have described upon our own species . . . which demand the most consideration."[28] Similarly, late Victorian critics of hunting were most concerned about the detrimental effects on humans when they characterized enjoyment of "the sufferings of the hapless victims of . . . butchery" as "a remnant of the barbarism in our natures," one that would "slowly but surely die under the influence of a higher and a gentler civilization."[29] In general, humanitarians felt that, as Arthur Helps wrote, "culture of a high kind, such as exists in the higher classes everywhere" would inevitably lead to "a thoroughly good treatment of animals."[30] Thus in adults as well as children, the treatment of animals could be seen as an index of the extent to which an individual had managed to control his or her lower urges. If animal suffering was caused by people in need of moral uplift, then to work for the protection of the brute creation was simultaneously to promote the salvation of human souls and the maintenance of social order.

It is, therefore, not surprising to find William Wilberforce and other Evangelicals among the earliest advocates of humane legislation, as it is not surprising that Puritans had been among the first to urge the suppression of cruel animal sports more than a century earlier. The connection between middle-class social discipline and religious morality was strong in the charitable organizations and movements that assisted and inspired eighteenth- and especially nineteenth-century English social reform, and Evangelicals were particularly instrumental in merging religion and philanthropy.[31] The humane movement has frequently been compared to other Evangelically supported crusades that combined concern for suffering with suppression of license and maintenance of social order. For example, the antislavery movement was fueled by indignation about the unregeneracy of the slaveowners as well as compassion for their oppressed chattels, and factory reform legislation was designed not only to improve working conditions but to provide a more efficient labor force as well.[32] Similarly, the National Society for the Prevention of Cruelty to Children, a late Victorian offshoot of the RSPCA, aimed to impose moral discipline within the family at the same time that it safeguarded the well-being of children.[33] This is not to deny that supporters of the humane movement were directly and simply concerned with animal suffering, as reformers of other abuses were also genuinely moved by the plight of those they wished to rescue. The pathetic descriptions and heightened emotional tone that characterized the publicity disseminated by the RSPCA left no room for doubt about the sincerity of the authors' compassion or the strength of the feelings they expected to arouse in their readers. An early leaflet entitled "To the Friends of Humanity" included typically heartrending descriptions of such abused beasts as "the dust-cart horses . . . weak, old, lame" and "the poor harmless milch asses, which go great distances . . . banged by a fellow with a thick cudgel."[34]

Yet the sincere sympathy documented by such statements and corroborated by the energetic prosecutorial and legislative activities of the RSPCA had certain limits, which reflected the analytical function of anticruelty rhetoric. By and large these limits corresponded to the line dividing the lower classes, already implicitly defined as cruel and in need of discipline, from the respectable orders of society. Sometimes this division led humanitarians to value animals more than the vulgar humans who abused them; one indignant lover of horses complained that "the lower class of persons, to whom the care of the horse is intrusted, frequently possess less sense than those noble animals, which groan under their tyranny."[35] Those unsympathetic to the humanitarian cause frequently wondered why people professedly sensitive to the sufferings of animals were less concerned with the tribulations endured by many human beings. *Punch* hammered at this theme year after year, refusing to celebrate the humanitarianism of laws stipulating, for example, that a woman who had put out a man's eye received only the same fine as a man who beat a horse, or that a farmer could be imprisoned for neglecting to feed his cows but not for denying food to paupers.[36]

If the social map projected by their crusade led humanitarians to treat groups they castigated for cruelty almost as exiles from the human community, it produced a reciprocal blindness to potential abuses committed on the other side of the social divide. Even some animal advocates occasionally criticized what they viewed as the unduly narrow focus of the humane establishment, which, though alert to the brutality of members of the lower classes, was less sensitive to the pain caused by their superiors. Although the RSPCA occasionally directed harsh words at upper-class pastimes like steeplechasing, which it characterized as "a cruel practice indulged in by many persons whose education and fortune should lead to better deeds," it showed little inclination to utilize its legal apparatus in such cases. As the society's prosecutor told a magistrate who expressed the desire to convict steeplechasers as well as horse beaters, "there were much greater obstacles in the way of obtaining convictions for that kind of cruelty to horses than the public imagined."[37]

Every so often, the RSPCA actually attempted to suppress rather specialized elite abuses, such as cruelty to polo ponies or cropping the ears and docking the tails of show dogs. But usually it acted in accordance with the opinion of Viscount Mahon, the chair of the society's 1839 general meeting, who did not feel that "innocent amusements, such as fishing and shooting, come within the objects of the Society" so long as sportsmen were careful "to protect from causeless pain those sources of our amusements, and incentives to wholesome exercise."[38] Many of the society's most distinguished members were also, for example, enthusiastic fox hunters or grouse shooters and perceived no incongruity between their humane and their sporting avocations.[39] The strength of this position was indicated by the fact that entrants in one of the society's early essay competitions felt obligated specifically to exempt hunting from their strictures, citing in justification the "artfulness of the creatures pursued" or its design "by Providence to check the redundance of other creatures."[40] This position remained rather constant, despite the public embarrassment it intermittently caused. At the end of the nineteenth century, for instance, the radical humanitarian Henry Salt criticized John Colam, the secretary of the RSPCA, as a fence-sitter on the issue of the Royal Buckhounds, which were under attack from the left wing of the humane movement for hunting tame deer.[41]

Although these limitations provoked continuing criticism of the RSPCA, they were also a major source of the society's strength. The identification of cruelty as a lower-class propensity implied a rhetoric of moral distinction which potential patrons found comforting and attractive, and which, indeed, had probably guaranteed that the society would surmount its early obstacles. The potent double appeal of the young organization was clear from the records of discussion at the founding meeting in 1824. According to the chairman, their object was not only "to prevent the exercise of cruelty towards animals, but to spread amongst the lower orders of the people . . . a degree of moral feeling which would compel them to think and act like those of a superior class."[42] If cruelty to animals represented, in general, the triumph of humankind's baser nature, the kind of cruelty that individual humanitarians found most distressing was likely to signal what they considered the most dangerous threat to social order. In the view of the RSPCA and its supporters, that threat came from the uneducated and inadequately disciplined lower classes; and it was their duty, once the source had been identified, to counter it.

Case by Case

The *Annual Report* of the RSPCA appeared early each summer, after the annual meeting. Its ostensible purpose was to inform absent members about the proceedings and, more generally, about the society's activities, finances, and membership. But as organized animal protection did not exist in a social vacuum, so the annual reports referred both implicitly and explicitly to the human context of animal suffering. If humanitarian concern crudely distinguished the indecent and the decent— those in need of restraint and those morally empowered to restrain them—the annual reports contained a wealth of detail designed both to reemphasize the dichotomy and to inspire their genteel audience with horror and outrage. Thus the rhetoric of animal protection simultaneously isolated and stigmatized a large segment of the Victorian public.

The complex interconnections between the society's animal and human concerns structured the reports on legal prosecutions that occupied up to fifty pages of each *Annual Report*. The amount of space devoted to them in the expensively produced document signaled their importance, especially since, in the aggregate, they must have appeared somewhat repetitive and predictable to regular readers. Their most obvious function was to demonstrate the energy of the RSPCA's staff and the efficacy of its program. The cases usually featured the secretary of the society as the prosecutor or one of the inspectors as a witness, or both, and, with a few exceptions, they showed the society triumphant. Cases that did not result in convictions were not selected for inclusion unless they made some special point about the difficulties facing the humane movement or the shocking cruelties perpetrated in the absence of adequate regulation and enforcement.

The cases summarized in each *Annual Report*, although numerous, represented only a fraction of those actually prosecuted in the course of the year. (The percentage varied. In the earliest annual reports it was sometimes as high as 20 percent, but later settled down in the vicinity of 5 percent.) A second rhetorical function, both more subtle and more important, guided the winnowing process. (That the significance of such reports in anticruelty rhetoric was not limited to celebrating legal triumphs was corroborated by their parallel role in the publications of the Association for Promoting Rational Humanity towards the Animal Creation, which although it shared the RSPCA's general goals, did not devote any of its resources to actual enforcement.)[43] The principle of selection was not revealed in the superficial structure of the cases. All fit into the same rough narrative framework; an abuse took place, the offender was apprehended, and finally justice was meted out in court. Within this framework, however, there were large variations. Some cases were very brief, others as long as ten pages. Some incidents were recounted in the formulaic language of the courtroom—for example (this entry is quoted in its entirety), "*William Baker,* a donkey driver, was convicted by the Rev. Mr. BARROW, upon the evidence of Joseph Willy, for wantonly and cruelly beating a donkey on the 10th of September—

fined 16s. 6d."[44] Others elicited vivid descriptions. Most dealt with common offenses, but a few opened surprising vistas of cruelty. Despite their apparent diversity, in the aggregate the cases explicated the frequency, nature, and meaning of cruelty to animals. They illustrated the intensity of the struggle between the forces of order and disorder in Victorian society, alerting readers to the quarters from which the gravest challenges might be expected.

Like the laws that the RSPCA was organized to enforce, the reports on legal prosecutions implicitly identified the lower classes as the source of brutality. In its original version Martin's act covered only livestock animals and horses, which were usually in the hands of their lower-class caretakers. Although the law was revised in 1835 and again in 1849 and 1854 to cover domestic animals not previously protected, the overwhelming majority of prosecutions continued to concern draft horses and livestock abused by butchers and drovers. Among the prosecutions selected for narrative description in the annual reports from 1857 through 1860, for example, 82 percent of the offenders belonged to the lower classes, and for 6 percent more there was no indication of social status. The statutory penalties also made it clear that the laws were not designed to discourage affluent malefactors. The "Act for the More Effectual Prevention of Cruelty to Animals," which superseded all previous humane legislation when it was passed in 1849, stipulated maximum fines of £5 or less for most offenses.[45] The reports of prosecutions were full of poor offenders who were committed to jail because they could not pay a mitigated fine of £1 or £2, but such penalties were only an annoyance to even the moderately prosperous. So widely was it understood that the lower classes were the target of the anticruelty laws that one witness before the Royal Commission on Vivisection, which in 1876 was considering whether to apply those laws systematically to scientific experimentation, stated flatly that the laws were intended "for the ignorant, and not for the best people in the country."[46]

Thus the most appalling cruelties were often associated with the most routine economic activities. The horses and other draft animals that filled the streets suffered most frequently. The selected reports of prosecutions reflected this preponderance. Even though horses did not figure in them quite as often as they figured in the prosecutions, they constituted the majority of described victims. For the period 1857 through 1860, for example, when the *Annual Report* included a breakdown of total convictions, making it possible to compare them to the group selected for detailed description, cruelty to horses accounted for 84 percent of the total convictions and 60 percent of the narrative reports. The reports repeatedly described a scene that crystallized all the elements of mistreatment that RSPCA members found most disturbing. The suffering animal was a particularly noble and selfless servant, and the abuser was a rough member of the urban proletariat. Worse still, the cruelty was ordinarily perpetrated in the public street, with insolent disregard for both the feelings of onlookers and the prohibitions of the law.

If an animal was unwilling or unable to go as fast or as far as its driver wished, he might try any number of unacceptable ways to persuade it. Beating was the most common tactic, and the arsenal enumerated in the reports on prosecution included not only whips, straps, and sticks, but also chains, shovels, pitchforks, knives, and a variety of other hardware. One driver was apprehended while "beating his horse in the most unmerciful manner" although it could only drag one of its hind legs. "The poor animal was covered with sweat, and in the greatest possible agony;

" Hansom, Miss ! Yes, Miss ! Cattle or Dog Show?"

An emaciated cabhorse transporting an aficionado of prize animals.
From *Punch,* 1862.

and although [it was] wholly unable to move, the prisoner continued beating it on the sides with the sharp edge of a steel stay busk, having broken a thick stick over it, a part of which he still carried." When ordered to stop, "he commenced a fresh attack with his iron weapon upon the mutilated sides of the poor animal."[47] If simple beating did not work, more drastic methods might be employed. A Shadwell carman whose horse could not drag a heavy cart up a hill "procured a quantity of straw and lighted a fire under the animal's belly, the flame burnt strongly and severely scorched the tender parts of the body."[48] A Kent farmer cured a horse of obstinacy by fastening a cord "around the poor animal's tongue . . . the pain causing it to rear. Grub [the farmer's accomplice] jerked the cord and dragged five inches of the tongue out, and a dog that was standing by at the time ate it up."[49]

Horses were not the only victims of this kind of cruelty. The reports included many accounts of donkeys beaten either by their drivers, "human brutes," or by the "heavy men and women" who paid to ride them, especially at seaside resorts.[50] Dogs that drew carts (not prohibited in London until 1839, or in the rest of England until 1854) might be forced to drag a heavy load—six hundredweight plus the defendant's wife in one instance—and beaten with "a heavy chain . . . fixed in such a manner as to enable him to beat them without attracting general observation"; they might be raced until their tongues "were hanging out of their mouths, and they were foaming excessively."[51]

Livestock on the way to market were under similar pressure. An impatient cattle drover might "strike the animal a tremendous blow on the rump . . . so violent . . . that it cut a piece of flesh out." Or, like Joseph Millet of Bristol, he might have first beaten the ox "over the nose and head in a most brutal manner," then "called for a saw, with which he deliberately cut off a part of each of the horns; the blood poured out in streams, and the wretched animal, suffering intense agony, roared out in the most piteous manner."[52] A sheep that could not keep up with its flock was beaten "over the head and back" with "severe blows" by the drover, who finally "repeatedly pulled pieces of the wool from its back." The report emphasized that "the sheep must have suffered great pain," comparable to "the pain that a person would suffer from having handfulls [sic] of hair pulled from his head."[53] A Wolverhampton pig driver was convicted of cruelly beating some pigs who fell down frequently because "the feet of many of them were bleeding, and dreadfully sore,

Drovers beating cattle on their way to market.
From the *Illustrated London News*, 1849.

and the hoofs of some of them only hanging on by a thin piece of skin."[54]

Even if an animal did not require unlawful punishment to keep moving, its driver might be liable to prosecution if it were not fit to work. Such cases provided some of the most graphic descriptions of the physical consequences of cruelty. One horse whose owner was prosecuted for this offense had "both knees broken: the flesh was cut through and the bone and sinews exposed: . . . a white froth and matter was running from the knees down to the hoofs."[55] Another had "a deep wound in the . . . back nearly as large as the crown of a man's hat, in a state of suppuration and sloughing, and water oozing out and running down its sides; the back bone was entirely raw for half its length; its nostrils were bleeding, and its mouth jagged and cut by the bit"; another "must have been driven for a considerable distance with one of its fetlocks out of joint, the hoof being turned upwards which caused the bone of the leg to protrude and bear part of the weight of the body." Most of the victims of this kind of abuse were cabhorses or carthorses, but almost any working animal was a candidate. In 1866 a menagerie keeper named James Edmonds was convicted of using an unfit camel with "a bad wound on the near leg as wide as a man's two hands and putrid matter issuing from it" to draw a van containing wild animals.[56]

Ill treatment of draft animals and livestock destined for the butcher had a superficial economic explanation which, to some extent, veiled the bad character of the drovers, cabmen, and other laborers who inflicted the pain, although it did not mitigate their wickedness. When the victims of cruelty were pet animals, however, the wanton and malicious brutality of the perpetrators, usually also identified as members of the lower classes, seemed both starker and more threatening. The dogs and cats who suffered were often the cherished companions and alter egos of people like the readers of the *Annual Report*; lurid reports of their torments invited RSPCA members to perceive themselves as embattled participants in the struggle—even as potential victims— rather than just benevolent onlookers. (Intensifying and complicating their engagement was their indirect implication in the animals' torment, since in many cases pets accustomed to trusting people were easily lured by passing malefactors.) The compilers of the annual reports described more pet abuse cases than their proportions in the actual convictions would have justified. From 1857 through 1860 canine and feline victims accounted for only about 2 percent of the convictions, but they figured in 13 percent of the reports. The narratives emphasized both the gratuitousness and the grotesqueness of their sufferings, and the corollary moral depravity of their torturers. Tenderhearted readers must have shuddered when they read of a stray dog hung from a tree then "most savagely kicked and stoned" so that "one of his eyes was cut completely out, and it was otherwise so seriously injured, that it was necessary to kill it," or a Skye terrier "completely saturated" with turpentine, then covered with straw and set afire, so that "the dog was literally roasted to death, uttering the most excruciating cries, and the limbs dropping from the body."[57] One cat had "the skin of its tail drawn completely off" by a tavern patron who "used either a knife or his teeth"; another had "its nose bitten entirely off, and one tooth taken away" by a neighbor who "enticed the cat within his clutches by words of endearment."[58]

In cases where the goriness of the details or the attractiveness of the victims could not be counted upon to provoke appropriate horror and disgust, the reports often provided emotional guidance by recording the reactions of upstanding witnesses. Readers too would find a half-starved dog with an open wound drawing a cart "a most revolting spectacle," or a flogged mare standing in a pool of her own copiously flowing blood "quite heart-sickening"; they could sympathize with the housewife who turned away from the sight of straw being lighted under the

WHAT HAVE WE DONE THAT WE SHOULD BE SKINNED ALIVE?

Potential victims of thieves who might skin them alive
and leave their bodies in a back alley.
From Thomas Foster, *Philozoia*, 1839.

hind legs of a horse "as it made her quite ill."[59] They could imagine
themselves among the crowds that had gathered to cry "shame" on a
carman beating his horse with a shovel and to "express their abhor-
rence" of a drover who set his dog on a cow that had fallen in the street,
then poked out the stricken animal's eye with his stick.[60] They could
understand why the display of thirty-eight ears that a grazier had cut
off his oxen "created quite a sensation" in the courtroom, and why even
the other criminals waiting to be transported to prison "vented their
indignation" with "yells and execrations" against a man convicted of
skinning cats alive.[61]

Readers' sympathy was further engaged and their indignation heightened by the descriptions of the animal victims. Some characterizations
simply appealed to the sense of fair play by emphasizing the power-
lessness of animals against ill-disposed humans. Thus a beaten goat was

a "poor animal," a cabhorse with sores rubbed open by its harness was a "poor horse," and a tortured cat was a "poor puss."[62] Or the victim's inexperience might be emphasized, as with the beaten donkey that was just a "young creature."[63] Another sort of characterization stressed the animals' good moral character, presumably in response to the frequent claims of accused miscreants that they had only been punishing laziness, insubordination, or aggressiveness. Thus a savagely beaten flock was composed of "fat sheep—not inclined to run about," a flogged bullock had been "walking quietly and slowly," and a stabbed dog was "a very quiet, inoffensive animal and very fond of children."[64] It was often pointed out that tortured cats were "heavy with kitten."[65] The more blameless the victims, the more horrifying the crimes and the more depraved the perpetrators. The physical descriptions of the offenders as they appeared in the courtroom often reinforced this estimate of their moral characters. "A low costermonger" was convicted for beating his dog; two "great hulking fellows" were charged with skinning a cat alive; and "a rough, dirty, brutal-looking fellow" had barbarously whipped a pair of carthorses.[66] Another cat skinner was characterized as "a dirty and repulsive-looking middle-aged man . . . whose flesh was begrimed with filth."[67] Their brutal and ugly appearance made a suggestive contrast with that of the "poor animals" they had tortured.

Finally, some characterizations made claims about the intrinsic worth of the maltreated animals. Cats, oxen, donkeys, horses, and dogs might all be described as "fine" or "remarkably fine," which was an appreciative general appraisal of their size, beauty, and vigor. Or their status might be more specifically ascribed. Some animals had an easily certifiable cash value. A dog stabbed by a butcher was "a valuable animal of the bull species, and kept for breeding purposes"; one stabbed by a greengrocer was a St. Bernard worth more than £20.[68] Others, like a cat belonging to "a respectable farmer," which had been "first wounded with a gun, and afterwards tortured in a very brutal manner," derived their rank from their owners.[69] Whatever its source, the value of the animal seemed to make the offense more reprehensible. And praise of the victims in such terms inevitably suggested a favorable comparison between them and their tormentors. Through a combination of documentary evidence and emotional appeals, the animal victims of cruelty were gradually conflated with their respectable human protectors, who might also need to defend themselves against vicious predation from below.

Enforcing Public Discipline

The annual reports on prosecutions thus emphasized the ubiquitousness of evil and chaos under the thin veneer of social discipline. The very activities that were necessary to maintain an advanced, prosperous, and highly organized society nurtured forces that could undermine and destroy it. Constant vigilance was required, the reports implicitly suggested, to combat these forces, and using several subtle arguments they encouraged respectable citizens, who might not ordinarily participate directly in law enforcement, to join the battle. The vivid description of abuses laid the groundwork by stirring up readers' feelings of moral outrage. The repeated emphasis on the shocking or horrifying nature of cruelty to animals presented offenses as intentional lower-class assaults on more refined sensibilities.[70] The weakness of the victims, the fact that most of the offenders were from the lower classes, and the frequent mention of reporting or even apprehension by those other than constables all encouraged readers to understand, exercise, and perhaps even enjoy the power implicit in their superior social standing.

The exercise of this power was not confined to the sphere of rhetoric and example. The RSPCA devoted as much energy to enforcement as to lobbying and public education, and it urged its individual members not only to encourage and exemplify good behavior, but also to work actively to suppress vicious practices. As the society announced in the introduction to its pocket guide to humane legislation, "The object of this Society is to prevent the cruel and improper treatment of Animals. The Committee earnestly solicit the co-operation of the Police Authorities and the Public."[71] Even the Association for Promoting Rational Humanity towards the Animal Creation, which reserved its funds only for propaganda activities, had included the establishment of "surveillance by means of *respectable* agents" as the final item in a list of its objects.[72]

The encouragement of activism, which was rather unusual among respectable reformist organizations, had been implicit in the humane movement from the beginning. The legislation that inspired it, Martin's act of 1822, provided for punishment but not enforcement, and subsequent extensions of legal protection for animals followed the same pattern. Martin himself recognized that it was up to committed private citizens to implement the law. Thus three weeks after his bill became law, the energetic sixty-seven-year-old legislator made the first arrests under its provisions, nabbing two horse beaters; subsequently he apprehended coachmen, carters, cabmen, and drovers for abusing the animals in their charge. He also employed an inspector to help him in his surveillance and prosecution, as did the Reverend Arthur Broome of the SPCA.[73] Indeed, the major purpose of the new organization was to institutionalize the enforcement of Martin's act, under which, in its first year of operation, the society conducted 147 successful prosecutions. Following the example of its founders, the society enforced the law through hired proxies. It employed only a few constables at first, but the corps had grown to 8 by 1855, to 48 by 1878, and to 120 by 1897. Over the same period the number of successful prosecutions increased proportionately, peaking at over 8,000 per year before horses, the most frequent victims of prosecuted offenses against the animal protection laws, were replaced by motor vehicles.[74]

By maintaining what amounted to a private police force, the society defined itself as a quasi-governmental institution and its mission as the surveillance and control of the dangerous perpetrators of cruelty to animals. This whole-hearted endorsement of interventionist law enforcement seemed particularly powerful and daring in 1824, when the regular police were still new and widely resented as invaders of the privacy of citizens. Yet the new society did not hesitate to identify its inspectors with the police. They wore badges and were selected for sobriety, firmness, and responsibility. They were expected to patrol their beats—hotbeds of cruelty like the Smithfield market or the routes of omnibuses—with authority and courage. Knowledge of and feeling for animals were not prerequisites for would-be inspectors, but previous police or military experience was an advantage.[75] (The RSPCA was to continue in advance of public opinion on the issue of enforcement versus privacy; the 1895 *Annual Report* complained that "the doctrine of the sacredness of alleged rights of the citizen, the domicile, and of private property, is a British fetish, and is responsible for the closure of private places against Officers of the Society. A sealed door bars mines, slaughter houses, and laboratories." In a similar vein, the proprietor of a turn-of-the-century home for stray cats lamented that she could not "rescue the cats of Slumland" from their impoverished owners at will, because "there is far too much prominence given to the rights of property and far too little to the rights of animals.")[76]

Those officially charged with enforcing the law were not always flattered by this imitation. Although some magistrates welcomed the society's prosecutions from the beginning, many viewed its inspectors with suspicion. When, in 1834, financial pressures forced the temporary discontinuance of the inspector corps, the move was explained at the annual meeting as partly "in deference to the general feeling of dislike by Magistrates and distrust of persons coming under the denomination of 'hired informers.'" In 1841 the RSPCA complained gently in a letter to the commissioner of city police that its constables were unable to obtain convictions unless their testimony was corroborated by a regular policeman. Even several decades later the society occasionally felt constrained to remind magistrates of the extent to which it depended on them: thus the "respectful" suggestion that if they would impose severer sentences, "the poor brute servants of man would soon be protected from violence. Many offenders are tenderly dealt with, owing to an impression that the Officers of this Society exaggerate the guilt of the accused."[77]

On the whole, however, relations between the animal protection movement and the law enforcement establishment were good. Indeed, the RSPCA was unusual among nineteenth-century reform movements in maintaining a cooperative rather than an antagonistic relationship with the officially constituted authorities.[78] In part, this conciliatory posture embodied a restatement of the disturbing prevalence of cruelty. The turf was too large to be either patrolled or defended by the society's hired inspectors; they were simply the vanguard, blazing a trail which others were welcome to follow. The RSPCA solicited all the help it could get from both magistrates and police. Members of the judiciary, upon whom the society's inspectors depended to convict the miscreants they had nabbed, were repeatedly courted in the annual reports. The early reports, for the period when the activities of the humane inspectorate were mostly confined to London, even singled out particularly well-disposed magistrates for praise. And the reports were pleased to recount praise from the bench, as when the magistrates of Worthing, to which several constables had been temporarily dispatched, "expressed their approval of the Society's proceedings, and said that the inhabitants . . . were much indebted to the Society for its humane and praiseworthy interference."[79] The society also encouraged the regular police to watch out for cruelty to animals by presenting "suitable rewards" to constables who arrested or reported offenders. Such incentives might be handed directly to the exemplary officers—for example, in 1837 Serjeant Hooker of the London force received £1 for helping to apprehend a man who was trying to make a horse walk with a dislocated fetlock joint—or they might be deposited with police authorities as an incentive, like the two sovereigns given to the commissioners of the metropolitan police in 1833, for distribution among the officers at Pimlico.[80]

RSPCA cooperation with the police also symbolized the relation prescribed by the society between individual members of the humane movement and lower-class abusers of animals. More animals were being mistreated than any corps of private or public officials, however capable and dedicated, could possibly protect; in addition to governmental authorities, the RSPCA wished to enlist the sympathetic public in its campaign to enforce the anticruelty laws. This rather startling mobilization of the respectable part of the citizenry to report its errant neighbors was justified by arguments that recalled an imagined former state of society in which impromptu surveillance and enforcement was routine. Humane legislation was only necessary, according to one legal member of the society, because although "long before the existence of the Act the higher classes of society inflicted summary chastisement on the lower classes who were guilty of cruelty . . . now the liberty of the lower orders had arrived at such a pitch that if a gentleman . . . witnessed any act of cruelty, he dared not inflict any punishment on the perpetrator."[81] The goal of the society's public education program was not simply to acquaint people with the extent of animal suffering, but also to inspire them to do something about it—to encourage them to take sides in the struggle to purge society of a dangerous evil. While the new organization was still struggling to establish an effective working relation with the police, its committee worked to engage the "respectable Residents" of various London neighborhoods to participate in enforcement.[82] The seemingly endless stream of pamphlets and other publications that flowed from RSPCA headquarters celebrated the progress of enlightenment and the extension of legal protection for animals, but it also let responsible citizens know how to join personally in the struggle to suppress violators of the anticruelty statutes.

Vigilante action was encouraged by both example and precept. Many

of the cases recorded in the annual reports included grateful acknowl-
edgment of the assistance of passers by. In case readers did not take the
hint, the society was prepared to be more explicit, stating that "it is not
generally known, that . . . any one may take out a summons for a case
of cruelty which he has witnessed, and obtain certain conviction, without the need of *any other* witness."[83] Finally, around 1861, it published a
manual called *Cruelty to Animals*, which was updated as the laws changed.
It included reprints of all the laws under which offenders might be apprehended, as well as a large selection of sample prosecutions (to illustrate the normal procedures and kinds of evidence required) and some
practical suggestions for novice enforcers. Many of these suggestions
were very detailed and explicit. For example, a citizen wishing to report
an unfit cabhorse would have to note the name, address, and badge
number of the driver, as well as the name, address, and number of his
vehicle. The next step in the investigation required checking the animal
for wounds and noting how old they seemed to be, whether they were
discharging pus or other matter, and whether they were being rubbed
by the harness. It was also "important to remember the exact words of
accused when stopped, which frequently amount to an admission of
guilt." The results of this inspection could be communicated to the society in person or by letter, and if the evidence was deemed sufficient
the RSPCA would prosecute the case at no expense to the whistle-
blower, as long as he or she was deemed a "respectable person."[84] Thus
implicitly members of the "respectable" public were defined as active
soldiers in the society's campaign against cruelty.

Resistance and Denial

The RSPCA's maintenance of a private constabulary, and especially its
attempt to mobilize its predominantly middle-class adherents as an aux-
iliary army, represented a shift from the realm of rhetorical manipulation, where the treatment of animals metonymically identified the social and moral status of human beings, to the realm of political coercion
and physical punishment. This transformation did not go unremarked
or unprotested. Questions of turf arose between the society and the
police and magistrates whose territory it invaded, but these were relatively easily resolved through genteel negotiation and the experience
of cooperation. More serious challenges came from those who had been

defined as in need of discipline. Although lower-class abusers of animals could not effectively protest the society's characterization of them while it remained exclusively rhetorical, they mounted aggressive challenges to every attempt to translate it into action. Sometimes they seemed to cherish their offensive treatment of animals as a means of self-expression, or even to flaunt it as a counter to the interpretation of their behavior imposed from above. Such resistance could be "for the sake of a 'lark,'" as in the case of street urchins who rubbed dogs with irritating oils, then released the howling animals to bolt through the streets and terrify the populace, or they could be in deadly earnest. In rural East Anglia maiming of livestock and pets—with techniques that ranged from tongue cutting to laming to disembowelling—was occasionally used by farm workers as a means of exerting pressure on their employers or paying them back.[85] In either mode, the rebellion thus provoked confirmed humanitarians' worst fears.

Signs of this troubling defiance were everywhere—especially since it was widely believed that habitual brutality to animals on the part of members of the lower classes resulted from their general inability or disinclination to "subjugate the passions."[86] The RSPCA reports on prosecution often noted that the offender was "enraged" or "in a great passion," or "a most savage, passionate man" with "no control over himself."[87] These same passions were blamed for the provocative misbehavior of such people toward members of their own species, which those concerned with preserving social discipline found equally disturbing. For this reason many reports of prosecutions stressed the insubordination of the accused almost as heavily as the sufferings of the animal victims. And it was not only the enforcers who perceived this double significance in animal cruelty cases. Offenders also understood the confrontations not as simple legal matters, but as opportunities to resist the assertion of moral superiority and political dominion.[88] Few accepted their arrests—which were emblematic of a systematic attempt to curtail traditional practices—without protest, and many resented even a warning from constables or other passers-by that what they were doing was against the law. Typical were a butcher caught stabbing a ram, who responded to remonstrance with "a loud laugh and coarse talk," and a horse beater who became "exceedingly abusive" to a "highly respectable" witness.[89] A man arrested for starving an ass threatened to burn a copy of the anticruelty act brandished by an officer to prove that neglecting animals was illegal.[90] More vigorous resistance was also relatively common. A man caught whipping his dog team redoubled his abuse in an attempt to outdistance the constable, and a gypsy arrested for donkey beating tried to convince a mob of bystanders to rescue him by force.[91] Occasionally miscreants received double citations—one for cruelty and one for assaulting a constable.

Apprehended violators did not behave much better during their trials. In the dock many were reported to be unconcerned about the crimes of which they were accused, "treating the matter with much contempt," or laughing during the examination of witnesses.[92] They undermined the seriousness of the courtroom by producing barefaced lies when asked to explain their conduct. A driver who had beaten his horse with a shovel at first denied all charges, then said that he had used a spade, not a shovel, and had only pushed the animal gently, not beaten it. An eating-house keeper who had been seen rushing from behind his counter to stab a stray dog "declared most solemnly that he did not stab the dog, but that it was accidentally injured."[93] Sometimes they directly challenged the authority and dignity of the magistrate. It was reported that a shopkeeper convicted of abusing a dog concluded his trial by "declaring his intention to serve the dog so again if it came near his premises," and a drover about to be carted off to prison "in a most insolent tone told the magistrate that he was much obliged to him."[94]

If trivial acts of individual defiance threatened the social order projected by humane rhetoric, organized animal combats where crowds gathered to enjoy the mayhem and to gamble on the outcome could be considered powerful, premeditated challenges. Sometimes animal baiting overlapped with the world of unquestioned criminality: according to Pierce Egan, Slender Billy (a notorious criminal who was hanged in 1812) was also famous as a manager of badger baits and dog fights.[95] Even when no lawbreaking was involved, such occasions smacked of the self-consciously unsavory and disreputable. Although in earlier periods animal combats had appealed to spectators of all ranks, by the beginning of the nineteenth century they were generally considered to be the province of the vulgar. In 1801 Joseph Strutt noted in his survey of English recreations that "bull and bear-baiting is not encouraged by persons of rank and opulence in the present day; and when practised . . . it is attended only by the lowest and most despicable part of the people."[96] When Martin described the goings-on at the "Westminster

Thomas Rowlandson, *Watching a Dog Fight*, 1818.

Pit" to his fellow legislators in 1822, he emphasized both the degrada-
tion of the habitués—"the lowest miscreants" and "the vilest of mankind"—and the violence of the entertainment. A fight between a monkey called Jacco and a dog called Puss had lasted half an hour and
resulted in the mutilation and painful death of both combatants; when
no special encounter was scheduled, equivalent excitement was provided by the single bear and fifty to sixty badgers kept on hand for
baiting.[97] The defiance implicit in the combination of low company and
brutal entertainment was even more obvious in the north of England,
where animal combats often occurred in conjunction with traditionally
saturnalian rural festivals.[98]

Although it had deplored them from the beginning, the RSPCA was
unable to prosecute animal sports until 1835, when Martin's act was
extended to cover wanton cruelty (there had been some legal question
about whether it was technically cruel to let innately aggressive animals
fight each other, no matter how bloody the result) and to prohibit the
keeping of premises for "fighting or baiting any bull, bear, badger, dog,
cock, or other kind of animal, whether of domestic or wild nature."[99]
The latter provision made it possible to prosecute people for provoking

fights between creatures, like birds and wild animals, that were not protected under the more general parts of the act. The society rapidly capitalized on this new opportunity, reporting a steady flow of animal-baiting convictions after 1836. The numbers were not enormous—in most years, there were fewer than ten—but the way in which the cases were presented emphasized their significance. In the five years after 1835 they accounted for two-thirds of the cases more than a page long in the reports of prosecutions, and several decades later, when only about 5 percent of the total cases prosecuted were selected for description, every single cock-fighting or dog-fighting case was described. The interest of RSPCA supporters was apparently echoed by the public at large, for this was also the aspect of the society's enforcement work most likely to be reported in the general press.

Why did it make such good copy? Certainly, animal combats were inhumane by the standards of the society. But the reports of prosecutions made it clear that the RSPCA's concern with animal baiting and fighting had at least as much to do with human discipline as with animal pain. The heightened descriptions of the animals' suffering and the invitations to sympathize with them that provided the main narrative interest in the reports of prosecutions for other crimes were much less frequent and striking in animal combat cases. In many instances the descriptions were quite perfunctory, a mere recital of the boilerplate language necessary to convince a magistrate that an offense had been committed. A witness to a dog fight noted only that the dogs were "very much worried"; a witness to a cock fight only that "several cocks were killed during the fight"; a witness to a badger bait only that the dog "drew the badger out" of the box in which it had been confined.[100] The ordeal of the primary victim in the Stamford bull running, against which the RSPCA conducted its first and most highly publicized campaign under the 1835 legislation, was described in barely greater detail. In the event, which was an annual tradition of the Lincolnshire market town, a bull was first chased through the streets by people armed with sticks, then baited by dogs. The animal was described only as having been "beaten and cruelly used," then "tormented and cruelly lacerated."[101]

More vivid were the characterizations of the human participants and spectators. At Stamford these were "a large assemblage of between 200 and 300 persons of the lowest description," who, after tormenting the bull all day, in the evening dragged it around the town "and halted in front of various houses, particularly those of the inhabitants who were known to be adverse to such cruelties, &c, where loud yells, &c, were set up by the mob."[102] At a bull bait in Lavenham, a Suffolk village, "about two hundred persons were assembled, and during the baiting the greatest uproar prevailed, and language of the most filthy and disgusting description was indulged in"; afterward "riot, drunkenness and disorder" continued until early the next morning.[103] London dog pits were "the rendezvous of the lowest classes"; they might attract a crowd of over one hundred people, composed of "many gentlemen's servants and coachmen, as also thieves and blackguards of the lowest kind."[104] Occasions at which such groups congregated were seriously objectionable on several grounds: "so distressing to the feelings of the humane inhabitants . . . so demoralizing to the lower classes, and attended with such riotous and dangerous consequences."[105]

Thus, even more than reports of quotidian anticruelty prosecutions, descriptions of animal combat cases depicted active resistance to the moral and social discipline that the humane establishment was attempting to enforce. And this resistance was not confined to the realm of imagination. Attending a bull bait or a cock fight was a dangerous activity for an RSPCA inspector or for anyone suspected of collecting evidence for the authorities. In 1838 the Stamford magistrates and the RSPCA needed twelve London policemen as well as a troop of dragoons to enforce the ban on the bull running.[106] Less spectacular occasions also often turned into literal confrontations between the forces of order and disorder. A cock pit raid during which patrons and inspectors had fought several pitched battles (and from which several of the inspectors, who were badly outnumbered, emerged seriously beaten) was headlined "Desperate Assault upon the Society's Constables"; most of the five pages devoted to the incident described the human combats.[107] A plainclothes police constable who was recognized at a dog fight was assaulted by both men and dogs before reinforcements rescued him. The constables then rounded up a few of the participants (many escaped through the windows); and, when they escorted their prisoners into the street, they were "assailed by a shower of stones and brickbats, hurled at them by the mob, who had collected in great numbers."[108] At such moments the connection between cruelty to animals and general resistance to social discipline could not have seemed clearer.

A bull baiting scene.
From Edward Jesse,
Anecdotes of Dogs, 1846.

The RSPCA's efforts at social engineering were explicitly directed at the lower orders of society. But a more powerful, if less frequent and less rowdy, challenge to the social map on which those efforts were based came from quite a different direction. The predilections of some members of the upper classes implicitly undermined the division between vulgar cruelty and the respectable humaneness that structured the RSPCA's rhetoric. Combats involving large wild animals might attract the most distinguished spectators. The duke of Cumberland staged a fight between a stag and a tiger at Windsor in 1764, and Wombwell's lion bait more than half a century later appealed to a broad audience and received national coverage.[109] A few members of the higher orders even enjoyed the less exalted combats staged at the lowly pits. A police constable found "several persons dressed as *gentlemen*" (the emphasis indicated his astonishment) at a dog fight, and bull-baiting crowds sometimes included "persons who call themselves *respectable*."[110] Oxford undergraduates were reputed to buy a great many live rats for their dogs to bait.[111]

Perhaps more troubling to the guardians of order, some people of great local prestige abetted and encouraged the organizers of animal combats. The earls of Derby patronized cock fighting in mid-nineteenth-century Lancashire. Indeed, cock fighting was traditionally associated with the aristocratic sport of horse racing; and presumably the Lancashire matches were governed by the rules that were printed in each *Racing Calendar* until 1840, several years after cock fighting had become illegal.[112] In many places it had been customary for the borough to underwrite these amusements, and one of the reasons the Stamford bull running proved so hard to suppress was that "the Mayor himself, as well as several of the Aldermen, were subscribers to the annual *sport*."[113] By and large, such cases showed traditional provincial authorities ignoring or rejecting new standards of behavior promulgated by interfering do-gooders from London. As the defense attorney in a Newcastle cock-fighting case stated, "This prosecution was commenced by parties who did not reside upon the spot, who had no interest in the welfare of the inhabitants of this town . . . No attempt whatever had been made on the part of the authorities here to put it down, but they had to wait until a party came down from London to correct their morals and reform their manners."[114]

The editors of the RSPCA annual reports, however, did not see it that way. They viewed such behavior as simply anomalous, like that of the errant members of the upper and middle classes whom they were occasionally forced to prosecute for offenses that were less exciting but equally déclassé. Cruelty to animals was supposed to characterize the most dangerous members of society, not those on whose responsible shoulders the social structure rested. Sometimes this cognitive dissonance led to simple denials that an individual could simultaneously be respectable and violate the animal protection laws. For example, two men arrested for horse beating were only "according to their own description 'gentlemen.'"[115] But in other cases it was not possible to deny the gentility of the offenders. This made their behavior particularly heinous. Thus when a London gentleman concerned in the East India trade was convicted for roasting his cat slowly on a jack, "his position in society, and his education, required that a severe example should be made." The magistrate agreed with the RSPCA prosecutor and sentenced him to jail for one month.[116]

Lapses of this kind were particularly distressing from the perspective of the society's members and supporters. They suggested that resistance to the humanitarian program of social discipline was not confined to those beyond the pale of breeding and education—that some of those who should have been marching under the humanitarian flag had deserted to the enemy. For this reason the society was extremely disappointed in Sir Isaac Goldsmid's response when several laborers were arrested for working unfit horses on his farm. The RSPCA prosecutor explained how the system should have worked: "From the distinguished position occupied by Sir Isaac Goldsmid . . . if an explanation had been offered as to the circumstances under which these horses had been allowed to become so neglected, and had a satisfactory undertaking been obtained that nothing of the kind should occur again, it was probable the Bench would not have been troubled with this prosecution." On the contrary, however, Goldsmid had attempted to impede the society's efforts in every way possible.[117]

There was, however, a silver lining to such class apostasy. It was these prosecutions of gentry who somehow transgressed the boundaries between classes that allowed the RSPCA to feel "grieved at an imputation that they allow themselves to be either seduced or terrified into an allowance of cruelty by persons in high and aristocratic circles, while they inflexibly prosecute the misdeeds of cabmen, drovers, and persons of inferior rank."[118] Prosecuting the anomalous transgressions was not quite the same as perceiving the cruelty of genteel pastimes; in a sense, in these cases, the crime defined the criminal. If members of the upper classes acted exactly like cabbies, they would be treated with similar severity. Even when translated into action, the RSPCA's rhetoric was largely determined by the powerful metaphor equating cruelty to animals with social deviance.

The Hardest Case

The resistance of those who practiced vivisection, commonly understood as dissecting a live animal or performing some other painful operation on it for scientific purposes, to RSPCA surveillance and discipline could not be explained away so easily. Unless it was considered to include the skinning of live cats or, as was seriously suggested in the *Fortnightly Review*, the favored methods of castrating cattle, sheep, and pigs,[119] vivisection was the exclusive prerogative of the responsible and the highly educated. It occurred only in scientific experiments and demonstrations, and as part of medical and veterinary education. Most of this work was done by certified professionals, although some scientific amateurs maintained home laboratories for parallel endeavors. For example, Everett Millais, a prominent dog fancier, apparently experimented on his own animals while attempting to develop a vaccine for distemper.[120] From one point of view vivisection seemed analogous to other attempts by similar people to manipulate the animal kingdom—scientific taxonomy and stock breeding among them. Thus, unlike genteel aficionados of cruel sports, vivisectors could not be represented as having violated the carefully drawn boundaries of the RSPCA's social map. An incontestably respectable activity that required subjecting animals to pain challenged the social categories that underlay the RSPCA's interpretation of cruelty.

Whether because they sensed this inconsistency or because more widespread abuses absorbed their attention, those who managed the society in its first decades paid relatively little attention to vivisection. When they had to take a position, they usually equivocated. The prospectus drawn up at the initial meeting in 1824 foreshadowed the line that the mainstream humane movement was to take throughout the century: "However justifiable it may be to conduct certain experiments of a painful nature, under the control of a benevolent mind . . . all must agree 'that Providence cannot intend that the secrets of Nature should be discovered by means of cruelty.'"[121] Their attempt to posit a distinction between inflicting pain during "justifiable" experiments and mere cruelty showed the founders of the society uneasily desiring to spare animals without discouraging research. Scientists, in their view, automatically belonged in a different moral category from drovers and omnibus drivers. The veterinarian William Youatt was able to distinguish along these lines between experiments that "have been instituted from an honest love of truth, and . . . have borne on points of considerable importance" and those—worthy only of "detestation"—that had been inspired by "a vain and interested motive."[122] If the RSPCA as an organization walked the fence, however, individual members occasionally endorsed less moderate positions. Martin told the governing committee that vivisection was "too revolting to be palliated by any excuse that Science may be enlarged or improved by so detestable a means," and in 1827, the society published a pamphlet in which several dozen physicians and surgeons undertook to discourage "physiological butchery."[123]

By and large, however, members of the humane establishment had little trouble averting their collective eyes from the issue. The predilections of English scientists made it easy to assuage the anxieties that cropped up from time to time in the open discussions after the RSPCA's annual meetings. In 1847, for example, R. D. Grainger, a physician and a Fellow of the Royal Society, rose to assure his fellow humanitarians that although foreign experiments on animals might be reprehensible, those carried on in England did not deserve condemnation.[124] Grainger's remarks smacked a little of self-interest, but they also reflected the divergent concerns of English and continental biological research in the middle of the nineteenth century. English scientists tended to avoid vivisection, either because they shared the religious and moral biases that made it distasteful to their lay countrymen or because the natural theology that determined their view of the organic world led them in other directions.[125] Gradually, however, it became clear that the most promising research was being pursued in the laboratories and on the operating tables of French and German physiologists, and by the 1860s the English scientific establishment, undeterred by the reservations of humanitarians, had begun systematically to encourage the incorporation of vivisection into research and training.[126]

STUPIDITY AND SCIENCE.

(Meeting of Medical Professors.)

Operating Professor. "By this experiment we have ascertained that we can alleviate the sufferings of thousands of our fellow-creatures! I may further add—"
Policeman (interrupting). "No, you mayn't! we've had enough o' this sort o' thing! You must move on!"   Professor. "Move on? We can't move on if you interfere!"

Resistance to regulating experimentation on animals. From *Punch*, 1876.

The resulting increase in experimentation on live animals outraged at least part of the RSPCA's constituency, and in response to their indignation, the editors of the *Annual Report* began to pay more consistent attention to vivisection. Starting in 1862 the year's developments were collected under a separate heading. The society also devoted more of its public relations and enforcement resources to this issue. In 1864 it offered a prize of £50 for the best essay answering the following two questions: "1. Whether vivisection were necessary or justifiable (when performed as at certain veterinary schools) for the purpose of giving dexterity to the operators? 2. Whether it is necessary or justifiable for the general purposes of science, and if so, under what limitations?" The winners answered both questions in the negative.[127] The RSPCA's involvement in antivivisection activity peaked in 1874, when it used Martin's act to prosecute the French physiologist Eugene Magnan and three English doctors who had helped him for attempting to perform an experimental vivisection (injecting a dog with absinthe to induce epilepsy) at the annual meeting of the British Medical Association. The prosecution failed on a legal technicality, but the case received enormous publicity and generated widespread sympathy for the critics of vivisection.[128]

The time seemed ripe for straightening out the law; and, according to Frances Power Cobbe, who became the best-known spokesperson for the antivivisection movement, "the great and wealthy RSPCA was obviously the body with which it properly lay to promote the needed legislation."[129] But that was not exactly what happened. Instead of leading the antivivisection procession, the RSPCA soon became, next to experimenters themselves, one of the favorite targets of antivivisectionist brickbats. This was not because the society had gone over to the enemy, although it never went so far as to urge the prohibition of all experiments on live animals. The well-prepared testimony that John Colam offered in 1876 before the Royal Commission on the Practice of Subjecting Live Animals to Experiments for Scientific Purposes recommended the prohibition of all painful experiments and all vivisections, whether painful or not, simply for demonstration or training purposes. Despite Colam's carefully reasoned arguments and the more impassioned presentations of other humane activists, the Parliamentary reaction to the commission's report was more heavily influenced by the energetic pro-experimentation campaign mounted by physiological researchers and their supporters. The Cruelty to Animals Act of 1876 could easily have been understood as a protection for vivisectors rather than a constraint on them. It set up a licensing system that made approval for painful experiments relatively easy for scientists to gain, and it offered no firm protection for dogs and cats.[130] In addition, those strictures provided by the act were difficult to invoke. As the society's handbook wryly cautioned would-be enforcers, "this Act is complex—its provisions can hardly be applied by the police; much less by individuals."[131]

The failure to enact effective antivivisection legislation exposed a double fault in the rhetoric of the humane movement. The scientific community, many members of which considered themselves committed humanitarians, had organized effectively to resist subjecting its activities to the same surveillance and restraint considered appropriate for members of the working classes whose professional responsibilities might similarly induce them to inflict pain on animals. That many RSPCA members sympathized with this position, which implied that not all cruelty was equally reprehensible and threatening, was suggested by the rapidity with which the society put the vivisection controversy behind it. In dealing with experimentation cases the society settled down to work within the limitations of the law;[132] but for the most part, doubtless with some relief, it refocused on the issues that had traditionally concerned it. A survey carried out in 1881 by antivivisectionists indicated a striking lack of interest in vivisection among mainstream humane organizations. Only about 11 of the 118 local prevention of cruelty societies had gone on record against vivisection. Many of the secretaries who responded claimed that they were antivivisectionists themselves, but that their steering committees were divided or felt that their organizations should not take a stand. The Deal branch of the RSPCA had actually been founded on the understanding that "vivisection should be an open question." And some of the societies were inclined to take the scientific side. The committee of the Wakefield branch was opposed to vivisection "as *Amusement*, but not for Scientific Purposes," and the president of the Ryde society was reported to be "a strong advocate of vivisection."[133]

The defection of antivivisectionists from the mainstream humanitarian ranks may have signaled a more profound challenge to the interpretation of cruelty embodied in RSPCA rhetoric. Several societies devoted exclusively to the cause of antivivisection had been founded in 1875, when it became clear to antivivisectionists that the RSPCA's commitment to their cause left something to be desired—most importantly Cobbe's Victoria Street Society for the Protection of Animals from Vivisection but also George Jesse's fringe Society for the Total Abolition and Utter Suppression of Vivisection. Their members felt the 1876 act as a more profound blow than did moderate animal lovers. In her autobiography Cobbe said that "the world has never seemed to me quite the same since that dreadful time." She even feared that she "brought fresh danger to the hapless brutes for whose sake, as I realized more and more their agonies, I would have gladly died."[134] In response to this disappointment, antivivisectionists stepped up their flow of propaganda, recruited more members, and attacked the scientific and medical establishments with increasing enthusiasm.[135] And they abandoned hope of achieving their ends through the legislative process. Instead, they planned to "rouse the public conscience" directly, to which end, after a year and a half of publication, the editors of the *Zoophilist* (the monthly journal of the Victoria Street Society) decided to provide "a smaller quantity of purely scientific matter, and a larger one of matters political, social, and moral."[136] By 1892 the Victoria Street Society alone had published 320 books, pamphlets, and leaflets, of which over 270,000 copies had been distributed. (This figure was not achieved by waiting for potential readers to ask. For example, antivivisectionists received permission to pass out leaflets at the first St. Bernard breed show in 1882; and many of the visitors were reported to have "accepted them with alacrity.")[137]

At first, it seemed that the antivivisectionists' attempt to mobilize public opinion might succeed. The Royal Commission of 1876 had been constituted in response to strong and widespread public pressure. When Cobbe was organizing the Victoria Street Society, she had no trouble finding earls and bishops to adorn the roster. But gradually the tide of public support receded. To more than scientists, antivivisectionist polemics began to seem, as *Nature* put it in 1882, characterized by "bitterness and ill temper," in contrast to the "calm and tolerant spirit" of their physiological antagonists.[138] Even new recruits within the movement did not always understand why it was necessary to espouse such extreme and rigid positions. In 1886 the *Zoophilist* devoted a leading article to reminding stragglers why antivivisection was "a case of all or nothing."[139] The appeal of the antivivisectionist case was also weakened by proofs of the medical benefits of research on living animals; the discovery of the diphtheria antitoxin in 1894, which promised to save thousands of lives each year, was a decisive blow.[140] By the early years of the twentieth century antivivisection had become a fringe movement, appealing to an assortment of feminists, labor activists, vegetarians, spiritualists, and others who did not fit easily into the established order of society.[141]

The antivivisectionists' predilection for emotional appeals and uncompromising positions was both a symbol and a symptom of the gulf that separated them from the mainstream humane movement. Antivivisectionists understood the meaning of cruelty differently from the humanitarians who dominated the RSPCA. Both groups viewed the abuse of animals as indicating what was worst in human nature and therefore most dangerous in human society. But they disagreed about the nature of the threat. The RSPCA feared social chaos and therefore defined cruelty as the disturbing behavior of the common people, which presented the most obvious challenge to the smooth operation and continued progress of England's complex and sophisticated society. Antivivisectionists saw the greatest danger in that very progress and sophistication; among their most powerful weapons was the emotionalism that, in another arena, the humane establishment was committed to suppressing.

Their antagonist, as the antivivisectionists saw it, was science itself. The first issue of the *Zoophilist* included among "our opponents" the Royal College of Physicians; the Royal College of Surgeons; the Royal Veterinary College; the professors of medicine and anatomy at the universities of Oxford, Cambridge, Dublin, Edinburgh, Glasgow, Aberdeen, and London; the Local Government Board; the Royal Gardens at Kew; the Royal Society; and a host of other scientific and medical authorities.[142] Antivivisectionist appeals characterized scientists in terms that recalled the image of the lower classes presented by the reports on prosecution in the RSPCA's annual reports. They denigrated the hard-fought claims of Victorian doctors to social prestige, placing them on the same level as attorneys and others "distinguished for their grasping dishonesty and insincerity"; they asserted that medicine "should be understood to be a *parvenu* profession, with the merits and defects of the class."[143] Although the "Pecksniffs of Medicine" claimed to be inspired by concern for humanity, they did not care "really very much for their human fellow-creatures unless so far as attending them helps to fill their own pockets ... and to surround their heads with coronas of scientific glory."[144] This sordid materialism not only prevented experimenters from recognizing that the soul, rather than the body, was the most important part of people (and also of animals, according to some antivivisectionists),[145] but it put their own souls in jeopardy as well. The practice of vivisection led to a *"new vice"* of "scientific cruelty," which seemed much more alarming than "the careless brutal cruelty of the half-savage drunken drover, the low ruffian who skins living cats for gain, or of the ... Spaniard, watching the sports of the arena with fierce delight in the sight of blood and death ... It is not like most other human vices, hot and thoughtless. The man possessed by it is calm, cool, deliberate ... understanding ... the full meaning and extent of the waves and spasms of agony he deliberately creates."[146]

Thus science became conflated with evil itself, an attitude that precluded any cooperation with its representatives, even when there was no immediate prospect of vivisection. For example, when in 1882 the distinguished veterinarian George Fleming refused to condemn vivisection unconditionally, the antivivisectionist members of the board of the Battersea Home for Lost and Starving Dogs (the first institution of its kind when founded in 1860, and, although ridiculed at first in the press, a very popular one)[147] tried to vote him off the board. After their attempt failed, they resigned themselves.[148] This was a relatively trivial episode in the antivivisectionists' war on science, but the focus of their anxieties in this small case illuminated their general fears. The Battersea Home symbolized the sentimental attachment of many Victorians to their pets (a feeling that was even more powerfully and frequently expressed among antivivisectionists than within the humane movement proper); they wanted a board untainted by support for vivisection to ensure that none of the rescued dogs ended on a laboratory table—a fate worse than death. Suggestively, a very laudatory and sympathetic account that appeared in the *Strand Magazine* identified "the Infirmary—which is practically the condemned cell—the Lethal Chamber, and the Crematorium" as "perhaps the most important part of the Battersea Home."[149]

The antivivisection movement was a way of rejecting a social order that allowed scientists to appropriate animals for experimentation with the unthinking confidence that they were serving the ends of progress. It abjured a set of values that prized progress above all else, preferring a more spiritual code. (The quasi-religious dimension of the movement was powerful, but imprecise, so it could appeal to both an orthodox clergyman like Cardinal Manning and a thoughtful atheist like Henry Salt.) Thus it offered a radical critique of Victorian materialism.[150] Antivivisectionists saw scientific experimentation on animals as a defilement of both nature and human nature, a symbol of what was wrong with a world in which people had assigned the highest priority to themselves, their reasoning power, and the gratification of their desires.

When vivisection was understood in this way, all other animal abuses seemed insignificant. And many antivivisectionists did not worry about them, making themselves vulnerable to charges of hypocrisy. An earnest clergyman, explaining the painful deliberations that had convinced him that vivisection was justifiable, noted that many antivivisectionists approved of fox hunting and battue shooting, which he characterized as "the slaughter of multitudes of helpless creatures."[151] *Punch* satirized this

inconsistency repeatedly, asking why antivivisectionists were unconcerned with the skinning of live eels or the boiling of live lobsters or
the slaughter of livestock without anesthesia.[152] Undeterred by such
criticism, antivivisectionists attacked the RSPCA for squandering its resources on "the suppression in the public streets of lame horses and
starving donkeys and other unsightly victims of the guinea-less" while
ignoring the torments of "any number of cats and dogs whose howls
can never pain their fastidious ears."[153] To concentrate on public instances while ignoring "the slow, deliberate, exquisite tortures inflicted
by vivisection" was to give in to "the eager efforts of vivisectors to dis-
tract our attention from their own doings to those of the careless
butcher or drunken costermonger."[154]

But most humanitarians did not agree. Distressed as they were by any
animal pain, they believed that the sufferings of animals used in scientific experiments were justified by the potential medical benefits of the
research, benefits not restricted to humans. In other words, the mainstream humane movement approved of science. Doctors and naturalists
were traditional allies of the RSPCA; indeed, some of the expert testimony it had used in a series of cases against the common practice of
transporting calves to market upside down had been gathered in the
laboratory.[155] More generally, science was part of that inexorable process of improvement in humankind and society which, humanitarians
confidently expected, would gradually eliminate even the desire to torture animals. Cruel scientists were perceived as the exception, not the
depressing rule. They therefore required individual correction, but they
did not impugn the enterprise of which they were unworthy parts. The
RSPCA continued to reserve its systematic surveillance for cruelties
that threatened to disrupt, rather than to sustain, the orderly hierarchy
of Victorian society.

Although the RSPCA emerged relatively unscathed from the antivivisection crisis of the 1870s, the feebleness of the resulting legislation
underlined a sustained failure that shadowed the general success of the
humane movement. Despite the time, energy, and money devoted to
education and enforcement, abuse of animals continued. The *Voice of
Humanity* had complained in 1833 that, ten years after the passage of
Martin's act, "we cannot boast of the *suppression* of *any* ONE *species of bar-
barity*."[156] By the end of the nineteenth century only baiting large animals had been suppressed. Because its rhetorical program involved the

manipulation of people as well as animals, the RSPCA encountered more trouble with implementation than did practitioners of natural history or animal husbandry. Humanitarians provoked sustained resistance with both their attempts to manipulate social reality through categorization and their attempts to exert more direct control through surveillance and enforcement. Therefore it was not surprising that the RSPCA's constituency should embrace the chance to participate actively in social regulation provided by a related issue that threatened human health as well as animal happiness.

CHAPTER FOUR

Cave Canem

Rabies was only one of many contagious diseases that affected domesticated animals during the nineteenth century, and it was not unique in being transmissible to human beings. Its economic impact was limited, since its main victims were dogs, few of which contributed significantly to English industry and commerce. In any case, even in bad years the animal death toll numbered only in the hundreds, far fewer than the many thousands that might be claimed by such livestock scourges as rinderpest, hoof and mouth disease, or pleuropneumonia.[1] Yet it provoked a public response unparalleled in scale and intensity. Much more typical was the discussion generated by serious livestock epizootics. For example, in the summer of 1865, for the first time in almost a century, English cattle began to die of rinderpest. By the time the infection subsided more than a year later, over half a million animals had perished. Both the magnitude of the resulting economic disaster and fears for the soundness of the food supply prompted widespread concern; on behalf of the nation, the archbishop of Canterbury acknowledged general transgression and prayed for the pestilence to be lifted.[2] Most of the discussion of this crisis, although highly charged, was conducted in a more pragmatic key. The viewpoints that predominated were those of the farmers and merchandisers who depended financially upon the threatened herds and those of the veterinary experts and public health officials professionally responsible for containing the disease.[3] Eighteenth-century outbreaks of rinderpest had provoked similar rhetoric, heavy on economic calculation and technical analysis, and the official management of the disease had been notably measured, rational, and effective.[4] Since active engagement with the problem of rinderpest was confined to a relatively small circle, worry about its causes and effects was usually short-lived. The eighteenth-century epizootics inspired speculations about the disease that were uniformly ignored by later scientists working on the general problem of contagion; no one consulted them until rinderpest itself threatened once again.[5] Nonspecialist interest was still more evanescent; once over, even a catastrophic visitation left few traces in public consciousness.

The Rabies Mystique

Rabies, in contrast, maintained a continuously high public profile. It preoccupied a large and varied selection of English citizens from approximately the middle of the eighteenth century to the end of the nineteenth century. Newspapers reported frequently on outbreaks of the disease in animals, and invariably on the gruesome sufferings of humans who contracted it; any perceived rise in local incidence could provoke a frantic outcry. On the national level, Parliament regularly debated bills to prevent the spread of hydrophobia[6] and to compensate dog bite victims. Rabies was the subject of inquiries by august government committees in 1830, 1887 (twice), and 1897.[7] Participation in this discussion was not limited to those with professional expertise or special interest in its subject, nor was it structured by the rational argumentation of technical exchange. The disease inspired a combination of horror and compulsive fascination reminiscent of that triggered by devastating human scourges from the east—cholera, or, further back, bubonic plague.[8]

The intensity of the public reaction to rabies bemused many contemporary observers. The unpleasant characteristics of the disease provided one possible explanation, and the medical specialists who dealt with rabies on the most literal level tended to choose this practical interpretation of its power to terrify. Writing in 1872, George Fleming, the distinguished veterinarian whose *Rabies and Hydrophobia* became the standard work on the subject, identified three distinct causes of the hysteria excited by rabies. First, because the disease could incubate for many months, an exposed person, usually understood as one who had been bitten by an infected dog, had to endure a long period of dreadful anxiety. (It was not always possible to tell whether a dog was rabid, even if it was caught, and not every bite of a rabid animal actually caused disease in the victim.) Second, rabies caused excruciating pain and certain death. And third, the carriers of infection, who should logically have been shunned, were cherished companions.[9]

It was this combination of familiarity and danger—of protracted doubt and, should infection have occurred, absolute certainty—that made Charlotte Brontë choose rabies as a convenient *deus ex machina* in the novel *Shirley*, when she needed to soften her prickly and unapproachable heroine. After being bitten by an apparently mad dog, Shirley became increasingly depressed and, as a result, unable to resist the sympathy offered by her destined husband. Confessing her secret dread—she had told no one of the incident and had bravely cauterized the wound herself—provided some relief, and his reassurance, offered on the spot with great confidence, did the rest: "I doubt whether the smallest particle of virus mingled with your blood; and if it did, let me assure you that—young, healthy, faultlessly sound as you are—no harm will ensue . . . I shall inquire whether the dog was really mad. I hold she was not mad."[10] As the mystery surrounding the disease had enhanced Shirley's terrors, so it made it easy for the strong-minded hero to dismiss them. Once hydrophobia had served its romantic purpose, in a single chapter named after the aggressive dog, it vanished from the plot.

Although the unpleasant prognosis for a rabies victim was more than sufficient to explain the fears of those who had been exposed to infection, it was harder to account on such grounds for the anxiety that any report of the disease provoked among many who had never been near a rabid animal. Even during epizootics, people were not, after all, at very high risk. Both the geographical range of rabies and its frequency of incidence seem to have increased during the nineteenth century,[11] but the human death toll was never very high. Seventy-nine people died in 1877, by far the worst year on record. Two years later, in 1879, thirty-five people died of rabies; two years earlier, in 1875, forty-seven (which worked out to two rabies deaths per million of population). In 1862 only a single person died of rabies in England and Wales. According to a more graphic calculation, the average English citizen of the later nineteenth century was more than ten times as likely to be murdered as to die of hydrophobia.[12] The medical profession tacitly acknowledged the infrequency of human rabies by ignoring the disease. Although scientific descriptions of its symptoms and progress were readily accessible, hydrophobia did not figure prominently in medical education. Few doctors had ever seen it, and fewer still were able to recognize a case. Small as it was, therefore, the reported number of human rabies deaths might have been exaggerated as a result of alarmist misdiagnosis.[13]

Rabies was much more common in dogs, although there were probably far fewer rabid animals on the loose, even at times of maximum outcry, than the volume of public discussion suggested. Although veterinarians were a great deal better than doctors at diagnosing rabies, reliable figures were harder to come by for dogs than for human beings. During most of the nineteenth century the only available counts were of dogs destroyed by the local police on suspicion of madness. These statistics were widely perceived as unreliable. It was variously estimated that three-quarters of the dogs so identified were merely epileptic or unpleasant looking, that less than 5 percent were mad, and that 99 out of 100 had "suffered as martyrs most innocently and unjustifiably."[14] During its first seventeen years of operation, London's Battersea Home for Lost and Starving Dogs received over 150,000 animals, of which only 1 was rabid. In his testimony before the Select Committee of the House of Lords on Rabies in Dogs in 1887, a veterinarian named William South challenged the committee members and his fellow witnesses to remember a single mad dog they had seen on the streets. Apparently no one volunteered an example.[15]

Thus rabies may have been more threatening as a metaphorical disease than as an actual one, and the attention it commanded may have been the result of its complex and sometimes conflicting rhetorical functions rather than of its potential impact on public health. The relatively small number of afflicted animals and their minimal economic importance paradoxically enhanced the symbolic significance of a rabies outbreak; the limited influence of rabies on concrete human interests removed certain constraints on exegesis. The public health bureaucracy, which overlapped with the mainstream humane movement and the scientific establishment, understood rabies as yet another manifestation of unsettling social forces. Since, in the worst case, rabies control was a matter of human life and death, it provided more persuasive justification for a wide-reaching program of social discipline than did cruelty to animals. The most compelling alternative interpretation stressed not the figurative overtones of the disease, but those of regulation itself, in tandem with the close emotional connection that existed between many dogs—the most likely potential rabies victims—and their human masters. At issue was control over the rhetorical arena in which the meaning of both the animals and the disease was defined. For those concerned primarily with social order, the rhetorical context provided by the deadly zoonosis transformed the significance of dogs; for those who worried more about their relationship with their animals, the significance of dogs was absolute, and their medical and legal contexts needed to be reinterpreted accordingly. This metaphorical load was so heavy that it conditioned not only the terms of public discussion but pragmatic decisions about prevention and prophylaxis as well.

Panic and Purity

The pattern of public response to rabies outbreaks demonstrated the extent to which the disease existed in the realm of rhetoric. The first alert was ordinarily sounded by the press, rather than by medical authorities or government officials, and it was often couched in terms that seemed calculated to inspire and exacerbate fear. After an apparently mad dog had bitten a number of other canines, for example, the *Exeter Flying-Post* characterized the consequent risk of disease as "a very dreadful Consideration, which should *alarm* Persons of all Ranks" and regretted that "it does not appear that the Inhabitants are at all apprehensive that e're long, they may suffer it themselves or be the Spectators of it in their dearest Friends."[16] Announcements like this often triggered a "general alarm," usually grossly disproportionate, in the view of less excitable commentators, to the number of documented cases. Sometimes these relatively sober citizens suggested explicitly that both published reports and the anxiety they generated were products of overstimulated imaginations. Responding to one of the first of these recurrent overreactions, in the second half of the eighteenth century, Daniel Peter Layard, the physician to the princess dowager of Wales, wondered whether the apprehension that had "spread all over the cities of *London* and *Westminster,* was occasioned by any real cause, which infected dogs." He speculated that the panic was the result of mass hysteria.[17]

Even in the face of an incontestable epizootic, public alarm was frequently characterized as excessive—a response more to the idea of the disease than to the disease itself. During the outbreak of 1877 few observers suggested that the incidence of rabies had not increased. But even so, editorialized the *Times*, "it would be scarcely an exaggeration to say that something like a panic has been produced." *Punch's* canine mascot agreed that the public had overreacted, blaming the press for fanning the flames of anxiety during the so-called silly season of summer, when Parliament was not in session and there was little political news: "It occurs unto your *Toby* / His opinion to express, / That reports of hydrophoby / Only come in the recess."[18] Reasoned analyses, although proffered during every rabies panic for over a century, had little effect. The letters columns of periodicals evidenced, according to one dog lover, "how mischievous and melancholy the effects of timorous and ignorant delusions are"; when fear was running high, a single loose animal on a city street could provoke pandemonium. If a suspicious dog was spotted during a period of heightened anxiety, according to one London police official, "as a rule, people lose their heads at once . . . and the whole street is in an uproar immediately."[19]

In its extreme form rabies hysteria could persuade healthy people to fancy themselves ill. Sometimes psychosomatic symptoms occurred as a result of feared exposure; as the physician Robert Hamilton stated in 1785, such anxiety "disturbs the mind, and induces a train of symptoms, in many respects resembling what would have really taken place, was the true disease present." But more frequently, as his contemporary Layard noted, complaints appeared in people at no risk of developing rabies. He found this kind of hydrophobia "complicated by *Hypochondriac* or hysterical symptoms," for which he prescribed "exercise, company, and diversions," much easier to treat than the real thing, which he called the "confirmed state" of hydrophobia.[20] Imaginary rabies could torment the relatively sophisticated as well as the credulous. One medical student produced hysterical symptoms of hydrophobia for twenty-four hours, until a friend who knew his weakness for porter tricked him into drinking some, at which point his ability to swallow convinced him that he was still healthy.[21] If medical expertise could not prevent such unnecessary suffering, neither could cumulative public experience. Similar psychosomatic symptoms appeared during every rabies outbreak. During a panic period more than half a century after the one described by Layard, William Youatt noted that "hydrophobia has been produced in the human subject by the power of imagination ... but ... has materially differed from rabies in its symptoms, progress and termination." Later still Fleming also noted the existence of a "kind of mental hydrophobia" in people whose minds were "affected by thinking of the malady."[22]

If hysterical sufferers presented dramatic evidence of the extreme terror provoked by even the rumor of rabies, they also illustrated the extent to which public understanding of the disease was derived from a set of shared fears and fantasies. The notion that people who had had no contact with rabid animals could develop rabies was only one of many widespread misunderstandings, the appeal of which was impervious to empirical counterdemonstration. Their very persistence suggested that part of the fascination of rabies might lie in its ability to inspire or accommodate these imaginative flights, which could reach lurid or mystical heights. An account of a young man who on his wedding night was "seized with the most exalted rabies, and murdered his bride by literally tearing out her entrails with his nails and teeth," implied that bystanders might be endangered as well as appalled by the unfortunate human victims of hydrophobia.[23] A mother whose child had been bitten by a demonstrably healthy dog asked the Clerkenwell magistrate for permission to destroy it on the grounds that the child would go mad when certain planets crossed in the heavens. After the magistrate dismissed her request as "foolish twaddle," she vowed to poison the animal.[24]

Especially in the absence of a comprehensive scientific explanation of its transmission and incubation (which was unavailable until the 1880s), rabies offered people generous space for rhetorical manipulation, and they defended that territory against the efforts of experts who struggled vainly during every outbreak to correct their misapprehensions. In 1830 Youatt insisted that an offensive smell and the tendency to run with the tail between the legs were not symptoms of rabies, nor did healthy dogs instinctively detect and shun dogs that were rabid. (An example of what he was up against appeared the same year in the intellectual and progressive *Westminster Review*, where it was asserted that rabies was caused by dog bite, but not necessarily by the bite of a rabid dog. The determining factor was supposed to be the size and shape of the wound.) In 1861, several epizootics later, George Henry Lewes, a general writer on scientific subjects, lamented that "very few persons

know . . . the signs and symptoms of the disease." Instead they erroneously supposed that mad dogs feared water, that rabies only occurred
during the dog days of summer (originally named after Sirius, the dog
star, rather than any terrestrial animals), that all mad dogs foamed at
the mouth and ran around biting people, and that a person bitten by a
dog that subsequently went mad would inevitably also contract rabies.[25]

These fantasies may have indicated a source of the public obsession
with rabies that was somewhat obscured by the energetically reiterated
fear of suffering and death. Like cholera and bubonic plague, rabies was
a "shock disease," and like them, it was associated with disorder, dirt,
and sin.[26] The rhetoric of purity and contamination structured the discussions both of scientific and bureaucratic rationalizers and of their
most ignorant and panic-stricken charges. Rabid dogs were viewed as
not only dangerous, but also unclean; their disease was a kind of pollution. In India, where corpses were more readily available to roaming
carnivores than in England, rabies could be linked to the most profound
transgression of which an animal was capable. David Johnson, a military
surgeon in Bengal, attributed the large number of rabid dogs and jackals
there to "the number of putrid human carcasses which they have to feed
on." Explaining the extent to which "that frightful disease, hydrophobia"
prevailed among wild dogs and jackals, the *Field* noted that "these animals are addicted to carrion in the most advanced stages of putrefac-
tion, and by indulging these polluted appetites . . . they incur . . . the
most loathsome diseases, disgusting . . . to behold and dangerous to
approach."[27] Within the more restricted range of possibilities open to
English canines, rabies was often connected with excrement. It could
arise, one veterinarian speculated, as a result of dogs' exposure to their
own "dung and urine." Dogs who lived in filthy cellars and scavenged
their food from dunghills might also be more susceptible. Obsession
with excrement was occasionally cited as a symptom of the disease. In
1847 the journal of the Veterinary Medical Association retailed a report
of a mad dog who "had been observed to pass his excrements, and immediately to eat them; and, although a dog of very cleanly habits in the
house, he had voided great quantities of urine on the drawing-room
carpet, the corner of which he had afterward eaten, as well as a small
woolen mat that lay upon the stairs." Lewes more primly warned that "if
the . . . well-behaved dog misconducts himself in the rooms where,
hitherto, he has been perfectly clean, and if he is seen *perseveringly* ex-

amining and licking those places, he may at once be pronounced mad."[28]

Thus rabies was defined as more than a misfortune; it was a sin that the afflicted animal had somehow deserved or brought on itself. Consequently, infection was a kind of contamination—a moral as well as medical catastrophe. In *The Jungle Books* Rudyard Kipling called hydrophobia, to which the ignoble jackal Tabaqui was particularly liable, "the most disgraceful thing that can overtake a wild creature."[29] The official and scientific vocabularies applied to English canines reinforced this notion of blame. Healthy dogs were "innocent," other dogs were "suspected," and all dogs should be "narrowly watched."[30] So deeply embedded was the rhetoric of guilt and transgression that it was adopted even by those who were troubled by the application of quasi-moral categories to sick dogs. One dog lover complained that "the dog has often been accused of madness without a fair trial"; another characterized the consequences of the 1886 Dog Order as "a persecution unexampled in history." A relatively detached analyst, who could see what was funny about people who attacked "the recent police interference with the liberty of the British dog," worried that dogs had to "do penance for their liability to rabies."[31]

Although infection was the most obvious and direct way for humans to be tainted by guilty dogs, canine pollution could be transmitted to people on the metonymic as well as the literal level. Legal convention endowed dogs with a hierarchy of moral attributes and, moreover, it clearly associated the character of an animal with that of its owner. Frederick Lupton, a solicitor who wrote in 1888 about laws relating to dogs, divided them into four categories, at once legal and moral: ferocious (naturally savage); dangerous (sometimes, but not always savage, such as guard dogs and rabid dogs); mischievous (destructive, such as those that jumped on people, damaged furniture or crops, or chased poultry or game); and harmless (tame and gentle, as dogs should be). Dogs in the first three categories were considered likely to violate the law, in which case their owners would be responsible for the harm they did.[32] This responsibility was, in the first instance, financial, but it might not stop with compensation. Since the owner had formed the dog's nature, went the reasoning behind this implicit assertion, he or she had in some way participated in the animal's transgression and was also subject to chastisement and special restraint.

Defining rabid dogs as guilty rather than sick transformed an epizootic from a medical problem into a police problem. From this point of view the main job of disease control was intensive moral surveillance of the dog population, in order to purge it of the errant members who had deviated from standards of moral as well as physical soundness. During officially recognized outbreaks, officers on the beat had to identify canine offenders—either suspicious-looking dogs or, depending on the time and place, dogs who were unregistered or unmuzzled—and arrest or kill them. This was, as the police commissioner of London made clear in his testimony to the House of Lords Select Committee, a job that the police loathed, and they were eager to mitigate the burden it imposed.[33] The connection between infection and moral deviance offered a means to this end. In theory this correlation made it possible to predict from an animal's character whether it was likely to contract and spread rabies, a prediction that would enable the police to identify and isolate or kill potential carriers—best of all before they got sick and threatened to contaminate others. Deciding whether any particular types of dogs were especially liable to infection or especially dangerous when infected meant deciding whether some dogs were intrinsically worse than others; the figurative link between dog and owner meant that such judgments in effect identified suspicious or troublesome kinds of people. The health professionals, government officials, and well-regulated citizens who cared most about controlling rabies unearthed many candidates for special opprobrium.

The Guilty Parties

The rhetoric of official rabies control often resembled a bolder version of that of the anticruelty movement, fortified by the executive powers derived from the perceived danger to human health. It similarly divided society into respectable and dangerous classes—potentially offensive dogs were invariably identified by their social status, which reflected that of their owners, rather than their biological category or breed—and it located the most urgent threat to health and safety among the disorderly poor. Thus the aggressive sporting and hunting dogs kept by members of the lower classes emerged as the most suspicious element of the canine population. Youatt identified poaching dogs ("the cur and the lurcher") in the country and fighting dogs in the towns as the principal propagators of rabies, along with other social ills. Dog pits were, he felt, "nurseries of crime" as well as of disease. The viciousness of such dogs—their inbred eagerness to attack other animals, even rabid ones, as well as people—made them more likely to contract rabies, according to another veterinarian, and more likely to spread it widely once they became ill. In 1833 a surgeon warned the members of the Society for the Prevention of Cruelty to Animals that "a rabid fighting dog is equally formidable with any of the wild beasts in the Zoological Gardens." The ferocious temper of the dogs duplicated that of their masters. When Stuart Russell, the chief constable of the West Riding of Yorkshire, long a focus of rabies, testified before the Dog Laws Committee in 1897, he singled out sheepdogs for special blame, explaining that they were the "class of dog" kept by butchers, a class of men that the chief constable also found violent and disruptive.[34]

The pet dogs of the poor were equally objectionable, if less aggressive—living emblems of the depravity of their owners. Those responsible for maintaining public order considered such animals an unwarranted indulgence that led to the neglect of important social duties. Russell also complained of colliers who "have more dogs than they know what to do with" and "starve their children and feed their dogs on legs of mutton." This was a concrete version of a general complaint about people who, although they could "scarcely maintain their large families, still think it necessary to keep a dog or two hanging about their heels." More alarming, dogs intensified the squalor that characterized impoverished dwellings. Fleming painted a distressing picture that conflated physical and moral contamination: "Currish brutes . . . living with their owners in the most miserable and badly ventilated dwellings . . . and contributing to make these dwellings still more insalubrious by absorbing their share of the oxygen . . . and poisoning the atmosphere by their filthiness. Even without their tendency to become rabid, these parasites are a nuisance, and a source of waste and insalubrity."[35] Just as the allegation that fighting dogs tended to contract and spread rabies could be seen as an extension of the tactics used by anticruelty crusaders to suppress the dog pits, of which they disapproved on other grounds, so the parallel accusations lodged against the pets of poor people more powerfully prosecuted a long-standing campaign by their betters. In 1795, for example, the *Times* printed a rather preachy set of rules entitled "The Way to Peace and Plenty" (actually two sets, one for

"I 'M SURPRISED TO FIND THAT YOU KEEP A DOG, TOMKINS! WHY, YOU CAN BARELY
KEEP YOUR WIFE! WHAT ON EARTH DO YOU FEED HIM ON?"
"WELL, I GIVES 'IM CAT'S-MEAT. AND WHEN I CAN'T AFFORD THAT, WHY, 'E 'AS TO
'AVE WOT WE 'AVE."

A dog seen as an unwarranted luxury. From *Punch*, 1897.

the poor and one for the rich), which instructed humble citizens to "Keep no dogs: for they rob your children, and your neighbours." Almost a century later the regulations governing the Peabody Model Dwellings, part of a paternalistic scheme to assist the worthy poor, expressly forbade residents to keep dogs (they also could not hang their washing out on lines or paper their walls, and their children were forbidden to play in the corridors).[36]

Whereas pet dogs were seen as most threatening to the owners who unwisely nurtured them, neglected mongrels were believed to endanger society at large. They were often turned out-of-doors after they had passed the puppy stage, either because they were no longer cute and amusing to children, or because their owners wished to avoid paying the licensing tax due on dogs more than six months old. Once liberated, they dispersed their taint throughout the metropolitan streets, and when well-meaning admonition was no longer an option, sterner expressions of establishment disapproval could be invoked. The *Illustrated London News* described the vagrant animals as "pariahs . . . poor dissipated canine ne'er do wells . . . having above all things a dread of the police, whom they dodge with preternatural sagacity."[37] "Herds" of such dogs were observed to "infest every avenue of London." Not only were they deemed scavengers, who carried parasitic diseases and fouled the streets; they were also considered more vulnerable to rabies than "well-bred dogs"—and "with that class of animal you never know when you may be snapped at by them." Like the people who had set them loose, they were "idle and disorderly," constant threats to public order and safety.[38] If they bit and then, as was likely, ran off never to be recognized again, their respectable victims would be in for prolonged mental agony at least. Newspaper reports often emphasized the social standing of rabies victims, implicitly suggesting that they had been bitten by animals of lower rank. The *Times* described one casualty as "a respectable young man . . . a clerk in the Goods Department at Camden-Town Station, and residing with his wife and three young children in a cottage home in the village of Bushey." The solution to this particular problem had been clear enough, if impracticable, since at least the middle of the eighteenth century: "Were the common people prevented from keeping dogs, many accidents of this kind would be prevented."[39]

Animals associated with the lower classes may have offered the most obvious challenge to the social discipline symbolized by rabies control, but they were not the only potential source of trouble. Also singled out were animals from the other end of the social scale—the pets and sporting dogs of the rich. Here the rhetoric of the administrators and medical experts diverged from that of the RSPCA and other mainstream humane organizations. Disruption from above was thus transformed from an anomaly, undermining the neat division between the respectable and the suspicious, to a predictable consequence of disturbing proclivities of the upper classes, proclivities strongly suggested by the language used to describe their animals. Indeed, from the solid middle it might be difficult to distinguish the threats posed by the extremes. According to one observer, dogs in "a starving diseased . . . state, or in constant habits of fatness and luxurious indolence" were "equally dangerous."[40] Like the poor, the rich could be considered both unproductive and unruly.

Testifying before the House of Lords Select Committee in 1887, one veterinarian asserted that "it is twenty to one that it is the best-kept dogs which spread rabies." His professional colleagues, many of whom despised expensive useless dogs, tended to agree. Fleming thought that "the cruel custom of pampering and overfeeding dogs" predisposed them to contract rabies. In addition to wasteful, ostentatious consumption, pampered pets symbolized the risk of corruption inherent in rarefied bloodlines, with their inevitable suggestion of incest. Other witnesses attributed the alleged special susceptibility of luxury dogs to inbreeding, which had made "their whole nervous system . . . debilitated or exhausted" or to the prevalence of exotic foreign (mainly German and French) bloodlines.[41] Such analyses mingled disapproval of the idle, luxurious lives of the dogs and of their indulgent masters—or, more often, mistresses; they implicitly asserted a moral standard according to which unrestrained indulgence of appetite was a source of risk and contamination.

If dogs' appetite for food could predispose them to rabies, their appetite for sex was still more dangerous. Dog lovers often claimed that naturally affectionate male dogs could be driven mad—that is, made to develop rabies—if deprived of the opportunity for sexual intercourse. This diagnosis blamed human beings, but its logic could easily be reversed to blame the concupiscent animal. Even veterinarians who doubted that rabies could arise spontaneously might make an exception in this case. Fleming conceded in his treatise that "there may be some foundation for the supposition that intense sexual excitement may produce rabies"; a colleague reported that he had "known a dog go mad when you take it from a bitch."[42] The overfed dogs of rich mistresses were commonly assumed to suffer most severely from thwarted sexual urges. The interconnection of sex and sin and rabies could be discreetly suggested: "all veterinary surgeons have noted that male animals, and those habitually confined [and] richly fed ... are far more liable to contract rabies." Or it could be asserted more directly: "the first sexual excitement in the young dog [can be] followed by symptoms wonderfully like dumb rabies ... usually ... amongst ladies' pets, young dogs in full habit of body." As a result of this powerful association with lust, rabies was occasionally confused with another kind of contaminating disease. According to one Yorkshire farmer, "as long as bitch whelps are slaughtered wholesale," thus depriving male dogs of opportunities to mate, "so long shall we have rabies or ... some form of *syphilis*."[43]

The aggressiveness of aristocratic sporting dogs constituted yet a graver challenge to law and order; these active animals acted as vigorous disseminators of infection rather than stagnant pools where it could fester. The genteel rural pastimes of shooting and fox hunting required canine auxiliaries, and both kinds of dogs were accused of special susceptibility to rabies. Harrison Weir, a breeding expert, identified retrievers as prone to rabies in a letter to the *Times*, but most experts did not consider them the chief culprits. Rather, the packs of highly trained and carefully bred foxhounds that dotted the Victorian countryside seemed to be constantly at risk. The informal logs of small kennels repeatedly recorded rabies outbreaks, like the one at Beachborough in the summer of 1795, where eight hounds died of "madness or inexperience," and the sporting press routinely publicized the larger-scale misfortunes suffered by more important hunts, such as the destruction of a harrier pack in Lancashire or the cancellation of the Royal Calf Hunt because of rabies in the Royal Buckhounds. If of sufficient magnitude, such catastrophes might also be featured by general-audience periodicals. Thus the *Times* lamented that "a very heavy loss has befallen the Essex Hunt, in the enforced total destruction of the bitch pack ... one of the finest bred and best hunting packs in the whole kingdom."[44]

One explanation of this inveterate scrutiny was the fact that many members and aspiring members of the upper classes were enthusiastic fox hunters, and the periodical press catered to their recreational interests. These proclivities also determined the composition of the House of Lords Select Committee on Rabies, most of whose members were also distinguished as sportsmen. Viscount Cranbrook, the committee chairman, bred retrievers, for example; the earl of Kimberley was "in his youth a vigorous rider to hounds ... until late in his life a capital shot ... and in all respects a good representative of the country gentleman"; and the earl of Onslow was "a keen sportsman and an ardent whip."[45] The practical nature of their concern often surfaced during their examination of expert witnesses, whom they pumped for useful advice on such topics as how to prevent the spread of rabies once it had broken out in a kennel; their relatively frequent requests for information about controlling rabies outbreaks in deer parks were probably similarly motivated.[46]

It was not, however, clear to the members of the select committee and their ilk that their interest in maintaining healthy hound kennels and deer parks was identical to that which prompted insistent public attention to the problems with these facilities. Because rabies inevitably carried a hint of contamination, some sportsmen felt this intense scrutiny as hostile and resented the metonymic criticism leveled at them through their animals. In 1874 the eccentric Grantley Berkeley, an accomplished amateur pugilist as well as both a Master of Fox Hounds and a Master of Stag Hounds, castigated "the cry pervading certain classes of society, falsely, cruelly, and ignorantly raised to condemn the beautiful creature, the noble, graceful, useful foxhound, for the possession of a deadly disease from which he never really suffered."[47] Less excitable members of the rural elite also worried about the moral implications of unusual susceptibility to rabies in animals that were closely associated with upper-class proprietors. It was, after all, the aggressiveness and independence characteristic of the best foxhounds that supposedly inclined them to go mad, and their inbred predilection for chasing other animals over vast tracts of countryside that made them particularly liable to spread the disease if, in its early, restless stages, they escaped from their kennels. If foxhunting symbolized the easy sway the gentry and aristocracy held over Victorian rural society, the prevalence of rabies in hound packs suggested some danger in that domination.

The dogs of the rich may have posed, in the view of those concerned with enforcing public health regulation, dangers equivalent to those posed by the dogs of the poor, but their owners did not allow these accusations to remain unanswered. Unlike the mongrels and curs whose lowly social status made them vulnerable at once to the rhetorical and the police powers of their detractors, the moral character of elite animals was vigorously defended, either by the tactic of angry denial adopted by Berkeley or, less crudely and more effectively, by the appropriation of the terms in which the criticism was couched. Thus a dog's pedigree, cash value, or genteel environment might be cited as evidence of its respectability. According to the editor of one fancying periodical, rabies rarely occurred in the kennels of exhibitors and breeders, because "such valuable animals" were "secluded and . . . well looked after," and the same was claimed of many hound packs. Notices of rabies outbreaks in kennels often included a mystified statement that no source of the infection could be discovered, which implicitly relocated foxhounds and other dogs of the wealthy on the social map, within rather than outside the zone of respectability and virtue. It followed that stigmatizing infections must have come from elsewhere—imported by an interloper of lesser degree, like the "half-wild tom cat" that caused one Mr. J. Buckley Rutherford to destroy "a fine kennel of dogs," or the wandering mongrel that burst into James Brierly's yard at Mossley Hall and bit his "famous Bloodhound Dog 'Mow.'" Even rabies in deer parks could be interpreted in this way; when nearly one hundred of the animals in Stainborough Park succumbed to the disease, they were pointedly described as "otherwise innocent and playful," presumably in contrast to the "mad dog" who was "said to be roaming about the locality, and which is supposed to have communicated the contagion."[48]

Not all rabid animals could be easily located on a social map that connected their disease with their owners' status. If the rhetoric of virtue and vice that structured the analysis of veterinary experts, public health officials, and others who shared their point of view provided a consistent and even gratifying interpretation of the incidence of rabies among animals associated with the highest and lowest ranges of human society, it could not explain the occasional affliction of dogs belonging to the middling orders. The intrusion of moral and physical taint into their well-regulated domestic precincts seemed both shocking and anomalous—a violation of the logic of social categories so profound as to be comprehensible, if at all, only in terms that transcended the merely material. Even those strongly inclined to pragmatism and common sense were apt to offer quasi-religious analyses of such visitations. Thus the judge and naturalist William Broderip reflected, "That these faithful creatures should be subject to the most frightful and fatal of diseases . . . is one of those inscrutable dispensations that sets all our philosophy at nought." David Low, Professor of Agriculture at the University of Edinburgh and a prolific writer on animal husbandry, suggested that the susceptibility of beloved dogs to rabies was a divinely wrought irony, intended to teach their owners humility.[49]

The bitterness of this irony was exacerbated by the close sentimental as well as physical association between many middle-class dog owners and their animals. More than metonymic representatives of their owners, cherished pets often enjoyed privileged status as actual members of the family circle. As a result, if they became rabid they exposed their human intimates to heightened risk. Since rabies is transmitted in the saliva of the infected animal, a sick pet could be most dangerous when most loving. And, according to Fleming, a dog in the early stages of rabies might be more affectionate than usual, sticking to its owner's side and eagerly licking his or her hands with "perfidious caresses . . . Judas kisses."[50] The increased danger was rhetorical as well as physical. If few people contracted rabies from their afflicted pets, anyone whose animal succumbed was bound to suffer on the figurative level. Even if the disease was defined as a divine visitation or scourge, its powerful taint inevitably undermined the moral status of the establishment in which it had managed to flourish. Alongside the stereotyped image of the strange mad dog that appeared suddenly, foaming and furious, spreading panic and death through a quiet village or a respectable city street, emerged an alternative icon, less violent but perhaps more sinister: the cherished pet who, secretly harboring the disease, became a sort of fifth column, a symbol of latent contamination and decay.

Divine intervention was difficult to challenge as an explanation of this ostensibly paradoxical juxtaposition, but it failed to provide either the intellectual or the social solace offered by the systematic equation of virtue and health, wickedness and disease. Denial was the only rhetorical strategy left to the virtuous owners of afflicted dogs, under pressure to defend both the general accuracy of their social map, with its neat division between the upright and the deviant, and the particular purity of their homes. Sometimes they tried to suggest that their animals behaved better when rabid—were more thoughtful and generous—than those associated with less respectable citizens. One member of the House of Lords Select Committee suggested that if an affectionate and responsible dog felt rabies coming on, he might try to "slip out of his master's house, as though unwilling to remain with friends he had loved so well after becoming to them a source of danger and disease." Some owners recited tales of dogs that gratefully accepted the ministrations of their owners without trying to bite them. Others tried to console themselves with scattered evidence that rabid pets might not be as destructive, at least to their human families, as mad strangers. Though seldom given to sentimentalism, Fleming agreed that occasionally the affection of a dog for its master was so strong that it overwhelmed the "rabic impulsion—that ferocious and altogether morbid instinct that impels it to bite . . . everything animated."[51]

Suggestions of this kind, which attempted to mediate between the incomprehensibility of contamination and the fact of infection, constituted a tricky and only partially persuasive maneuver. Absolute denial was easier to articulate and more satisfying emotionally; in its radical restructuring of reality it restaked some of the rhetorical claims challenged by rabies outbreaks among respectable pets. The eagerness of middle-class dog owners to attribute rabies to mongrels and curs, foxhounds and lapdogs, and foreign dogs of all sorts—alien animals belonging to alien and ill-regulated people—found its corollary in their refusal to recognize their own household companions as potential victims. It was frequently remarked that many people remained convinced of the blamelessness and invulnerability of their animals even during local epizootics, when at least a few rabid animals demonstrably roamed the streets. In warning of the danger posed by an outbreak in 1773, the *Exeter Flying-Post* specifically addressed fond owners: "Let no one be lulled to Security by imagining *his* Dog escaped the Evil." Like other rhetorical manipulations inspired by rabies, this one died hard. According to a veterinary surgeon who testified before the House of Lords Committee a century later, "in cases of rabies, it always seems to be the last thing suspected by the owner."[52] This reluctance was also expressed on the communal level, in the form of strong local resistance to official recognition of a rabies epizootic. In 1890, for example, the dog owners of Kent banded together to protest the "vexatious, arbitrary, and tyrannical interference" on the part of the Board of Agriculture, which had required that the dogs of the adjoining counties of south-eastern England, as well as those of the metropolis, be muzzled during a London outbreak.[53] These country gentlemen resented being tarred with the brush of urban disorder and crime more than they feared the spread of rabies among their animals.

Official Victorian reaction to another socially loaded affliction revealed analogous tensions between ideological convictions and stubborn medical realities, and a similar tendency to privilege the figurative rather than the literal in their resolution. Although it occurred at all levels of society, veneral disease was primarily associated with the lower classes. Female prostitutes, in particular, were assumed to be its source; they symbolized the same combination of deviance and contamination as did the street dogs of London and the northern industrial towns. Large-scale attempts to control venereal disease were triggered when it became a threat to national security. By 1864 almost one-third of the army suffered from either gonorrhea or syphilis, with the navy infected at a lesser, but still alarming rate. In response, the Contagious Diseases Acts of 1864, 1866, and 1869 imposed compulsory medical examinations of suspected prostitutes—a category which was often interpreted as including any female of humble social position—in designated garrison towns and ports. Although it was well known that venereal disease could spread from men to women, and even from the rich to the poor, there was no complementary requirement for the soldiers and sailors known to be infected in such large numbers. Indeed, most army regiments had abandoned compulsory venereal disease examinations several years earlier because they were humiliating to the rank and file and distasteful to the medical officers.[54] As with rabies, an epidemiological crisis was interpreted by authorities primarily as a rhetorical occasion— an opportunity to reiterate social understandings. At least in the case of diseases that carried a heavy emotional and moral charge, blame was more important than prevention.

Control and Prevention

For much of the nineteenth century the medical theory promulgated by public health officials, scientists, and other experts provided no more comprehensive explanation of the pattern of rabies outbreaks and the course of the infection in individuals than did their rhetorical interpretation. This lack of preventive and curative power did not, however, deter those charged with safeguarding the health of the populace from taking vigorous action on its behalf; on the contrary, many rabies control measures, especially those implemented during the second half of the Victorian period, were notable for their intrusiveness. In part this response was justified and required by a public sufficiently alarmed to demand a show of official protection. If "Cave Canem," who thundered in a letter to the *Times*, "I suppose that even the most unreasoning lovers of animals would admit that it would be better to exterminate dogs than to allow the increase of hydrophobia," represented an extreme opinion, many of his compatriots implicitly agreed that the threat of rabies justified an extraordinary amount of governmental meddling with the domestic arrangements of British citizens.[55] As Fleming argued, both the nature and the scale of the problem demanded the subordination of individual inclination to the common good identified by experts: "When a destructive disease threatens ... domestic animals ... it should be the duty of all concerned to obey the dictates of science and experience, in order to avert danger and loss ... Individual efforts go for little. It is on the strict observance of sanitary laws, and to the wise measures prescribed by authority, that reliance must be placed."[56] But the community of enlightened administrators, scientists, doctors, and humanitarians also had other reasons for eagerly embracing the proffered opportunity for action. Like offenses against humanitarianism, the spread of rabies symbolized more profound social problems. The perceived danger to human life licensed them to express in regulations and enforcement attitudes previously confined to the realm of rhetoric.

The lack of consensus about the causes and transmission of rabies gave experts and officials a great deal of room to maneuver in designing public health policies. It was universally recognized that the disease could spread through the bite or scratch of an afflicted animal, but protracted controversy raged about whether that was the only way to go mad. A profound schism separated those who thought that rabies was transmitted from animal to animal (and human) exclusively in saliva and those who adhered to the theory of spontaneous generation, which identified more varied sources of danger. The former materialistic view, which became known as the inoculation theory, was not confirmed until Pasteur's experiments of the 1880s, although as early as 1794 it had inspired a Manchester physician named Samuel Argent Bardsley to propose eliminating rabies in the United Kingdom by confining every British dog for a period of eight months and imposing a quarantine on imported dogs.[57] The plan was never seriously considered for implementation, at least in part because Bardsley's fundamental assumptions directly contradicted the conviction of many scientists and medical experts, as well as dog lovers, that rabies could arise in dogs and even in people who had had no contact with diseased animals, as a result of exposure to a variety of external, noninfectious agents. Depending on which authority was consulted, these included not only overfeeding and sexual frustration, but also cold weather, wet weather, hot weather, thirst, hunger, confinement, terror, pain, and other violent emotions.[58] As empirical evidence slowly accumulated, it corroborated Bardsley's point of view, but spontaneous generation retained a sentimental appeal. Not even the repeated and authoritative assertions of Youatt could undermine the widespread conviction that circumstances might trigger rabies in an unfortunate or unhappy animal.[59]

As a result, until the last decades of the nineteenth century most official rabies control measures were structured by the rhetoric of social engineering rather than that of medical science. They worked by stigmatizing and restricting dangerous human groups, based on their metonymic association with animals alleged to be at special risk. Dog licensing, the earliest, least onerous, and most widespread form of rabies control, exemplified this approach: since the licenses were designed to be carried by owner rather than animal, they could even seem to certify humans directly rather than through a canine intermediary. And indeed, licenses always served multiple purposes, some of them explicitly concerned with maintaining order among the human masses. An early veterinary proponent of a dog tax noted that as well as helping "in regard to the prevention of Hydrophobia," such a levy would also "prove of public utility . . . in a political view." Such "political" considerations sparked the initial imposition of dog licensing in 1796: it found favor both as a revenue measure and as a possible means of discouraging the rural poor from owning poaching dogs.[60] The Bill to Prevent the Spreading of Canine Madness, which was proposed but not passed in 1831, similarly illustrated the tendency to conflate rabies control with social taxonomy. It made several provisions for outbreaks: magistrates were empowered to order all dogs confined, dogs were required to wear tags identifying their owners, and owners of mad dogs were made financially liable for damages to any people and animals that they bit in their frenzy. None of these measures would have done much to stem a rabies epizootic, but each made it easier to distinguish guilty dogs from innocent ones belonging to responsible owners.[61] Like licensing regulations in general, the bill assumed that ownership by a respectable person, defined as someone with both the means and the inclination to pay for registration, offered minimum assurance that a dog was not at risk.

Poor dog owners almost inevitably came up short in these attributes, and consequently compulsory licensing was strongly endorsed by those who viewed the urban canine proletariat as the reservoir of rabies. It offered a legal means of examining and circumscribing at least one facet of the lives of the unruly poor, as well as a chance to rid city streets of a dangerous nuisance. If the paupers, shoemakers, and tailors who turned their dogs out into the street every day "to get their living where they could find it" were unlikely to bother with the formality and expense of licenses, critics argued, then they should not be allowed to keep dogs. If there was no one to license the "untaxed dogs without owners" that abounded in London and other large cities, then those animals had no business roaming the streets. Occasionally, enforcement of licensing laws produced some tear-jerking copy, like the story of the "miserably clad" old woman who was fined 25s. by the Preston Town Council for not having licensed "a diminutive white dog with beautiful curly hair," although she wept bitterly and protested that, being blind and toothless, it just sat by the fire and never hurt anyone. For every such episode, however, there were numerous counterexamples discouraging sentimentality about the relation of the urban poor to their dogs. In general, William Hone, a strong supporter of punitive licensing, warned in his *Every-Day Book*, "few poor men in towns keep dogs but for the purpose of sport . . . to fight them . . . drawing badgers . . . baiting bulls . . . or otherwise brutally misemploying them."[62]

Licensing also identified another dangerous class—dog owners who, although well able to afford to register their animals, chose not to submit themselves to official surveillance. In 1877 Gordon Stables guessed that fewer than 40 percent of British dogs had been properly registered, mostly by "the poorer middle classes." He complained that "many so-called gentlemen, in good position of life" neglected to get licenses, because their prosperous and respectable appearance guaranteed that the police would never ask to examine them; keepers of hound kennels might delay registering their young dogs until they had decided which ones were good enough to be kept. These scofflaws often assumed that their elevated social position exempted them from the obligation to comply with petty rules. As one "Friend of Dogs" put it in a periodical that catered to genteel sportsmen, licensing regulations were not intended to be enforced equally and indiscriminately against "the worthless cur and the valuable pointer or house-dog."[63] And enforcers of the dog laws seemed to corroborate this judgment; derelictions on this level did not represent as profound a social threat as did those of the poor. If an affluent owner was apprehended, he or she could easily rejoin the ranks of the respectable with a few readily available shillings.

Although licensing was, at least in principle, thorough in its categorization of the dog-owning public, it operated unobtrusively; animals carried no visible sign of their status, other than the appearance of their owners. Moderate surveillance seemed sufficient in the absence of infection, but during times of unusual alarm officials might feel the need to intensify their struggle against the disease. The escalation functioned primarily in the symbolic sphere. The Metropolitan Streets Act of 1867 gave the London commissioner of police the authority to order the most dramatic means of separating, so to speak, the sheep from the goats: muzzles, made of wire or stiffened leather, to be worn by all unled dogs. After several decades of testing in the metropolis, this power was extended to local authorities by the Rabies Orders of 1886 and 1887.[64] The enthusiasm with which most veterinarians and public officials endorsed muzzling focused on its rhetorical effect: muzzles were more visible than registration tickets carried in owners' pockets, and so potentially dangerous dogs were obvious at a glance. This was much more important than any direct protection that muzzling offered against dog bite, except perhaps to the dogs themselves, since muzzled dogs were often reluctant to challenge unmuzzled dogs to fight. Occasionally muzzling advocates claimed that if a muzzled dog should develop rabies, it would be unable to bite anybody, but this argument was recognized to be relatively weak. In the first place, muzzled dogs would be responsibly owned and thus not reckoned as likely rabies victims. Furthermore, a furious mad dog would probably be able to destroy its muzzle.[65] The charm of the muzzle resided in its power to signal danger, not to prevent the spread of infection.

Official support for muzzling orders may have also reflected the fact that they tended to be enforced more vigorously than mere licensing

THE DOG SCARE.

THE POLICEMAN AS HE OUGHT TO BE (PROPERLY PROTECTED) OUTSIDE THE
SIX-MILE METROPOLITAN RADIUS.

The police war on dogs. From *Punch*, 1886.

orders. Although in theory the same sanction buttressed both kinds of regulation, the prosecution and punishment of dogs caught *in flagrante* occurred much more frequently when muzzling was the issue. According to the medical officer of Nottingham, muzzling orders, strictly enforced, had effectively stemmed a serious rabies outbreak in that city during the winter of 1886–87.[66] Strict enforcement meant killing all unmuzzled dogs, a duty that police carried out with energy and often in full view of the public. Their normal method was to beat the offending animals to death on the spot. This technique aroused the consternation, not only of the poor, whose dogs were most likely to suffer, but also of their betters, who urged "the desirability of preventing shocking scenes being enacted in the presence of children and ladies in open thoroughfares by the use of police truncheons." Ordinary human-strength truncheons did not always prove adequate for this purpose; their frequent dog patrols forced the London police to replace them with a sturdier model.[67]

Thus muzzling demonstrated the power of governmental authorities to interfere in ordinary life and the violence deemed necessary to suppress some kinds of threatening behavior. Urban streets full of muzzled dogs suggested not only the docility of both canines and humans, but also the omnipresence of regulation, which restricted the freedom of owners as well as that of their animals. Many dog owners resented this implicit celebration of official intrusion into what they regarded as the sphere of private autonomy. As a result, the rhetorical effectiveness of muzzling sparked resistance among law-abiding dog owners. The resistance took several forms, most of which focused on alleged practical drawbacks of muzzling rather than on the dog owners' resentment of meddling experts. Proprietors of working dogs like sheep-herding collies and foxhounds pointed out that their animals were rendered useless by such a device. Many dog owners considered the muzzle "a species of torture." Ill-fitting muzzles could irritate a dog's skin, causing pain and inflammation; although they were ostensibly designed to allow free access to water, many muzzles prevented animals from drinking. Queen Victoria herself urged that "muzzles, except in the case of very savage dogs, should not be used." Even the Royal Society for the Prevention of Cruelty to Animals, which normally supported the authorities, voted in 1883 to condemn compulsory use of muzzles. Instead, it endorsed filing dogs' teeth as a more effective and humane means of preventing "the poisonous virus from being conveyed from a rabid dog to other animals, including human beings."[68] The ultimate use of the muzzle as a symbol of unjustifiable regulation may have been the warning, published by the Ladies' Kennel Journal in 1897, that the Board of Agriculture, having admitted the impossibility of muzzling cats, was considering killing them all.[69]

This tension between self-righteous enforcers and pet owners resentful of official attempts to control their behavior and that of their animals persisted even after Pasteur's research provided the scientific rationale for the offensive policies. Indeed, relations between the regulators and the regulated may even have deteriorated. Not only did Pasteur's discoveries vindicate the policies of surveillance and punishment that had increasingly been favored by medical experts and national public health

"PREVENTION BETTER THAN CURE."
(Poor Pussy's Scratch is as bad as her Bite.)

Muzzling cats, a more difficult proposition than muzzling dogs.
From *Punch*, 1889.

authorities, they also encouraged officials to extend these measures and to enforce them more vigorously. Pasteur successfully inoculated the first human being, a nine-year-old boy who had been severely bitten on the hands and legs by a certifiably mad dog, which virtually guaranteed that he would contract rabies, in July of 1885. As it happened, the initial

flush of publicity heralding this successful intervention coincided with
an upswing in British public concern.[70] Human rabies deaths, which had
leveled off after the bad year of 1877 to an annual average of approximately thirty-four (still greater than the pre-1860 rate), peaked again
at sixty in 1885; among the first patients who flocked to Pasteur's clinic
for preventive vaccination were seven London bobbies bitten in the line
of duty.[71] The panic routinely fueled by the press further supported the
official predilection for vigorous and wide-ranging regulation.

Nevertheless, before committing itself wholeheartedly to escalated
enforcement based on Pasteur's work, the government carefully established an elaborate structure of corroborative authority. In 1886 the
Local Government Board appointed a "Committee to inquire into M.
Pasteur's Treatment of Hydrophobia," which was composed primarily of
scientists. The committee members visited Pasteur's laboratory, and its
secretary Victor Horsley duplicated his experiments; they expressed
complete approbation of Pasteur's methods and results.[72] Impressed as
they were with Pasteur's vaccine, however, the members of the Local
Government Board Committee advised against a policy of universal inoculation. Although it might have seemed attractive as a symbol of
thorough prophylactic management, committee members did not believe it "would be voluntarily adopted by all owners of dogs, or could
be enforced on them." Any attempt at implementation might have
backfired, thus circumscribing rather than extending the sphere of official influence. Instead, using scientific advances to provide a renewed
license for policies developed to serve rhetorical purposes, they suggested a combination of more familiar tactics: destruction of stray dogs,
taxes on "useless dogs" to discourage people—especially poor people—
from keeping them, a quarantine on dogs from foreign countries where
rabies outbreaks were in progress, and compulsory muzzling during rabies emergencies.[73] Similarly, although they advocated the establishment of a vaccination facility in England, the members of the House of
Lords Select Committee on Rabies, which met in the summer of 1887,
recommended that the government rely on vigorous application of conventional measures—muzzling and the slaughter of ownerless dogs—
for its main offensive against rabies and the fear of hydrophobia. They
also suggested that dogs wear badges to prove they had been licensed,
and that the symptoms of rabies be detailed on the back of the licenses
dog owners carried. And they emphasized the need for rigorous en-

forcement in densely populated areas—the urban and industrial slums that harbored the most threatening segments of the human and canine populations.[74]

Pasteur himself would have endorsed these recommendations. Because the sea presented an insurmountable barrier to migrating wild animals (or roving domestic ones) that might carry rabies, Pasteur had been puzzled by the British interest in large-scale vaccination. "You do not require it in England at all," he told Horsley. "I have proved that this is an infectious disease: all you have to do is to establish a brief quarantine covering the incubation period, muzzle all your dogs at the present moment, and in a few years you will be free."[75] And in fact that is, more or less, what happened. The combination of muzzling and quarantine meant that in 1902 Britain was declared free of rabies—as it was again in 1922, after the eradication of an outbreak caused by smuggled animals.[76]

Although the plan was simple and in the end effective, implementation proved rather complicated. The fact that the highest scientific and political authorities had joined to endorse a sensible campaign to eliminate a widely dreaded menace did not guarantee universal cooperation. Indeed, it sometimes seemed to guarantee the reverse. As long as enforcement of antirabies measures was left in the hands of local author-

SIR WALTER DE LONG SETTETH HIMSELF TO MUZZLE DOGS.

The official enforcement of muzzling. From Carruthers Gould, *Froissart's Modern Chronicles*, 1902.

ities, who were sympathetic to local dog lovers and therefore reluctant to declare outbreaks, control regulations seldom went into operation. The statistics gathered by the departmental committee appointed by the Board of Agriculture to inquire into the laws relating to dogs made this point with incontrovertible clarity. In 1889, when the Board of Agriculture had assumed responsibility for issuing local muzzling orders, there were 312 reported cases of rabies in dogs and 30 registered human deaths from hydrophobia. In 1892, after four years of central regulation, the numbers had fallen to 38 and 6, respectively, and the local authorities were allowed to reassume their responsibilities. Only three years later there were 672 cases of rabies in dogs and 20 human deaths. As a result, the Board of Agriculture once again took charge of rabies control, with demonstrable effectiveness. But even when the end was in sight, the clamor continued. In *Froissart's Modern Chronicles* (1902), the satirist Carruthers Gould recounted that the antirabies regulations—especially muzzling—"sorely vexed all those who possessed dogs, and they leagued themselves together saying that the law was an evil one, and that Sir Walter de Long [that is, Walter Long, then president of the Board of Agriculture] should be put down."[77]

Defenders of Innocent Dogs

If resentment of intrusive rabies control measures and harsh enforcement was widespread among ordinary dog owners, it did not reflect profound disaffection from the authorities that imposed them. In most cases the resistance simply expressed divergent understandings of what action was appropriate at specific times—to what extent government should dictate behavior within the family and whether individual dogs or groups of dogs should be included within the stigmatized category of animals at special risk. Indeed, when the aggrieved dog owners of Kent complained formally to the Board of Agriculture about government interference between them and their dogs,[78] the implicit assumptions on which they based their protest signaled their underlying acceptance of official rhetoric. Like policy makers and enforcers, they interpreted rabies as a marker for human groups that also represented contamination, sin, and social danger, and they understood public health regulation as an appropriate means of identifying and defusing such threats. What they disliked was being classed, albeit respectfully and temporarily, in the dangerous category.

More radical critics, mostly drawn from the ranks of antivivisectionists and often with ties to the anti-inoculation movement, objected to
antirabies regulation on rhetorical as well as pragmatic grounds. They
professed a love of dogs so intense as to verge on the ideological. To an
even greater extent than the administrators and experts whom they castigated, they understood rabies as primarly a moral problem, emphasizing issues of purity and contamination. In a complete figurative reversal,
however, rabies became the symbol of corruption not on the part of
diseased animals and their owners, but on the part of the people responsible for their persecution; the regulators who saw themselves as
representing progress, enlightenment, and social discipline, were reinterpreted as agents of contamination, apostasy, and decay. Confirming
the division between antivivisectionists and members of the mainstream
humane movement, radical critics of the public health establishment
isolated themselves from others with superficially similar concerns by
targeting science as the agent of corruption rather than of cleansing.
An index of their distance from the consensus that developed in the
1880s among scientists, officials, and self-proclaimed enlightened dog
owners was offered to the House of Lords Select Committee by George
R. Krehl, the editor of the *Stockkeeper, Kennel, and Fanciers' Chronicle*. He
disdainfully characterized anyone who did not share these views as "un-
scientific," implicitly equating the scientific and the good.[79]

As they abandoned the opposition between good, clean, safe dogs
and bad, dirty, dangerous dogs, these dissenters replaced it with one in
which all dogs were innocent and any evil they did was the fault of
wicked human beings. One advocate of this perspective testified to the
House of Lords Select Committee that muzzling "developed the rabitic
matter in the blood of the dogs."[80] Animals were not surrogates of their
owners but more generally represented a range of human victims of the
increasingly intrusive state, and rabies regulation became part of a larger
pattern of persecuting dogs in order both to license many sins of authorities and to blame dogs for them. Thus the *Zoophilist* asserted during
the heated debates of 1886 that "the hydrophobia scare has been made
the excuse for every kind of brutal treatment towards dogs, and the
public, at the instigation of the doctors, are becoming, like children
under a vulgar and silly nurse, first terrified out of their senses and then
pitilessly cruel."[81] Even the least powerful people could become the
agents of their superiors' evil. George Jesse, an eccentric dog lover who
documented what he considered the national war against dogs in a se-

ries of enormous scrapbooks, scrawled the following explanation in the margin of a brief newspaper notice that a ten-year-old girl had been bitten by a dog: "No doubt the little wretch teased it."[82]

When the authorities acted on their own behalf, they came in for much harsher, shriller criticism. Jesse characterized a doctor who wrote to the *Standard* urging licensing and, if rabies threatened to become prevalent, compulsory muzzling, as a "vile vivisector."[83] And such direct attacks constituted only one-half of a double rejection of scientific progress. The other was implicit in the interpretation of rabies put forth by antivivisectionists and their sympathizers. The moralized metaphorical terms in which they conceived the issue had little reference to the physical realities of disease. Indeed, from their perspective, rabies itself did not present a problem. What was troublesome was the tendency of people to perceive it as a problem, and therefore to try to solve it by means that inevitably encouraged the spread of corruption. Purging rabies of its physical component and translating it entirely into the figurative realm allowed critics to treat the evidence offered in expert discussion of the disease as similarly insubstantial, to be taken into account only on the basis of its moral persuasiveness. The radical resistance to official rabies control measures came to unite behind a set of alternative opinions that had been abandoned by the forces of progress, among them the theory of spontaneous generation, which was attractive because it contended that dogs were put at risk of contracting rabies by human cruelty or human neglect. As a correspondent who styled himself "Sirius" wrote to the *Times*, "were all owners of dogs to give them good food, abundant exercise, and above all kind treatment, I believe that hydrophobia would be scarcely ever heard of."[84]

This insistent retreat to the metaphorical level led to claims that rabies was much less common than was generally understood. Grantley Berkeley for one asserted that "nothing can be more mischievous, or . . . more ignorant, than classifying what is called 'rabies' with the fearful and always fatal malady of hydrophobia, for it is impossible to understand what 'rabies' means, descanted on as it has been of late by erring and blatant individuals."[85] At the extreme, this recourse led to the flat denial that the disease existed. Instead, it was portrayed as the construction of those who wished for an excuse to persecute dogs and people. According to the *Worcestershire Chronicle*, "there is no such thing as hydrophobia from dog bite, but there is a very widespread disease of insanity arising from an unnatural and causeless distrust of dogs, which appears to affect people long before they have been bitten by them." The *Kennel Review* defined hydrophobia as "a peculiar madness that seizes men and impels them to destroy dogs." A similar view was expressed by Surgeon General Charles Alexander Gordon in his testimony to the House of Lords Committee. Representing a substantial body of antimodernizing opinion within the medical profession, he dissociated rabies from dog bite with less humor but equal conviction: "It is not a specific disease . . . but . . . simply a complication or condition arising in the course of certain other diseases."[86] A Brighton surgeon named Robert White attributed the idea that the bite of a rabid dog produced hydrophobia to "nothing more than one of the instances of deliramenta among the learned that occasionally creep forth"; if analyzed carefully, he claimed, all cases of human hydrophobia would prove to be misdiagnoses of other diseases. Dr. White had, at least, the courage of his convictions. He allowed himself to be bitten by a rabid dog in substantiation of his theory, and, luckily for him, he did not become ill.[87]

Because of its influence in legitimizing public antirabies campaigns, Pasteur's work offered a compelling target for reinterpretation. Antivivisectionist criticism of Pasteur, his experiments, and his vaccine continually disparaged—whether implicitly or explicitly—the reality of rabies: both his methods and his results were recast as part of a moral rather than a scientific exchange. Such essentially ad hominem estimates might be relatively generous in their denial of significance; for example, Anna Kingsford, an antivivisectionist who had also studied medicine on the Continent called his work "very brilliant, but . . . not solid." More typical were the suggestion of Gordon Stables that "Pasteur . . . has proved nothing and done *much* harm" and that of John H. Clarke, one of Kingsford's coadjutors, that "M. Pasteur's excuses and inconsistencies are of exactly the same kind as those of the vulgar quack to be found in every country market-place and every country fair." The secrecy with which Pasteur surrounded his experiments and the jealousy with which he guarded his vaccine were also frequently cited as evidence that he was morally defective, as was the terrible suffering endured by the many animals that had to be artificially infected with rabies so that their spinal cords could be extracted and ground up.[88]

Pasteur's rabies vaccine was, from this point of view, not a cure but an egregious example of the power of science to contaminate. By turning

ARGUMENTUM AD HOMINEM.

"OH, JOSEPH! TEDDY'S JUST BEEN BITTEN BY A STRANGE DOG! DOCTOR SAYS WE'D BETTER TAKE HIM OVER TO PASTEUR *AT ONCE!*"

"BUT, MY LOVE, I'VE JUST WRITTEN AND PUBLISHED A VIOLENT ATTACK UPON M. PASTEUR, ON THE SCORE OF HIS CRUELTY TO RABBITS! AND AT *YOUR INSTIGATION*, TOO!"

"OH, HEAVENS! NEVER MIND THE RABBITS *NOW!* WHAT ARE ALL THE RABBITS IN THE WORLD COMPARED TO *OUR ONLY CHILD!*"

The anti-vaccinationist's dilemma. From *Punch*, 1889.

laboratory animals into "cesspools of disease," he was actually spreading
rabies; "wherever a Pasteur Institute has sprung up," charged Thomas
Dolan, a Yorkshire physician, in 1890, "the number bitten by *rabid* dogs
has increased."[89] The dangers posed by the vaccine were alleged to be
psychological as well as physical. The number of people who went to
Pasteur's laboratory for prophylactic inoculation turned out to be much
larger than predicted by the number of previously reported hydrophobia cases; many who would not have become ill or who were not in
actual danger must have availed themselves of the new treatment. Pasteur concluded from this stampede that "rabies is a far more common
disease than is generally supposed," but his antivivisectionist critics
viewed it as part of his self-aggrandizing plan to "innoculate the world
with the virus of fear." As Jesse explained in a letter to the *British Medical
Journal,* "the practical results of Monsieur Pasteur's proceedings since
January, 1881 have been panic, a senseless and cowardly alarm, an increase in fear and death, and the brutal massacre of innumerable innocent, intelligent and affectionate animals."[90]

Human beings might put themselves at even greater risk by venturing
inside the institutes. Then, as now, a small percentage of the people
treated with rabies vaccine after being bitten by infected animals nevertheless contracted the disease and died. In such cases, antagonists of
rabies prophylaxis claimed, the victims had been murdered by science.
On September 4, 1886, for example, a man named Goffi, who worked
as a laboratory assistant at the Brown Institution (an animal hospital
and experimental center that was itself a frequent target of antivivisectionist outrage), was bitten by a rabid cat. He was quickly dispatched
to Paris for inoculations. As Jesse queried in a letter to the *Standard,*
"after being inoculated by a Rabid Cat, and Monsieur Pasteur he soon
died. Which, oh! 'Learned Man,' was the author of his death?" A French
doctor who carried his opposition to Pasteur across the Channel was
more moderate in his tone but more positive in his assertion: "There is
not the slightest doubt that, if Goffi had remained quietly in England,
instead of running to Paris, he would today be performing his duties at
the Brown Institution."[91]

And rabies might not be the only polluting disease to fester in the
reprobate air of the Pasteur Institutes. Kingsford evoked a more complex system of contamination when, in a speech to the North London
Anti-Vivisection Society, she described Pasteur's treatment facilities:

"Dr. Grancher [Pasteur's colleague] . . . uses . . . one syringe and needle to inoculate in rapid succession all the motley file of clients . . . Russian peasants . . . half-wild Arab peasants . . . unkempt and unclean . . . Italian donkey-boys and mountaineers . . . well-dressed women and dandies of the first water . . . Ah! if some of the patients bring no disease in their blood, is it certain they will go away without any?" Kingsford asked her audience to shudder not at an animal-borne biological threat, but at one mediated through the apparatus of the laboratory.[92] If they abandoned themselves to the ministrations of experts, humans might join animals as victims of scientific progress.

Thus the antagonists on both sides of the rabies debate were as concerned with metaphorical issues as with medical ones, and they fought their most heated battles over rhetorical territory. At issue in the largest sense was the source of social danger—for they agreed in perceiving society as threatened and rabies as the symbol of that threat. To policy makers rabies represented the refractory groups whose animals were prone to contract it, whereas their radical critics identified official regulation as both emblem and agent of contamination and decay. A vision of social order maintained only by vigorous discipline of potentially chaotic elements countered a vision of traditional social order compromised by arbitrary official interference. Correspondingly, the antagonists in this debate offered alternative understandings of the figurative significance of animals, which inevitably represented the organic forces suspected by one side and cherished by the other. The regulators perceived animals as confined within their metonymic roles—completely the products of human manipulation—whereas antivivisectionists granted them greater rhetorical autonomy. The socially grounded interpretation of rabies may have contributed as much to the ultimate triumph of the public health establishment as did the efficacy of the regulations implemented. The rhetoric that structured official attempts to control rabies reiterated a widespread Victorian understanding of animals as subordinate to human needs and desires. And this subordination was not confined to everyday contexts. That it extended into the realm of fantasy and imagination was evidenced by the large crowds attracted by the exhibitions of captive wild animals that became increasingly common in English towns and cities during the nineteenth century.

PART III

Animals and Empire

CHAPTER FIVE

Exotic Captives

In 1824 Sir Stamford Raffles returned to England after a distinguished career empire-building in the East Indies. There, when his official duties permitted, Raffles had devoted himself to zoology and botany. He discovered many new species, several of which, including a gibbon with black fur and an enormous parasitic flower that smelled like rotting flesh, were named in his honor; he also amassed a substantial private museum of animal and plant specimens as well as a small domestic menagerie containing tigers, bears, orangutans, gibbons, and monkeys. Raffles's activities as a naturalist echoed his concerns as a colonial administrator: he made discoveries, imposed order, and carried off whatever seemed particularly valuable or interesting. The maintenance and study of captive wild animals, simultaneous emblems of human mastery over the natural world and of English dominion over remote territories, offered an especially vivid rhetorical means of reenacting and extending the work of empire, and Raffles intended to continue his colonial pursuits in this figurative form after returning to the center of English power and enterprise. But this turned out to be more difficult than he had anticipated. When the ship on which he was sailing back to England burned at sea, he lost his raw material—"a living tapir, a new species of tiger, splendid pheasants, &c., domesticated for the voyage," along with all his preserved specimens.[1] And he did not find much to replace it; the great capital offered little scope for the systematic appropriation, scientific or otherwise, of the animal kingdom. Although London boasted several permanent menageries and a shifting panoply of more modest zoological exhibits, they catered to a larger, less knowledgeable, and more passive audience than Raffles envisioned; as a result, they were designed, in his view, to titillate the curiosity of the multitudes rather than to celebrate the achievements of the few. This was, in Raffle's view, a serious national scientific and political gap. To repair it, he began to organize what eventually became the Zoological Society of London. He projected a collection of captive wild animals that would serve not just as a popular symbol of human domination, but also as a more precise and elaborate figuration of England's imperial enterprise.

Old or New Emblems

Raffles may have interpreted the metaphorical significance of the crowd-pleasing exhibits and menageries too narrowly. The use of wild animals as tokens of political submission had ancient roots; for millenia kings and emperors had maintained menageries to symbolize the extent of their sway.[2] The oldest animal collection in London represented this tradition—a cruder and more forceful version of the rhetoric of conquest that Raffles planned to embody in the Regent's Park Zoo. This was the royal menagerie, which had moved to the Tower of London from Woodstock during the reign of Henry IV and which, like many regal collections, specialized in ferocious animals. Although the variety and abundance of its stock varied according to the zoological proclivities of the reigning monarch, it usually offered at least lions, leopards, tigers, and bears.[3] Beginning in the late seventeenth century, citizens who wished to admire symbols of triumphant individual enterprise as well as those of national prestige could visit the numerous exotic animal displays that mirrored the spread of British commercial influence throughout the globe. Advertisements for these captive attractions often stressed their uniqueness, which, in addition to piquing curiosity, suggested that the animal had been captured in virgin territory or by means of unusual ingenuity or force. In about 1795 one showman offered "a most stupendous elephant," allegedly "the only animal of the kind seen in this Kingdom for upwards of TWENTY YEARS." A llama from Peru, billed as "the first that has ever been offered to the inspection of a British Public," was displayed in the Haymarket in 1805. Well into the nineteenth century metropolitan crowds would flock to see a sufficiently remarkable single animal, such as the so-called bonassus (probably an American bison) that was admired by Queen Caroline and described by its promoters as "the only one that was ever imported into this king-dom—*The sight of which instantly impressed every beholder with that magnificent idea of wonder which no words can describe.*"[4]

The better-stocked menageries that tended to replace exhibits of single animals during the nineteenth century more forcefully embodied the symbolism of conquest and acquisition; many impressive animals behind bars presented a more striking spectacle of dominion than did one or two. And although they might not have met Raffles's standards for precise signification, their numbers suggested that many Londoners appreciated their patriotic message. In 1805 George Wombwell organized the first large-scale traveling menagerie.[5] His success attracted competitors, and by 1825 London's Bartholomew Fair boasted at least two major menageries besides Wombwell's.[6] Even the Tower Menagerie, which entered one of its cyclical declines at the end of the eighteenth century, could inspire the admiration of a country visitor. In 1794 Richard Hodgkinson, a Lancashire estate agent, found the motley collection of big cats a "curiosity" well worth the ninepence it cost him to view it (if Hodgkinson had brought a pet dog or cat from Lancashire, he could have contributed it in lieu of admission, then watched it fed to the lions).[7] The major zoological attraction of early nineteenth-century London was known through several transfers of ownership as the Exeter Change Menagerie. When Hodgkinson's business took him to London again in 1819, he pronounced it "the largest collection I had ever seen."[8] It was housed in a general-purpose commercial building in central London, and visitors had to climb a flight of stairs to reach the main exhibits—two rooms packed with animals in cages barely large enough to allow them to turn around. In 1812 the fuller of the rooms housed two tigers, a lion, a hyena, a leopard, a panther, two sloths, a camel, many monkeys, and a tapir. Despite this congestion, visitors found the menagerie a pleasant resort; one reporter praised the proprietor for the "extreme attention bestowed on the removal of everything offensive."[9]

Londoners were not alone in their desire to view exotic animals in chains and cages; to meet provincial demand, exhibitors regularly traveled up and down the country. In 1783, for example, "all Admirers of the Wonderful Productions of Nature" in the vicinity of Norwich were

The Exeter Change Menagerie, which was located in the heart of commercial
London. Thomas Hosmer Shepherd, *View of Exeter 'Change*, 1829.

invited to an innyard near the marketplace to see a lion, a hunting tiger
(probably a cheetah), a porcupine, a wolf, "an Astonishing Animal
called, The MOON ACT" which bore "A strong Resemblance of the Human Species," "A Beautiful Creature, called, The WANDEROO, Being the
only one of that Species ever seen in Europe," and a "FEMALE SATYR
or Aethiopian Savage."[10] In 1806 Exeter was visited by a "noble Lion and
Lioness, Panthers, Leopards, Hyaena, Lynx, Kangaroo, Ostrichs, and
upwards of a hundred other animals and birds." The highlights of a
menagerie that arrived there in 1812 were a lion (improbably alleged
to be "absolutely the only one travelling this kingdom"), a lioness, a pair
of tigers, a zebra, both a spotted and a striped hyena, and a pair of
kangaroos.[11] (That carting dangerous animals over rough country roads
opened new sources of hazard as well as of profit, was illustrated in 1816
when a lioness from Ballard's menagerie escaped from her wooden
wagon and immediately attacked one of the horses drawing the Exeter
mail coach.)[12]

And if these popular exhibitions effectively symbolized expanding
English influence over remote exotic territories, Raffles may also have

underestimated the extent to which the broad public they served shared and appreciated his rhetorical goals. Few English citizens were likely ever to wield the kind of power represented by the animals' captivity, but since that power was exercised by their countrymen over nature or the human inhabitants of distant lands, all could take vicarious pleasure in the evidence of its magnitude. Even the pricing policies of many exhibitions clearly indicated that interest in caged wild animals extended far beyond the ranks of the educated and the wealthy. Thomas Shore, who proclaimed himself "willing to accommodate every Class of Persons," charged a shilling for "ladies and gentlemen" who wished to view his menagerie, but only sixpence for "tradesmen" and threepence for "working people"; a regular daily admission to the short-lived Manchester Zoological Gardens also cost a shilling, but children and servants could get in for half-price.[13]

By excluding the large popular audience for wild animal displays, Raffles burdened his projected menagerie with a double symbolic load. He attempted to make it the emblem not only of English hegemony in colonial territories, but also of analogous class relationships at home.

Crowded conditions inside the Exeter Change Menagerie.
From Rudolph Ackermann,
Repository of Arts, Literature, Commerce, Manufactures, Fashions, and Politics, 1812.

As a result, he planned an institution that would serve only elite participants (whether direct or indirect) in the enterprise of imperial acquisition and domination. It would serve as both a treasure house of exotic
animals and an illustration of the techniques of management and organization that enabled the agents of British government and commerce
and, more abstractly, science to dominate vast territories. Early in 1825
he began to canvass friends and acquaintances for subscriptions to what
he described as "a grand Zoological collection in the metropolis." The
enthusiastic response suggested that other mandarins also recognized
the rhetorical gap that his project was designed to fill. By mid-May
Raffles had accumulated sixty-six signatures, including those of aristocrats like the marquess of Lansdowne and the Earl Spencer as well as
such scientific luminaries as Sir Humphry Davy. A year later nearly two
hundred subscribers had promised to pay the introductory fees of £3
and the annual dues of £2, and the Zoological Society of London was
ready to be launched.[14] Even the government offered concrete encouragement, although not in the form of cold cash, as some of the early
patrons had hoped; instead, it provided a tract of land in the northeast
corner of Regent's Park. And when the zoological gardens opened in
1828, they were an immediate success. In 1829 the governing council
happily reported that "the resort to the Garden has far surpassed the
most sanguine expectations . . . 112,226 persons have visited it during
the last year."[15]

These people were not, however, the miscellaneous curiosity seekers
who flocked to see Wombwell's traveling collection or the menagerie at
Exeter Change. The official rhetoric of the Zoological Society emphasized that they were distinguished by their ability to appreciate and, at
least figuratively, participate in the grand appropriative enterprise, the
fruits of which were metonymically displayed in the cages and pens.
This ability was signaled in several ways. Most blatant, admission was
restricted, at least in the intention of the society's council, to visitors
belonging to the classes that produced officers, administrators, and
commercial entrepreneurs. The nature of their interest in the animals
was inveterately described as scientific, which both distinguished it
from the ignorant gaping attributed to the excluded multitudes and allied it to the project of intellectual appropriation that often shadowed
the extension of English political influence. Correspondingly, the Zoological Society described its own institutional purposes as primarily

scientific. The society presented itself and its patrons not as gratifying idle or selfish ends, but as fulfilling a patriotic obligation—a version of noblesse oblige. A prospectus distributed in 1826, when the Zoological Society's menagerie was still in the planning stages, described its purposes in terms of national priorities and national service. Most important was to remedy the lack of a necessary icon: "It has long been a matter of deep regret to the cultivators of Natural History, that we possess no great scientific establishments either for teaching or elucidating Zoology; and no public menageries or collections of living animals where their nature, properties and habits may be studied." The "great objects" of the society would be "the introduction of new varieties, breeds, and races of animals for the purpose of domestication . . . with the establishment of a general Zoological Collection, consisting of prepared specimens in the different classes and orders."[16]

From the beginning, official Zoological Society pronouncements emphasized the scientific proclivities of its visitors. The introduction to the first official guide to the zoological exhibits proposed to "afford some instruction" by explaining the "scientific qualities" of the exhibits.[17] In 1835, after almost a decade of operation, the council interpreted the continuing appeal of its collection of living animals in a similar vein, attributing it to "the number, the variety, and (in many instances) the rarity of the animals."[18] And this scientific focus was expressed concretely, as well as in the language of promotional literature. The menagerie animals were readily available for approved research purposes; for example, an inquisitive naturalist was allowed to "make experiments on the *hollow-horned Ruminants* . . . respecting the growth of their horns and the use of the lacrymal sinus." In addition, the zoo was from the beginning very generous with its carcasses. One anatomist was sent the hearts of certain dead animals, another their diseased joints. A Fellow of the Zoological Society requested the "testes of the Society's lion, in the event of the death of that animal" (the council decided to give him only one); the surgeon general of Ireland requested the head of the kangaroo in the same unfortunate eventuality. Often, the council did not wait to be asked. When an elephant died in 1847, it was immediately cut up and distributed to several scientific institutions for study.[19] The needs of scientists also influenced the selection of animals for the living collection at Regent's Park. As *Nature* reminded its erudite readers later in the century, "While the supply of lions, tigers, elephants, and other well-known animals must always be kept up for the delectation of the ordinary public," the Zoological Society also took pains "to acquire animals of specially scientific value, in which the casual observer would take little interest."[20]

Although not all the early visitors to the zoo could appreciate the subtlest scientific points illustrated by the collection, they were always seen as a select group. The physical relation of the menagerie to the rest of Regent's Park symbolically reiterated the association between its zoological riches and human privilege. Two rustic gates separated the scientific enclave from the larger tracts dedicated to strolling or to such frivolous diversions as a diorama representing the Roman colosseum. Immediately inside the segregated precincts, a terrace offered early patrons a chance to look down on those outside—as well as to admire views of the London suburbs—before beginning their promenade past the animals.[21] The landscaping thus manifested official Zoological Society policy. In his energetic efforts to recruit subscribers, Raffles had limited his attention to members of the social and scientific elites, and after his death in 1826 the new society continued to court the prominent and powerful. Appropriate class standing was, however, the only pre-requisite for admission; within these limits the society cast its net widely. In 1827 the council ordered that "cards of invitation . . . be issued to such members of both Houses of Parliament, as well as to such other persons as may be likely to forward the views of the Society." And it was early resolved that "Ladies, proposed by any Member of the Council, be admitted as Members of the Society on the same terms, and with the same privileges, as Gentlemen Subscribers."[22]

The main privilege of membership was access to the gardens. Sundays were reserved for members and their guests, and on other days, "strangers," as nonsubscribers were termed in the regulations, could "be admitted . . . by Orders from Fellows, upon payment of 1s." In comparison with the prices charged for other live animal displays, 1s. was not prohibitive—Londoners and visitors had long been willing to pay half a crown or 2s. to admire the much smaller and less attractive menagerie at Exeter Change.[23] But by requiring that nonsubscribers be personally vouched for by subscribers, at least to the limited extent of a written request for admission, the council attempted to ensure that its patrons would be drawn from a restricted circle. One "Constant Reader" complained to the Tatler of "every care having been taken 'to prevent the contamination of the Zoological Garden by the admission of the poorer classes of Society.'"[24] But it turned out to be difficult to maintain the exclusiveness of the gardens on this basis. By 1834, according to one scientific journalist, it was "well known that admission to the privileges of a Fellow of the Zoological Society is a matter of no great difficulty"; the required recommendation and election were "little more than forms." Once elected, subscribers apparently were willing to request admission for second-hand and more distant acquaintances without inquiring carefully into their character or intellectual qualifications, and, according to *Punch*, those who could not scare up even a tenuous connection to a subscriber could buy a ticket to the Regent's Park Zoo in one of the neighboring public houses.[25]

The Right Note

To some extent the clamor for tickets was a function of fashion, for the impressive, if exclusive crowds drawn to the Regent's Park Zoo in its first years were responding to the lure of a modish novelty as well as to the charms of the animal collection.[26] But the zoo's attractiveness was also an index of rhetorical miscalculation on the part of Raffles and his successors. English citizens of all classes recognized the fledgling Zoological Society as a more elaborate iteration of a symbol of imperial dominion with which they had long been familiar. And this recognition was echoed on a more literal level by the established metropolitan menagerists, who regarded the new collection not as a scientific or metaphorical innovation, but as an upstart competitor or colleague. Within a decade of the new zoo's establishment, both the major London collections emphasized the extent to which its goals and audience overlapped theirs by attempting to merge with it. In 1826 Edward Cross, the proprietor of the Exeter Change Menagerie, tried to get in on the ground floor by offering both "his services in the management of the Society's Menagerie, and . . . the whole of his present collection for sale on such terms as might be agreeable to the Society." The members of the Zoological Society's council, chary of Cross's vulgar impresarial inclinations, decided that they were not "prepared to enter into the consideration of this proposal," and they subsequently also rejected Cross's offer to sell just his menagerie for £3,600. Five years later, however, they accepted with alacrity "his Majesty's most gracious offer . . . of the Collection of Wild Animals . . . now in the Tower," a gift with no awkward human strings attached.[27] William IV's generosity may have indicated admiration for the young society or boredom with the royal animals; it simultaneously marked the end of the royal collection and confirmed the quasi-official status of the Regent's Park Zoo as the national repository of wild beasts and the symbol, for a large segment of the populace, of Britain's spreading global influence.

Failure to acknowledge this expanded significance might have pragmatic as well as rhetorical implications. Ultimately it was simple economics that forced the Zoological Society to include a broader audience within its rhetorical orbit. After the novelty of its menagerie wore off, attendance declined and the society faced a serious financial crisis. As a result, in 1846 its newly appointed secretary D. W. Mitchell persuaded the council to open the gates to anyone willing to pay the admission fee, whether or not the money was accompanied by a voucher from a fellow.[28]

The London Zoo was not alone in feeling this pressure to reconstrue. In general, zoos that misrepresented their public significance were likely to suffer financially. Thus, several provincial zoos that had emulated the elitism of Regent's Park foundered on this figurative rock. The Leeds Zoological and Botanical Gardens, which opened in 1840 to serve "people principally of the higher classes of society," was bankrupt within eight years; the planned Birmingham Zoological Gardens, of which the 1835 prospectus similarly aimed at an audience composed exclusively of "gentlemen," never got off the ground.[29]

As the Council of the Zoological Society began to encourage the patronage of visitors who could not have dreamed of paying an annual subscription or applying for membership, it also implicitly incorporated them into the institution's underlying symbolic project.[30] When the council noted with gratification the "increasing popularity of the Society's Gardens amongst that class of visitors who resort to them on the national holidays," it was, in part, redefining and expanding its national mission. Serious interest in the Regent's Park Zoo among the vulgar was both an agent and an index of their improvement, and hence another symbol of English progress and enlightenment. Although the new brand of visitor was inclined to enjoy such vulgar pastimes as "lying on the grass . . . enjoying their repast *al fresco*," one approving observer concluded that their "quiet demeanour . . . established the fact that . . .

there are no people who more highly appreciate such rational amusements than the intelligent mechanics, or the working classes of this country." A commentator in the *Quarterly Review* applauded the rise in working-class visitors to the zoo between 1848 and 1854 in more pragmatic terms; many of the 135,712 additional zoogoers "were, no doubt, rescued, on those days at least, from the fascinations of the public-house."[31] Along similar lines, in 1841 the Royal Zoological Society of Ireland, the sister institution of the Zoological Society of London, had happily announced the "success of the measure of opening the Gardens at hours suitable to the working classes at one penny admission." Its council stressed that its pleasure did not arise so much from the effect on the funds of the society, as from a feeling that "the admission of not less than 100,000 persons this year is a carrying out of the great principle of the Society, the spread of useful information . . . a powerful aid to the confirming of the people in their improved habits."[32]

Provincial and proprietary societies with fewer wealthy subscribers catered even more assiduously to their humbler clients, similarly emphasizing the elevating influence of their exhibits. Thus the prospectus of the Rosherville Zoological Gardens, established in Kent in 1837, promised special consideration for those who came with curiosity but not much knowledge: "That those visitors who are not conversant with Zoology and Botany may not be left to wonder, as at other gardens, what is the nature of this animal or that plant, some of the most distinguishing facts in the natural history of each will be written on labels near it."[33] The obituary for George Wombwell in the *Times* stated that "no one probably did more to bring forward the study of natural history among the masses." And as late as 1858 the proprietor of Edmonds menagerie (a descendant of Wombwell's original collection) was praised for instructing "the labouring classes, who have not the advantage of zoological gardens, as to the forms and peculiarities of living creatures, which many know by pictures only."[34]

This emphasis on improvement was incorporated into the menageries' rhetoric of dominion, as the visitors in need of refinement were figuratively assimilated to those who came to admire their own reflected glory. Even the most vulgar patrons were expected to view a visit to a zoological garden or traveling menagerie as more than mere diversion; it gave them a chance not only to admire the conquests of their more fortunate countrymen, but also, in a shadowy way, to participate in them. A diminished version of the scientific enterprise, mediated through the inexpensive guidebooks sold at most zoos and menageries, often symbolized more energetic forms of appropriation. Thus the official *Companion to the Royal Zoological Gardens, Surrey* included a long entry about the elephants, which alluded to such technical matters as the geographical distribution and natural habitat of the species, its diet, longevity, and social behavior.[35] The guide to the Liverpool Zoological Gardens modestly claimed to provide only a "List of the Animals," but individual entries for the pelicans, the American black bear, the lions, the tiger, the lion-tiger (a cross between the two), the leopard, the wolves, the polar bear, the ichneumon, the elephants, the rhinoceros, and the ostrich each ran to over half a page of quasi-scientific description. Large traveling menageries like Bostock and Wombwell's (another descendant of Wombwell's) also sold annotated lists of their collections, which doubled as retail catalogs as well; thus readers might be warned at the beginning that since "management are continually supplying and exchanging specimens with Zoological Gardens, the following exhibits . . . are subject to occasional variations."[36]

Even the novelties that the managers of every live animal collection learned were necessary to ensure steady attendance had to be presented in terms that indicated their relation to the rhetoric of empire, rather than that of idle entertainment. The extravagant tone and typography of the posters traveling menageries used to lure crowds at fairs and markets seemed indistinguishable from the announcements for circuses and other frivolous diversions, but their content promised new intellectual and geographical horizons. For example, Thomas Shore offered a reward of £500, headlined in large print, to "any Person who ever saw, in any other Travelling Menagerie, A Black Tyger, His being the ONLY ONE in Europe." When Wombwell procured a pair of rhinoceroses, he advertised them as "Those Rare and Wonderful Animals, the . . . Unicorns of Scripture . . . and The Largest Quadruped in the World," with the qualifier, "the Elephant excepted," in much smaller type on the next line. Kendrick's menagerie vaunted "Two Surprising Nylghaws," and a French exhibitor crossed the Channel with a gnu that he advertised as "that curious animal . . . one of the most Extraordinary Productions of Nature!"[37]

Similarly, when the Council of the London Zoo realized that its future financial health required "a due sucession of novelties"—a result of examining the attendance figures from 1850, the first year that the celebrated hippopotamus Obaysch arrived, which at 360,402 showed a dramatic increase over the 168,895 of the previous year—the enterprising Mitchell introduced a system that was referred to as "starring."[38] This meant ensuring that there was always at least one attractive new animal on display. (More than one was even better. In 1876 visitors flocked to the London Zoo to see a collection of animals that included four elephants, five tigers, and seven leopards, as well as zebus, monkeys, antelopes, deer, wild goats, and bears, all donated by the Prince of Wales after an extensive tour of India.)[39] But the animals selected for stardom, which often included elaborate coverage in the national and metropolitan press, were never offered as mere curiosities; rather, they were presented in terms of their scientific or political significance, as evidence of British ability to subdue exotic territories and convert their wild products to useful purposes. Thus the pair of "graceful" clouded tigers was "not only one of the most beautiful objects in the menagerie ... but one of the rarest," since no others had ever reached Europe alive. The choiropotamus or red hog of the Cameroons was remarkable for having escaped for so long the observation of naturalists eager to discover species that might improve domestic livestock breeds. Pigs were, as it happened, in special need of such melioration, and the stud services of the zoo's relatively trim specimen were suggested as a possible corrective of "the somewhat over-bloated candidates for porcine honours at the ... Smithfield Club."[40]

Shows of Power

In thriving menageries the defining symbolism was embodied in every aspect of the exhibits, as well as expressed in public pronouncements and policy formulation.[41] It was implicit in the very composition and structure of a collection. Animals that roamed free and often dangerous in their native wilds were confined in small cages and placed along well-marked paths, in manicured parks that seemed natural only in contrast to the surrounding urban landscapes. The horticultural displays that routinely adorned the borders, often composed of plants from all over the world, emphasized the artificiality of the setting, as did the man-made lakes featured by every zoo spacious and prosperous enough to install one. Zoos explicitly encouraged visitors to enjoy the contrast between the wild beasts and their intensely cultivated surroundings. The Liverpool Zoological Gardens advertised its "ten acres of ground, tastefully laid out in Walks, Lawns, and Shrubberies"; the guidebook to the Belle Vue Zoological Gardens in Manchester boasted that "the Great Lake ... has recently been considerably enlarged."[42] Like other guidebooks, it implicitly structured visitors' experience of the gardens. No matter what the shape of the zoo they described, nineteenth-century guidebooks were inveterately linear, prescribing a single route through the exhibits, from the entrance to the refreshment stand. Thus, in their physical design, zoos reenacted and celebrated the imposition of human structure on the threatening chaos of nature.

The Zoological Society of London carried this strategy of appropriation and control to a rather rarefied intellectual extreme. It strove to realize in its collection what one reviewer of zoo guidebooks identified as the goal of the whole science of zoology: "to furnish every possible link in the grand procession of organized life."[43] Thus the Zoological Society pursued as its "principal object ... to present as many types of form as possible, with the view of illustrating the generic variations of the Animal Kingdom," while most of its sister institutions followed the alternative policy denigrated at Regent's Park as the accumulation of "a mere mass of species from which comparatively little can be learnt."[44] The animals at the London Zoo were conceived of as part of an interrelated, graduated zoological series—as a living representation of the standard vertebrate taxonomical categories. New animals, especially if they were not likely to enhance attendance significantly, might be described in terms of their place in the larger order. Two jaguars purchased in 1875 were said to have "raised the series of larger members of the cat genus ... to 20"; the kiang, or Tibetan wild horse, donated in 1859 was particularly valued because "the Zoological Society of London, with the object of completing its series of wild species of the genus Equus ... have long been anxious to procure living specimens."[45] When, as was the case at Regent's Park beginning in 1840, animals were arranged taxonomically, the exhibits showed nature not only confined and restrained, but interpreted and ordered.

Although few menageries could aspire to this high standard of acquisition and control, to most zoogoers the simple spectacle of wild animals in cages was impressive enough. And this spectacle was not

From "A Day at the Zoo," a game in which Victorian children
pasted bars over animals.

exclusively visual. Victorian zoos were designed to allow a great deal of
interaction between the animals and their admirers, if not quite so much
as had some of their predecessors. (For example, the Tower Menagerie
had owned a jaguar "so mild as to lick the hands of visitors"; and Wombwell's famous lion Nero, who declined to be baited by dogs, had allowed
human "strangers to enter his den, and even put their heads within his
jaws.")[46] But there was ample opportunity for visitors to enjoy simultaneously the thrill of proximity to wild animals and the happy sense of
secure superiority produced by their incarceration. Only the exceptional visitor, such as the critic Leigh Hunt, found this relationship
other than pleasant. He was struck by the animals' "quiet . . . and the

human-like sort of intercourse into which they get with their visiters" and ended his tour of the London Zoo feeling melancholy about their captivity.[47]

The most natural way for most visitors to interact with the animals was to feed them, an act which symbolized both proprietorship and domination. Most zoos encouraged this activity. The first elephants in the collection of the London Zoo were reported to "have a keen relish for buns and biscuits, which are vended on the spot for their benefit and the gratification of the visitors." Their successors shared the same tastes. When the celebrated Jumbo was about to depart for the United States, his admirers expressed their regret with farewell gifts including fruit, cakes, oysters, and a variety of alcoholic beverages. At the end of the century a zoo book for children encouraged them to befriend the elephants by offering them fruit and biscuits; the children of Sir William Henry Flower, the late nineteenth-century president of the Zoological Society, remembered feeding the elephants with the "crunchy biscuits" that keepers always carried in their pockets.[48] A *Punch* cartoon of 1871, which showed a group of dyspeptic animals commiserating after a bank holiday, suggested that bears were the most frequent recipients of such donations. "Bruin" complained that "there were 31,457 people here yesterday. They gave me 31,457 buns." Feeding the bears was exciting as well as entertaining. They were more dangerous, or at least more ferocious, than the large herbivores, and they were willing to perform for their treats. According the the guidebook to the Liverpool Zoo, "they eagerly climb a pole placed in their den, if any spectator will take the trouble to raise a piece of bread or cake towards the top of it, by means of a long staff provided for that purpose." At the London Zoo, which provided similar ursine accommodations, competition among the bears to reach the head of the pole—"a monopoly the more irritating, inasmuch as that elevation generally leads to the acquisition of the good things in the power of a generous public to bestow"—enhanced the spectacle. (How good these "good things" were might be open to question: one human consumer who tried the buns sold in the London Zoo pronounced them "stale" and "an insult to one's dinner.")[49]

Other opportunities for interaction with zoo animals also encouraged visitors to think of them as temporary possessions or playthings. Camel and elephant rides were traditional features of both zoos and traveling menageries. At first, the London Zoo allowed the keepers to

Feeding the bears at the Regent's Park Zoo.

pocket the proceeds, but by the end of the nineteenth century this activity was producing £700 annually for the Zoological Society. This success led the zoo administration to hope that llamas, which bred freely in the zoo, could also be trained to the saddle.[50] Although wild sheep could not be ridden, they were reported to "show their gratitude to any one who will scratch them with his cane just beyond the reach of their horns by licking his hand with their long black tongue." Still smaller animals, if they were tame enough, could be fondled, like a pair of beavers displayed at Exeter Change in the 1820s or a chinchilla exhibited later in the century at Regent's Park. Ladies were assured by one guide that it would do them no harm, because "its claws are so short that it is unable to inflict the slightest scratch, and I never found it particularly given to biting."[51]

This proximity to the animals presented occasional hazards. Monkeys, whom visitors were apt to tease, might tease back. Few were so vigorous as the menagerie baboon that "attempted to seize every person who came within the reach of his chain," but many snatched hats from the heads of ladies and gentlemen who pressed against the bars of their cages. Children were warned that, although monkeys provided "plenty of amusement . . . at the expenditure of a few nuts or a bun," they also "have sharp nails and sometimes resent the playing of tricks."[52] Patting an elephant would contaminate "lily-white gloves" with the train oil with which its skin was rubbed to keep it in condition, and the "moisture from his trunk" would not "improve the lustre of either silk or satin." Excessive proximity might also result in a flowered hat being devoured (especially if its owner were also wearing a floral fragrance).[53] Llamas had "an insane love of spitting at those who approach too close . . . that has ruined many a good hat and coat."[54]

Not much was made of these episodes, although occasionally an unhappy visitor would be quietly reimbursed for damages. In most cases such contretemps were treated rather humorously, as gratifying evidence that the animals which could be approached so casually really were dangerous. And in any case, visitors—interpreting too literally the metaphorical invitation embodied in the exhibits—did their share of harm in return, although zoos and zoo guidebooks featured prominent requests not to tease the animals.[55] Most injuries to zoo animals resulted from improper feeding. The ostrich responded to the overfed bear in the *Punch* cartoon that he would prefer too many buns and too much ginger beer to what he was fed: bottles, brown paper, and rusty nails. If such behavior was deemed malicious, it could lead to criminal charges: in 1852 the London Zoo prosecuted two "well-dressed young men" for "wantonly injuring a badger, by administering to it some gin."[56] Occasionally the consequences of visitors treating the animals too familiarly were more serious. In 1864 a young seal in the Dublin Zoo died after being injured by visitors, and in 1879 the death of an experienced elephant keeper in the London Zoo of injuries inflicted by an animal "whose trunk had pleasantly inserted itself into so many pockets, and whose back had borne so many happy children" was attributed to "some mischievous person" who "prodded the animal from behind with a stick or umbrella, or else pulled its tail."[57]

Although lions and tigers were too dangerous to feed or scratch, the lion house, where the abject captivity of the king of beasts provided the most conclusive evidence in the zoo of the human triumph over nature, was an essential component of any successful zoo or menagerie. Therefore, the high mortality rate among the big cats in the early years of the London Zoo—the average lifespan of its first lions, tigers, leopards, and pumas was about two years, which meant that one of them died each month—was especially alarming to the Council of the Zoological Society. Not only did each death represent a significant financial loss, but it made the zoo a less appealing destination as well for "general visitors," who found the "Carnivora . . . one of the most attractive portions of the Collection."[58] More modest establishments also felt the need to tantalize the public with large collections of carnivores. In 1841 visitors to the Liverpool Zoo could admire lions, tigers, lion-tiger hybrids, leopards, and jaguars, as well as a lynx, an ocelot, a margay, and several hyenas (which are not felines but were frequently exhibited with them in nineteenth-century zoos, presumably because they produced a similar frisson on the part of visitors). Forty years later the Bristol Zoo's display included specimens of the leopard, cheetah, puma, tiger, and lion, as well as a variety of smaller wild cats. At about the same time Bostock and Wombwell's Royal Menagerie was traveling with six or eight leopards, a lynx, approximately ten lions, two tigers, a puma, and a jaguar.[59]

The posters advertising traveling menageries telegraphed the source of these creatures' appeal. Thomas Shore invited the public to admire his "fiery" lynx and "noble" lions; Isaac Van Amburgh, an American lion tamer, performed with a menagerie of "ramping leopards" and "tigers of the jungle."[60] And if the simple confined presence of such ferocious beasts was thrilling—as one visitor commented of the lion room in the Exeter Change Menagerie, "we are . . . surrounded . . . by death under its most frightful form; and yet we hold our life as securely as if we were seated by our own hearths"—the sight of them eating was still more gratifying. Feeding time emphasized both their ferocity and their captive condition, the former making the latter the more remarkable. Zoos and menageries frequently noted it in their publicity. Some menagerists capitalized on its attractiveness to charge spectators an extra fee, as Cross had done at Exeter Change; others followed the practice of the Tower Menagerie and offered it as an extra inducement to pay the general admission.[61]

The bloodier the spectacle, the more reassuring it must have been to the audience to know that humankind had conquered the animal kingdom. It was advertised in 1806 that when the duke of Cumberland visited Polito's menagerie, he "could scarce express his gratification at being so highly delighted with the great Bengal Tyger devouring a whole bullock's head, horns and all!" A biographer of Van Amburgh noted proudly that the young Queen Victoria had visited several of his lion-taming performances. After one, she lingered "for the purpose of seeing the animals in their more excited and savage state during the operation of feeding them." So that the Queen would not be disappointed, the animals "had been kept purposely without food for six and thirty hours." Although she indulged it in private on this occasion, the Queen's taste was shared by many of her fellow citizens. A journalist who visited the London Zoo in 1870 described the feeding of the carnivora as "the crowning point of the show," enthusiastically reporting their anticipatory "bellowing, roaring, and growling," "how they drag and tear the big bone or lump of raw meat," and "how true the animals are to their savage instincts, even in confinement."[62]

If dangerous animals that expressed their wild nature within the confines of zoos were regarded with grisly satisfaction and even complacency, animals that violated the carefully drawn boundaries by which they were circumscribed provoked reciprocal anxiety. Private attempts to contain and domesticate them were suspect when they did not conform to conventional notions of confinement. Walter Lionel Rothschild's juvenile attempts to maintain a menagerie at Tring, his father's

Hertfordshire estate, succumbed to local protests about a walleroo (a member of the kangaroo family) that turned on children who teased it and a tame wolf that fought with aggressive neighborhood dogs. And fears about the liberation of more securely confined animals were never far from the surface. In 1874 the explosion of a boatload of gunpowder in the vicinity of Regent's Park provoked expressions of relief that "the effect of the explosion in the Zoological Gardens was not so serious as might have been expected," although the zoo suffered only minor damage (a single hole in the glass roof of the aviary). The elands, antelopes, and deer were startled and ran around their enclosures for a while; the elephant, hippopotamus, rhinoceros, and giraffes were observed to be "very much excited." But most worthy of note, according to *Nature*, was something that neither happened nor came close to happening: "It was fortunate . . . that none of the large carnivora were liberated."[63]

Exotic animals that escaped received no quarter, unless someone with a financial interest in their welfare was close at hand. Thus when one of Wombwell's baboons escaped in Glasgow, frightening a church congregation and then entering a public house, his keepers, who had followed in hot pursuit, offered him "spirituous liquors" until he could be easily overpowered. And when a large and expensive tiger escaped from Jamrach's, the most extensive dealer in wild animals in Victorian Britain, the proprietor strolled out with an iron bar in his hand and reclaimed his investment, forcing the animal to relinquish a small boy he was carrying in his mouth.[64] More characteristic, however, was the fate of a troop of Wombwell's monkeys that escaped when their caravan overturned near Carlisle. The local farmers pursued them with dogs, resulting in what a newspaper characterized as "one of the most ludicrous chases ever beheld in this part of the country." Similarly, in 1830 the sentries at the Tower of London, who had no stake in the welfare of its menagerie, immediately shot a newly arrived tiger that escaped from its cage.[65]

Stern retribution awaited even well-known and well-loved captives who strayed from the straight and narrow path. Before he was executed in 1826, Chunee, a massive Indian elephant, had lived in England for sixteen years, first as a stage performer and then as one of the star attractions of the Exeter Change Menagerie. He was considered a "remarkably docile" animal. The carpenter who built a new cage to house Chunee's increasing bulk and strength, reported that the elephant "accommodated himself to his wishes in every respect"; his keeper was able to sleep "in the den within reach of the trunk."[66] But beginning in about 1820 Chunee experienced annual attacks of what was diagnosed as sexual excitability, under the influence of which he threatened his keepers and tested the bars that confined him. For several years Cross, the proprietor of Exeter Change, trusted the stout cage and massive doses of laxatives to confine him until the fit had passed.[67] Each year, however, Chunee grew more furious during these periods and cleverer at identifying and refusing his medicine; finally it was feared that he would burst from his "den" and either liberate the lions and tigers confined in neighboring cages or crash through the floor (only that under his cage was reinforced to bear his weight) into the shops below.

Once he had been defined as a threat to public safety, Chunee's fate was sealed, although his death sentence proved agonizingly difficult to implement. He refused a proffered dose of arsenic, and the shots of three rifles only maddened him further. Soldiers were called in, and they discharged volley after volley without killing him; the coup de grace was finally administered by a keeper with a sword. The struggle lasted over an hour, during which the elephant roared and lunged constantly. A young eyewitness remembered that the noise of his agony had been much more alarming than that made by the soldiers' guns.[68] It was never conclusively established that Chunee's spells were likely to produce the disastrous consequences forecast by the most apprehensive. But once his proprietor and the guardians of public order perceived his liberation as a real possibility, neither the elephant's history of good behavior, nor his considerable value as an attraction (he was worth about £1,000 alive, but only £50 as skin and bones) could preserve him. The uneasiness provoked by the idea of wild animals loose in civilized Britain was not simply a prudent response to their capacity for doing harm; it inversely figured the domination symbolized by their captivity.

National Pets

What distinguished Chunee's death from that of Wombwell's monkeys or the Tower tiger was its impact on the popular imagination. Instead of being buried on the back pages of local newspapers, it was extensively covered by the national press. The *Times* printed letters criticizing the decision to kill Chunee as well as the manner in which he had been confined; magazines featured both sentimental and humorous poetry

AN EXACT REPRESENTATION OF THE MANNER OF

DESTROYING THE ELEPHANT,

On Thursday, March 2nd, 1826, at Exeter Change, Strand.

The death of this stupendous Animal was accomplished by the discharge of 152 Musket Balls, which were lodged in various parts of its body. It was about 22 years old, and has been exhibited at the Change 17 years; was the largest in the Kingdom, and was valued at upwards of £1000— It was dissected on Sunday by Dr. Brookes, Waring, Clarke, Spurzheim, Mr. H. Mayo, Morgan, Yarrall, C. Hawkins, Bell, and other Surgeons. Its Skin weighed One Ton, for which Mr. Cross was offered Fifty Pounds.

Printed and Published at 28, Bowling Green Lane, Clerkenwell.

The death of Chunee.

on the subject; prints and broadsides portrayed the gruesome details of the killing; and a play called *Chuneelah; or, The Death of the Elephant at Exeter 'Change* enjoyed a successful run at Sadler's Wells.[69] Nor was Chunee's demise a nine days' wonder. A decade later the author of an article on the Regent's Park Zoo included a fond digression on the slain pachyderm, who had not even lived there: "Poor Chuny, who was obedient even in death, for amid the shower of balls that struck him, he knelt down,—even in his mortal agony he knelt down at the well-known command of his keeper,—to present a more vulnerable point to his murderers."[70] Had Chunee been simply a captured wild animal resisting human domination, his death would have been, in the view of the British public, neither remarkable nor regrettable. But Chunee's long and celebrated captivity, during most of which he was noted for his tractability and friendliness, had made him a familiar personality. Many had seen him and many more had read about him, even before his spectacular execution. Not only had he been captured and restrained, but he had also been sentimentalized and, symbolically at least, domesticated, converted into a kind of public pet.

Chunee was the first of a series of zoo dwellers to achieve similar positions in the hearts of the nineteenth-century British public. Predictably, most of his successors resided in the Regent's Park Zoo, which was both the largest and the most heavily publicized in the nation. The infant Obaysch, touted as the first live hippopotamus to visit Europe since the days of the Roman Empire, was a celebrity from the moment he arrived in 1850, along with a portable bath, a retinue of native human attendants, and enough cows and goats to provide him with milk on the long journey from Egypt.[71] Crowds gathered at the stations to greet the special train that carried Obaysch to London, where, during his first year, he attracted such throngs that at times "some difficulty was found in making arrangements for their passage through the house in which the hippopotamus bath is placed."[72] Among the creatures with whom he shared his celebrity, most numerous were a succession of gifted chimpanzees. Of one, who resided in the London Zoo during the 1880s and 1890s, a journalist claimed that "paragraphs and articles relating to . . . Sally . . . would fill many goodly volumes."[73] Consul, a young male chimpanzee who lived in Manchester's Belle Vue Zoological Gardens at about the same time, rivalled Sally both in popular affection and literary notoriety. Like her, he was considered highly "educated"; one photograph showed him fully clothed, including a hat, with a cigarette in one hand and the other on a table next to a bottle and glass. And when he died an admirer was moved to ask: "Then who says/ Thou'rt not immortal? That not mortal knows,/Not e'en the wisest—he can but *suppose*."[74]

Menageries encouraged this tendency to convert their exhibits into

The celebrated and accomplished Consul.

mascots; thus in 1891 a stall selling photographs of favorite animals opened in the center of the Regent's Park Zoo.[75] But candidates for such symbolic translation had to be carefully chosen. It took more than simple novelty, for example, to make an enduring star. Interest in most curiosities faded after a few months of exposure; like an anteater that arrived at Regent's Park in 1853, they tended to enjoy only a brief moment of glory. The giraffes imported from the Sudan in the 1830s were widely ballyhooed but never became individual personalities known by name to a wide public; nor did the large predators stocked in generous numbers by most zoos. When "the old patriarch lion, who has so long been an ornament to the carnivora house, and the admiration of visitors" died, he was identified only as "a large and very valuable animal."[76] To win the permanent affections of the British public, a wild animal had to be impressive, whether in size like the elephant or the hippo, or in mental power, like the chimpanzee, but it could not seem too dangerous or independent. The lion might fittingly symbolize Britain in its dealings with other nations, but the national imagination was not attracted by the notion of a leonine pet.

Zoo pets represented not Britain, but their native territories, which were invariably British colonies in Africa and Asia, and never colonies

which, like Canada and Australia, had significant European populations.
It is probably no accident that they were often accompanied by exotic
human attendants who, like the Arabs in Obaysch's train, were presented in the press as equally curious if not equally lovable. Corrobo-
rating this rhetoric of dominion was the tendency of the royal family,
after William IV had contributed the Tower animals to the Zoological
Society of London, to regard the Regent's Park Zoo as the appropriate
repository of symbolic acknowledgments of Britain's international position. Queen Victoria routinely consigned to the Zoological Society
the "stream of barbaric offerings in the shape of lions, tigers, leopards,
&c., which is continually flowing from tropical princes"; and her eldest
son followed suit, donating not only animals he accumulated when
touring the outposts of Empire as Prince of Wales, but also gifts such as
the five lions and two zebras he received from Emperor Menelik of
Abyssinia on his coronation as Edward VII.[77]

If the royal family considered the London Zoo a metaphorical extension of its private domains, so too, although doubtless in an attenuated
sense, did many ordinary visitors to Regent's Park. After the governing
council abolished admission restrictions, the zoo emerged as a national
public institution, which reflected its glory on all British citizens. And
this glory was not solely political or military, whether represented by
animals that had been captured in the field, or those that had been
presented to the Queen as tribute, or those that had been adopted at
exotic postings as regimental pets and then relinquished to the zoo
when they grew unmanageable. In a more pragmatic sense the zoo illustrated Britain's economic prowess; the variety of the animals was "a
proof that our commerce is pushed to the ends of the earth!" (Another
index of this mercantile association was the stream of contributions
from the Hudson's Bay Company in the Zoological Society's early
years.)[78] Even the scientific side of the zoo testified to the superior com-
petence of Britons, who were able to maintain so many exotic species
in confinement and to manipulate and study them, so that they were
better understood and appreciated than by the peoples who had lived
among them for millennia. Perhaps it was in order to make this point
on the spot that the East India Company had established a small zoological garden in Barrackpore in 1804; at about the same time, which
was several decades before there was any equivalent on home soil, English settlers at Capetown could enjoy "a large menagerie, containing

Exotic captives and their keepers. G. Scharf, 1835.

the most remarkable beasts and birds indigenous to Africa, or brought
from other parts of the world."[79]

As the emblem of British domination over its colonial empire, the
London Zoo also inevitably came to symbolize Britain's competition for
preeminence with western rivals. Helping to stock it became a quasi-
official duty for consuls and other colonial officials, whose frequent gifts
were recorded with gratitude in the Zoological Society's proceedings.[80]
From the beginning the London Zoo was measured against its European
competitors. Indeed, a primary motive for its establishment had been
Britain's shameful lack of an institution for the study of living exotic
animals, despite being "richer than any other country in the extent and
variety of our possessions," while its neighbors could boast "magnificent
institutions" devoted to this purpose.[81] Cause for embarrassment
quickly faded, however. Soon after it was stocked, the Zoological Society's menagerie was proclaimed "the most extensive assemblage of living Quadrupeds and Birds ever exhibited in this, or perhaps in any
other, country"; after a few decades it was without question "the finest
public Vivarium in Europe."[82] But the struggle continued; the society's
judges never allowed it to rest comfortably on its considerable laurels.

When, for example, the first live pandas appeared in zoos elsewhere in Europe, *Nature* goaded Regent's Park to a parallel act of symbolic acquisition: "As France and Russia can now both boast of specimens, England, whose interests in China are so predominant, surely ought to be able to obtain some likewise."[83]

This competitive national pride was insulted in 1882, when P. T. Barnum, the American entrepreneur, arranged to purchase Jumbo, an enormous African elephant who had been for many years the pride of Regent's Park. Many of the children who had ridden on his back, as well as their parents, felt personally bereft when they heard of his projected departure. (Ironically, the Council of the Zoological Society decided to sell Jumbo because he was following in Chunee's footsteps and becoming difficult to control; zoo administrators feared an accident, something they were reluctant to reveal at the time of the sale.) There was a public outcry, including letters to the editor criticizing the sale as "a disgrace to English lovers of animals," and an attempt orchestrated by the *Daily Telegraph* to get Barnum to cancel his purchase for an offered £100,000 (about one hundred times the best guess of the purchase price).[84] But in the voluminous pamphlet literature that registered this national trauma, humanitarian concerns were incontestably secondary to those of patriotism. The problem was not that Jumbo would suffer under the big top, but that the United States had managed to wrest him from Britain. In one such doggerel, entitled *The Farewell of the Zoo Pet*, Jumbo assured his fans that "I love old England's dear little girls and boys"; in another he announced that "I love the brave old British flag, of it my boys I'll always brag,/And you must clearly understand, I do not care for Yankee land." Jumbo was a valued chattel, and the British public had a hard time giving him up to a transatlantic rival.[85]

Private Preserves

Maintaining exotic animals in captivity was a compelling symbol of human power. Transporting them safely to England and figuring out how to keep them alive were triumphs of human skill and intelligence over the contrary dictates of nature; access to their native territories symbolized English power and prestige. Most visitors to Victorian zoos, viewing the confined and uprooted creatures, were content to bask in this reflected glory. But for some people caged wild animals presented

BAD NEWS FOR JUMBO.

SOLD TO BARNUM FOR £2000

For 21 years a faithful servant I've been, yet they say I'm wild now I am out of my teens,
And to get rid of me, they have taken some gold, its all on account because I've grown old,

JUMBO'S DEPARTURE.

Farewell to England, the home of my youth; farewell, dear young friends, for in truth.
When far away over the sea, poor old Jumbo will ne'er forget thee.

Popular expressions of regret and resentment at Jumbo's departure.
From *The Farewell of the Zoo Pet*.

a further challenge. Physical domination and confinement was only the first stage in a process that would eventually overcome the animals' wild nature altogether. From this perspective the ultimate goal was domestication—ostensibly so that they could serve pragmatic human ends, but actually as a crowning metaphorical demonstration of human ascendancy. Most of those involved in organized efforts to domesticate exotic animals were either scientists with a professional interest in illustrating the power of human intellect over nature, or magnates and officials with a social or political interest in emphasizing their dominion over other people. If the rhetoric of public zoos engaged the lowest common denominator of national pride, that of acclimatization and domestication expressed the special figurative concerns of the elite audience that Raffles had envisioned when he planned the Zoological Society of London.

An essential preliminary to this project was inducing wild animals to breed in captivity, and here the concerns of domesticators converged with those of the managers of public live animal collections. Most substantial zoos made at least some attempt to encourage their animals to breed.[86] Baby animals boosted attendance; they were cheaper than imported animals; and if there was no permanent room for them in their natal collection, they could be sold or traded when they grew older. The annual reports of the Zoological Society of London included detailed accounts of zoo births. The society's officers took pride in the fecundity of their giraffes and hastened to procure a new male lion for breeding when an incumbent passed his prime.[87] In 1864 the annual report of the Bristol Zoo announced that "your Committee have also paid attention to the breeding of animals, with the view of having an annual supply of stock for sale." This scheme had already succeeded with lions and nilgais; the next candidates for exploitation were leopards and llamas. Several years later the zoo management celebrated a successful tiger birth—an unusual feat in the nineteenth century, much more difficult than the breeding of lions.[88]

Zookeepers' interest in breeding captive wild animals was not entirely pragmatic; the reluctance of zoo stock to reproduce was regarded as a challenge. Some menagerists interpreted this challenge as a scientific problem to be solved by the application of reason. For example, the officials of the Dublin Zoo, which became famous for its success in breeding lions and other large carnivores, seduced its charges with "per-

fect quietness and seclusion, a variety of natural food, and as large a
space for exercise as possible"—all rare commodities in nineteenth-
century wild animal collections.[89] But most menagerists conceived the
challenge as defiance of human authority. Thus, when discussing this
problem in *The Variation of Animals and Plants under Domestication*, Darwin
used the language of intention and resistance to suggest, "It is notorious
that many animals . . . refuse to breed in captivity."[90] From this point of
view it was not surprising that zoo ruminants, the wild relations of domestic farm animals, were much more prolific than carnivora. And this
may also explain why both zoos and private menagerists were willing
to undertake heroic measures, involving expense and risk that far outstripped the potential rewards of a successful mating, to bring breeding
pairs together. In 1837 the Bristol Zoo sent its female leopard to the
male in Regent's Park for stud services; and the earl of Derby sent what
he called his Kepul doe to the stag in Regent's Park for the same purpose, although, as he confided to Sir Robert Heron, a fellow enthusiast,
"I shd have *preferred* his coming to her."[91]

The desire to triumph over obstacles mounted by nature may also
explain the Victorian fascination with hybrids, which explicitly violated
natural categories. Even small-scale breeders might be tempted by the
opportunity to cross their pets or chattels with wild animals. Sometimes
these amateurs were more enthusiastic than realistic in their plans. One
Alfred Tichborne wrote Frank Buckland, the popular naturalist, about
his intention to mate a vixen with his terrier dog. And a cross between
a stag and a mare was actually reported in a credulous veterinary magazine.[92] In zoos hybrids between wild animals and their close domesticated relatives were relatively common. Typical pairings included an
English cow and a Brahman bull, a yak and a zebu, a quagga and a horse,
a zebra and a donkey, and English red deer and various exotic cervids.[93]
If crossing a domesticated and a wild species symbolized human ability
to surmount natural obstacles, hybrids between two wild species made
the same point more forcefully. The most publicized nineteenth-
century crosses were called ligers or tigons or, in the more plodding
phrase allegedly coined by King William IV, lion-tigers. They were
bred by Thomas Atkins, first in his traveling menagerie and later in the
Liverpool Zoological Gardens, and they were celebrated as "the greatest phenomenon that has occurred in the history of these animals . . .
the most implacable enemies in the forest . . . it remained for the Pro-

Friendship between a lion and a tiger in Atkins's Menagerie.

prietor of these Gardens to prove, that under the dominion of man even the most savage spirits may be subdued."[94]

From the point of view of most breeders of wild animals, however, Atkins's boasting was premature; successful captive reproduction represented the beginning rather than the culmination of their efforts. Complete domestication implied that the resulting offspring would be dedicated to human purposes. Although cloaked in the rhetoric of public service, in fact this enterprise embodied the most powerful possible symbol of possession and control. Wild animals were to be raised as livestock, not because their flesh would improve the national food supply, but because those with the wealth and skill to breed them wished also to appropriate them as completely as possible. The failure of attempts to translate the high-minded rhetoric into practice clearly indicated that the demand for exotic flesh was both limited and figurative. The first goal mentioned in the "Prospectus" of the Zoological Society of London was to introduce new varieties of animals for "domestication or for stocking our farm-yards, woods, pleasure-grounds, and wastes."[95] To make good on this commitment, which was close to the hearts of some of the most influential fellows, the young society quickly established a breeding farm at Kingston Hill, not far from the city. Little demand emerged for the products of this venture, outside of stock breeders who wanted to distinguish their herds and flocks with an infusion of exotic blood and were willing to pay stud fees that ranged from 5s. for a zebu to £1 for a Brahman bull to £2 for a zebra. In 1833 the council voted to sell the farm and end its adventure in commercial wild animal husbandry.[96] That few members of the British public relished even the idea of eating strange meat was illustrated by the strong emotions aroused by the rumor, current in 1855, that a 5,000-pound elephant carcass had found its way to the knackers, and thence to the sausage makers. As Peter Lund Simmonds, who yearned for such delicacies as dog, monkey, and puma, lamented, a boring and monotonous allegiance to beef in all forms was the "national weakness" of the British.[97]

The rare spirits who shared Simmonds's predilections were apt to be indulging more than a gustatory appetite. Such feasts expressed more than simple culinary flexibility; they enabled those who represented the elites of wealth and knowledge figuratively to reenact their positions at the table. Thus scientists might sample the flesh of exotic animals as part of their intellectual appropriation of the natural world. Darwin and a group of his Cambridge friends met occasionally to eat "birds & beasts which were before unknown to the human palate." As a child Frank Buckland had dined on hedgehog, puppy, and crocodile at the table of his father, a distinguished geologist and clergyman; as an adult he arranged with the Regent's Park authorities to sample any interesting creature that died at the zoo. Guests at his London home might be treated to panther (dug up after being buried for several days and judged *"not very good"*), elephant trunk soup, or roast giraffe.[98] Parallel symbolism clearly informed the regulations of the Raleigh Travellers' Club, which was founded in 1826 with a membership limited to forty distinguished travelers. At each fortnightly meeting a member provided a dinner of animals and plants from whatever exotic territory he had recently conquered.[99]

The small number of wealthy landowners who, throughout the nineteenth century, maintained breeding menageries on their estates, were drawn from the same ranks as those acquisitive club members. Some animals were included in these collections because they appealed to the aesthetic sensibility or intellectual curiosity of their owners—an example of a menagerie selected on this basis was that of Walter Lionel Rothschild, which ran to ostriches and kangaroos as well as more conventional species—but most menagerists restricted their attention to creatures that might conceivably be eaten. Thus Lord Powerscourt introduced Japanese deer on his Irish estate in the 1850s, and several decades later Sir E. G. Loder stocked his Sussex park with mouflons (European wild sheep), Japanese deer, gazelles, hog deer, Indian black buck antelopes, and American turkeys. Between 1892 and 1905, the duke and duchess of Bedford imported forty-six species of exotic deer, sixteen of antelope, two of gazelles, four of goats, and five of sheep, among others. Many of these bred successfully in the enormous grounds at Woburn Abbey. Reiterating the evocative combination of ingestion and power, the *Field* urged proprietors of "our country seats" to naturalize the edible eland and kangaroo in their parks.[100]

The most impressive private menagerie of the nineteenth century was organized along such appropriate lines. Edward Smith Stanley, the thirteenth earl of Derby, had been interested in natural history since his youth.[101] Although he was a founding member of the Zoological Society in 1826 and took an active part in related scientific activities, his zoological projects remained relatively modest in scale while his father controlled the family estate at Knowsley, near Liverpool. A letter written by the then Lord Stanley to his father's steward in 1830 suggested the restrictions under which he labored as well as his designs for the future. He explained that he had been reluctant to purchase a lot of eight deer because they would have had to be confined to a paddock, but "as I have this Evening obtained my father's permission to turn my Deer into the Park," the sale could be concluded.[102] When his father died in 1834, the new earl began converting the park at Knowsley into a princely collection of living animals.

When the menagerie was cataloged before being auctioned off at his death (his son had no more sympathy for his avocation than his father had had), it included 345 mammals, representing 94 species, of which over one-third had bred in the park, as well as a much larger number of birds. About a hundred acres at Knowsley were devoted to their accommodation, and the payroll listed thirty attendants. Estimates of the annual cost of maintaining the animals varied from £10,000 to £15,000.[103] In scale Derby's collection rivaled that of a national institution like the Zoological Society of London, of which he served as president for many years, but the distribution of species within it was quite different from the Noah's ark assortment characteristic of zoological gardens. Deer and antelope accounted for most of the species, with some wild bovines, sheep, goats, llamas, and zebras; there were also a few curiosities like kangaroos, lemurs, and armadillos. The animals had not been gathered "for the gratification of whim, for the sake of mere collecting, or for ostentatious display," but to experiment with the "breeding of such beasts as would be likely to be ornamental or useful if successfully naturalized in this country"; most of them were, at least in theory, candidates for the stewpot.[104]

Although Derby's efforts to naturalize and domesticate exotic animals ended with the dispersal of his menagerie, the torch he had let fall was soon rescued by societies dedicated to subjugating previously untamed species. The Acclimatisation Society of Great Britain, which was founded in 1860, largely at the instigation of Buckland, institutionalized the rhetoric of private domesticators. It survived only through 1866, when it could muster a mere 270 members (90 of them life members who could not quit); this narrow base of support provided additional evidence of the rarefied appeal of the enterprises it was designed to forward. Nevertheless, the society cherished ambitious objectives, which included a wide variety of manipulations of exotic species—naturalizing them in Britain; perfecting, propagating, and hybridizing them once domesticated; and shipping native English species to the colonies in exchange. The objectives of the society were couched in the familiar language of patriotic service, but its activities made it clear that its underlying concern was consumption. Besides meetings, its first public activity was a dinner, held in 1863, at which the menu included birds' nest soup, kangaroo steamer, kangaroo ham, Syrian pig, Canadian goose, curassow, Honduras turkey, leporine, and Chinese sheep.[105]

This miscellaneous feast suggested that the Acclimatisation Society catered to a generalized and profound acquisitiveness. Its activities during its few years of operation showed a parallel lack of system and restraint. It imported sheep from Brittany, deer from Japan, asses from Catalonia, and wombats from Australia; a survey conducted by the society just before its demise elicited suggestions for new target species ranging from tapirs to camels to yaks to muskrats. One enthusiastic correspondent even suggested naturalizing the leopard and the jackal.[106] Acclimatization, in this expanded sense, followed empire, and it was no accident that much of the society's correspondence involved British officials in British colonies. This pattern of acquisition reflected that of a magnate like the earl of Derby, who similarly involved colonial officials in his quest for new specimens (one thanked the earl profusely for stating "your wishes relative to the introduction of Singhalese animals into England" but regretted that "my engagements at Columbo place it out of my power to collect myself"), and who also gloried in possession for its own sake. Even when his collection had grown to enormous proportions and his physical vigor was failing, he still made long lists of species yet to be acquired and tamed.[107] If there was anything remotely worth having in the world, in this view, the British should be sure to have it.

The political dimension of acclimatization was also illustrated in an inverted way by the societies established by English colonists in Australia, who wished to impose their presence on a very alien landscape. Although the stated objectives of the Acclimatisation Society of Victoria, which was founded in 1861, echoed those of the British society, the Australian acclimatizers were more interested in supplanting the native fauna than in supplementing it. They lamented the "paucity of

SOUTH AFRICAN SMITHFIELD SHOW.

The ultimate goal of acclimatization. From *Punch,* 1898.

serviceable animals in this Colony," proposing to remedy the lack with such useful creatures from England as the roe deer, the partridge, the rook, the hare, and the sparrow. They complained that "while Nature has so abundantly furnished . . . the natural larder of every other similarly situated country . . . with a great variety, and a profusion . . . of ruminants good for food, *not one single creature of the kind inhabits Australia!"* And even when, as happened quickly, imported rabbits and sparrows began to despoil gardens and fields, the rhetoric of conquest by assimilation continued. "The acclimatisation . . . of every good thing the world contains" was celebrated as "about as legitimate an enterprise as can be conceived"; acclimatizers were urged to continue their efforts until "the country teemed with animals introduced from other countries."[108]

Thus acclimatization offered the very powerful a figurative reenactment of their commanding positions. For this reason English acclimatizers were undeterred by their persistent lack of commercial success (although some exotic varieties of deer became completely naturalized in private English parks, and a few even escaped and established wild populations).[109] It quickly became clear that the animals already domesticated were better adapted to fulfill human needs in the English climate than any exotic species; in any case, as a writer in *Nature* reminded enthusiasts near the end of the century, "no addition of any practical importance has been made to our stock of truly domestic animals since the commencement of the historic period of man's life upon the earth."[110] But that was beside the point. Like their more conventional neighbors who bred fat cattle, private menagerists used their ability to confine, produce, and ingest wild animals within their own domains to celebrate their own splendid preeminence among their fellow humans and their dominion over nature.

CHAPTER SIX

The Thrill of the Chase

The menageries of nineteenth-century England offered a stately, highly structured display of some of the more exotic spoils of empire, impressive symbols of British domination both of vast tributary territories and of the natural world. The serene confidence of achieved mastery was, however, only one side of imperialism, and not the only one to stir the imagination of stay-at-home patriots. At least equally compelling was the more romantic, violent, and dangerous process of confrontation and conquest. Although the overt symbolism of zoological gardens tended to overshadow this darker reading of imperialism, it was implicitly embodied in the capture and transportation to Europe of the tigers, elephants, and antelopes that ended up sedately marshaled for the edification of the Victorian public.

The Source

The men who brought wild animals back to England had experienced the risks and excitement of the exotic frontier; they were human symbols of the outward thrust of British influence. In the eighteenth century and the early part of the nineteenth century, when the emphasis of British expansion was economic, most live animals arrived with sailors returning from trading voyages. East Indiamen constituted a particularly rich source of stock for menagerists, whose agents raced for first choice of each cargo. Sometimes they did not wait for ships that might be carrying wild animals to dock, but boarded them as they entered the Thames estuary. This direct and rather chaotic contact between supplier and consumer was soon superseded by the emergence of a group of middlemen, dealers specializing in live animals. At first they were often menagerists wearing a different hat—both Wombwell and Pidcock, the founder of the Exeter Change Menagerie, also operated beast shops—but the establishments of their successors developed stronger affinities with the animals' sources than with their destinations. That is, they became part of the boundary between the African or Asian wilds and the streets of urban Britain; they were agents of the process of imperialism rather than exhibitors or celebrants of its results.[1]

The largest and most renowned wild animal shop in Victorian London was operated by Charles Jamrach from 1840 until his death in 1891. So closely was he associated with his trade that near the end of the century one sporting author referred casually to "some Indian Jamrack" as the appropriate purchaser of a pair of tiger cubs.[2] His shifting collection of exotic animals rivaled the permanent stock of many public menageries; a visitor who came to examine the big cats could stay to admire "springboks, baboons, and elephants without end."[3] Located in large but cramped premises in the unsavory neighborhood of the London docks, Jamrach's establishment mediated between the sedate precincts of Regent's Park, Knowsley Park, and the other menageries that were its most important customers, and the mysterious and dangerous localities from which its stock had come. The route to the rooms and outbuildings where the animals were kept led through settings increasingly remote from the everyday London world. The room that opened onto the street was ordinary enough, at least for an animal dealer's shop, being filled with birds; but after walking through the countinghouse, the visitor arrived in "one of the most extraordinary apartments we have ever seen," a large chamber filled with South Sea island weapons, heathen deities, assegais from Zululand, Buddhas, and other human artifacts from the native countries of the captive animals. On the other side of this exotic divide were the wild creatures themselves.[4]

The animals' quarters reinforced the sense of strangeness and remoteness. The cages were arranged for commercial convenience—that is, to make the premises hold as much merchandise as possible—rather than for aesthetic or taxonomical purposes. The result was a confusing and in some cases frightening jumble of animals, with predators and their prey closely juxtaposed; one visitor observed leopards and black-buck caged side by side. Where public menageries generally avoided even the subtlest suggestion of the violence of nature, Jamrach's emphasized the inherent savageness of wild animals. Visitors were warned not to approach the jammed-in cages too closely, because they contained "not the half-domesticated creatures of the Lion House at the Zoo, but the wild and savage denizens of tropical jungles, captured but not yet cowed, or even reconciled to the proximity of man." Even an apparently "gentle" seal was capable of taking a large bite out of a passing umbrella handle. As a final signal of the shop's intermediate or transitional status, the animals were frequently kept in their traveling containers, no matter how small and flimsy.[5]

The establishments of Jamrach's competitors were similarly liminal. William Cross of Liverpool, the grandson of Edward Cross of Exeter Change and the Royal Surrey Zoological Gardens, also maintained an extensive inventory of animals; a single small advertisement listed a mongoose, a "monster" elephant, two zebras, a llama, a tiger, a "monster" mandrill and several other baboons, seventy monkeys, a brown bear, and a pair of "large" antelopes, among much other stock. Like Jamrach's, Cross's was located in an insalubrious neighborhood, unlike those to which its patrons were accustomed. And again, access to the animals was through an antechamber stocked with miscellaneous exotica—"mummies and Burmese idols . . .—weapons of savage warfare"—which allied Cross's emporium with the "obscure Malayan districts" and "African kraals" where his name was allegedly as well known and well respected as that of Queen Victoria.[6] Less grandiose establishments could also seem to be transported pieces of the empire, although the tiny shops found near the London docks and on the quays of other great port cities were apt to evoke its more sordid and less exhilarating aspects. In the condescending characterization of Carl Hagenbeck, Jamrach's German counterpart, rival, and occasional collaborator, these were "untidy," "generally evil smelling," and "crowded with parrots and monkeys and similar casual acquisitions from sailors." Both the filth of these shops and the character of their merchandise were more reminiscent of the rough waterfront quarters of exotic ports, where sailors might buy such creatures from native entrepreneurs, than of the imperial frontier, where sportsmen conquered more dangerous game on its own ground.[7]

As the focus of empire shifted from commerce to territorial acquisition and administration during the nineteenth century, the imperial frontier moved from ports like Capetown and Singapore to the untamed interior or bush. Simultaneously, the Englishmen who encountered the frontier were less likely to be merchants than members of more dynamic and predatory (and frequently overlapping) groups, such as explorers, military officers, civilian administrators, sportsmen, and professional hunters and collectors. And they used more exciting methods than simple purchase to acquire their stock. Young animals were considered preferable to older ones as captures because they were more adaptable and easier to transport; for most big game species this meant shooting a mother to get a juvenile. In a few cases the mother was not apt to put up much of a fight; one of the many orangutans shot out of the Malayan treetops by Alfred Russel Wallace, who spent most of his scientific career collecting natural history specimens, fell to the ground with her unharmed daughter in her arms. But many wild mothers were more inclined and better able to protect their offspring. One valiant tigress defended her litter against both guns and sticks before she was shot and the cubs captured. A lioness with cubs was characterized as "one of the most savage of animals"; and once she was out of the way, the cubs themselves were likely to prove "fierce, strong, and vicious." An early nineteenth-century sportsman described the task of catching a young Indian rhinoceros as prohibitively "arduous" and "hazardous"; he did not see how it could be managed unless by shooting the mother "when she might be at the pile, attended by her calf."[8]

Once the animals were caught, transportation and maintenance posed problems that were in some ways more complex, if less alarming. After capturing two lion cubs in the Somali bush, one late nineteenth-century sportsman had to cope with elaborate export restrictions at the coast, then provide appropriate means of confinement (the simpler ones, such as large dog collars, proved inadequate) for the voyage home, on which their passage cost almost as much as that of a first-class human passenger. Proper food was a continuing problem, and there were the British authorities to be dealt with at the other end. Despite his efforts, the cubs died soon after they arrived in Britain.[9] Daunting as the risks and the subsequent administrative challenges were, however, they seem to have attracted rather than discouraged hunters.

Almost every variety of English citizen that ventured into the wild savanna or jungle was apt to emerge with young animals of the most prized big game species. The explorer Dixon Denham, who searched for Lake Chad in the 1820s, accumulated a virtual menagerie in the course of his travels; near the end of the century the Stanfords, a wealthy couple on a safari vacation, returned to England with a young oryx and four leopard cubs.[10] If triumphant sportsmen had second thoughts about bringing their prizes home, they could dispose of them at the nearest large town. The stream of animals flowing out of the bush was so large in rich game areas that the local functionaries were apt to develop it into a profitable sideline. Vice-Consul Petherick of Khartoum, for example, acted as agent for various European zoological societies. At Entebbe, toward the end of the nineteenth century, British officials would accept young, healthy wild animals, which were valued at the rate of 3 rupees for a bush pig, 90 for a zebra, 300 for a hippopotamus, and 3,000 for an elephant, in lieu of taxes.[11]

In some cases hunters caught young animals on speculation—the £60 paid for a juvenile rhinoceros in mid-century India went some way toward defraying a junior officer's hunting expenses—but the adventurers who lived in the territories where they hunted usually kept their living trophies.[12] Indeed, any British regimental headquarters or official residence in Africa or India was apt to include a miscellaneous accumulation of half-tamed fauna. The chief engineer at Berbera put up guests on the veranda of his bungalow, near a cage containing a fifteen-month-old-lion; when Sir Harry Johnston was special commissioner of Uganda, a chimpanzee, several baboons, an eagle, and a baby elephant had the run of Government House, while his antelopes, zebras, leopards, and serval cats lived outside. The "rearing of wild animals" was general among Britons resident in India at the beginning of the nineteenth century, according to an observer who considered the practice "very imprudent," although he conceded that a semidomesticated tiger was more trustworthy than a leopard or a bear in the same condition. Near the end of the century an officer who still mourned a ten-month-old tiger that had died of teething difficulties (he also regretted not having managed to shoot its mother) regarded his menagerie—which had included leopards, bears, deer, antelope, monkeys, and birds—as no more than the usual "Anglo-Indian fashion."[13] Collections offered diversion and occupation in lives that could often seem confined and boring. And they were constant reminders of the hunting expeditions during which they had been procured, a symbol of the force and power that supported and validated the routinized day-to-day domination of the empire.

Alive or Dead

Nevertheless, live animals that required special handling and expensive maintenance offered at best an attenuated or indirect representation of the grand process of imperial annexation and control. Only the actual capture, which normally required the death of at least one animal, evoked the repeated conflicts that attended the spread of British dominion in Asia and Africa and that excited expansionist sentiment at home. Dead wild animals, especially if there were a lot of them, symbolized the British suppression of the Afghans or the Ashante more compellingly than their pampered captive cousins. Rows of horns and hides, mounted heads and stuffed bodies, clearly alluded to the violent, heroic underside of imperialism.

The mere size of even zoologically oriented collections, such as those in William Bullock's "London Museum," opened in 1812, or in the short-lived museum of the Zoological Society of London, testified to the vigor of colonial appropriation. Each stuffed animal represented a bloody triumph in the field, an impression that might be enhanced by arrangements and backgrounds (introduced in London by Bullock) designed to suggest the animal's native territory. The museum that the earl of Derby maintained in addition to his menagerie contained over twenty-five thousand specimens. The most attractive specimens were those that were hardest to kill. A "splendid collection of objects, illustrative of the zoology of Central Africa" that visited London in 1837 was touted as including three species of rhinoceros. Later in the century Walter Lionel Rothschild converted his enormous private collections into a public museum. Although the heart of the museum was entomological, the biggest draws were the exotic carnivores and a white rhinoceros, which had been specially "shot for Mr. Rothschild by Mr. Coryndon."[14] This symbolism was not seriously compromised by the fact that at least some stuffed specimens had died peacefully in English captivity. But it was generally agreed that specimens killed in the wild, especially large carnivores, were preferable for scientific study and public display, because confined menagerie animals had no opportunity to exert their bones and muscles "in a violent manner," and their skeletons were consequently less fully developed.[15]

More exciting, however, were collections structured to emphasize not the variety of nature but human domination of it. The India Museum was founded in 1801 by the East India Company as a concrete metropolitan representation of its commercial and political influence; it soon accumulated the largest collection of South Asian zoological specimens in Britain and by the 1840s attracted between ten thousand and twenty thousand visitors per year. The theme of conquest was implicitly expressed by the centerpiece of its natural history display: a tiger and a panther snarling at brightly colored tropical birds.[16] Big game trophies figured frequently in expositions celebrating commercial and industrial prowess. The Great Exhibition of 1851 featured a range of trophies, from British birds to Indian game (the latter considered the "most attractive" dead animals in the exhibition by one aesthetically oriented guidebook). At the Crystal Palace these displays were ostensibly presented as examples of fine craftsmanship; but on subsequent occasions similar offerings seemed simply to embody the aggressive national spirit. Britain's contribution to the International Exhibition of 1862 included "two very fine tigers, shot by Colonel Reid"; "a very fine group of a lion and tiger fighting" was part of one British entry in the Paris Exhibition of 1867; and the American Exhibition of 1887, held in London, was graced by a collection of hunting trophies, "the best of its kind that has ever been brought together," which had all "been secured in the wildest parts of North America by the prowess of British sportsmen."[17]

That the appeal of such trophy displays rested upon their celebration of naked force was perhaps best illustrated by the popular successes of two mighty hunters, both of whom reaped the spoils of the chase a second time on the book, lecture, and exhibition circuit back in England. The careers of Roualeyn Gordon Cumming and Frederick Courteney Selous bracketed the most vigorous period of imperial expansion. Gordon Cumming, like many young men, was drawn to imperial service at least partly by the promise of big game hunting. He entered the East India Company's Madras cavalry in 1838 but could not endure the climate; then he returned to Scotland, where he found the deer stalking too tame; next he enlisted in a Canadian regiment, but North America failed to provide the hunting opportunities he had anticipated, so in 1843 he joined the Cape Mounted Rifles. When his military duties did not leave him enough time for sport, he resigned his commission in order to "penetrate into the interior farther than . . . civilized man had yet trodden—to vast regions which would afford abundant food for the gratification of the passion of my youth—the collecting of hunting trophies." For five years he supported himself as an ivory hunter, abandoning the field in 1849 not because he was "in the slightest degree satiated," but because elephant hunting was "too rapidly wearing down my constitution."[18]

Gordon Cumming returned to England intending to capitalize on his African experiences. He brought with him not only the trophies he had amassed during his sojourn in the bush, but also a Bushman boy named Ruyter and one of the huge, heavy Cape wagons that had carried his supplies and his prizes in the bush. The total cargo (not counting Ruyter) weighed more than thirty tons and formed the core of a "museum" that one admirer described as "such as never yet was achieved by the personal labour and energy of a single man."[19] He coordinated his publicity cleverly, publishing a popular narrative of his adventures, *Five Years of a Hunter's Life in the Far Interior of South Africa*, in 1850, the same year that he opened his London exhibit. It throve for the next eight years, and his occasional tours of the provinces were equally successful. The public flocked to see "the immense variety of tusks, antlers, horns, bones, skulls, teeth," which, according to the *Illustrated London News*, were "especially attractive to holiday visitors." Those who wanted more than just a look at the trophies and the large canvases that Gordon Cumming commissioned to illustrate his most dramatic adventures could pay from 1s. to 3s. to hear the "lion-slayer" describe his adventures to a musical accompaniment; he lectured nightly, with a Saturday matinee.[20]

What drew visitors to this vast collection of animal remains was the compelling way in which it testified to Gordon Cumming's stature as "the greatest hunter of modern times"—"bold, enterprising, and skilful." Each trophy represented "a select specimen of some fierce and formidable, or shy and wary animal, and most of them were obtained by undergoing extraordinary perils, hardships, and fatigues."[21] And viewers who wished to admire these qualities, the same that were needed in nonsporting encounters on the imperial frontier, were also gratified by the gross physicality of Gordon Cumming's evidence. It made it easy to controvert those "Cockneys" or "sceptical people, whose acquaintance with savage nature is derived solely from an occasional visit to a menagerie," who might suggest that accounts of sporting prowess were exaggerated and that sportsmen did not represent the most admirable British

The Lion-Slayer at Home,
232, PICCADILLY.

MR. GORDON CUMMING
DESCRIBES WHAT HE SAW AND DID IN AFRICA
EVERY EVENING AT EIGHT O'CLOCK.
ALSO
A Morning Entertainment
EVERY SATURDAY AT THREE O'CLOCK.
ILLUSTRATIONS BY FIRST-RATE ARTISTS, AND APPROPRIATE MUSIC.

ADMISSION—ONE SHILLING, TWO SHILLINGS, & THREE SHILLINGS.

Drawing the crowds to admire Gordon Cumming's hunting prowess.

type. In Gordon Cumming's museum there was no question that he was a "trustworthy narrator"; even a visitor who declared himself "bored to death" with the exhibition acknowledged that it attested the hunter's "courage and energy."[22]

If Gordon Cumming appeared to be motivated primarily by the love of sport and spoil, Frederick Courteney Selous presented a more austere and explicitly imperialistic figure. By the time he began to lecture in Britain—in 1895, after more than twenty years as an ivory hunter and specimen collector in southern Africa—he had also participated in the military adventures that led to the British acquisition of Rhodesia. It was this colonial service that the duke of Fife stressed in presenting Selous to a crowd that had packed the Great Hall of the Imperial Institute. Although Selous's contemporary reputation was as "a great traveller and an intrepid sportsman," the duke predicted that in the future he would be "known as one of those who had advanced the cause of civilization and helped to extend the British Empire."[23] Despite the automatic cheers that greeted this announcement, the audience had really come to hear about Selous's hunting exploits. The lecturer obliged by recounting three perilous encounters in the bush—one with lions, one with elephants, and one with hostile natives—which commanded the "rapt attention" of his listeners for more than an hour and a half. Similar subject matter subsequently produced similar results at the Exeter Hall, the London Institution, and other forums. Selous self-consciously avoided the exaggeration and hoopla associated with figures like Gordon Cumming and Buffalo Bill (who also enjoyed an enormous English vogue); and he resisted some public demand—fueled by his lectures and his books, *A Hunter's Wanderings in Africa* (1881) and *Travel and Adventure in South-East Africa* (1893)—for him to mount a "demonstration" of lion killing. Although he did not open his collection of trophies to the public for a fee, as had his more flamboyant predecessors, he used it in the same way to validate and define his prowess as a frontiersman.[24]

Selous had begun his collection of African mammals in 1874, and even when hunting specimens on commission from museums or other collectors, he reserved the "best" trophies for himself. He was strikingly generous in these appropriations. When Selous's widow donated the accumulated trophies to the British Museum (Natural History) in 1919, there were approximately 500 specimens, including at least 19 lions, 18 kudu, 11 eland (kudu and eland were considered the noblest quarries among the African antelopes), and 10 rhinoceroses. If the public had to wait to see the collection in its full glory, sample views were available to those who attended Selous's lectures. Because, as he explained to one audience, he had no lantern slides to illustrate his narrative, he arranged on the platform "certain of the most remarkable lions and other animals which have fallen to the lecturer's gun." They offered both dramatic background for and persuasive corroboration of his stories.[25]

More than sheer numbers was required to constitute an impressive trophy collection; prizes could easily lose their symbolic force in the process of preservation. The *Field*, which regularly covered big game hunting along with English rural diversions, used the window of its London office to display such models of the taxidermist's art as a massive American bison, the "finest" stuffed gorillas in the market, and a "beautiful" tiger. These trophies represented the highest ideals of the magazine and its readers.[26] Their physical perfection reflected a great deal of technical ingenuity and careful craftsmanship—the combination of manual and intellectual skill that distinguished the English colonialist from his native charges. The splendid specimens had been carefully skinned and dried in the field, a delicate operation that sportsmen were advised to oversee personally. Trusting "native servants or agents," as one guidebook put it, opened the door to several hazards. At the most practical level, the hard-won prizes might rot or be devoured by insects if improperly preserved. In addition, natives were unlikely to understand the aesthetics of taxidermy, which required that hides be removed with as few holes and tears as possible. One sportsman reported himself "thoroughly disgusted" at being deprived of what he "was inclined to believe would have turned out a new antelope"; one of his attendants spoiled it by knocking off the horns. In Islamic areas hunters had to reach a compromise with their servants on the subject of *halal* (the ritual slitting of the throat of a slain animal to drain it of blood) before an expedition began; with careful explanation, it was considered possible to satisfy the demands of religion and sport simultaneously.[27]

Maintaining the integrity of the remains was only the first step in producing a prize worthy of public display. To present an effective symbol of the hunter's heroic appropriation, a trophy needed to evoke the aspect of the animal that had provoked and justified the killing. Thus many intrinsically impressive specimens emerged as inferior trophies because of failures in taxidermic interpretation or transformation. Often, according to one connoisseur, "graceful outlines . . . expressive attitudes, and . . . sleek, glossy coat" turned into a "stiff, gaunt, distorted form . . . with its round staring eyes, its withered ears, lips, and nostrils . . . which bear not more resemblance to the extremities of the living creature than Yorick's skull to the living face."[28] The nobler the slain animal, the more difficult it was to reproduce its living fire. Sportsmen were advised to note carefully the appearance of their victims before and just after they killed them, lest "the taxidermist at home may be led to a wrong conclusion"; but even so, according to the catalog, in most of the heads of North American game in the American Exhibition "the outlines have been altogether lost in the stuffing." When he shot a "magnificent" eland, Selous hoped to see him "set up in a manner that would recall to my mind, in some degree, the splendid creature he looked when alive, though I was fully aware how difficult it must be to mount these large skins so as to do them justice."[29]

Although the ostensible criterion by which such efforts were judged was realism, in fact the most acclaimed taxidermy made its subjects seem dangerous and powerful. Thus the stuffed gorillas that Paul du Chaillu displayed in 1861 had been made to appear as menacing as possible—perhaps even to the extent (alleged by some of du Chaillu's detractors) of producing artificial bullet wounds in the front to disguise the fact that they had been shot from behind, in the act of fleeing. The hard-to-please cataloger of the American Exhibition of 1887 singled out four grizzly bears for praise—whole stuffed animals, standing erect, as if ready to attack. And the naturalist Frank Buckland was full of admiration for a pair of tiger cubs that occupied the *Field* window in 1863. Although killed very young, when still smaller than house cats, they had been "stuffed in the threatening, ferocious attitude assumed by their full-grown parent," which he found "much better . . . than stuffing them as helpless, stupid-looking cubs."[30]

The Image of the Hunter

If the spoils of the big game hunter powerfully evoked the conquest and domination of exotic territories, written accounts made his exploits seem still more inspiring and more widely accessible. The connection between triumphing over a dangerous animal and subduing unwilling natives was direct and obvious, and the association of the big game hunter with the march of empire was literal as well as metonymic. By the beginning of the nineteenth century big game hunting was an integral part of the life of the British administrative and military community in India, and A. C. McMaster, whose subcontinental service came later in the century, traced this habit of conquerors even further back. When he asserted that "almost all Eastern soldiers have been sportsmen," he appended Alexander the Great to the list of British notables.[31] The gratifications of hunting overlapped significantly with those of dominion, whether they were profound—"the grim and silent satisfaction of looking over the trophies . . . which bring vividly to memory some successful shot, or closely contested struggle"—or petty, such as the pleasure one group of young officers found in shooting the bats considered sacred by the inhabitants of the Indian town where they were quartered.[32]

Ultimately, the hunter emerged as both the ideal and the definitive type of the empire builder. Even before his participation in the British annexation of Mashonaland, when he was renowned exclusively as a slayer of elephants, Selous was the hero of many boys preparing for colonial service at public schools. The arrival of big game hunters in regions previously untrodden by Europeans was seen as the harbinger of civilization; one mid-century journalist attacked critics of hunting by presuming that "it will hardly be maintained that the range of discovery is to be narrowed, and a huge portion of the globe left unexplored, merely out of deference to . . . delicate feelings." When late Victorian imperialists began to worry about the waning of national purpose, they attributed this enfeeblement of spiritual and bodily vigor to the exhaustion of the "new world of Sport . . . still begirt by the remoteness, difficulties, and dangers which . . . fire the hunter's imagination," and which had lured at least two generations of doughty Englishmen into the hearts of Africa and Asia. But if there were no virgin hunting grounds left, there were still stalwart sportsmen; according to a fin de siècle Edinburgh reviewer, "it is a sure sign that the race of men who made the Empire are not likely to be extinct when the hardships as well as the hazards only lend additional attraction to wild shooting."[33]

Such paragons were not only the subjects of patriotic accolades. Even more than trophy collections, narratives written by the potent protagonists fanned public appreciation of the heroic big game hunter. It seemed to one reviewer of these accounts that "the born sportsman is generally a born writer"; an author explained the same phenomenon somewhat differently, noting that "any one who has devoted himself to Indian field-sports for some years . . . must have been singularly unfortunate if he has not sufficient facts . . . to fill a book." The stream of sporting adventure flowed so copiously from the presses of London publishers that eventually, in the view of a relatively jaded reader, "people have been so overdone with howdahs, and . . . hair-breadth escapes, and griffins spearing a sow by mistake, that they had rather face a royal Bengal tiger in his native jungle than in the Sporting Magazine." By the last quarter of the century the situation with regard to African exploits was similar; one sporting author rather unself-consciously began his book by lamenting that "every person visiting South Africa, who has shooting proclivities, and is gifted with the smallest powers of description, deems it his duty to the world at large, to give information regarding the sport to be had."[34]

Apparently, however, this surfeit existed only in the eye of particularly jaundiced beholders. The demand for the literature remained strong. Both general audience magazines and highbrow reviews regularly carried hunting articles, as, more frequently, did the *Field* and other periodicals concerned with outdoor recreation; there was also a market for much more specialized publications like the *Oriental Sporting Magazine* and the *Oriental Sportsman's Newspaper.*[35] Successful sporting narratives might spark a continuing spiral of demand. Samuel White Baker's *Rifle and Hound in Ceylon*, originally published in 1853, was reprinted six times and his *Albert Nyanza* of 1866 ten times before the end of the century. In 1889 a writer of self-proclaimed seriousness of purpose in the *Journal of the Bombay Natural History Society* irritably acknowledged the existence of a large public appetite for dramatic hunting tales: "Books of sport are written to be read by the masses," he complained, "and the first idea of the author is to romance."[36] In some ways the most important members of this audience were young readers, many of whom later recalled that sporting narratives inspired them to prepare for a career of exotic service. Selous himself credited William Baldwin's *African Hunting from Natal to Zambesi*, published in 1864, with sending him to Africa.[37]

Hunting narratives had not always enjoyed such a wide audience. The first books dealing specifically with the chase of exotic big game appeared early in the nineteenth century, probably because, as Theodore Roosevelt (who collected such works) speculated, before then "the men who went on long voyages usually had quite enough to do simply as travellers"; they had no energy to spare for superfluous adventures.[38] These early works were apt to be, like Thomas Williamson's two-volume *Oriental Field Sports*, which appeared in 1807, beautifully illustrated and expensively executed. They appealed to the same elite audience that consumed the books on exotic natural history often produced by the explorers who had no time for sport. Indeed, works such as John Barrow's *Account of Travels into the Interior of Southern Africa* (1801, 1804) and Samuel and William Daniell's *Sketches Representing the Native Tribes, Animals, and Scenery of Southern Africa* (1820) incorporated some of the first descriptions of big game hunting near the Cape of Good Hope.[39] According to William Cornwallis Harris, his narratives of African hunting in the 1830s were meant for his "brother officers in India, with whom I have often stalked the forest and scoured the plain"; and this exclusive group accounted for about half of the four hundred subscribers to his *Portraits of the Game and Wild Animals of Southern Africa*, an enormous illustrated folio.[40] This was, in any case, the traditional audience for hunting literature, which, like the activity it described, had long been associated with upper-class hegemony.[41] Thus an elaborate Restoration compendium like Richard Blome's *Gentleman's Recreations* had devoted one of its three parts to "Horsemanship, Hawking, Hunting, Fowling, Fishing, Agriculture & c." and a second to "A Compleat Body of all our Forest, Chace, and Game Laws as they are at this Time." And thus, more than a century and a half later, Matthew Arnold characterized the English upper classes as "barbarians" with a "passion for field sports."[42]

By Arnold's time the passion for field sports, or at least for vicarious participation in exotic field sports, had spread far beyond the original barbarians, although even at the end of the nineteenth century, there persisted a subgenre of big game literature that Roosevelt called "these short and simple annals of the rich," by which he meant unembellished accounts of expensive hunting vacations.[43] But in the second half of the nineteenth century most narratives of Asian and African sport explicitly invited a much broader range of readers to share the excitement. To some extent this was a direct result of the popularization of the subject by Gordon Cumming and his ilk. In addition, the development of steam transportation made it easier for prospective hunters and (especially) prospective writers of hunting narratives to reach the haunts of exotic game; as early as 1854 a reviewer complained of his boredom with the sporting adventures of "the Cockney who goes out for a winter's excursion" in India.[44] The expansion of British colonial territories in Asia and Africa required increasing numbers of civilian officials and military officers to administer and defend them, and they too contributed to the flood of sporting literature. But most important was the fact that the imperialist adventure, in which Britain appropriated exotic territories and subjugated alien peoples, allowed even humble citizens to engage, at least by proxy, in a kind of metaphoric reenactment of conquest that had previously been confined to the privileged classes.

Narratives of big game hunting varied in many particulars: the length of the trip, the location of the hunting grounds, the number of European participants, the character and situation of the narrator. Whatever the ostensible reason for the excursion into the bush, however—whether the protagonist was an explorer, a naturalist, a commercial adventurer, or an official on holiday—the narratives shared a conventionalized format that emphasized the difficulties and dangers encountered by the hunter in order to magnify his eventual triumph. A first-person narrator was invariably at the center of the story. His dominating position was consolidated both by the inevitably reiterated "I" and by the predictably chronological structure of the narrative. Brief safaris might be presented in something close to diary form, as was the seventh earl of Mayo's, when he offered the public a slightly revised version of the daily journals he had kept on a four-month tour of Abyssinia. For works that covered a longer period, such as Baldwin's chronicle of eight years in the bush, more editorial digestion and selection was necessary, but the ultimate source was the same: "my journals . . . written sometimes in ink, but often in pencil, and gunpowder, tea, etc., in Kaffir kraals or wagon bottoms."[45] In either case the plot resembled that of a picaresque novel, focused squarely on the protagonist as he moved along a road (actually a trail in most hunting narratives) and through a series of adventures.

In this unremitting spotlight, the protagonists often presented themselves with modest, and even whimsical understatement. They insistently exposed their failures and frustrations—a litany of bad luck ("whenever anything large appears I always seem to have dust shot in my gun") and bad judgment (on the part of a "dreadfully annoyed" sportsman who had spared a wild boar, thinking it was a donkey). One hunter characterized his experience of sport as "crawling in breathless and perspiring silence on my stomach for about 500 yards . . . to be rewarded . . . by the view of a hartebeest shambling awkwardly away with a derisive and malevolent look in his eye."[46] Selous himself demurred at the suggestion that the large numbers of animals he had killed meant that he was a crack marksman. Elephants were, he pointed out, much larger and therefore easier to hit than the creatures normally hunted in Britain, and his reputation had often embarrassed him when he missed easy chances in front of "an English gamekeeper or a Scotch ghillie." In the same deprecatory vein, the most ferocious game might be whimsically or derisively nicknamed. Thus the wild boar was familiarly apostrophized as "piggy," and the tiger as "pussy" and "stripes." Even triumphs might be described with ostensible diffidence. According to one sportsman, "the story of the bagging of my first Uganda elephant is rather amusing, because he behaved distinctly improperly and was a cause of great annoyance to me, besides boring one of my men to bitter tears."[47]

Rather than undermining the stature of the hero, such rhetoric implicitly enhanced it. Abjuring braggadocio and hysteria, the hunter used his tone to display the manly British qualities of coolness, restraint, and humor. By defining certain kinds of setbacks as trivial and by similarly minimizing easy victories, he established a context in which more serious challenges, dangers, and triumphs could be accurately appreciated. For, as their manifest content made clear, big game narratives were not primarily about petty irritations and minor gratifications; that is, sporting expeditions, even those undertaken for recreational purposes, were not to be understood as mere parties of pleasure.

Meeting the Test

Instead, hunters presented their pastime as composed, like other imperial activities, of a series of increasingly difficult obstacles to be overcome by superior intelligence, skill, courage, and force. The initial problems were apt to require managerial talent. Unless the sportsman happened to live in a well-stocked big game district, organizing a hunting trip was a complicated and expensive procedure. When preparing for a year-long trip into the interior of Africa in the 1840s, Gordon Cumming amassed enough supplies to make him independent of both native Africans and Boers. These included 300 pounds each of sugar and rice, 5 pounds of pepper, 2 cases of gin, 24 boxes of snuff, 50 pounds of tobacco, 300 pounds of colored beads; equipment for cooking, blacksmithing, carpentry, and tailoring; 7 guns of various sorts; 10,000 bullets as well as tools and raw materials for making more; and £200 in cash. Several years earlier Harris had estimated that a South African expedition of similar duration cost £800.[48]

In India hunting trips did not usually last so long or traverse such uncertainly populated territory, but the predictable presence of native villages brought its own problems. These settlements did not offer accommodations considered fit for Europeans or even for their horses, so sportsmen still had to carry their own tents, food, and cooking equipment. Furthermore, because the villagers provided an audience of subject people who had to be suitably impressed, hunting parties were advised to take along a small company of sepoys; the similar custom of wealthy Indians had "created in the minds of the inferior classes an opinion, that to be without such a retinue proceeds from a want of dignity, or from a want of importance, and produces, on many occasions, very unpleasant dilemmas." In general, Indian sportsmen traveled more luxuriously than their African colleagues; as one sportsman put it,

in preparing for a tiger shoot "almost as many details have to be provided for as are required . . . for the conduct of a campaign." This grandeur was epitomized by the expedition mounted for the Prince of Wales
in 1876, on which he was accompanied by nine thousand people and
proportionate numbers of elephants, camels, and horses. The party was
supplied with every comfort of European civilization; at one point the
sportsmen roused a tiger from its hiding place by bombarding it with
Apollinaris water bottles.[49]

By the end of the nineteenth century improved rail transportation in
both India and Africa had eased some of the logistical problems of organizing an expedition, but the diminishing numbers of big game animals in the more accessible hunting grounds meant that sportsmen had
to make sure that the quarry they sought still existed and that they
would be able to shoot it legally. Usually this merely entailed examining
the game laws and licensing regulations of the territory in question, but
sometimes access to game posed a more complex and delicate problem.
In many Indian districts, where there were more prospective hunters
than the territory could accommodate, permission to shoot depended
on special connections to the presiding British officer; similarly, in regions still under Indian control, the rajahs preferred to share their sport
only with officials who could repay the favor in some way.[50]

Only after these preliminary strategic difficulties had been negoti-
ated could the sportsman head for the haunts of wild game, where he
was likely to encounter more tangible hardships. Most obvious were
those provided by the environment. Even near the end of the century,
when the lot of sportsmen had been eased by railroads, river steamers,
and the suppression by British soldiers of the most aggressive indigenes,
one manual warned that in the African bush hunters should expect, at
least, to lose their way and to experience dreadful thirst.[51] The life of
an elephant hunter was agreed by all who experienced it to be "one of
incessant hardship and danger."[52] According to Harris, those accustomed to the luxury of Indian sport could not imagine the "toils, trials,
and troubles, that beset the wanderer in the African desert." He painted
a painful picture of himself struggling back to camp after a day in the
field, laden with weapons, hunting gear, venison, and "the weight of the
ponderous trophies which had fallen to my rifle."[53] Yet India offered its
own hazards, mostly connected with the "infernal climate." Isabel Savory warned women who might be contemplating a tiger hunt not to

set out "without being prepared for a great deal of discomfort." The best season for shooting tigers in the Terai was during the last six weeks of the hot weather, and the best time of day was at noon, when the tigers descended to the swamps to cool themselves. Hunters had to endure not only the heat, with no mitigating wet towel, but parching thirst and the burning metal of their guns. The sport was, however, so fascinating that many unwisely exposed themselves to these inconveniences for protracted periods and suffered "the most pernicious consequences" to the constitution as a result.[54]

Even ostensibly solitary hunters did not expect to brave the dangers posed by climate and terrain in total isolation. To be really alone in the wilds was a fearful prospect, which not even the boldest and most seasoned adventurer would encounter willingly. Selous once experienced what he referred to as "the full horror" of this position, when villagers who had welcomed his retinue treacherously attacked them during the night. As "a solitary Englishman, alone . . . in the middle of a hostile country, without blankets or anything else but what he stood in, and a rifle with four cartridges," he wandered for days before finding some of his surviving servants; they were "mightily glad" and also extremely surprised to see him, for they had automatically given him up for dead.[55] In both India and Africa hunters were invariably accompanied by a train of native attendants, who were not considered to provide companionship, but who cooked, set up camp, and carried baggage. Besides these relatively menial tasks (although the bush dinners cataloged by some hunters made the cooks, at least, seem like persons of consequence),[56] natives also ordinarily performed one much more skilled function. Without trackers, or shikaris as they were known (with many orthographical variations) in India, there could be no hunting; that is, the desired quarry would not be found. English sportsmen were full of praise for "the extraordinary, intuitive knowledge which a few *shikaris* possess"; they freely acknowledged that "the white man can never hope to compete successfully with the black man in following the spoor of big game."[57]

But they found little else to praise about the human inhabitants of big game hunting grounds, who at best presented an endless series of obstacles to efficient management. In the view of sporting authors, the native character varied little from continent to continent. The Kirghiz, who guided hunters to the *ovis poli*, a wild sheep that provided the most coveted trophy in the mountains of northern India, was "a lazy man, and will not go a yard on his legs if he can avoid doing so." One African sportsman considered the indolence of the natives "the greatest obstacle to sport in this country"; another called Hottentots "necessary evils . . . lazy, useless dogs, receiving high wages and doing nothing, wanting to be masters, and making the trek very unpleasant."[58] This systematic disparagement was not restricted by race; subject white peoples were tarred with the same brush. To make his point clear to the home audience, one author compared the Hottentots' reluctance to work with that of the Irish. And although a few English hunters, including Selous, appreciated the "simple kindness and great hospitality" of the Boers, who had been the first European colonizers of southern Africa, most of his fellow Britons despised them as ignorant and indolent, "hardly one remove from the Kaffirs."[59] Despite his decreed dominance, the hunter was both dependent on and vulnerable to indigenous peoples, and sporting narratives often distilled the disquiet and revulsion they inspired by comparing them unfavorably to wild animals. Thus Samuel White Baker found the "antelope tribe . . . more agreeable than . . . the human inhabitants" of Africa; William Cornwallis Harris asserted that "in point of personal attractions, the pig-faced baboon, odious and disgusting though he be, has . . . perhaps rather the advantage of the genuine Bushman."[60]

In addition to laziness and insubordination, native Asians and Africans were frequently accused of cowardice. Sometimes these accusations functioned simply to illustrate and thereby maintain British superiority, as on one occasion when Selous swam to retrieve a hippopotamus carcass. He remarked that "it is very foolish doing this sort of thing in a river full of crocodiles, especially . . . when the water is warm, but one cannot help it, if only to show the natives that a white man will do what they dare not attempt."[61] But more often they were adduced as evidence of a kind of treachery, paradoxically both unthinkable and, in these circumstances, inevitable. If big game hunting was a metaphor for conquest, the native attendants filled the role of the commanding sportsman's foot soldiery. When real danger materialized, however, the scenario that unfolded might be very different from the battle behavior of trained British troops; the natives were likely to flee, abandoning their leader to face peril alone. Often such pusillanimity had serious consequences, as when a group of "numerous and armed" African retainers left a hunter to be mauled by a leopard, or when a "well-known sportsman" named Captain Smith was "severely injured" by a bear after his Indian attendants had run away.[62]

In the end, having surmounted the obstacles posed by red tape and geography, climate and human nature, the hunter had to meet his central test in isolation. One writer, somewhat disingenuously omitting the influence of weapons on the outcome, summarized the confrontation between sportsman and lion as "pluck against pluck—cucumber coolness and nerves of steel, against fangs and claws."[63] Even if his servants or fellow sportsmen were nearby, they were not acknowledged as participants in the hunter's tête-à-tête with his prey; indeed, sporting parties often subdivided every day, with each hunter taking a different direction, in order to ensure solitary engagements.[64] And while the peripheral obstacles could be surmounted by intelligence and perseverance, these admirable qualities were not sufficient to overcome the ultimate challenge posed by a dangerous and enraged quarry. That required the raw force and the delight in violence that hunting narratives were structured to emphasize and celebrate.

Although such intense confrontations were far from the rule, they

The ideal of hunting: individual confrontation.
From H. A. Leveson, *Hunting Grounds of the Old World*, 1860.

occupied more than their share of space. The occasional sporting author might minimize "the supposed dangers of jungle life," noting that
even when a water buffalo charged, "a steady shot . . . will always floor
him, or at any rate turn him from his attack"; but most narratives gave
the reverse impression. They devoted only perfunctory attention to
routine hunting episodes, dismissing in a few sentences the easy kills
that accounted for the vast majority of trophies.[65] This was true even if
the victim belonged to a particularly impressive species or if the bag
was distinguished for its size or variety. Gordon Cumming mentioned
only in passing that he "came upon an extremely old and noble black
rhinoceros lying fast asleep . . . I fired from the saddle"; with similar
offhandedness William Henry Drummond noted that he had killed
three rhinoceroses, two buffalo, a hyena, and a water antelope in one
night while safely concealed near a water hole.[66]

Big game narratives lavished space and emotion on the much rarer
encounters that allowed the sportsman to act his prescribed heroic
part—encounters in which the quarry was difficult to locate and dangerous when cornered, and in which a real (or at least plausible) threat
to the hunter's life counterpointed his ultimate triumph. An article in
Fraser's Magazine devoted four closely printed columns to the pursuit of
a single man-eating tiger, which eluded its stalkers (an "indefatigable"
English officer and his Indian attendants) for days while killing villagers
in their vicinity; the "blood-stained grass" that marked the sites of its
"horrid feasts" underscored "the monster's" malevolence. When it was
finally tracked down and wounded, it charged the hunter and attacked
the hindquarters of his elephant; at point-blank range the sportsman
"put the muzzle of his rifle to the skull of the tiger and blew it into fifty
pieces." The episodes that Selous chose to enlarge upon told a similar
story of risk and violence, as when a buffalo he had shot turned out to
be stunned rather than dead and rose to charge him as he leaned over
it, or when he had to aim "right for the open mouth" of a "wounded and
furious lion" that was about to jump one of his servants.[67] Paradigmati-
cally, such encounters resulted in the absolute domination of the hunted
animal by the sportsman—that is, in a splendid corpse lying at his intrepid feet. This tableau offered a rather abstract and general symbol of
English hegemony, but it also made a strong concrete statement about
the nature or sources of the power that supported it. The sportsman
had triumphed as a result of his ability to deploy superior physical

More typical odds. From Thomas Williamson,
Oriental Field Sports, 1807.

force, to reenact on a personal level the violent appropriation that underlay the serene majesty of empire.

The uncompromisingly physical nature of this domination was underscored by the two most frequently emphasized features of the climactic scene: a precise anatomical and ballistic analysis of how the kill was accomplished and a sentimentalized description of how the animal faced its demise. After a fast-moving, emotionally charged chase narrative, the account of the decisive moment was often coldly technical. Thus one sportsman shot a running buffalo "right through the spine and lungs"; another's first shot at a leopard "had taken her in the centre of the belly, and torn quite half of the intestines away"; another noted of a tiger that "a bullet from my gun entered his ear, and went crashing through the centre of his brain, as accurately as though I had measured the cavity with a pair of compasses."[68] As the animal was reduced to its component parts in these descriptions, the hunter became embodied in his rifle and ammunition. At the climax of an exciting elephant stalk, Selous coolly commented, "I took a careful aim for the ridge of bone which [runs] . . . from the root of the tail to the top of the back. My bullet, a solid toughened 540-grain missile, propelled by only 75 grains of powder, struck him exactly in the centre of the bone and stopped him instantly."[69] Such comments were often jarring; they interrupted the narrative flow and implicitly shifted its subject from romantic adventure to calculated butchery. Neither the frequency of these awkward statements nor their repeated occurrence precisely where they seemed most discordant was accidental. They were insistent reminders that the pursuit of big game, which could be celebrated in the mythic terms of high romance, was also, and importantly, a brutal act of violence.

As the hunts selected for extended discussion were those that showed the sportsman in the most heroic light, so writers tended to focus on the final struggles of only the noblest quarry—which meant those that fought most tenaciously to the end. For example, "the finest" of a group of nine female elephants encountered by Harris responded ferociously to his initial volley: "Streaming with blood, and infuriated with rage, she turned upon us with uplifted trunk, and it was not until after repeated discharges, that a ball took effect in her brain." Isabel Savory praised the "magnificent pluck" and "implacable defiance" shown by a boar of "grim, devilish temper" that "charged time after time at his pursuers" and required to be speared three times before it fell.[70] Descriptions of the animals' death scenes provided a counterpoint to both the passionate aggression of the chase and the detached efficiency of the slaughter. In addition to admiration, they seemed to offer a measure of sympathy, at least to the extent of converting the quarry, however briefly, from object to subject.

Occasionally this sympathy became explicit; after the quarry was safely bagged some hunters expressed regret at having killed it. Pangs might assail the sportsman who had destroyed a wild mother, whether her offspring had shared her fate or been orphaned, like the zebra foal that one rueful hunter discovered standing near his prize's body.[71] Sometimes even the most enthusiastic hunters seemed vulnerable to softer feelings. The nearly insatiable Gordon Cumming was reluctant to shoot wild dogs (among the most ferocious predators of the African plains) because the "jolly hounds . . . reminded me . . . of . . . my own noble deer-hounds." After the irreversible fact, sportsmen could even entertain second thoughts of an aesthetic nature. Giraffes were frequently cited as animals whose beauty and mildness made them problematic targets.[72] But the most frequent inspiration for such misgivings was the magnificence of the fallen foe. The sight of a slain tiger inspired one philosophical hunter to lament that she could "not help feeling sorry to see such a noble beast laid low." (She immediately went on to comment that "so great are the rejoicings when she is brought triumphantly into camp . . . that one's regrets are soon forgotten.") The conqueror of an Indian bison confessed "some feeling of remorse, however slight and fleeting, and regret that he would roam his forest solitudes . . . no more."[73]

The sympathy evinced by such responses was, however, barely skin deep. The fallen animal soon resumed its status as object, and the hunter as quickly prepared to fire again. A sportsman who wrote under the pen name "Maqaqamba" confessed that although he regretted every giraffe he shot, in the excitement of each new chase "away fly conscience, philosophy, and all such abstract considerations."[74] And the expression of regret for an especially noble antagonist served as clearly as the animal's physical remains to enhance the stature of the hunter. The appropriation implicit in the hunter's triumph also transcended the physical—although the physical appropriation could occasionally be startlingly profound, as when, having brought down "a beautiful cow" gemsbok with "two bullets in her shoulder," Gordon Cumming "milked her into my mouth, and obtained a drink of the sweetest beverage I ever tasted."[75] Along with the hide and horns, the victorious sportsman assumed the admirable moral qualities of his vanquished foe—and their shared ferocity and courage might elevate them both above lesser human types. Savory made the lesson explicit, concluding her description of the plucky boar at bay with the statement that "humans would do well if they could play the game of life as nobly, and meet death as callously."[76]

Sporting authors attempted to codify these concerns under the rubric of "good sport," which turned out to mean sport that allowed the hunter to display the most devastating physical aggression. Animals were endlessly compared according to the amount or quality of sport they provided—or, using a less veiled alternative vocabulary, the degree of danger they posed to the hunter. Drummond ranked the rhinoceros first among African animals, because it was liable to charge without provocation; then the lion, because "escape from its clutches is rare"; and then the buffalo, because of "the sudden and vicious nature of its charge." The elephant came last, because it lacked vindictiveness and would abandon pursuit even when its assailant was in full view.[77] Although these species offered "sporting replete with danger, and of real

interest," not every individual would provide equally good sport. As one
seasoned hunter warned enthusiastic tyros, "you will probably hunt
them nine times without seeing a charge ... and [the quarry] will die
with no more danger to yourself than if he had been a snipe."[78]

Such disappointing behavior might reflect the animal's weariness or
bad temper, but it might also result from the hunter's method of attack.
As one writer pointed out, "even the lion, that is a dangerous, bold, and
therefore worthy antagonist if met on foot at early dawn by his kill,
appears a very different creature if potted from a safe perch in a tree, or
brought to a stand by a pack of dogs."[79] Consequently, when "good
sport" was the main desideratum, sportsmen strove to stage confrontations in which the animal would be inspired to struggle rather than to
give up; a hierarchy of sporting techniques paralleled that of game animals. Practices that distanced the animal from his antagonist ranked
lowest; at the top were those that offered "the glorious chance of getting
badly hurt."[80] Barely in the category of sport were techniques that transformed hunters from participants into spectators. Thus coursing deer
with tame cheetahs was described as "despicable ... fit only for the false
and effeminate natives of India," and the elaborate game drives staged
by Indian (and some Anglo-Indian) potentates were "amusing for once,
afterwards ... merely disgusting."[81] This objection also applied to
smaller scale beats; according to the bloodthirsty Samuel White Baker,
even driving for tigers was apt to prove a "constant disappointment."
Another unsporting way to avoid the risk and trouble of entering a
predatory animal's environment was to offer it live bait in the form of a
tethered goat or bullock. Sitting in the dark waiting for a leopard or
tiger to turn up was denigrated as "weary work and poor sport."[82]

The best sport required the hunter to prove his personal physical
mettle—to overcome a dangerous and powerful animal on its own
terms. As a result, the fiercest opponents were often also the most attractive. In Africa that meant the lion, of which one sportsman asked
his readers, "when all your adventures pass in review before you, do you
not linger longest and with keenest pleasure upon the memory of ...
your fairly won triumphs over the maned monarch of the African hunt-
ing-veldt?" In Asia the tiger occupied a parallel position and provided,
in the eyes of some hunters, "the most exciting and glorious sport."[83]
But most aficionados celebrated pig sticking, in which horsemen armed
with spears chased wild boars, as "the very prince of sport" and "the

Pig sticking, the most glorious sport, according to
many Anglo-Indian hunters. From *Ackermann's Sporting Scraps*, 1850–51.

most delightful, noble, and exciting of all sports." It epitomized the
challenge sought by big game hunters. In part this reflected the nature
of the quarry. Although boars would fight furiously when cornered,
they were not dangerous unless provoked; thus exposure to their on-
slaught was entirely the consequence of the hunter's own aggressiveness
and daring (not always the case in encounters with big cats). The attractiveness of pig sticking also reflected the protocols of the sport. The
use of the spear rather than the gun allowed the hunter a uniquely immediate and physical participation in the death. It was little wonder
that, for many Anglo-Indians, "so great is the entertainment it affords,
that the pursuit of it becomes an infatuation."[84]

To the Victor the Spoils

In the view of its chroniclers big game hunting generously rewarded
both individual participants and the colonial order to which they belonged. Brother sportsmen experienced intense camaraderie in wilder-
ness encampments where, at the end of a successful day, the quarry "was
toasted in bumpers of Burgundy and Claret, with a spirit that roused

the excited feelings of the party to a pitch of enthusiasm"; in later years and safer places it was still "pleasant, sitting over a fire, talking to congenial companions about sport, . . . to fight our battles with big game over again." This enjoyment derived ultimately from the satisfaction of a lust for blood—the "insatiable desire for *slaying* something" cited by one sporting author—that was celebrated as a component of the English national character; it was both a sign and a support of imperial destiny.[85] Harris characterized killing game as a "passion . . . one of the most powerful affections of the human mind"; Baldwin could "imagine no greater enjoyment than in shooting . . . till every bone in my body ached"; and White delighted in "whole hecatombs of slaughter."[86] Each slain animal represented a personal assertion of dominance. Harris viewed his sporting mission as to effect the "humiliation of every wild beast." When Gordon Cumming saw five bull elephants walking in front of him and felt "that you can ride up and vanquish whichever one you fancy," he found the experience "so overpoweringly exciting that it almost takes a man's breath away."[87]

If the chance of violent domination was the main component of Gordon Cumming's enjoyment of the "intense and maddening excitement of the chase," it was complemented by a sense of "unrestrained freedom."[88] He was the lord of all he surveyed, and accountable to no one. And the primary liberty of hunting—to wander and kill at will—was reflected in a range of secondary releases from social convention, which were appreciated not only by men who had embraced bush life more or less permanently, but also by those on leave from the elaborately structured routine of colonial service. A Royal Artillery captain relished the opportunity to "feel like a wild man—to throw off all the restraints imposed by the rules of society." These restraints were symbolized by the "all-important" dress code of British colonial installations, which in the bush was "a dead letter." One happy hunter exulted that "a blue and white shirt and a stout pair of gaiters, with the addition of a cap and shoes, are all that I burden my body with."[89] The joy with which officers and officials embraced their release from "the *désagréments* of artificial existence" suggested some of the psychological hazards of tropical service; and official concern about preserving stocks of game at the end of the nineteenth century corroborated the need to maintain this "element of health" in the lives of men stationed for long periods in debilitating climates. As a veteran sportsman put it, "When bile and nervousness become too intolerable; when you feel yourself too shaky and cross and yellow-faced for anything; get a leave of absence, and ride into the jungle."[90]

Big game hunting also maintained and developed the qualities required in colonial officers and administrators in more positive and direct ways. Enthusiasts like Baker considered it "the best possible guarantee for the development of those manly attributes of mind and body which we are all taught to admire," and even a critic of blood sports admitted that they had some "justification, as means of development of physical manhood and sources of health and vigour." For young men posted to remote stations, who were at some risk of falling into dissolute ways, hunting might prove their moral as well as their physical salvation; a day in the field would leave them "too tired and too hungry to again go forth, yet invigorated and strengthened." A civilian official who was also a sportsman could be expected to be a "straightforward, honorable man," one likely to display "real feelings of humanity" in appropriate circumstances. Even extended sporting expeditions were not considered mere wasted time by the military hierarchy; in the view of his superiors the enthusiastic hunter was "exercising many of the faculties needed by the good soldier in action."[91]

As hunting success became an index of personal or professional worth—or as the bush became a figurative extension of the district office and the parade ground—intense competition developed over the testimonials of prowess. Sometimes the object of contention was simply credit for a shared kill, which was determined by a rigidly enforced convention "in order to avoid continual disputes": it belonged to whoever had landed the first shot or, in pig sticking, the first spear, even though he or she might have played "a very insignificant part" in the actual death. Attributions were eagerly coveted. Even Selous, whose tally of victims was immense, would not let any of the natives who accompanied him carry guns because "I very much object to any of my servants claiming an elephant which I think I have killed myself."[92]

But the real focus of competition was on the accumulation of objective correlatives, which could be counted, measured, assessed, and compared. Trophies sometimes functioned simply as synecdochic proof that the hunter had vanquished a given adversary. Following this custom, one sportsman who had turned soldier during the Matabele War preserved the ears of a slain African assailant. More conventionally, the deaths of animals too large (or shot in too great quantity) to be easily transported were commemorated in this way. Thus the Prince of Wales returned from India with the tail of an elephant he had shot (he had cut it off himself, amid the cheers of a crowd of onlookers). To one veteran sportsman a buffalo's tail—a "poor old dried bit of skin and hair . . . valueless as regards money"—was the coveted prize of a memorable chase.[93] Trophies collected in this spirit were essentially notches on a stick—even if they were more substantial, like "the mighty tusks of the huge African elephant, the skins of the lion, the leopard, and the cheetah . . . besides those of many an African antelope," which, according to one hunter, "told silently of stirring adventures in the bush."[94] Like the detailed tallies of daily and monthly bags that many sporting authors included in their narratives, such trophies made a crude equation between hunting prowess and numbers of animals killed.

But many hunters, especially as improved rifles made shooting of even very large animals easier, and diminishing game populations made massive bags seem wasteful and vulgar, turned to modes of accumulation based on connoisseurship rather than simple arithmetic. They amassed their trophy collections with increased subtlety and restraint, although no less competitively; indeed, a standard based on both physical force and judicious discrimination was more appropriate to the magisterial functions exercised by the colonial ruling class than one based on force alone. Desirable trophies needed to represent something more than just the death of an animal. In some cases the additional criteria derived from natural history. Simple rarity made the skin of the snow leopard "one of the most precious trophies a hunter can possess" and the horns of the roan antelope "more eagerly sought for" than the trophies of all but a few "animals in the whole African catalogue."[95] On a grander scale sophisticated sportsmen sought to collect series of all the game in a particular region. Thus one hunter boasted that "my collection of horns and *exuviae* . . . extended to every known species of game quadruped in Southern Africa," and another that he had "either killed or been present at the death of nearly every kind of wild beast found in India." A still more elaborate goal was projected by a hunter who desired for each species he shot "specimens of the skin of both sexes."[96]

The most refined discriminations combined aesthetic and quantitative considerations. Hunters whose goals were determined by these de-

Hippopotamus trophies. From Denis David Lyell,
Hunting Trips in Northern Rhodesia, 1910.

manding criteria tried hard to ascertain in advance that their intended prey was worth killing; they derived "no satisfaction whatever in killing an inferior head." Such self-imposed restrictions reduced the chances of success as well as the number of targets, because the "coveted prize . . . is often in the center of the herd and nothing can be done to obtain it."[97] Ostensibly, desirable trophies were distinguished by beauty. Thus Selous, his judgment honed by vast experience, was particularly anxious to secure prizes whose superior qualities could be described in the language of art: "a large lion with a fine mane," a "superb . . . koodoo bull . . . his horns . . . perfectly symmetrical, very long, and beautifully twisted," and a male lechwe antelope whose "elegant lyrate horns" were among the "handsomest of trophies."[98] To develop a similarly discriminating eye, the novice sportsman was advised to view the heads and horns on display at the American Exhibition of 1887, which were remarkable for both "size and beauty."[99] Their impressionistic component, however, compromised the utility of purely aesthetic standards. They did not offer a firm basis for ranking rival Nimrods; they needed to be supplemented by a criterion that allowed verifiable comparison.

Reducing any particular animal to a set of standardized statistics was

An African bag. From C. V. A. Peel, *Somaliland*, 1900.

no simple task. First, it had to be established what parts of the animal
were to be measured, and how (the branching antlers of deer and the
spiral horns of antelope presented special problems), and when (skins
often changed size soon after they were removed). In addition, hunters
needed guidance about the range within which their trophies could
reasonably be expected to fall. When he published *Records of Big Game*,
Rowland Ward, the premier taxidermist of late Victorian London, tact-
fully billed his compilation as an aid to "sportsmen and scientific men
who are interested to see comparable measurements at a glance"; but it
was doubtless also a restraint to hunters whose claims about the size of
their trophies tempted their readers to fancy, as one reviewer of the
literature of tiger shooting put it, that they "had served in the Ma-
rines."[100] A sportsman could be admired not only for accumulating
prizes but also for being "averse to guess-work . . . and most particular
in his actual measurements." One punctilious chronicler of his own exploits shifted breathlessly from bagging his markhor (a large wild goat)

to careful measurement with tape, which showed the horns to be forty-three and one-half inches around the curve and eleven and one-quarter inches in circumference.[101] This arena of competition combined the two attributes that distinguished colonial officials, at least in their own estimation. Accurately measuring trophies required the administrative virtues of rationality, precision, and truthfulness, while collecting a worthwhile trophy involved the exercise of force.

Furthermore, the criterion of size reintroduced the equation between the power of the quarry and the prowess of the sportsman who vanquished it. And size, or even strength, was not the only determinant of perceived power. Even before game laws made it illegal to shoot the females of many species, males were universally preferred as trophies. Sometimes there were quantifiable explanations for this preference. For example, in certain deer and antelope species only bucks had antlers or horns; in others, like the eland, in which the bull was "larger, fatter, and . . . tougher," the male was more imposing. But maleness also had intrinsic value. Thus one sportsman noted with disappointment that a tiger "of great size," which had given him an "extraordinary amount of trouble" turned out to be "only a tigress." The cataloger of Selous's vast collection emphasized that it was composed almost entirely of "mounted heads of adult male individuals." And conversely, one veteran Anglo-Indian found shooting female elephants inconceivable, although they gave "as good sport as males" and, indeed, usually charged first, because of his romantic "consideration for their sex."[102]

If big game hunting offered British officials respite from occupational stresses and made them better at their jobs, in some cases it could also constitute part of their imperial duty. When natives were threatened by wild animals, especially by man-eating predators, business and pleasure overlapped. One district officer, stationed in the midst of the Indian jungle, closed his court "*instanter* . . . whenever news was brought of a tiger, panther, or bear anywhere within twenty miles." He smugly noted that the natives appreciated this policy, because "during the time of my predecessor (who did not shoot) these creatures had increased to a very serious extent."[103] The provision of such services was not disinterested, however; at least in the retelling of sporting authors it filled several rhetorical functions. It emphasized the physical and moral superiority of Europeans to non-Europeans. One hunter had "never heard of natives attempting to destroy wolves . . . unless under the influence and guid-

ance of some European"; according to another, man-eating tigers were
"too cunning and dangerous to be frequently shot by native shikarries."
The urgency with which beleaguered natives besought valiant sportsmen to rid them of such scourges—one gratified hunter reported that
"the natives . . . hearing of our arrival, wait upon us, imploring us to rid
them of the lions that are preying on them"—reinforced their sense of
the fitness of the structure of colonial domination.[104] Correspondingly,
sportsmen found alterations in this relationship disquieting. From the
less expansive viewpoint of the fin de siècle, the younger brother of the
great Gordon Cumming regretted the old days in Ceylon, which had
then been populated by "a grateful people . . . ready to bless the white
man, who freed them from the incursions of dangerous foes."[105] In their
absence, it was less easy to understand big game hunting, or the imperial appropriation it symbolized, as equally beneficial to the rulers and
the ruled.

The Rules of the Game

One reason natives ceased to express their gratitude to English sportsmen was that the ferocious beasts from which they had previously required to be delivered troubled them less frequently. Throughout the
empire the dense accumulations of animals that had dazzled early adventurers were disappearing. What had seemed "a fairy-land of sport"
in the 1830s was only a memory at the end of the century; one experienced sportsman dismissed it with the past tense—"South Africa was,
of course, the hunter's paradise." Within a similar period the Nilgiri
mountains in India had ceased to be "happy hunting grounds." Bison,
sambur, bears, and wild sheep had all been driven off; "an occasional
tiger . . . is mobbed and slaughtered by the united efforts of a dozen
'sportsmen' of sorts."[106] As the balance of population in the bush shifted
to include more hunters and fewer animals, the code of sport altered
correspondingly. By both rhetoric and example, sportsmen who considered themselves enlightened attempted to replace an ethic that celebrated unbridled violence with one that emphasized discrimination and
restraint.

The proposed change required hunters to abandon cherished attitudes that were deeply embedded in the language of earlier sporting
literature. Harris complacently recalled firing into a herd of zebras and

antelopes and "leaving the ground strewed with the slain"; the *Field* recounted with approval a tale of "immense slaughter" and "carnage." George P. Sanderson, who supervised the official elephant catching establishment at Mysore, referred complacently to his hunting exploits as his "butcher's bill."[107] Relish for indiscriminate killing also surfaced in the tallies of victims featured in most big game narratives. A good day's bag might include 29 buffalo ("considerably the largest [number] I have ever seen killed in one day") or 9 bears ("the biggest bag on record").[108] The yield of an expedition or, as some martial sportsmen preferred to call it, a "campaign" could run to 150 hippopotamuses and 91 elephants ("a most splendid hunt").[109] The cumulative slaughter of a career provided the most satisfying figures of all. Thus one officer "bagged forty-four rhinoceros, twenty-eight tigers, innumerable buffaloes and deer" in his seven years stationed in Assam; had he been unencumbered by military obligations, he asserted, he "could have slain ten times what I did, but . . . marching . . . sadly interferes with sport." And on a still grander

An Indian bag. From Horace Gordon Hutchinson, ed.,
Big Game Shooting, 1905.

scale, one Bengal planter was reported to have killed between 400 and 500 tigers, another more than 1,000.[110]

During the final quarter of the nineteenth century such large numbers occurred less frequently in big game narratives. "Slaughter" and related terms, which had been used as colorful synonyms for sport, were increasingly opposed to a moralized ideal of hunting. As one writer expressed the distinction, "there is reasonable sport, and there is useless and unconsidered slaughter"; even the previously bloodthirsty *Field* began to condemn the "butchery" practised by many "so-called 'sportsmen,'" which it characterized as "grossly unsportsmanlike," "very selfish," "foolish," "wicked," "disgusting," and "tigerish." Conversely, in a review of Edward North Buxton's *Short Stalks*, Theodore Roosevelt praised him as "a skilled hunter, but not a game butcher."[111] In order to avoid castigation as slaughterers of game, sportsmen had to realize that "the actual killing of an animal . . . is not sport, unless the circumstances connected with it are such as to create that peculiar feeling which can only be expressed by the word 'sport.'" A "fair sportsman" wished simply to experience that heady sensation, not "to make a holocaust of game."[112]

Sportsmen who limited themselves to moderate bags demonstrated the unselfishness that was the cardinal virtue of the new sporting order. The consideration that was supposed to characterize their behavior extended even to animals; "true sportsmen" were presumed to be "humane."[113] Sometimes the exercise of humaneness simply meant not causing unnecessary pain, in particular, not attempting shots when the animal was likely to be wounded rather than killed, and not leaving wounded animals to suffer. It would be, therefore, "a most unsportsmanlike proceeding" for rhinoceros hunters "to risk wounding one of these rare and wonderful animals." Sometimes humaneness meant giving the quarry a sporting chance; one hunter confessed that when shooting tigers from a *machan* or blind, he "always had the feeling that . . . I was an unworthy foe—a mere assassin." Fair hunting certainly excluded "all such mean and cowardly contrivances as spring-guns, traps, and poisoned carcasses."[114] In most cases what was prescribed as humane treatment of animals turned out also to benefit brother sportsmen. Practices that gave hunters too large an advantage threatened to deplete stocks of game. One hunter fumed that "the rascally trick of poisoning kills with strychnine" had destroyed the tiger hunting in the Godavery jungles of southern India; incredibly, he reported, "a man who called

The spoils of a tiger hunt. From Isabel Savory,
A Sportswoman in India, 1900.

himself a sportsman" had introduced "this abominable practice." Another warned enthusiastic marksmen that "in the vicinity of ground
where they can be speared from horseback," the killing of wild pigs "by
other means is as unpardonable as that of the fox in the hunting-
countries of England."[115] Overall, the new code of sportsmanship encouraged big game hunters to reconceive their pastime as a complex
cooperative venture, in which the interests of many individuals were
inevitably involved even when the sportsman seemed most isolated.

Not every human predator in the African and Asian wilds was, however, included in the hunting community constituted by the revised
rhetoric of sportsmanship. The code of self-restraint and consideration
for others promulgated in late Victorian sporting literature implicitly
claimed the diminishing zoological resources of the savanna and the
jungle for those who hunted for pleasure. Simultaneously it denied the
right to hunt of the numerous other people who roamed the bush, most
of whom killed to satisfy material rather than emotional needs. Most
frequently criticized was the killing of animals for practical gain rather
than spiritual satisfaction, whether done for subsistence by native "pot-
hunters" or for profit by professional ivory collectors "pursuing . . . their
work of slaughter." Even an ostensible sportsman who sold some of his

trophies when he returned to Britain might find his enterprise castigated as "a tradesman's job."[116]

These criticisms clearly reflected a moral assumption about the hierarchy of motives for killing, but they also attempted to enforce a hierarchy of privilege among humans. Sordid motives were most commonly attributed to groups that sporting authors had other reasons to
disparage. A sportsman who advocated "the absolute suppression of 'the
nigger with the gun'" pointed out that natives were so irredeemably
unsporting as to shoot females in preference to males, and to be "doubly
satisfied" if the victim turned out to be pregnant. The frequently denigrated Boer "skinhunters" were "the personification of ignorance and
brutality." And even among the colonizers, adherence to the sporting
code distinguished the British from their morally inferior fellow Europeans. It was asserted, for example, that "the Latin races and Latinized
races have no conception of 'the sporting idea' so dear to the average
Briton."[117]

But as hunting grounds became increasingly crowded, it became clear
that some of their countrymen were guilty of flagrant offenses against
good sportsmanship. Perhaps the most egregious example came in 1909
when "an Englishman—to his shame, be it said—collected a number of desperadoes and indiscriminately slaughtered thousands of elephants" in East Africa.[118] Sporting authors responded with a campaign
to disparage certain British hunters, in which they employed the familiar language of British class distinction, even though the evidence did
not particularly suggest such a correlation. It was, for example, an aristocrat, Randolph Churchill, whose letters to the *Daily Graphic* described
a trip to Mashonaland in terms "distasteful to . . . sporting readers, by
reason of the wilful destruction of life in a cruel and unsporting manner
. . . as well as the utter callousness displayed in the recital, to the sufferings of the hapless victims of that day of butchery and funk."[119] Nevertheless, sporting rhetoric usually insinuated that vulgar elements were
responsible for low moral tone in the bush. Sometimes the suggestion
was gentle and humorous, as in *Punch's* condescending lampoons of in-
competent, fearful, and unattractive bourgeois sportsmen. A series of
cartoons entitled "Hints to Beginners.—Big Game Hunting" carried
such captions as "Bear shooting. Some breeds of Bear can Climb; others
cannot. Hunters of Experience recommend the Latter for Sport"; and
"Lion Hunting. Be quite sure when you go looking for a Lion, that you

really want to find one." More seriously, elite sportsmen might imply that hunters who did not conform to the code were not their type; according to one, "with the indiscriminate gunner . . . the writer will surely fail to 'hit it off.'" The *Field* went even further. It characterized greedy hunters who shot enormous bags as "unscrupulous individuals" who could not even be numbered among "the respectable classes in England."[120]

Despite such vigorous denigration, the rhetorical efforts embodied in big game hunting narratives were only partially successful. In part, this may have been because their acknowledged purpose of moral improvement was, in fact, secondary to their latent purpose of protecting the favorite imperial diversion. As a result, sporting authors often expressed ambivalent or contradictory attitudes, most frequently by praising the feats or envying the opportunities of free-wheeling hunters of an earlier period. Inconsistencies of this kind were occasionally noted at the time; for example, one hunter did "not consider it just that Gordon Cumming, Oswell, and Sir Samuel Baker . . . should be lauded to the skies," while their modern equivalents were "branded as cruel slaughterers."[121] Perhaps a more important obstacle to implementing the new sporting ethic on a voluntary basis was that it served the interests of only a fraction of the people whose activities it was designed to control, many of whom were not, in any case, either able or inclined to appreciate English sporting commentary. But the hunters whose interests it did serve were powerful people, and the widespread concern about threatened big game that was aroused at home and in the colonies by hunting narratives allowed them to transform the protection of their symbolic pastime into an empire-wide legal priority.

The Beginning of the End

The imposition of official restrictions on big game hunting symbolized the replacement of a forceful, confrontative model of colonial domination by one with greater emphasis on stewardship. The timing of this shift probably reflected changed political as well as ecological perceptions; in any case, it occurred long after the initial recognition of the effect of European colonization on wild animal populations. The ruthless commercial exploitation of North American fur-bearing animals provided the first dramatic example. In 1830 one naturalist compared the 1743 harvest of Canadian beaver skins—over one hundred and fifty thousand—with the fifty thousand gathered over a territory four times as large in 1827.[122] During the same period, parallel (if less marked) tendencies were observable in British Asia. In 1831 an Indian sporting journal published "the dismal bodings of some of the people" that Nilgiri elk "will soon become extinct"; a few years later a veteran hunter confirmed that in the past tigers had been "more numerous . . . than they are now."[123] Even earlier, visitors to southern Africa routinely commented on the impoverishment of its originally rich and varied fauna. After his travels of 1797 and 1798, John Barrow complained that the Cape "affords but a narrow field for the inquiries of the Zoologist" because its wolves, hyenas, and antelopes had disappeared. A decade later William Burchell noted that the formerly common eland was "becoming daily more scarce," and the rhinoceros was "rarely to be met with." On his way to decimate the still numerous animals of the interior in the mid-1830s, Harris lamented, "Alas! in the Colony of the Cape . . . how have the wild sports dwindled from their former prosperity."[124] Before the end of the eighteenth century the southern tip of Africa had even lost a mammalian species—the blaubok, an antelope with a very limited range—to extinction.[125]

Despite Harris's elegiac tone, most of these observations were offered as matters of fact rather than of regret. If new territories were to be aggressively appropriated by Europeans who intended to exploit them more productively, their previous occupants would inevitably have to give way. Thus through most of the nineteenth century the British government of India encouraged hunters to clear the game from large areas, in order to make them available for cultivation. One complacent civil servant celebrated the "extermination of wild beasts in the great food-producing districts" as one of "the undoubted advantages which India has derived from British rule."[126] Observers in British Africa, where there was no centralized government to institute such a policy, agreed that game tended to retreat before what was uniformly and appreciatively described as "the advance of civilisation."[127]

The notions of "retreat to remote parts" and local extermination tended to recur in somewhat inconsistent juxtaposition.[128] That is, those who noticed that the game had vanished from a given locality assumed not that the animals had all been killed but that they had withdrawn to some wilder, less accessible place. And it was true that such territories were often more richly stocked. When Dr. Livingstone saw a herd of buffalo parading slowly before his campfire and numerous eland grazing fearlessly nearby, he deduced that he was the first white visitor in the neighborhood. By the 1880s, according to Selous, rhinoceros and Lichtenstein's hartebeest were "only to be met with in the 'fly' country"—the vast area within which horses and cattle quickly succumbed to sleeping sickness. Well into the second half of the century some sportsmen cherished the goal of discovering virgin hunting grounds, filled with animals that had not yet learned to fear men with firearms; one hunter on such a quest "expected to find plenty of big game, as it was a new country, and no English sportsman had shot over it previously."[129]

But as exploration and conquest shrank the blank spaces on the map, it became more difficult to believe that the animals that no longer inhabited colonized districts had simply decamped to parts unknown. Disquieting reports from across the empire told the same tale of diminishing game populations. Even an optimistic turn-of-the-century assessment of African hunting possibilities claimed only that "Africa . . . will not be shot out for many a long year" and admitted that there was "some element of truth" in the notion that it was "getting played out."[130] At about the same time, it became clear that not only were large areas at risk of losing their fauna, but in addition many whole kinds of animals were on the verge of vanishing permanently. The rapid disappearance of the vast bison herds that had roamed the Great Plains of North America shocked British sportsmen, even though bison hunting itself was considered no great loss—the excitement "soon palls" and "one Buffalo head is like another." Although Yellowstone National Park was founded in 1872 to protect the few remaining animals, the success of this pioneering preservation effort was long in doubt. Over thirty years later British preservationists cited the case of the North American bison as evidence that "if a species is . . . reduced to a single small herd . . . its ultimate total destruction is highly probable."[131] More disturbing to British sportsmen, because it happened in a part of the world for which their government was responsible, was the loss of the quagga, a striped relative of the zebra and the donkey that had once been numerous throughout southern Africa. As late as 1875 an expedition to Matabeleland found "more quagga and sable antelopes than any other game," but little more than a decade later it had disappeared completely, "shot down," according to one zoologist, "for the sake of its hide." Its extinction was castigated as an example of human "folly and greed" and as "a disgrace to our latter-day civilization."[132]

Gradually the point of view that had accepted the elimination of wild animals from appropriated districts as an inevitable by-product of progress was replaced by one that viewed them as a valuable resource requiring protection. Still symbolic of uncivilized nature, game no longer represented a serious threat; instead, it evoked the special kind of property—ambiguously neither public nor private—that Britons felt they possessed in their Asian and African territories. Gradually and piecemeal, late nineteenth-century colonial administrations throughout the empire placed legal restrictions on human exploitation of big game animals. Predictably, the most heavily settled jurisdictions were the first to adopt the codes. In Asia British efforts such as the Nilgiris Game and Fish Preservation Act of 1879, which protected bison, sambars, ibex, jungle sheep, deer, and hares, as well as a variety of birds and fish, and the Elephants' Preservation Act of 1879, which prohibited the killing of wild elephants unless they threatened human life or property, supplemented the extensive game reserves maintained by the rajahs who ruled the Native States.[133] In South Africa the hunting of buffalo, quaggas, zebras, hares, and antelopes was limited by a Natal ordinance of 1866; the Cape Colony extended systematic protection to elephants, giraffes, hippopotamuses, buffalo, zebras, quaggas, and antelopes in 1886, in the process repealing a few feeble restrictions enacted sixty years earlier. In the 1890s the first game reserves were established in southern and eastern Africa.[134]

If protection of their threatened game symbolized British stewardship of its colonies, then concern about the similar plight of creatures controlled by other powers may have been an oblique expression of Britain's claim to international preeminence. And pragmatically, international cooperation was necessary for preservation measures to work. Thus in 1900 representatives of the European governments with colonies in sub-Saharan Africa met in London and eventually signed the "Convention for the Preservation of Wild Animals, Birds and Fish in Africa," the substance of which had been proposed by the British delegation. The purpose of the convention was "saving from indiscriminate slaughter, and . . . insuring the preservation . . . of the various forms of animal life which are either useful to man or are harmless." Its provisions, which reflected the most enlightened contemporary sporting opinion, included absolute prohibitions on hunting the few species considered to be threatened with extinction (this short list included the giraffe, gorilla, chimpanzee, mountain zebra, wild ass, white-tailed gnu, eland, and the pigmy hippopotamus); the protection of females and young of other species; the establishment of quotas for individual hunters; the establishment of game reserves within which no hunting would be allowed; the prohibition of hunting during the breeding season; the requirement that hunters purchase licenses and that exporters of hides and horns pay duties; and the prohibition of such methods of killing as nets, pits, and dynamite.[135] That the other signatories may not have been so interested in preservation as the British was suggested by the official correspondence of the next decade, which contained frequent references to lack of cooperation on the part of the Belgians, Germans, and Portuguese. But the Colonial Office, sensitive to the desires of the sporting elite, was active in implementing the spirit of the convention, at least to the extent that successive colonial secretaries urged colonial administrators to embody its recommendations in their laws and to report regularly on their success in enforcing them.[136] Within a few years ordinances and acts on this model had been promulgated not only throughout British Africa, but as far afield as Malaya.[137]

Adopting regulations was one thing, however, and enforcing them was another. Although the Colonial Office was generous with encouragement for preservation, it was stingy with funds to pay for policing vast unsettled areas. As a result, few violations were punished. The government of Uganda, for example, prosecuted only eleven people for shooting prohibited animals in 1906, of whom six were excused on grounds of self-defense.[138] In addition, not all colonial administrators were equally enthusiastic about protecting big game. Many sympathized strongly with sportsmen and enrolled as members of the Society for the Preservation of the Wild Fauna of the Empire when it was founded in 1903—Sir Harry Johnston, recent high commissioner for Uganda, even joined such distinguished sporting authors as Selous, Edward North Buxton, Henry Seton-Karr, H. A. Bryden, and Abel Chapman when they called on the colonial secretary to promote the society's objectives. But some endorsed the discontent expressed by those with competing interests.[139] The multiplicity of opinion on this issue was an index of how complicated imperial overlordship had become; it could no longer be adequately represented by such straightforward dualities as European versus native or civilized versus wild.

Far from uniting the inhabitants of a given colony, or even the European inhabitants, attempts to protect big game animals seemed both to symbolize and to exacerbate their differences. Settlers often resented the superior privileges that game laws accorded civilian administrators, military officers, and sportsmen, licensing them to kill a few samples of most protected species, while restricting settlers to the most common antelopes. A more profound grievance reflected considerations of economics rather than status. Wild animals competed directly with humans for a finite amount of land; tracts set aside for game reserves could not be used for farming. As local planters in British Central Africa claimed in 1906 when they petitioned (ultimately with success) for the reduction of the Elephant Marsh Reserve, lions and other predators might emerge from the reserves to kill people and livestock; grazers and browsers from elephants to antelope might raid and trample crops; and wild animals might infect domestic animals with disease. Often complaints reflected the strength of the settlers' feelings more than the actual threat posed by the animals. For example, fears of contagion focused on sleeping sickness, to which many wild species were immune, even though prominent zoologists like Ray Lankester of the British Museum (Natural History) cautioned that there was no evidence that such animals could transmit the disease, and on rinderpest or cattle plague, which had demonstrably been introduced to both India and Africa by European cattle, and which had decimated indigenous bovines, deer, and antelope. Nevertheless, these representations were apt to be persuasive. In 1908 the game laws of British East Africa were restructured so as not to expose settlers to "the depredations of wild animals," and the governor promised that future enforcement would respect the principle that "the preservation of game cannot be allowed to interfere with the economic development of the country."[140]

Game laws also triggered expression of white hostility toward native Africans. Although settlers sometimes cited black farmers as fellow sufferers from the raids of wild animals on field and fold, more often they joined ranks with sportsmen to protest any special recognition of traditional hunting rights incorporated into the regulations. Hunters impatient of heavy license fees and restrictions on their bags regarded the local tribesmen as competitors with an unfair edge. One complained

that they "love to show their zeal toward the Government by reporting
. . . every . . . elephant . . . shot," while "cases of a native reporting another . . . for breaking the game regulations are extremely few." And as
settlers were impelled to find reasons that game deserved not to be
protected, whites responded that the natives deserved to lose their
hunting rights. Despite the incontrovertible association between the
advent of white hunters and the depletion of wild animal populations,
it was often alleged that natives with modern weapons, and not white
sportsmen, were responsible for the rapid disappearance of game. It
was, according to one sportsman, "not the British gunner, who shoots
. . . carefully and in a husband-like manner," who was "exterminating the
game of Africa" but "the African himself, who, armed with a cheap gun,
is dealing destruction daily and hourly, for ever creeping about the
bush, and with endless patience, manoeuvring until he can gain a certain shot."[141]

Thus the kind of domination represented by big game hunting had
altered significantly in the course of the nineteenth century. No longer
was it the emblem of armed European conquest of territories that
seemed particularly threatening and alien. Despite continual skirmish-
ing, the main task of the late Victorian empire was administration, and
the significance of hunting evolved to reflect this more sophisticated
and less overtly brutal assignment. Once practically a duty for any Englishman who found himself in the colonies, killing large wild animals
was redefined as a privilege for which the demand outstripped the supply. The sporting code, which had been rough and ready for most of
the century, especially in Africa, began to impose more self-restraint on
hunters; furthermore, it compromised the easy camaraderie of the field
by reintroducing the class distinctions of the old country. Hunting policy and rhetoric had to balance the competing interests of many groups,
rather than vigorously but unreflectingly prosecute a single appropriative purpose.

Nevertheless, big game hunting still represented dominion, even
though its primary mode was protection rather than unrestrained
slaughter. At the most basic level no threats were tolerated. Predators
were specifically excluded from protection under the convention of
1900 and under the many colonial ordinances based on its provisions.
In the first decade of the twentieth century the Indian government still
offered rewards for killing tigers and the Transvaal government still of-

fered rewards for killing lions. Sir Harry Johnston, an active preserva-
tionist, "never attempted to check the slaughter" of the hippopotamuses
in the Shire River, which he characterized as "very vicious and fond of
pursuing and upsetting canoes."[142] But these instances were exceptional;
in general, fewer and fewer threats were encountered. Big game hunting, the most atavistic and antagonistic connection between humans
and animals, became the fitting emblem of the new style in which the
English dominated both the human and the natural worlds. The need
to conquer through force had almost disappeared, leaving an urgent
new need to husband and manage, to protect and exploit.

Notes

Illustration Credits

Index

Notes

Introduction

1. Keith Thomas, *Man and the Natural World: A History of the Modern Sensibility* (New York: Pantheon, 1983), 97–98; William Shakespeare, *The Merchant of Venice*, act 5, sc. 1, ll. 133–134; Edward Payson Evans, *The Criminal Prosecution and Capital Punishment of Animals* (London: William Heinemann, 1906), 129–130, 10–11.

2. Following convention, I have used "animals" to refer to mammals other than human beings.

3. Evans, *Criminal Prosecution*, 256; Arthur Koestler, *Reflections on Hanging* (London: Victor Gollancz, 1956), 71–72.

4. *The England and Empire Digest* (London: Butterworth, 1976), II, 387, 395.

5. Not all of them are discussed in the following chapters, but those omitted, most notably fox hunting, coursing, and horse racing, follow patterns illustrated with different examples.

6. Thomas Bewick, *A Memoir of Thomas Bewick, Written by Himself*, ed. Iain Bain (1862; rpt. Oxford: Oxford University Press, 1975), 105. In addition to Bewick's autobiographical *Memoir*, Montague Weekley, *Thomas Bewick* (London: Oxford University Press, 1953), and Iain Bain, *Thomas Bewick: An Illustrated Record of His Life and Work* (Newcastle: Tyne and Wear County Council Museums, 1979), and a range of nineteenth-century appreciations, provide information about his life and work.

7. Bewick, *Memoir*, 107; S. Roscoe, *Thomas Bewick: A Bibliography Raisonné of Editions of the "General History of Quadrupeds," the "History of British Birds" and the "Fables of Aesop" Issued in His Lifetime* (London: Oxford University Press, 1953), 9; Roscoe presents the publishing history of *A General History* on pp. 5–38.

8. Connoisseurs began to appreciate Bewick's work before his death in 1828, and to accommodate them he produced several hundred volumes in each edition in the

relatively elaborate royal and imperial octavo formats, which could cost several times as much as the workaday demy octavos intended for ordinary readers. See, for example, the elaborate orders sent in on behalf of himself and his collecting friends by J. F. M. Dovaston, a connoisseur and amateur naturalist who became friendly with the elderly Bewick. Thomas Bewick, *Bewick to Dovaston: Letters 1824–1828,* ed. Gordon Williams (London: Nattali and Maurice, 1968), 26, 40–43; Thomas Hugo, *The Bewick Collector: A Descriptive Catalogue of the Works of Thomas and John Bewick* (1866; rpt. New York: Burt Franklin, 1970), I, xiv.

9. James Rennie, *Alphabet of Zoology, for the Use of Beginners* (London: Orr and Smith, 1833), 6.

10. Thomas Bewick, *A General History of Quadrupeds* (Newcastle: T. Bewick, 1824), 125–126, 167–168.

11. Quoted from an unidentified "local paper" in Robert Robinson, *Thomas Bewick: His Life and Times* (1887; rpt. Newcastle: Frank Graham, 1972), xxiv.

12. Quoted in Robinson, *Thomas Bewick,* 84.

13. See David Elliston Allen, *The Naturalist in Britain: A Social History* (1976; rpt. Harmondsworth, Middlesex: Penguin Books, 1978), chs. 2 and 3, for a discussion of how natural history became a fashionable pastime. Keith Thomas's *Man and the Natural World* includes the development of widespread interest in natural history as part of a survey of attitudes toward nature in early modern Britain.

14. For bibliographical information about the literature of natural history, see especially R. B. Freeman, *British Natural History Books, 1485–1900: A Handlist* (Folkestone, Kent: Dawson, 1980); also David M. Knight, *Natural Science Books in English, 1600–1900* (New York: Praeger, 1972), and *Zoological Illustration: An Essay towards a History of Printed Zoological Pictures* (Folkestone, Kent: Dawson, 1977); and S. Peter Dance, *The Art of Natural History: Animal Illustrators and Their Work* (London: Country Life Books, 1978).

15. George Shaw, *General Zoology; or, Systematic Natural History* (London: G. Kearsley, 1800), I, vii.

16. John Feather, *The Provincial Book Trade in Eighteenth-Century England* (Cambridge: Cambridge University Press, 1985), 33, 40; Charles Wilson, *First with the News: The History of W. H. Smith, 1792–1985* (London: Jonathan Cape, 1985), 31–32. See J. H. Plumb, "The Commercialization of Leisure in Eighteenth-Century England" and "The Acceptance of Modernity," in Neil McKendrick, John Brewer, and J. H. Plumb, *The Birth of a Consumer Society: The Commercialization of Eighteenth-Century England* (Bloomington: Indiana University Press, 1982), for an account of the commercial exploitation of literacy for leisure purposes and the spreading interest in science as a source of avocational activity.

17. Bewick, *Bewick to Dovaston,* 39. For additional information about natural history literature for children, see R. B. Freeman, "Children's Natural History Books before Queen Victoria," *History of Education Society Bulletin* 17 (1976), 7–21, and 18 (1976), 6–34; J. H. Plumb, "The First Flourishing of Children's Books," in *Early Children's Books and Their Illustration* (New York: Pierpont Morgan Library and Boston: David R. Godine, 1975), xviii–xix, xxiv; and Harriet Ritvo, "Learning from Animals: Natural History for Children in the Eighteenth and Nineteenth Centuries," *Children's Literature* 13 (1985), 72–93.

18. C. Kirke Swann, "Natural History Bookselling," *Journal of the Society for the Bibliography of Natural History* 6 (1972), 118. According to William Noblett, as early as the 1770s Benjamin White (the brother of Gilbert White of Selborne) both published and

stocked an unusual number of works about natural history; in addition, his shop served as a meeting place for naturalists. See Noblett, "Pennant and His Publisher: Benjamin White, Thomas Pennant and *Of London*," *Archives of Natural History* 11 (1982), 63, 65.

19. Susan Sheets-Pyenson, "War and Peace in Natural History Publishing: *The Naturalist's Library*, 1833–1843," *Isis* 72 (1981), 60.

20. In this case the publishers' optimism was less well founded. They had apparently overestimated the demand and competed too intensely for a relatively small market. Most of these ventures folded after a few years, and even the survivors could count on circulations of only about five hundred. Susan Sheets-Pyenson, "A Measure of Success: The Publication of Natural History Journals in Early Victorian Britain," *Publishing History* 9 (1981), 21–22, 29–31. For an analysis of the marketing strategy of one of the more successful periodicals, see her "From the North to Red Lion Court: The Creation and Early Years of the *Annals of Natural History*," *Archives of Natural History* 10 (1981), 221–249.

21. Edward Newman, "Preface," *Zoologist* 2 (1844), v; Edward Newman, "Preface," *Zoologist* 4 (1846), v.

22. G. R. de Beer, *Sir Hans Sloane and the British Museum* (London: Oxford University Press, 1953), 111, 121; Edward Miller, *That Noble Cabinet: A History of the British Museum* (Athens, Ohio: Ohio University Press, 1974), 71; Mildred Archer, *Natural History Drawings in the India Office Library* (London: HMSO, 1962), 1; Desmond Ray, *The India Museum, 1801–1879* (London: HMSO, 1982), 36–38.

23. Thomas Frost, *The Old Showmen and the Old London Fairs*, (London: Chatto and Windus, 1881), 161; Richard D. Altick, *The Shows of London* (Cambridge, Mass.: Harvard University Press, 1978), 35–49; Thomas Bewick, *The Watercolours and Drawings of Thomas Bewick and His Workshop Apprentices*, ed. Iain Bain (London: Gordon Fraser, 1981), I, 26–27. For an extended discussion of exhibitions of live wild animals, see below, Chapter 6.

24. Bewick, *General History*, 381; William Wood, *Zoography; or, The Beauties of Nature Displayed* (London: Cadell and Davies, 1807), I, 195.

25. Thomas Boreman, *A Description of Three Hundred Animals, viz. Beasts, Birds, Fishes, Serpents, and Insects* (1730; rpt. London: R. Ware, 1736), 0; Philip Henry Gosse, *Natural History: Mammalia* (London: Society for Promoting Christian Knowledge, 1848), iii.

26. George Thompson, *Travels and Adventures in Southern Africa, Comprising a View of the Present State of the Cape Colony with Observations on the Progress and Prospects of British Emigrants* (London: Henry Colburn, 1827), I, v.

27. "Suggestions Offered on the Part of the Literary and Philosophical Society of Liverpool, to Members of the Mercantile Marine, Who May Be Desirous of Using the Advantages They Enjoy for the Promotion of Science, in Furtherance of Zoology," *Proceedings of the Literary and Philosophical Society of Liverpool during the Fifty-First Session, 1861–62* (Liverpool: Thomas Brakell, 1862), Appendix II, 1, 2, 46.

28. *Encyclopedia Britannica; or, A Dictionary of Arts and Sciences, Compiled upon a New Plan* (Edinburgh: A. Bell and C. Macfarquhar, 1771), III, 326ff.

29. On the bestiary, see Montague Rhodes James, *The Bestiary, Being a Reproduction in Full of the Manuscript Ii.4.26 in the University Library, Cambridge . . . and a Preliminary Study of the Latin Bestiary as Current in England* (Oxford: Roxburghe Club, 1928); and T. J. Elliot, "Foreword," in *A Medieval Bestiary* (Boston: David R. Godine, 1971).

30. Edward Topsell, *The Historie of Four-Footed Beastes* (London: William Iaggard,

1607), 711–721, 103–107. Topsell's work was based on the five-volume *Historia Animalium* of the Swiss scholar Konrad Gesner, which had been published half a century earlier.

31. See Thomas, *Man and the Natural World*, 53–57, for a discussion of the understanding of these oppositions in early modern England.

32. Henry Peacham, *The Gentleman's Exercise . . . or, An exquisite Practice . . . for Drawing All Manner of Beasts . . .* (London: I. M., 1634), 51–52.

33. Joseph Strutt, *The Sports and Pastimes of the People of England . . . from the Earliest Period to the Present Time* (London: Chatto and Windus, 1876), 75; P. B. Munsche, *Gentlemen and Poachers: The English Game Laws, 1671–1831* (Cambridge: Cambridge University Press, 1981), 3–6.

34. For examples of the projects that engaged seventeenth-century naturalists in England, see Allen, *Naturalist in Britain*, 6–11; Thomas Birch, *The History of the Royal Society of London for Improving of Natural Knowledge from Its First Rise* (London: A. Millar, 1756–1757), I, 220, 393. On early English naturalists, see generally Charles E. Raven, *English Naturalists from Neckam to Ray* (Cambridge: Cambridge University Press, 1947).

35. Wood, *Zoography*, I, xvii. For some philosophical implications of Linnaean and related taxonomies, see Donald Worster, *Nature's Economy: A History of Ecological Ideas* (1977; rpt. Cambridge: Cambridge University Press, 1985), ch. 2.

36. William Swainson, *A Preliminary Discourse on the Study of Natural History* (London: Longman, Rees, Orme, Brown, Green, and Longman, 1834), 108; William Holloway and John Branch, *The British Museum; or, Elegant Repository of Natural History* (London: John Badcock, 1803), I, iii.

37. William Burchell, *Travels in the Interior of Southern Africa* (London: Longman, Hurst, Rees, Orme, and Brown, 1822–1824), II, 207.

38. Mary Trimmer, *A Natural History of the Most Remarkable Quadrupeds, Birds, Fishes, Serpents, Reptiles, and Insects* (1825; rpt., abridged, Boston: S. G. Goodrich, 1829), 4; [Stephen Jones], *The Natural History of Beasts, Compiled from the Best Authorities* (London: E. Newbery, 1793), ix. For a recent restatement of this point of view, see Robert Delort, *Les Animaux ont une Histoire* (Paris: Seuil, 1984), 217.

39. Charles Hamilton Smith, *Introduction to the Mammalia* (Edinburgh: Lizars, 1842), 74; William Swainson, *On the Habits and Instincts of Animals* (London: Longman, Orme, Brown, Green and Longmans, 1840), 176.

40. Smith, *Introduction to Mammalia*, 74.

41. Charles Darwin, *The Variation of Animals and Plants under Domestication* (New York: D. Appleton, 1892), II, 19–21.

42. Abraham Bartlett, *Wild Animals in Captivity*, comp. and ed. Edward Bartlett (London: Chapman and Hall, 1899), 23.

43. Francis Galton, "Gregariousness in Animals," *Macmillan's Magazine* 23 (1871), 353–357.

44. Charles Darwin, "A Preliminary Notice: 'On the Modification of a Race of Syrian Street-Dogs by Means of Sexual Selection,'" in *The Collected Papers of Charles Darwin,* ed. Paul H. Barrett (Chicago: University of Chicago Press, 1977), II, 279.

45. John Charles Hall, *Interesting Facts Connected with the Animal Kingdom* (London: Whittaker, 1841), 51. For further discussion of this comparison, which was originated by Buffon, who attributed the inferiority of American animals and humans to the newness and coldness of the continent, see Ray Allen Billington, *Land of Savagery, Land of*

Promise: The European Image of the American Frontier in the Nineteenth Century (New York: W. W. Norton, 1981), ch. 1. A later Darwinian variant stressed the dominance of northern, specifically European forms, over those native to the tropics and the southern hemisphere. Janet Browne, *The Secular Ark: Studies in the History of Biogeography* (New Haven: Yale University Press, 1983), 130. See Alfred W. Crosby, *Ecological Imperialism: The Biological Expansion of Europe, 900–1900* (Cambridge: Cambridge University Press, 1986), esp. ch. 6, for an explanation of the reality that underlay these perceptions.

46. Bartlett, *Wild Animals in Captivity*, 61.

47. Burchell, *Travels*, II, 328–329.

48. Richard Badham Thornhill, *The Shooting Directory* (London: Longman, Hurst, Rees, and Orme, 1804), ix.

49. T. W. Barlow, "A Few Words on the Question, Do the Inferior Animals Possess Intellectual Powers or Not?" *Zoologist* 3 (1845), 907; *The Natural History of Domestic Animals, Containing an Account of Their Habits and Instincts, and of the Services They Render to Man* (Dublin: J. Jones, 1821), v.

50. William Hamilton Drummond, *The Rights of Animals, and Man's Obligation to Treat them with Humanity* (London: John Mardon, 1838), 82.

51. They were frequently peddled in the streets of London by countrymen who had caught them. S. O. Beeton, *Beeton's Book of Home Pets* (London: Ward, Lock and Tyler, n.d.), 673–678; Henry Mayhew, *London Labour and the London Poor* (New York: Dover, 1968), II, 77.

52. *The Natural History of Domestic Animals*, 84, 106.

53. Edward Jesse, *Gleanings in Natural History, Third and Last Series* (London: John Murray, 1835), 175; *Animal Sagacity, Exemplified by Facts Showing the Force of Instinct in Beasts, Birds, &c.* (Dublin: W. Espy, 1824), 130–132.

54. Holloway and Branch, *British Museum*, II, 181.

55. Bewick, *General History*, 50; Thomas Bell, *A History of British Quadrupeds, Including the Cetacea* (London: John Van Voorst, 1837), 416.

56. Charles John Cornish, *Wild Animals in Captivity; or, Orpheus at the Zoo and Other Papers* (New York: Macmillan, 1894), 293. For a more systematic analysis of the replacement of the ox by the horse as a draft animal, see J. A. Perkins, "The Ox, the Horse, and English Farming, 1750–1850," Working Paper in Economic History (University of New South Wales, 1975).

57. The development of this genre has been documented in Judy Egerton, *British Sporting and Animal Paintings, 1655–1867: A Catalogue* (London: Tate Gallery, 1978), and Judy Egerton and Dudley Snelgrove, *British Sporting and Animal Drawings c. 1500–1850: A Catalogue* (London: Tate Gallery, 1978).

58. Bewick, *General History*, 3.

59. Holloway and Branch, *British Museum*, I, 145.

60. Philip Hamerton, *Chapters on Animals* (Boston: Roberts Brothers, 1874), 74.

61. Thomas Pennant, *British Zoology: A New Edition* (London: Wilkie and Robinson, 1812), I, 11.

62. Gosse, *Natural History: Mammalia*, 170; Edward Jesse, *Gleanings in Natural History, with Local Recollections* (London: John Murray, 1832), 244.

63. Hamerton, *Chapters*, 20.

64. William Swainson, *On the Natural History and Classification of Quadrupeds* (London: Longman, Rees, Orme, Browne, Green, and Longman, 1835), 137.

65. Bewick, *General History*, 325; William Broderip, *Zoological Recreations* (London: Henry Colburn, 1847), 175.

66. Darwin, *Variation*, II, 226.

67. The admiring view of canine character espoused by nineteenth-century naturalists was of relatively recent origin. For discussions of the less flattering opinions held in earlier periods, see William Empson, "The English Dog," in *The Structure of Complex Words* (New York: New Directions, 1951), 158–174, and Ronald Paulson, "The English Dog," in *Popular and Polite Art in the Age of Hogarth and Fielding* (Notre Dame, Ind.: University of Notre Dame Press, 1979), 49–63. In his autobiography Bewick echoed this view, noting that although dogs were loyal and servile to their masters, "to his own species he is ill-behaved, selfish, cruel, and unjust; he only associates with his fellows for the purpose of packing together to destroy other animals" (*Memoir*, 120–121).

68. Gosse, *Natural History: Mammalia*, 81.

69. Bell, *British Quadrupeds*, 195; John Timbs, *Strange Stories of the Animal World: A Book of Curious Contributions to Natural History* (London: Griffith and Farran, 1866), 19.

70. Hamerton, *Chapters*, 34.

71. Bingley, *Animal Biography*, I, 202.

72. John Church, *A Cabinet of Quadrupeds with Historical and Scientific Descriptions* (London: Darton and Harvey, 1805), I, n.p.; Swainson, *Habits and Instincts*, 71; Bewick, *General History*, 146–147.

73. [Eleanor Frere Fenn], *The Rational Dame; or, Hints towards Supplying Prattle for Children* (London: John Marshall, [c. 1800]), 36.

74. Bewick, *General History*, 377; Bell, *British Quadrupeds*, 354–355.

75. Francis T. Buckland, *Curiosities of Natural History, Second Series* (London: Macmillan, 1900), 69, 72–73; Harry Hopkins, *The Long Affray: The Poaching Wars, 1760–1914* (London: Secker and Warburg, 1985), 43.

76. See, for example, H. Sample, *Art of Training Animals: A Practical Guide for Amateur or Professional Trainers* (New York: Jesse Haney, 1869), 147; Pennant, *British Zoology*, I, 97.

77. Trimmer, *Natural History*, 25–26; [Fenn], *Rational Dame*, 38.

78. Louis Robinson, *Wild Traits in Tame Animals, Being Some Familiar Studies in Evolution* (Edinburgh: Blackwood, 1897), 277; Hamerton, *Chapters*, 52; Broderip, *Zoological Recreations*, 191.

79. Henry Anderson Bryden, *Kloof and Karroo: Sport, Legend and Natural History in Cape Colony* (London: Longmans, Green, 1889), 134; Robert Hamilton, *Amphibious Carnivora, Including the Walrus and Seals, Also of the Herbivorous Cetacea* (Edinburgh: Lizars, 1839), 153; Thomas Rowlandson, *Foreign and Domestic Animals Drawn from Nature* (London: Thomas Rowlandson, 1787); Bewick, *General History*, 205.

80. *The Natural History of Animals: Beasts, Birds, Fishes, and Insects* (Dublin: Smith and Son, 1822), 53.

81. Charles Knight, *Knight's Pictorial Museum of Animated Nature* (London: London Printing and Publishing Company, 1856–58), I, 83; Broderip, *Zoological Recreations*, 312; William Hone, *The Every-Day Book and Table Book* (London: T. Tegg, 1835), II, 360.

82. Bingley, *Animal Biography*, I, 122; Church, *Cabinet*, I, n.p.

83. George J. Romanes, *Animal Intelligence* (New York: D. Appleton, 1896), 387.

84. Wood, *Zoography*, I, 103; *Menagerie or History of Wild Beast's* [sic] (London: William Darton, [c. 1821]), n.p.

85. Broderip, *Zoological Recreations*, 269; Swainson, *Habits and Instincts*, 76.

86. Bewick, *General History*, 195.

87. [Jones], *Natural History of Beasts*, 117.

88. Bewick, *General History*, 244, 245; Thomas Williamson, *Oriental Field Sports* (London: Edward Orme, 1807), II, 109.

89. *The Animal Museum; or, Picture Gallery of Quadrupeds* (London: J. Harris, 1825), 93.

90. Church, *Cabinet*, II, n.p.; Bewick, *General History*, 201.

91. Bingley, *Animal Biography*, I, 269; Charles H. Ross, *The Book of Cats* (London: Griffith and Farran, 1868), 232; Bartlett, *Wild Animals in Captivity*, 31–32.

92. For full accounts of this event, see Hone, *Every-Day Book*, I, 978–993, and *Pierce Egan's Anecdotes (Original and Selected) of the Turf, the Chase, the Ring, and the Stage* (London: Knight and Lacey, 1827), 100–112.

93. Bennett, *Tower Menagerie*, 4–5.

94. Church, *Cabinet*, II, n.p.

95. Timbs, *Strange Stories*, 334.

96. Holloway and Branch, *British Museum*, I, 29.

97. William Swainson, *Animals in Menageries* (London: Longman, Orme, Brown, Green, and Longmans, 1830), 104; Church, *Cabinet*, II, n.p.

98. *Animal Museum*, 173.

99. Swainson, *Habits and Instincts*, 78–79; Rowlandson, *Foreign and Domestic Animals*, n.p.

100. Holloway and Branch, *British Museum*, I, 22.

101. Richard Lydekker, *The Great and Small Game of India, Burma and Tibet* (London: Rowland Ward, 1900), 289; Ray, *India Museum*, 21–24.

102. Pierce Egan, *Sporting Anecdotes, Original and Selected* (London: Sherwood, Neely, and Jones, 1820), 192–193; Evans, *Criminal Prosecution*, 160–165; Clifford Morsley, *News from the English Countryside, 1750–1850* (London: Harrap, 1979), 119; "A Child Partly Eaten by a Rabbit," *Field* 17 (1861), 107.

103. "The Lion of South Africa," *The Farrier and Naturalist* 1 (September 1828), 417.

104. Catton, *Animals*, n.p.

105. Swainson, *Habits and Instincts*, 186.

106. Bennett, *Tower Menagerie*, 75; Burchell, *Travels*, II, 285.

107. James Forbes, *Oriental Memoirs* (London: T. Bensley, 1813), IV, 81.

108. Edward Lockwood, *Natural History, Sport, and Travel* (London: William H. Allen, 1878), 237–238, 127.

109. Willoughby P. Lowe, *The Trail That Is Always New* (London: Gurney and Jackson, 1932), 87; Richard Owen, *Memoir on the Gorilla* (London: Taylor and Francis, 1865), 35; "The Gorilla," *Illustrated London News* 34 (1859), 348.

110. Bryden, *Kloof and Karroo*, 13.

111. Bingley, *Animal Biography*, I, 74; Thomas Belt, *The Naturalist in Nicaragua* (London: John Murray, 1874), 118.

112. Edward Tyson, *Orang-Outang sive Homo Sylvestris; or, The Anatomy of a Pygmie Compared with That of a "Monkey," an "Ape," and a "Man"* (1699; rpt. London: Dawson's of Pall Mall, 1966). See, for example, Hone, *Every-Day Book*, III, 758; Bewick, *General History*, 452–453. For some more erudite proponents of this connection, see Arthur O. Lovejoy, *The Great Chain of Being: A Study of the History of an Idea* (Cambridge, Mass.: Harvard University Press, 1936), 233–236. In the early eighteenth century the Hottentot was often cited as a link between apes and humankind. Artists also presented other primates in

the most human possible guise. Ellen K. Levy and David E. Levy, "Monkey in the Middle: Pre-Darwinian Evolutionary Thought and Artistic Creation," *Perspectives in Biology and Medicine* 30 (1986), 95–106.

113. [Thomas Boreman], *A Description of Some Curious and Uncommon Creatures Omitted in the Description of Three Hundred Animals* (London: Richard Ware and Thomas Boreman, 1739), 1.

114. Bingley, *Animal Biography*, I, 45–50; Jesse, *Gleanings in Natural History, Second Series* (London: John Murray, 1834), 40; Broderip, *Zoological Recreations*, 250; William Ogilby, *The Natural History of Monkeys, Opossums, and Lemurs* (London: Charles Knight, 1838), 70–71; "Importation of Another Specimen of the Chimpanzee," *Zoologist* 7 (1849), 2379.

115. *The Animal Museum*, 205.

116. Robert Jameson et al., *Narrative of Discovery and Adventure in Africa* (Edinburgh: Oliver and Boyd, 1830), 400–401.

117. For an extended discussion of the history of primate taxonomy, see Kristen Longenecker Zacharias, "The Construction of a Primate Order: Taxonomy and Comparative Anatomy in Establishing the Human Place in Nature, 1735–1916" (Ph.D. diss., Johns Hopkins University, 1980).

118. James Campbell, *Excursions, Adventures, and Field Sports in Ceylon* (London: T. and W. Boone, 1843), I, 333.

119. Forbes, *Oriental Memoirs*, I, 27–28.

120. Richard Lydekker, *Animal Portraiture* (London: Frederick Warne, 1912), 24.

121. "Monkeys," *Quarterly Review* 186 (1897), 419–420; Jameson et al., *Narrative of Discovery*, 405.

122. William Jardine, *Monkeys*, (Edinburgh: Lizars, 1833), 39.

123. Bell, *British Quadrupeds*, 195; Wood, *Zoography*, I, 1.

124. St. George Mivart, *The Cat: An Introduction to the Study of Backboned Animals, Especially Mammals* (New York: Charles Scribner's Sons, 1881), 491.

125. Bewick, *General History*, 452–453; Bingley, *Animal Biography*, I, 44–50.

126. Romanes, *Animal Intelligence*, 439; George J. Romanes, *Mental Evolution in Animals* (London: Kegan, Paul, Trench, 1883), inset, 352.

127. John Oliver French, "An Inquiry Respecting the True Nature of Instinct, and of the Mental Distinction between Brute Animals and Man . . . ," *Zoological Journal* 1 (March 1824), 2, 9. For a survey of changing human ideas about the intelligence of animals, see Stephen Walker, *Animal Thought* (London: Routledge and Kegan Paul, 1983).

128. Swainson, *Habits and Instincts*, 288–289.

129. These and other feelings were exhaustively explored in Edward Pett Thompson, *The Passions of Animals* (London: Chapman and Hall, 1851).

130. "Animal Phrenology," *The Farrier and Naturalist* 1 (February 1828), 71–75, and (March 1828), 106–109.

131. "Animal Phrenology," 72, 74–75, 106–107; Rennie, *Alphabet of Zoology*, 105; Hamilton, *Amphibious Carnivora*, 81.

132. Jesse, *Gleanings in Natural History, with Local Recollections*, 20, 96.

133. G. Romanes, *Animal Intelligence*, viii; G. Romanes, *Mental Evolution in Animals*, 234–235, 240; Ethel Romanes, *The Life and Letters of George John Romanes, M.A., Ll.D.* (London: Longmans, Green, 1896), 15.

134. Jesse, *Gleanings, Third Series*, 15–16, 34; Forbes Macgregor, *The Story of Greyfriars Bobby* (Edinburgh: Ampersand, 1981).

135. [Fenn], *Rational Dame*, 41.

136. *The Animal Museum*, 1.

137. Jameson et al., *Narrative of Discovery*, 423; William Rhind, *The Feline Species* (Edinburgh: Fraser, 1834), 147.

138. *Animal Museum*, 204; T. Teltruth, *The Natural History of Four-Footed Beasts* (London: E. Newbury, 1781), 72–73.

139. *Animal Museum*, 206.

140. Jardine, *Monkeys*, 91; Broderip, *Zoological Recreations*, 217.

141. See, for example, the orangutans in Bewick, *General History*; Edward Donovan, *A Naturalist's Repository of Exotic Natural History* (London: W. Simpkin and R. Marshall, 1822–1824), 2 vols.; Church, *Cabinet*; Knight, *Knight's Pictorial Museum*; and Lydekker, *Animal Portraiture.*

142. Frank Buckland, "The Gorilla," *Field* 17 (1867), 179; Swainson, *On the Natural History and Classification of Quadrupeds*, 98.

143. Charles Darwin, *The Descent of Man, and Selection in Relation to Sex*, (1871; rpt. Princeton, N.J.: Princeton University Press, 1981), 34–35.

144. The main differences between human and animal visages, according to LeBrun, were matters of detail and proportion, such as animals' eyes being nearer to their noses, and human eyebrows meeting over the nose whereas those of animals did not. Charles LeBrun, *Conference . . . upon Expression, General and Particular; and An Abridgement of a Conference . . . upon Physiognomy* (London: John Smith, Edward Cooper and David Mortier, 1701), 44–46.

145. Charles Darwin, *The Voyage of the Beagle* (1845; rpt. Garden City, N.Y.: Doubleday and the American Museum of Natural History, 1960), 433.

146. Arabella Buckley, *The Winners in Life's Race; or, The Great Backboned Family* (New York: D. Appleton, 1883), vi, 240, 285, 255. The gorilla had not been discovered when Bewick wrote, but Buckley and later popularizers simply attributed to it qualities already associated with other great apes.

147. For an exploration of the multivalence of Darwin's work, see Gillian Beer, *Darwin's Plots: Evolutionary Narrative in Darwin, George Eliot and Nineteenth-Century Fiction* (London: Routledge and Kegan Paul, 1983), ch. 4.

148. Charles Darwin, *On the Origin of Species* (1859; rpt. Cambridge, Mass.: Harvard University Press, 1964), 79.

149. For example, in the space of a few pages of *The Expression of the Emotions in Man and Animals* (1872; rpt. Chicago: University of Chicago Press, 1965), Darwin referred to Mr. H. F. Salvin's account of a tame jackal, Carpenter's *Principles of Comparative Physiology*, Müller's *Elements of Physiology*, and Mr. St. John's descriptions of his "tame Sheldrakes" (44–48).

1. Barons of Beef

1. Norman Comben, "The Durham Ox," *Veterinary History* 1 (1979–80), 40; D. H. Boalch, ed., *Prints and Paintings of British Livestock, 1780–1910: A Record of the Rothamsted Collection* (Harpenden: Rothamsted Agricultural Experiment Station, 1958), xvi. The

print was based on an oil portrait and dedicated to Lord Somerville, one of the leading aristocratic patrons of agriculture. Cadwallader John Bates, "The Brothers Colling," *Journal of the Royal Agricultural Society of England*, 3rd ser., 10 (1899), 15.

2. R. E. Prothero, *English Farming Past and Present* (1912; rpt. Chicago: Quadrangle Books, 1961; ed. G. E. Fussell and O. R. McGregor), 188; Robert Trow-Smith, *A History of British Livestock Husbandry*, vol. II, *1700–1900* (London: Routledge and Paul, 1959), 238, 188; Boalch, *Prints and Paintings*, xviii, 11–12.

3. Hutchinson, *Origin and Pedigrees of the Sockburn Shorthorns . . . in Prose and Verse* (London: Evans and Ruffy, 1822); Juliet Clutton-Brock, "British Cattle in the Eighteenth Century," *Ark* 9 (1982), 58.

4. Trow-Smith, *British Livestock*, 26. Such antiquarians also (erroneously) considered the white cattle preserved at Chillingham, Chartley, and several other English parks to be survivors of the original wild stock. Richard Lydekker, *A Guide to the Domesticated Animals (Other than Horses) Exhibited . . . in the British Museum (Natural History)* (London: British Museum, 1908), 1. For the history of sheep domestication, see M. L. Ryder, *Sheep and Man* (London: Duckworth, 1983). Judy Urquhart, *Animals on the Farm: Their History from the Earliest Times to the Present Day* (London: MacDonald, 1983) offers a general history of British livestock.

5. John Kenneth Bonser, *The Drovers, Who They Were and How They Went; An Epic of the English Countryside* (London: Macmillan, 1970), 17–20, 219.

6. John Saunders Sebright, *The Art of Improving the Breeds of Domestic Animals* (London: J. Harding, 1809), 3–4.

7. Roy Porter, *English Society in the Eighteenth Century* (Harmondsworth, Middlesex: Penguin, 1982), 381; John Stratton and Jack Houghton Brown, *The Meat Trade in Britain, 1840–1914* (London: Routledge and Kegan Paul, 1978), 3. Smug gastronomical comparisons persisted into the nineteenth century. As late as 1829, *The Quarterly Review of Agriculture* boasted that "the consumption of beef in that country, relative to the population, is only one-sixth what it is in England" ("On the Consumption of Beef in France," 1, 1828–29, 390).

8. For a description of the career of Arthur Young, who is generally recognized as the founder of the agricultural press, see John G. Gazley, *The Life of Arthur Young, 1741–1820* (Philadelphia: American Philosophical Society, 1973).

9. See Stuart Macdonald, "Model Farms," in *The Victorian Countryside*, ed. G. E. Mingay (London: Routledge and Kegan Paul, 1981), I, 214–226, on the spread of new techniques by example. Among others, the following have offered conservative estimates of the influence of the agricultural press: Nicholas Goddard, "The Development and Influence of Agricultural Periodicals and Newspapers, 1780–1880," *Agricultural History Review* 31 (1983), 116–131; G. E. Fussell, "Nineteenth-Century Farming Encyclopedias: A Note," *Agricultural History* 55 (1981), 16–20; R. A. Houston, *Scottish Literacy and the Scottish Identity: Illiteracy and Society in Scotland and Northern England, 1600–1800* (Cambridge: Cambridge University Press, 1985), 215–217.

10. R. A. C. Parker, *Coke of Norfolk: A Financial and Agricultural Study, 1707–1842* (Oxford: Clarendon Press, 1975), 117–118.

11. Rosalind Mitchison, *Agricultural Sir John: The Life of Sir John Sinclair of Ulbster, 1754–1835* (London: Geoffrey Bles, 1962), 137–182, 204–213; minutes of the Board of Agriculture, February 18, 1800, in the minute book for November 27, 1798–March 18,

1805, vol. B.VI, 92; John Sinclair, *The Correspondence of the Right Honourable Sir John Sinclair, Bart.* (London: Henry Colburn and Richard Bentley, 1831), I, xxv; Kenneth Hudson, *Patriotism with Profit: British Agricultural Societies in the Eighteenth and Nineteenth Centuries* (London: Hugh Evelyn, 1972), 23. For a brief history of the Board of Agriculture, see Ernest Clarke, "The Board of Agriculture, 1793–1822," *Journal of the Royal Agricultural Society of England,* 3rd ser., 9 (1898), 1–41.

12. Edwin James Powell, *History of the Smithfield Club from 1798 to 1900* (London: Smithfield Club, 1902), 27.

13. *The Smithfield Club, from 1798 to 1860* (London: Joseph Clayton, 1860), 3.

14. "On the Late Show of Fat Cattle at Smithfield," *Commercial and Agricultural Magazine* 2 (1800), 42–43.

15. Leonard Bull, *History of the Smithfield Club, from 1798 to 1925* (London: Smithfield Club, 1926), 6; "On the Late Show of Fat Cattle at Smithfield," 42; Powell, *Smithfield Club,* 2; *Smithfield Club,* 3.

16. "Smithfield Club Cattle Show," *Commercial and Agricultural Magazine,* n.s., 6 (1815), 419.

17. *Smithfield Club,* 4–5.

18. Bull, *Smithfield Club,* 42.

19. "Fat Stock and the Smithfield Show," *Illustrated London News* 23 (1853), 491.

20. Bakewell to Arthur Young, March 10, 1788, and Bakewell to Culley, May 30, 1789, in H. C. Pawson, *Robert Bakewell: Pioneer Livestock Breeder* (London: C. Lockwood, 1957), 172, 141.

21. John Martin Robinson, *Georgian Model Farms: A Study of Decorative and Model Farm Buildings in the Age of Improvement, 1700–1846* (Oxford: Clarendon Press, 1983), 85; Lucinda Lambton, *Beastly Buildings: The National Trust Book of Architecture for Animals* (London: Jonathan Cape, 1985), 108–109, 111.

22. "Annual Sussex Agricultural Society Meeting," *Commercial and Agricultural Magazine* 5 (1801), 142; Powell, *Smithfield Club,* 38–39. On the French and German appreciation of English agricultural improvement, see A. J. Bourde, *The Influence of England on the French Agronomes, 1750–1789* (Cambridge: Cambridge University Press, 1953), and Otto Ulbricht, *Englische Landwirtschaft in Kurhannover in der zweiten Hälfte des 18. Jahrhunderts* (Berlin: Duncker and Humblot, 1980).

23. John Fry, "On the Breeding of Stock," *Hippiatrist and Veterinary Journal* (January 15, 1830), 18; George Dobito, "On Fattening Cattle," *Journal of the Royal Agricultural Society of England* 6 (1845), 75; T. C. Hincks, *Hints for Increasing the Practical Usefulness of Agricultural Shows* (London: Ridgway, 1845), 33–34; "Breeding of Shorthorns," *Land and Water* 3 (1867), 41.

24. John Chalmers Morton, *The Prince Consort's Farms: An Agricultural Memoir* (London: Longman, Green, Longman, Roberts, and Green, 1863), 266–273.

25. David Low, *On the Domesticated Animals of the British Islands,* (London: Longman, Brown, Green, and Longman, 1845), 384–386.

26. Cited in Thomas Bell, *History of Improved Shorthorn Cattle* (Newcastle: R. Redpath, 1871), 102.

27. *British Farmer's Magazine* 1 (1827), 629; *British Farmer's Magazine* 4 (1830), 2; *British Farmer's Magazine* 5 (1831), 1; *Farmer's Magazine* 8 (1838), 1.

28. *Improved Short-Horns and Their Pretensions Stated* . . . (Liverpool, 1824), 10–11; *The*

Farmer's Friend: A Record of Recent Discoveries, Improvements, and Practical Suggestions in Agriculture (London: Smith, Elder, 1847), 5–6; James Dickson, "On the Application of the Points by Which Live-Stock Are Judged," *Quarterly Review of Agriculture* 6 (1835–36), 269.

29. *Commercial and Agricultural Magazine* 2 (1800), 291; *Commercial and Agricultural Magazine* 7 (1802), 309.

30. Archibald Constable, *Remarks on Livestock and Related Subjects* (Edinburgh: Archibald Constable, 1806), 5; Henry Berry, *Improved Shorthorns and Their Pretensions Stated* . . . , 2nd ed. (London: James Ridgway, 1830), 41.

31. "The Sussex v. Short-Horns Challenge Accepted," *Farmer's Magazine*, n.s., 3 (1839), 85; minutes of the Council of the Royal Agricultural Society of England, June 10, 1840, in the minute book for 1840–1845, vol. B.I. 11, 64.

32. Boalch, *Prints and Paintings*, includes representative samples of both genres.

33. "Preface," *Agricultural Magazine, and Journal of Scientific Farming* 1 (1845), n.p.

34. Cadwallader John Bates, *Thomas Bates and the Kirklevington Shorthorns: A Contribution to the History of Pure Durham Cattle* (Newcastle: Robert Redpath, 1897), 80; E. Heath-Agnew, *A History of Hereford Cattle and Their Breeders* (London: Duckworth, 1983), 30–31; Thomas Bewick, *A Memoir of Thomas Bewick, Written by Himself*, ed. Iain Bain (1862; rpt. Oxford: Oxford University Press, 1975), 140–141; Boalch, *Prints and Paintings*, xvii; Rosemary Treble, "The Victorian Picture of the Country," in *The Victorian Countryside*, ed. G. E. Mingay, I, 168. Similar distortions determined the representation of less prestigious animals. According to Julian Wiseman, illustrations of nineteenth-century pigs offer weak evidence for their actual appearance because "they were invariably commissioned by owners to show their own stock in its best light" (*A History of the British Pig*, London: Duckworth, 1986, 30).

35. *Annals of Sporting and Fancy Gazette* 2 (1822), 258; Lawrence Stone, *The Family, Sex and Marriage in England, 1500–1800* (New York: Harper and Row, 1979), 160–161.

36. Bates, *Thomas Bates*, 160; George Coates, *The General Short-Horned Herd-Book: Containing the Pedigrees of Short-Horned Bulls, Cows, &c* . . . (Otley: W. Walker, 1822), v.

37. For a survey of the development of the thoroughbred, see Roger Longrigg, *The History of Horse Racing* (London: Macmillan, 1972). The first complete *Stud Book* was published in 1791, but throughout the eighteenth century, genealogies of distinguished horses had appeared in racing calendars and other publications. For examples, see C. M. Prior, *Early Records of the Thoroughbred Horse* (London: "Sportsman Office," 1925), and *The History of the Racing Calendar and the Stud Book* (London: "Sporting Life," 1926).

38. Bates, *Thomas Bates*, 34.

39. John Claudius Loudon, *An Encyclopedia of Agriculture* . . . (London: Longman, Hurst, Rees, Orme, Brown, and Green, 1825), 961.

40. Genealogical catalogs of distinguished human beings appeared at about the same time as those of thoroughbred animals. The forerunner of *Debrett's Peerage and Baronetage* appeared in 1769 (it has been known as *Debrett's* since 1802). The first edition of *Burke's Genealogical and Heraldic History of the Peerage, Baronetage and Knightage* appeared in 1826, and *Burke's Genealogical and Heraldic History of the Landed Gentry* followed in 1833–1835.

41. C. David Edgar, "Honest Jack Althorp—Founder of the Royal," *Journal of the Royal Agricultural Society of England* 141 (1980), 18. Apparently even established aristocratic and gentry families were wont to maintain their pedigrees with determination and enthusiasm. Of the guardian of one of the human stud books, Edward A. Freeman

asked, "Does he not know, the manifest falsehood of the tales which he reprints year after year?" ("Pedigrees and Pedigree-Makers," *Contemporary Review* 30, 1877, 12). Most of Horace Round's *Peerage and Pedigree: Studies in Peerage Law and Family History,* 2 vols. (London: James Nisbet and St. Catherines Press, 1910) was devoted to "the rejection of fabulous pedigrees, the exposure of spurious records, and the substitution of fact for fiction in the realm of family history" (I, xiii).

42. Bell, *Shorthorn Cattle,* 96–97, 215.

43. J. A. Scott Watson and M. E. Hobbs, *Great Farmers* (London: Faber and Faber, 1951), 143; Bell, *Shorthorn Cattle,* 209, 313–314; Bates, *Thomas Bates,* 332–335.

44. Bell, *Shorthorn Cattle,* 92.

45. *Agricultural Magazine, and Journal of Scientific Farming* 1 (1845), 296; R. W. Dickson, *A Complete System of Improved Live Stock and Cattle Management* (London: Thomas Kelly, 1824), I, 35.

46. Henry Berry, "On the Present State of Some of the Improved Cattle of this Kingdom," *British Farmer's Magazine* 1 (1827), 461; J. Coleman, "The Cross-Breeding of Cattle," *Journal of the Royal Agricultural Society of England* 23 (1862), 352; "The Duke of Richmond's Cattle Show," *Agricultural Magazine and Plough* (1853), 43; Robert Smith, "Report on the Exhibition of Live Stock at Chester," *Journal of the Royal Agricultural Society of England* 19 (1858), 399–400.

47. H. J. Habakkuk has characterized the men "who advanced knowledge," as opposed to underwriting the testing and dissemination of new techniques, as "a mixed bag, but if one can generalize about them, they were farmers rather than landowners." See his "Economic Functions of English Landowners in the Seventeenth and Eighteenth Centuries" in *Essays in Agrarian History,* ed. W. E. Minchinton (Newton Abbot: David and Charles, 1968) I, 189–190.

48. Bates, *Thomas Bates,* 165.

49. According to Joan Thirsk, before 1750 there is little evidence for the selective breeding of any animals besides horses and, possibly, dogs. See her "Introduction," in *The Agrarian History of England and Wales,* vol. V, *1640–1750,* pt. 1, *Regional Farming Systems* (Cambridge: Cambridge University Press, 1984), xxix. For an excellent detailed analysis of animal breeding through the eighteenth century, see Nicholas Russell, *Like Engend'ring Like: Heredity and Animal Breeding in Early Modern England* (Cambridge: Cambridge University Press, 1986).

50. Nicholas C. Russell, "Who Improved the Eighteenth-Century Longhorn Cow?" in *Agricultural Improvement: Medieval and Modern,* ed. Walter Minchinton (Exeter: University of Exeter Press, 1981), 38–40; Trow-Smith, *British Livestock,* 84–89.

51. Thomas Wedge, *General View of the Agriculture of the County Palatine of Chester* (London: C. Macrae, 1794), 30; John Fox, *General View of the Agriculture of the County of Monmouth* (Brentford: P. Norbury, 1794), 14; Charles Hassall, *General View of the Agriculture of the County of Carmarthen* (London: W. Smith, 1794), 35; John Bailey and George Culley, *General View of the Agriculture of the County of Cumberland* (London: C. Macrae, 1794), 14.

52. Thomas Hale, *A Compleat Body of Husbandry* (London: T. Osborne, 1756), 209; Richard Bradley, *The Gentleman and Farmer's Guide for the Increase and Improvement of Cattle* (London: J. Hodges, 1739), 127–128, 131; John Sinclair, *The Code of Agriculture* (London: W. Bulmer, 1817), 84.

53. Minutes of the Board of Agriculture, May 20, 1801, in the minute book for November 27, 1798–March 18, 1805, vol. B.VI, 224. Many of Garrard's models still

exist. They have been described by Juliet Clutton-Brock in "George Garrard's Livestock Models," *Agricultural History Review* 24 (1976, part 1), 18–29. George Garrard, *A Description of the Different Varieties of Oxen, Common in the British Isles* (London: J. Smeeton, 1800), n.p.

54. Russell, "Who Improved the Eighteenth-Century Longhorn Cow?" 20–24; "Biographical Sketches of Eminent Agriculturists: Robert Bakewell," *British Farmer's Magazine* 2 (1828), 322; Thomas Bewick, *A General History of Quadrupeds* (Newcastle: T. Bewick, 1824), 63–65, 33–34.

55. John Lawrence, *A General Treatise on Cattle, the Ox, the Sheep, and the Swine* (London: H. D. Symonds, 1805), 384; John Sinclair, "Hints and Queries Regarding Cattle" *Commercial and Agricultural Magazine* 6 (1802), 257. Ambrose Blacklock, *A Treatise on Sheep, with the Best Means for Their Improvement, General Management, and the Treatment of Their Diseases* (Glasgow: W. R. McPhun, 1838), 118.

56. Gazley, *Arthur Young*, 14; Low, *On the Domesticated Animals of the British Islands*, 372–373; David Low, *The Breeds of the Domestic Animals of the British Islands* (London: Longman, Orme, Brown, Green, and Longmans, 1842), I, 46; George Culley, *Observations on Live Stock, Containing Hints for Choosing and Improving the Best Breeds of the Most Useful Kinds of Domestic Animals* (London: G. Wilkie and J. Robinson, 1807), 183; "Impressions of Robert Bakewell, by François de la Rochefoucauld," rpt. in G. E. Mingay, ed., *The Agricultural Revolution: Changes in Agriculture, 1650–1880* (London: Adam and Charles Black, 1977), 145.

57. Arthur Young, quoted in Gordon Edmund Mingay, ed., *Arthur Young and His Times* (London: Macmillan, 1975), 78; George Culley, *Observations on Livestock*, ix.

58. Gazley, *Arthur Young*, 272; Prothero, *English Farming*, 184.

59. Bakewell to George Culley, February 8, 1787, in Pawson, *Robert Bakewell*, 107.

60. Scott Watson and Hobbs, *Great Farmers*, 175; Low, *On the Domesticated Animals of the British Islands*, 373; Sebright, *Improving the Breeds*, 9.

61. *The Complete Grazier, or Farmer's and Cattle Breeder's and Dealer's Assistant . . . by a Lincolnshire Grazier* (London, 1833), 14; Russell, "Who Improved the Eighteenth-Century Longhorn Cow?" 27; J. M. Stratton and Jack Houghton Brown, *Agricultural Records in Britain, A. D. 220–1977*, ed. Ralph Whitelock (Hamden, Conn.: Archon Books, 1978), 67, 92.

62. T. Weston, "On the Smithfield Prize Cattle," *Commercial and Agricultural Magazine* 5 (1801), 383.

63. Arthur Young, "Experiment on the Comparison of Four Breeds of Sheep, Made by Order of His Grace the Duke of Bedford and Communicated by Him to the Board of Agriculture," pamphlet, rpt. from *Annals of Agriculture* 23, p. 465, item R3/2114/3 in the collection of the Bedford County Record Office. Records of the fattening properties of cattle, sheep, and pigs, observed at the Woburn estate farms 1802–1807, items R3/2114/4, R3/2114/5, R3/2114/7, R3/2114/11, R3/2114/20, R3/2114/22, R3/2114/31, and R3/2114/32 in the collection of the Bedford County Record Office.

64. Herbrand Arthur Russell, *A Great Agricultural Estate, Being the Story of the Origin and Administration of Woburn and Thorney* (London: J. Murray, 1897), 27; minutes of the Bedfordshire Agricultural Society, September 9, 1813 in the minute book for 1801–1814, vol. I, 143.

65. P. J. Perry, "The Shorthorn Comes of Age (1822–1843): Agricultural History from the Herd Book," *Agricultural History* 56 (1982), 565–566.

66. The acuteness of their fear reflected the aristocratic breeders' own oversan-

guine estimate of the influence of their precept and practice on ordinary farmers. In fact, slow communications and proverbial rural conservatism ensured that stock improvements of all sorts trickled into general use rather slowly, although the characteristics of elite herds from which show animals were selected might change rapidly in response to breeding fashions. G. E. Mingay, "The Agricultural Revolution in English History: A Reconsideration," in *Essays in Agrarian History*, ed. W. E. Minchinton (Newton Abbot: David and Charles, 1968), II, 21.

67. "Smithfield Club Prize Cattle Show," *Agricultural Magazine and Plough* (1847), 232; "The Cattle Show," *Illustrated London News* 9 (1846), 369.

68. *Commercial and Agricultural Magazine* 3 (1800), 401, 404.

69. John Farey, "Proceedings of the Smithfield Club," *Agricultural Magazine*, 2nd ser., 2 (1807), 13; "On Prize-Fed Oxen," *British Farmer's Magazine* 1 (1827), 483; Bates, *Thomas Bates*, 79.

70. "On the Excessive Fattening of Cattle," *Commercial and Agricultural Magazine* 4 (1801), 321; Lawrence, *General Treatise*, 387; "On Prize-Fed Oxen," *British Farmer's Magazine* 1 (1827), 485.

71. T. C. Hincks, *Hints for Increasing the Practical Usefulness of Agricultural Shows* (London, 1845), 16; "Miss Points," *British Farmer's Magazine* 2 (1828), 266; Youatt, *Cattle*, 526. For a recent analysis of the relation of fat to fertility in mammalian females, see Rose E. Frisch, "Fatness, Puberty, and Fertility," *Natural History* 89 (1980), 16–27.

72. Youatt, *Cattle*, 525; Richard Parkinson, *Treatise on the Breeding and Management of Livestock* (London: Cadell and Davies, 1810), I, 99–100, 307.

73. "The Fat Cattle Competition," *Punch* 17 (1849), 235; "A Darwinian Idea Suggested by the Cattle Show," *Punch* 49 (1865), 246; *A Reflective Letter Addressed to . . . the Royal Agricultural Society of England* (London: Seeleys, 1852), 5–7.

74. "Smithfield Club," *Commercial and Agricultural Magazine* 13 (1805), 431; Pawsey to Lady Lucas, December 25, 1805, item L30/11/215/167 in the collection of the Bedford County Record Office.

75. "Observations on the Christmas Cattle Show," *Commercial and Agricultural Magazine*, n.s., 5 (1815), 6–7; "Sporting Occurrences in December," *Annals of Sporting and Fancy Gazette* 1 (1822), 63; Thomas Hartwell Horne, *The Complete Grazier* (London: Baldwin and Craddock, 1833), 594.

76. "Smithfield Club Prize Cattle Show," *Agricultural Magazine and Plough* (January 1853), 35; "Smithfield Club Prize Cattle," *Illustrated London News* 23 (1853), 488; "The Smithfield Cattle Club Show," *Agricultural Magazine, Plough, and Farmer's Journal* (November–December 1857), 32.

77. Clarke, "Board of Agriculture," 38–40.

78. Minutes of the Council of the Royal Agricultural Society of England, July 15, 1839, in the minute book for 1838–1840, vol. B.I.10, 248; Richard Milward, "Report on the Exhibition of the Live Stock at the Gloucester Meeting of the Society," *Journal of the Royal Agricultural Society of England* 14 (1853), 456–457; J. Evelyn Denison "The Agricultural Meeting at Paris of 1856," *Journal of the Royal Agricultural Society of England* 17 (1856), 395.

79. Thomas Bell, *The History of Improved Short-horn or Durham Cattle and of the Kirklevington Herd* (Newcastle-upon-Tyne, 1871), 10; Culley, *Observations on Livestock* (London: G. G. and J. Robinson, 1801), 183; Thomas Hartwell Horne, *The Complete Grazier* (London: B. Crosby, 1807), 3–6.

80. Bell, *History,* 33.

81. Philip Pusey, "On the Present State of the Science of Agriculture in England," *Journal of the Royal Agricultural Society of England* 1 (1840), 17.

82. "Memorandum Smithfield Cattle Show for Ensuing Seasons," 1827, item Z355/373 in the collection of the Bedford County Record Office.

83. Hincks, *Hints,* 4.

84. For example, a typical entry in *A Catalogue of the Beasts, Horses, Sheep, Pigs & Poultry Shown at the Meeting of the Society at Gloucester, July 14th and 15th, 1853* (London: Royal Agricultural Society of England, 1853) read, "Nathaniel Bland, of Randalls Park, Leatherhead, Surrey, a 3 years and 10 months old red and white Bull, Wahnabee, bred by exhibitor; sire Puritan, dam Nectarine, sire of dam supposed to be Homer."

85. "On the Origin and Natural History of the Domestic Ox, and Its Allied Species," *Quarterly Journal of Agriculture* 2 (1830), 195–196; Pusey, "On the Present State of the Science of Agriculture in England," 17.

86. *Quarterly Journal of Agriculture* 8 (1837), 399.

87. "Smithfield Club Cattle Show," *Agricultural Magazine, Plough, and Farmers' Journal* (January 1854), 46–47.

88. *Punch* 6 (1844), 46.

89. "On the Origin and Natural History of the Domestic Ox . . . ," *Quarterly Journal of Agriculture* 1 (1828), 390; *Quarterly Journal of Agriculture* 11 (1840), 128.

2. *Prize Pets*

1. Judith Neville Lytton, *Toy Dogs and Their Ancestors, Including the History and Management of Toy Spaniels, Pekingese, Japanese and Pomeranians* (London: Duckworth, 1911).

2. Ibid., 11.

3. Ibid., 104, 107, 13, 40, 43.

4. Sydenham Edwards, *Cynographia Britannica* (London, 1800–1805), 7.

5. Lytton, *Toy Dogs,* 13, 46, 40, 58.

6. Rawdon B. Lee, *A History and Description of the Modern Dogs of Great Britain and Ireland,* (London: Horace Cox, 1893–94), II, 116–119; C. J. Davies, "Dog Breeding as a Business," *Dog Owners' Annual for 1902,* 36.

7. William Youatt, *The Dog* (New York: Leavitt and Allen, 1846), 24; Edward Ash, *Dogs: Their History and Development* (London: Benn, 1927), I, 95.

8. Dix Harwood, *Love for Animals and How It Developed in Great Britain* (New York: Columbia University, 1928), 23.

9. Carson I. A. Ritchie, *The British Dog, Its History from Earliest Times* (London: Robert Hale, 1981), 118–119. Arline Meyer has described one early painter of aristocratic dogs in "Household Mock-Heroics: The Dog Portraits of John Wootton (1682–1764)," *Country Life* (February 9, 1984), 340–342. The listings under "Dogs" in the Computerized Index of British Art at the Photograph Archive of the Yale Center for British Art corroborate this chronology.

10. Harwood, *Love for Animals,* 214–225; Christopher Smart, "Jubilate Agno," sections xix–xx. For brief discussions of the eighteenth-century beginnings of petkeeping among the middle classes, see Keith Thomas, *Man and the Natural World: A History of the Modern Sensibility* (New York: Pantheon, 1983), 117–119, and J. H. Plumb, "The Acceptance of Modernity," in *The Birth of a Consumer Society: The Commercialization of Eighteenth-*

Century England, ed. Neil McKendrick, John Brewer, and J. H. Plumb (Bloomington: Indiana University Press, 1982), 320–323. For a more sinister and metaphysical interpretation of this development, see Marc Shell, "The Family Pet," *Representations* 15 (1986), 121–153.

11. George R. Jesse, *Researches into the History of the British Dog* . . . (London: Robert Hardwicke, 1866), I, 24–25; Richard Allen, *A Souvenir of Newstead Abbey, Formerly the Home of Lord Byron* (Nottingham: Richard Allen and Son, 1874), 7–8; Richard D. French, *Antivivisection and Medical Science in Victorian Society* (Princeton, N.J.: Princeton University Press, 1975), 373–374; Lucinda Lambton, *Beastly Buildings* (London: Jonathan Cape, 1985), 174. Kathleen Kete discusses the parallel evolution of feeling and practice across the Channel in "The Culture of Pet-keeping in the French Nineteenth Century" (Ph.D. diss., in progress, Harvard University).

12. Ministry of Agriculture, Fisheries and Food, *Animal Health, a Centenary, 1865–1965: A Century of Endeavour to Control Diseases of Animals* (London: HMSO, 1965), 298; Geoffrey Wills, ". . . Whose Dog Are You?" *Country Life* (April 4, 1974), 804; "Canine Fashions," *Punch* 16 (1849), 53; Henry Mayhew, *London Labour and the London Poor* (New York: Dover, 1968), II, 48–49.

13. Advertisements bound at the end of Gordon Stables, *Ladies' Dogs as Companions* (London: Dean and Son, 1879); William G. Fitzgerald, "Dandy Dogs," *Strand Magazine* 11 (1896), 542–545.

14. Johannes Caius, *Of Englishe Dogges, the Diversities, the Names, the Natures, and the Properties*, trans. Abraham Fleming (London: A. Bradley, 1880).

15. Clifford L. B. Hubbard, *An Introduction to the Literature of British Dogs: Five Centuries of Illustrated Dog Books* (Ponterwyd, n.p., 1949) examines this development. See also Brian Vesey-Fitzgerald, *The Domestic Dog: An Introduction to Its History* (London: Routledge and Kegan Paul, 1957), 95–97.

16. Report from the Select Committee of the House of Lords on Rabies in Dogs, *Parliamentary Papers*, 1887, no. 322, vol. XI.451, p. 125; "Fancy Prices," *Kennel Gazette* 5 (1884), 41; "High Prices of Dogs," *Dog Owners' Annual for 1892*, 164. See also John K. Walton, "Mad Dogs and Englishmen: The Conflict over Rabies in Victorian England," *Journal of Social History* 13 (1979), 221–223.

17. C. J. Davies, *The Kennel Handbook* (London: John Lane, 1905), 34.

18. *The Complete Dog Fancier; or, General History of Dogs* (London: T. Hughes, 1824), 4.

19. Lee, *Modern Dogs*, I, 102; Grantley F. Berkeley, *Fact against Fiction: The Habits and Treatment of Animals Practically Considered* (London: Samuel Tinsley, 1874), I, 65; *Kennel Club Stud Book* 1 (1859–1874), n.p.; "Have Shows Improved Our Field Dogs?" *Sportsman's Journal and Fancier's Guide* 12 (February 15, 1879), 3; Davies, *Kennel Handbook*, 113.

20. See the leading articles in *British Fancier Annual Review for 1894* and *British Fancier Annual Review for 1895*, respectively; "Her Majesty's Favourites," *Kennel Review* 4 (1885), 212; *Notable Dogs of the Year and Their Owners* (London: A. D. Innes, 1896).

21. Charles Henry Lane, *All about Dogs: A Book for Doggy People* (London: John Lane, 1900), 316–317.

22. Lane, *All about Dogs*, 226; Henry Webb [Henry Fennel Whitcomb], *Dogs: Their Points, Whims, Instincts, and Peculiarities* (London: Dean and Son, 1876), 237; Lee, *Modern Dogs*, III, 298.

23. "Dogs up to Date: The Pug," *Dogs*, n.s., 1 (1894), 114; Hugh Dalziel, *The Collie:*

As a Show Dog, Companion, and Worker, rev. J. Maxtee (London: L. Upcott Gill, 1904), 9; Lane, *All about Dogs,* 27, 109; Lee, *Modern Dogs,* I, 130–131.

24. Parker Gillmore, *The Hunter's Arcadia* (London: Chapman and Hall, 1886), 70.

25. Lee, *Modern Dogs,* I, 168–169.

26. Ibid., III, 318–319; "Dog Shows," *Land and Water* 1 (1866), 59; "Colliers and Their Dogs," *Sportsman's Journal and Fancier's Guide* 9 (January 25, 1879), 8.

27. "A Dog of Dogs," *Punch* 10 (1846), 236.

28. George J. Romanes, *Animal Intelligence* (New York: D. Appleton, 1896), 441–442.

29. Gordon Stables, *Dogs in Their Relation to the Public (Social, Sanitary and Legal)* (London: Cassell, Petter and Galpin, 1877), 17; Benjamin Clayton, *Dogs: How to Breed and Treat in Health and Disease* (London, 1871), 6, 23; John Lawrence, *The Sportsman's Repository* . . . (London: Sherwood, Neely, and Jones, 1820), 56; Gordon Stables, *Ladies' Dogs as Companions* (London: Dean and Son, 1879), 22, 63; *The Dog Fancier, Containing Instructions for the Management of Dogs* (London: J. Bysh, 1861), n.p.

30. Stables, *Dogs in Their Relation to the Public,* 51; Everett Millais, *The Theory and Practice of Rational Breeding* (London: "Fancier's Gazette," 1889), x; F. A. Manning, "The History and Growth of the Kennel Club," *Dog Owners' Annual for 1890,* 147; Gordon Stables, "Breeding and Rearing for Pleasure, Prizes and Profit," *Dog Owners' Annual for 1896,* 166.

31. Caius, *Of Englishe Dogges,* 13.

32. Thomas Fairfax, *The New Complete Sportsman; or, The Town and Country Gentleman's Recreation* (London: Alexander Hogg, [c. 1770]), 125–126.

33. Edward William Bovill, *The England of Nimrod and Surtees, 1815–1854* (London: Oxford University Press, 1959), 68–69; Raymond Carr, *English Fox Hunting: A History* (London: Weidenfeld, 1976), 36–37.

34. "Fox Hound Kennel at Beachborough," Brockman Papers, vol. CXXXV, pp. 25b–24b (British Library Add. Ms. 45,202); Brierly to the earl of Derby, April 12, 1848, item 11/7/1, Correspondence of the Thirteenth Earl of Derby, Liverpool City Library; "Pillars of the Stud Book, No. XVI, Pugs," *Kennel Gazette* 5 (1885), 213–214.

35. Harriet Ritvo, "Pride and Pedigree: The Evolution of the Victorian Dog Fancy," *Victorian Studies* 29 (1986), 38–40; *Kennel Club Stud Book* 1(1859–1874), n.p.; Edward C. Ash, *The New Book of the Dog* (New York: Macmillan, 1939), 48–51.

36. Edwards, *Cynographia,* 7–8; Youatt, *Dog,* chs. 2–4; *Book of Sports, British and Foreign* (London: Walter Spiers, 1843), 77–78; Ritchie, *British Dog,* 189.

37. Richard Lydekker, *A Guide to Domesticated Animals (Other than Horses) Exhibited . . . in the British Museum (Natural History)* (London: British Museum, 1908), 29. Lee's *History and Description of the Modern Dogs of Great Britain and Ireland* allotted one volume to sporting dogs, one to terriers, and one to nonsporting dogs. Vesey-Fitzgerald, *Domestic Dog,* 172–173.

38. "The Title of Champion," *Field* 49 (1877), 387.

39. Ash, *Dogs,* I, 7–8; Hugh Dalziel, *British Dogs: Their Varieties, History, Characteristics, Breeding, Management and Exhibition* (London: "Bazaar" Office, 1879–80), 174–175.

40. Vesey-Fitzgerald, *Domestic Dog,* 143; Frank Pearce, "Preface," *Kennel Club Stud Book* 1 (1859–1874), n.p.

41. Lane, *All about Dogs,* v; "Dog Shows in 1889," *Dog Owners' Annual for 1890,* 195;

"Dog Shows of 1892," *Dog Owners' Annual for 1893*, 45–48; "The Dog Shows of 1895," *Dog Owners' Annual for 1896*, 42–48; "Dog Shows of 1897," *Dog Owners' Annual for 1898*, 52–57; "Dog Shows of 1899," *Dog Owners' Annual for 1900*, 84–90.

42. "Dog Show Notes," *Dog Owners' Annual for 1891*, 189–191.

43. Lane, *All about Dogs*, 314–315; L. K. A., "The Ladies Kennel Association," *Ladies' Kennel Journal* 1 (1894), 3; "Club and Kennel Notes," *Kennel Gazette* 19 (1898), 271.

44. Ash, *Dogs*, I, 7.

45. Robert Vyner, *Notitia Venatica: A Treatise on Fox Hunting* (London: Robert Vyner, 1847), 27; *Courser's Annual Remembrancer, and Stud Book* (London, 1854), 420.

46. Dalziel, *British Dogs*, 172–173; Hubbard, *Literature of British Dogs*, 41; "Fancy Pets," *Illustrated London News* 18 (1851), 91.

47. Lytton, *Toy Dogs*, 100; Dalziel, *British Dogs*, 173.

48. *Kennel Club Stud Book* 1 (1859–1874) n.p.; Walsh's account is reproduced in Ash, *Dogs*, II, 676–677.

49. Everett Millais, "The Kennel Club," *Dog Owners' Annual for 1893*, 52, 64; "Birmingham Cat Show," *Live Stock Journal and Fancier's Gazette* 2 (1875), 780. Despite protests, show animals continued to suffer throughout the Victorian period. In 1893 Gordon Stables, a well-known breeder and show judge, published *Sable and White: The Autobiography of a Show Dog*, a fictional exposé of dog show abuses, which was regularly reissued into the twentieth century.

50. Stables, *Dogs in Their Relation to the Public*, 34.

51. Ash, *Dogs*, II, 676–678.

52. Dalziel, *British Dogs*, 174, 183.

53. Vero Shaw, *"Don'ts": Instructions What to Avoid in Buying, Managing, Feeding and Exhibiting Dogs* (London: "Stock-keeper" Company, 1898), 33; Theodore Marples, *Prize Dogs: Their Successful Housing, Management, and Preparation for Exhibition from Puppyhood to the Show Ring* (Manchester: "Our Dogs," 1905), 87; Vesey-Fitzgerald, *Domestic Dog*, 147.

54. Gordon Stables, *Hints about Home and Farm Favourites, for Pleasure, Prizes and Profit* (London: Frederick Warne, 1889), 132; Davies, *Kennel Handbook*, 31–32.

55. Millais, "The Kennel Club," 55–56.

56. Frank Pearce, "Preface," *Kennel Club Stud Book* 1 (1859–1874), n.p.; Vesey-Fitzgerald, *Domestic Dog*, 147–148.

57. Millais, "The Kennel Club," 69.

58. F. A. Manning, "The History and Growth of the Kennel Club," *Dog Owners' Annual for 1890*, 138; Millais, *The Theory and Practice of Rational Breeding*, 80–81.

59. Stonehenge [J. H. Walsh], *The Dogs of the British Isles* (London: Horace Cox, 1866–67), preface; Stonehenge [J. H. Walsh], *The Dog: Its Varieties and Management in Health and Disease* (London: Frederick Warne, 1873), 87–88; "A Defined Standard of Points for all Breeds of Dogs," *Kennel Gazette* 8 (1887), 242.

60. "Pocket Beagles," *Dog Owners' Annual for 1897*, 65; Lee, *Modern Dogs*, I, 91–92; *Kennel Gazette* 20 (1899), 9; Shaw, *"Don'ts,"* 6; Walter Baxendale, "Dogs and Dogmen in 1897," *Dog Owners' Annual for 1898*, 44; "Kennel Club Show Report," *Kennel Gazette* 9 (1888), 53.

61. Edwards, *Cynographia*, n.p.; "On Beagles—Their Merits Appreciated," *Annals of Sporting and Fancy Gazette* 3 (1823), 314–315.

62. John Meyrick, *House Dogs and Sporting Dogs: Their Varieties, Points, Management,*

Training, Breeding, Rearing and Diseases (London: John Van Voorst, 1861), 19; "The Dogs of 1897: A Retrospect," *Kennel Gazette* 19 (1898), 63; C. H. Lane, "Beagles," *The British Fancier Annual Review for 1895* (Manchester), 69; Lane, *All about Dogs,* 20, 23.

63. "The Dogs of 1897: A Retrospect," 63.

64. "Review of the Year," *Kennel Gazette* 17 (1896), 15; Lane, *All about Dogs,* 20.

65. Pierce Egan, *Sporting Anecdotes, Original and Selected* (London: Sherwood, Neely, and Jones, 1820), 399.

66. Lane, *All about Dogs,* 179, 183; Davies, *Kennel Handbook,* 34; Edgar Farman, "Bulldogs," *Kennel Gazette* 15 (1894), 4–5.

67. Dalziel, *British Dogs,* 221; "The Bulldog," *Ladies' Kennel Journal* 4 (1896), 13.

68. Clayton, *Dogs,* 12; Meyrick, *House Dogs and Sporting Dogs,* 65; Edgar Farman, "The Bulldog Club," *Kennel Gazette* 19 (1898), 199.

69. William Youatt, *The Obligation and Extent of Humanity to Brutes, Principally Considered with Reference to the Domesticated Animals* (London: Longman, Orme, Brown, Green, and Longman, 1839), 169; Stonehenge, *The Dog in Health and Disease,* 132; Webb, *Dogs,* 162.

70. Farman, "The Bulldog Club," *Kennel Gazette* 19 (1898), 238, and 19 (1898), 199, 200.

71. Youatt, *Dog,* 150; Ephraim Watts, *The Life of Van Amburgh: The Brute Tamer* (London: Robert Tyas, n.d.), 39; Dalziel, *British Dogs,* 226; J. S. Pybus-Sellon, "Bull Dogs," *Kennel Gazette* 5 (1885), 144; "Dogs up to Date: The Bulldog," *Dogs* 1 (1894), 43; *Ladies' Kennel Journal* 1 (1894), 57; Edgar Farman, "Bulldogs," *Kennel Gazette* 17 (1896), 13.

72. *Sportsman's Journal and Fancier's Guide: Stud + Stable + Kennel + Curtilage* 12 (February 15, 1879), 9.

73. Farman "The Bulldog Club," *Kennel Gazette* 19 (1898), 471, and 20 (1899), 55; Lee, *Modern Dogs,* III, 237.

74. "Review of the Past Year," *Kennel Gazette* 12 (1891), 5–6; Lee, *Modern Dogs,* III, 220–221, 243.

75. Stonehenge, *The Dog in Health and Disease,* 133; Frank W. Crowther, "Bulldogs," *Kennel Gazette* 14 (1893), 11; Jesse, *Researches,* II, 390.

76. Calculated on the basis of lists published in *Dog Owners' Annual* for the years 1890–1896.

77. Vero Shaw, *The Illustrated Book of the Dog* (London: Cassell, Petter, Galpin, 1879), 74–75; D. J. Thomson Gray, *The Dogs of Scotland: Their Varieties, History, Characteristics, and Exhibition Points* (Dundee: James P. Mathew, 1891), 150; "Collies," *Kennel Gazette* 7 (1891), 7–8.

78. "'Specialism' in Dog Shows," *Kennel Gazette* 11 (1890), 193; Dalziel, *Collie,* 12, 15, 40; *Kennel Gazette* 5 (1884), 75.

79. Lee, *Modern Dogs,* III, 129; Dalziel, *Collie,* 9.

80. "Rabbits and Cats at Epworth," *Live Stock Journal and Fancier's Gazette* 2 (1875), 121; "Rabbits and Cats at Burton," *Live Stock Journal and Fancier's Gazette* 2 (1875), 468; J. G. Gardner, *The Cat, Being My Experience of "Poor Puss," with Hints for Feeding, Breeding, and General Management . . .* (Bromley, 1892), 21.

81. James Secord has described the mid-Victorian pigeon fancy in "Nature's Fancy: Charles Darwin and the Breeding of Pigeons," *Isis* 72 (1981), 163–186.

82. Charles Darwin, *The Variation of Animals and Plants under Domestication* (1868; rpt. New York: D. Appleton, 1892), I, 50.

83. Stables, *Hints,* 39.

84. Webb, *Dogs* 10; Harrison Weir, *Our Cats and All about Them: Their Varieties, Habits, and Management* . . . (Tunbridge Wells: R. Clements, 1889), 1–2; Frank Buckland, *Log Book of a Fisherman and Zoologist* (London: Chapman and Hall, 1875), 252–253; Philip M. Rule, *The Cat: Its Natural History, Domestic Varieties, Management and Treatment* (London: S. Sonnenschein, Lowrey, 1887), 62.

85. Gardner, *Cat,* 60; Gordon Stables, *"Cats:" Their Points and Characteristics with Curiosities of Cat Life, and a Chapter on Feline Ailments* (London: Dean and Son, 1876), 285; Gordon Stables, "The Domestic Cat," *Live Stock Journal and Fancier's Gazette* 2 (1875), 99, 141–161, 203–204.

86. Gardner, *Cat,* 60, 46–47; Francis Simpson, *Cats and All about Them* (New York: Frederick A. Stokes, 1902), 18, 96–97; C. H. Lane, *Rabbits, Cats and Cavies: Descriptive Sketches of all Recognized Exhibition Varieties with Many Original Anecdotes* (London: J. M. Dent, 1903).

87. John Jennings, *Domestic and Fancy Cats: A Practical Treatise on Their Varieties, Breeding, Management, and Diseases* (London: L. Upcott Gill, n.d.), 53.

88. Stables, "The Domestic Cat," *Live Stock Journal and Fancier's Gazette* 2 (1875), 246, and 2 (1875), 266.

89. Rule, *Cat,* 77–78; Frances Simpson, *The Book of the Cat* (London: Cassell, 1903), 98; "Cats at the Crystal Palace," *Ladies' Kennel Journal* 4 (1896), 257.

90. "Kit-Kat," *Ladies' Kennel Journal* 3 (1896), 35; "Miss Cunninghame's Siamese Cats," *Ladies' Kennel Journal* 5 (1897), 244.

91. Jennings, *Domestic and Fancy Cats,* 53; "Tortoiseshell Tom Cat," *Illustrated London News* 19 (1851), 382; "The Zoological Gardens," *Quarterly Review* 98 (1855), 246; Stables, "The Domestic Cat," *Live Stock Journal and Fancier's Gazette* 2 (1875), 162.

3. A Measure of Compassion

1. In a busy week, as many as 100,000 cattle and sheep might pass through the London streets on their way to Smithfield; in the year 1846, 210,757 head of cattle and 1,518,510 of sheep were slaughtered there. (John Timbs, *Curiosities of London,* London: David Bogue, 1855, 500; Richard Perren, *The Meat Trade in Britain, 1840–1914,* London: Routledge and Kegan Paul, 1978, 33.) The number of urban horses in Britain increased from about 350,000 in the 1830s to about 1,200,000 at the beginning of the twentieth century; most of the additional animals were used to haul omnibuses and other heavy vehicles in the growing towns. (F. M. L. Thompson, "Horses and Hay in Britain, 1830–1918," 59, and T. C. Barker, "The Delayed Decline of the Horse in the Twentieth Century," 102, both in F. M. L. Thompson, ed., *Horses in European Economic History: A Preliminary Canter,* Reading: British Agricultural History Society, 1983. Also in this volume Jennifer Tann's "Horse Power, 1780–1880" itemizes the various industrial uses of horsepower, see esp. 25–26.)

2. James Turner, *Reckoning with the Beast: Animals, Pain, and Humanity in the Victorian Mind* (Baltimore: Johns Hopkins University Press, 1980), 15; Antony Brown, *Who Cares For Animals? 150 Years of the RSPCA* (London: Heinemann, 1974), 10–11.

3. "The Lion Fight," *New Monthly Magazine* 14 (1825), 288; Edward Jesse, *Gleanings in Natural History, Third and Last Series* (London: John Murray, 1835), vi.

4. Alfred Charles Smith, "On the Persecution of Birds and Animals, Unhappily So General in This Country," *Zoologist* 11 (1853), 3901.

5. William Hamilton Drummond, *The Rights of Animals, and Man's Obligation to Treat Them with Humanity* (London: John Mardon, 1838), 5; "Abattoirs Contrasted with Slaughter-houses and Smithfield Market," *Voice of Humanity* 3 (1832), 5–6.

6. Christopher Hibbett, ed., *Queen Victoria in Her Letters and Journals* (London: John Murray, 1984), 205.

7. W. J. Stillman, "A Plea for Wild Animals," *Contemporary Review* 75 (1899), 674, 675–676; Brian Harrison, "Animals and the State," in *Peaceable Kingdom: Stability and Change in Modern Britain* (Oxford: Clarendon Press, 1982), 102–103. Evidence of the success of this public relations campaign appeared in such places as "Orthodox Cruelty to Animals," *Punch* 45 (1863), 157.

8. Turner, *Reckoning with the Beast*, 39.

9. Edward G. Fairholme and Wellesley Pain, *A Century of Work for Animals: The History of the R.S.P.C.A., 1824–1924* (New York: E. P. Dutton, 1924), 23.

10. *Sixth Report and Proceedings of the Annual Meeting of the Society for the Prevention of Cruelty to Animals, 1832* (subsequently referred to as *Annual Report* for a particular year).

11. See, for example, *Cruelty to Animals: Suggestions, Acts of Parliament, Prosecutions* (London: R.S.P.C.A., n.d.). The first reference to this pocket-sized tract was in the *Annual Report* for 1861; internal evidence suggests that the edition cited was published in the 1880s.

12. Turner, *Reckoning with the Beast*, 16–17; Fairholme and Pain, *A Century of Work*, 22–23.

13. Turner, *Reckoning with the Beast*, 39; Fairholme and Pain, *A Century of Work*, 25–26, 39–40; Wellesley Pain, *Richard Martin, 1754–1834* (London: Leonard Parsons, 1925), 132, 140.

14. Fairholme and Pain, *A Century of Work*, 23, 49–53.

15. Brown, *Who Cares For Animals?* 16.

16. Turner, *Reckoning with the Beast*, 40–45; Fairholme and Pain, *A Century of Work*, 60–71.

17. Quoted in Clifford Morsley, *News from the English Countryside, 1750–1850* (London: Harrap, 1979), 157; William B. Daniel, *Supplement to the Rural Sports* (London: B. and R. Crosby, 1801–1813), 478.

18. Harrison, "Animals and the State," 91; Fairholme and Pain, *A Century of Work*, 71–72, 89; *Voice of Humanity*, prospectus appended to 3 (1833), 6–7.

19. David Owen, *English Philanthropy, 1660–1960* (Cambridge, Mass.: Harvard University Press, 1964), 179–180.

20. "The Bulldog," *Ladies' Kennel Journal* 4 (1896), 14.

21. Keith Thomas, *Man and the Natural World: A History of the Modern Sensibility* (New York: Pantheon, 1983), 152–159; Robert Malcolmson, *Popular Recreations in English Society, 1700–1850* (Cambridge: Cambridge University Press, 1973), 118. John Passmore traces the relation of the Christian tradition to the development of humanitarian sentiment in "The Treatment of Animals," *Journal of the History of Ideas* 36 (1975), 195–218. In the eighteenth century writers began to systematize these scattered attempts to control cruelty to animals. David Hume discussed animal sympathy in his *Treatise of Human Nature* (1739), and John Hildrop criticized cruelty to animals in *Free Thoughts on the Brute Creation* (1742). Humphrey Primatt's *Dissertation on the Duty of Mercy and Sin of Cruelty to Brute Animals* (1776) laid the religious foundation for later humanitarians, while Jeremy Bentham, in remarks scattered through his writings, gave them secular support. For an elaborate

analysis of the awakening of sentimentalism in the eighteenth century, see Dix Harwood, *Love for Animals and How It Developed in Great Britain* (New York: Columbia University, 1928).

22. For the development of children's literature in the eighteenth century, see F. J. Harvey Darton, *Children's Books in England: Five Centuries of Social Life* (1932; 3rd ed. rev. Brian Alderson, Cambridge: Cambridge University Press, 1982); J. H. Plumb, "The First Flourishing of Children's Books," in *Early Children's Books and Their Illustration* (New York: Pierpont Morgan Library and Boston: David R. Godine, 1975); Samuel F. Pickering, *John Locke and Children's Books in Eighteenth-Century England* (Knoxville: University of Tennessee Press, 1981); and Isaac Kramnick, "Children's Literature and Bourgeois Ideology: Observations on Culture and Industrial Capitalism in the Later Eighteenth Century," in *Culture and Politics from Puritanism to the Enlightenment,* ed. Perez Zagorin (Berkeley: University of California Press, 1980), 203–240.

23. Eleanor Frere Fenn, *The Rational Dame; or, Hints towards Supplying Prattle for Children* ([c. 1790]; rpt. London: John Marshall, [c. 1800]), vi.

24. Samuel Jackson Pratt, *Pity's Gift: A Collection of Interesting Tales to Excite the Compassion of Youth for the Animal Creation; from the Writings of Mr. Pratt, Selected by a Lady* (Philadelphia: J. Johnson, 1808), v–vi.

25. Sarah Kirby Trimmer, *Fabulous Histories: Designed for the Instruction of Children, Respecting Their Treatment of Animals* (London: Whittingham and Arliss, 1813), I, 86.

26. As far as children are concerned, at least, recent research has shown that this identification may have some empirical validity. See Stephen R. Kellert and Alan F. Felthous, "Childhood Cruelty toward Animals among Criminals and Noncriminals," *Human Relations* 38 (1985), 1113–29.

27. "Traffic," in John Ruskin, *The Crown of Wild Olive* (1866), collected in *The Complete Works of John Ruskin,* ed. E. T. Cook and Alexander Wedderburn (London: George Allen, 1905), XVIII, 433.

28. *Cursory Remarks on the Evil Tendency of Unrestrained Cruelty; Particularly on that Practised in Smithfield Market* (London, 1823), 9–11.

29. Florence Dixie, "The Horrors of Sport," *Westminster Review* 137 (1892), 49–50; George Greenwood, "The Ethics of Field Sports," *Westminster Review* 138 (1892), 172.

30. Arthur Helps, *Some Talk about Animals and Their Masters* (London: Strahan, 1872), 9.

31. Owen, *English Philanthropy,* 94; Brian Harrison, "Philanthropy and the Victorians," in *Peaceable Kingdom: Stability and Change in Modern Britain* (Oxford: Clarendon Press, 1982), 227–229. For an analysis that connects humanitarianism to the evolving free market economy, see Thomas L. Haskell, "Capitalism and the Origins of the Humanitarian Sensibility," *American Historical Review* 90 (1985), 339–361, 547–566.

32. Harrison, "Animals and the State," 84–85; Thomas, *Man and the Natural World,* 184–185.

33. George K. Behlmer, *Child Abuse and Moral Reform in England, 1870–1908* (Stanford: Stanford University Press, 1982), 12, 16. Behlmer has also compared the child protection movement to mid-nineteenth-century attempts to control baby farming and venereal disease (34–35).

34. Reprinted in *Annual Report,* 1836, 72–73.

35. William Hone, *The Every-Day Book and Table Book* (London: T. Tegg, 1835), I, 799.

36. "Eyes and Asses," *Punch* 6 (1844), 174; "Veterinary Poor-Law," *Punch* 48 (1865), 143.

37. *Annual Report*, 1849, 10; *Annual Report*, 1853, 82.

38. *Annual Report*, 1839, 24.

39. Behlmer, *Child Abuse*, 139; Harrison, "Animals and the State," 117.

40. William Youatt, *The Obligation and Extent of Humanity to Brutes, Principally Considered with Reference to the Domesticated Animals* (London: Longman, Orme, Brown, Green, and Longman, 1839), 110; Drummond, *Rights of Animals*, 44.

41. Henry Salt, *Animals' Rights Considered in Relation to Social Progress* (1892; rpt. Clark's Summit, Pa.: Society for Animal Rights, 1980), 74–75; George Hendrick, *Henry Salt: Humanitarian Reformer and Man of Letters* (Urbana: University of Illinois Press, 1977), 63.

42. Quoted in Fairholme and Pain, *A Century of Work*, 54–55.

43. For example, the "Police Reports" section of the *Voice of Humanity* 3 (1832), 10–11, recounted trials for burning a horse, skinning cats alive, and tearing off a bullock's tail.

44. *Annual Report*, 1841, 116.

45. *Cruelty to Animals*, 13–33.

46. Quoted in Harrison, "Animals and the State," 90.

47. *Annual Report*, 1837, 82.

48. *Annual Report*, 1844, 71.

49. *Annual Report*, 1850, 98.

50. *Annual Report*, 1841, 109.

51. *Annual Report*, 1839, 60; *Annual Report*, 1841, 117.

52. *Annual Report*, 1842, 67, 77–78.

53. *Annual Report*, 1841, 82.

54. *Annual Report*, 1844, 84.

55. *Annual Report*, 1840, 76.

56. *Annual Report*, 1844, 65; *Annual Report*, 1849, 66; *Annual Report*, 1866, 123–124.

57. *Annual Report*, 1853, 143; *Annual Report*, 1857, 67.

58. *Annual Report*, 1861, 61; *Annual Report*, 1855, 87.

59. *Annual Report*, 1839, 67; *Annual Report*, 1838, 64; *Annual Report*, 1847, 79.

60. *Annual Report*, 1844, 73; *Annual Report*, 1846, 75.

61. *Annual Report*, 1859, 104, 53.

62. *Annual Report*, 1846, 101; *Annual Report*, 1842, 49; *Annual Report*, 1851, 111.

63. *Annual Report*, 1837, 79.

64. *Annual Report*, 1838, 66; *Annual Report*, 1857, 48; *Annual Report*, 1859, 45.

65. *Annual Report*, 1837, 84.

66. Ibid., 78; *Annual Report*, 1838, 69; *Annual Report*, 1857, 32.

67. *Annual Report*, 1859, 52.

68. *Annual Report*, 1861, 79; *Annual Report*, 1849, 71.

69. *Annual Report*, 1854, 101.

70. There was an element of hypocrisy here, since some necessary activities, such as butchering, were recognized as inevitably offensive, yet none but the most extreme humanitarians suggested doing away with them. The only solution was to avert the eyes. This point was made clearly in an early nineteenth-century drawing manual, which stated that the butcher was "no very fit subject for the artist"; his profession was

"exceedingly shocking" and had "a very savage appearance." Slaughtering should not only be eliminated in art, it "should be concealed as much as possible from public view." William H. Pyne, *Microcosm; or, A Picturesque Delineation of the Arts, Agriculture, Manufactures &c. of Great Britain* (London: W. H. Pyne and J. C. Nattes, 1806), I, 13.

71. *Cruelty to Animals,* 4.

72. "Proceedings of the Association," *Voice of Humanity* 3 (1833), 79.

73. Fairholme and Pain, *A Century of Work,* 30–31, 53; Pain, *Martin,* 77–91.

74. Fairholme and Pain, *A Century of Work,* 59; Harrison, "Animals and the State," 92.

75. See Harrison, "Animals and the State," 92–97, for a more elaborate discussion of the nineteenth-century RSPCA inspectorate, which occasionally helped out the regular police on nonanimal matters. Behlmer, *Child Abuse,* 162–163, has compared the RSPCA inspectors to the force set up by its daughter organization, the National Society for the Prevention of Cruelty to Children.

76. *Annual Report,* 1895, 147; Kale Cording, *Waifs of a Great City; Being More about the Beggar Cats of London* (London: Gilbert and Rivington, 1907), 26–27.

77. Minutes of the annual meeting, April 30, 1834, in SPCA Minute Book 1, commencing March 1832, 139; minutes of the committee meeting, December 6, 1841, in RSPCA Minute Book 4, commencing July 1840, 217–218; *Annual Report,* 1861, 75.

78. Harrison, "Animals and the State," 83.

79. *Annual Report,* 1842, 77.

80. *Annual Report,* 1845, 89; *Annual Report,* 1837, 82; minutes of the committee meeting, November 5, 1833, in SPCA Minute Book 1, commencing March 1832, 107. Subsequently this procedure was formalized, so that constables were to report cruelty cases to their superiors, who had to both verify the convictions and approve the rewards (*Cruelty to Animals,* 4). In any case, the RSPCA relied less heavily on the police as its own force expanded. The *Annual Report* for 1836 (55) noted that 100 policemen had received gratuities for testifying in 80 prosecutions, but the police appeared as witnesses in only 6 percent of the cases selected for discussion in the *Annual Reports* for 1857 through 1860.

81. *Annual Report,* 1853, 154.

82. Minutes of the committee meeting, August 13, 1832, in SPCA Minute Book 1, commencing March 1832.

83. *Annual Report,* 1847, 81.

84. *Cruelty to Animals,* 8–13.

85. Grantley F. Berkeley, *Fact against Fiction: The Habits and Treatment of Animals Practically Considered* (London: Samuel Tinsley, 1874), I, ix–x; John E. Archer, "'A Fiendish Outrage'? A Study of Animal Maiming in East Anglia: 1830–1870," *Agricultural History Review* 33 (1985), 147–157.

86. Hone, *Every-Day Book,* I, 945.

87. *Annual Report,* 1858, 36, 77–78.

88. For a discussion of a related French confrontation in which the workers took the initiative, see Robert Darnton, "Workers Revolt: The Great Cat Massacre of the Rue Saint-Severin," in *The Great Cat Massacre and Other Episodes in French Cultural History* (New York: Basic Books, 1984), 75–106.

89. *Annual Report,* 1856, 62; *Annual Report,* 1845, 74.

90. *Annual Report,* 1839, 62.

91. *Annual Report,* 1840, 81; *Annual Report,* 1843, 70.

92. *Annual Report,* 1858, 50; *Annual Report,* 1843, 56.

93. *Annual Report,* 1844, 73; *Annual Report,* 1842, 49.

94. *Annual Report,* 1849, 71; *Annual Report,* 1844, 85.

95. Pierce Egan, *Sporting Anecdotes, Original and Selected* (London: Sherwood, Neely, and Jones, 1820), 239.

96. Joseph Strutt, *The Sports and Pastimes of the People of England* (1801; rpt. London: Chatto and Windus, 1876), 349.

97. Pain, *Martin,* 67–69.

98. John K. Walton and Robert Poole, "The Lancashire Wakes in the Nineteenth Century," in *Popular Culture and Custom in Nineteenth-Century England,* ed. Robert D. Storch (London: Croom Helm, 1982), 105–106; Douglas A. Reid, "Interpreting the Festival Calendar: Wakes and Fairs as Carnivals," in *Popular Culture and Custom in Nineteenth-Century England,* 128, 133–135.

99. *Cruelty to Animals,* 15–16.

100. *Annual Report,* 1840, 64; *Annual Report,* 1841, 135; *Annual Report,* 1845, 95.

101. *Annual Report,* 1836, 65.

102. Ibid.

103. *Annual Report,* 1843, 80, 82.

104. *Annual Report,* 1838, 61, 63.

105. *Annual Report,* 1839, 83.

106. Ibid.

107. *Annual Report,* 1838, 83–88.

108. *Annual Report,* 1852, 73–74.

109. Morsley, *News from the English Countryside,* 49; Hone, *Every-Day Book,* I, 978–999.

110. *Annual Report,* 1837, 80; *Annual Report,* 1838, 82.

111. Morsley, *News from the English Countryside,* 26.

112. Walton and Poole, "The Lancashire Wakes," 106; C. M. Prior, *The History of the Racing Calendar and the Stud-Book, from Their inception in the Eighteenth Century, with Observations on Some of the Occurrences Noted Therein* (London: "Sporting Life," 1926), 198.

113. Malcolmson, *Popular Recreations,* 118; *Annual Report,* 1836, 64.

114. *Annual Report,* 1850, 120.

115. *Annual Report,* 1843, 68.

116. *Annual Report,* 1853, 83–87.

117. *Annual Report,* 1854, 111–112.

118. *Annual Report,* 1844, 135.

119. James Cotter Morison, "Scientific *versus* Bucolic Vivisection," *Fortnightly Review* 43 (1885), 249–252.

120. *Zoophilist* 10 (1890), 34.

121. Fairholme and Pain, *A Century of Work,* 191.

122. Youatt, *Obligation and Extent of Humanity to Brutes,* 197.

123. Minutes of the committee meeting, April 25, 1832, in SPCA Minute Book 1, commencing March 1832, 19; Richard D. French, *Antivivisection and Medical Science in Victorian Society* (Princeton: Princeton University Press, 1975), 28.

124. *Annual Report,* 1847, 36.

125. Lloyd G. Stevenson, "Religious Elements in the Background of the British Anti-Vivisection Movement," *Yale Journal of Biology and Medicine* 29 (1956), 154–157; Ger-

ald Geison, *Michael Foster and the Cambridge School of Physiology: The Scientific Enterprise in Late Victorian Society* (Princeton: Princeton University Press, 1978), 18–19; L. S. Jacyna, "Principles of General Physiology: The Comparative Dimension to British Neuroscience in the 1830s and 1840s," in *Studies in the History of Biology,* vol. VII, ed. William Coleman and Camille Limoges (Baltimore: Johns Hopkins University Press, 1984), 48.

126. French, *Antivivisection,* 39–46.

127. E. Westacott, *A Century of Vivisection and Anti-Vivisection: A Study of Their Effect upon Science, Medicine and Human Life during the Past Hundred Years* (Ashingdon, Essex: C. W. Daniel, 1949), 1–2.

128. French, *Antivivisection,* 59–60; Frances Power Cobbe, *Life of Frances Power Cobbe* (Boston: Houghton Mifflin, 1894), II, 568–569.

129. Cobbe, *Life,* II, 569.

130. See French, *Antivivisection,* chs. 4 and 5 for a full discussion of the debate surrounding the passage of the 1876 act.

131. *Cruelty to Animals,* 47.

132. Harrison, "Animals and the State," 90.

133. *Zoophilist* 1 (1882), 169–171.

134. Cobbe, *Life,* II, 596.

135. Cobbe, *Life,* II, 599ff.; George R. Jesse, "Publications of Vivisection," book 1 (scrapbook deposited in the British Library); French, *Antivivisection,* ch. 8.

136. *Zoophilist* 3 (1883), 140; *Zoophilist* 2 (1882), 197.

137. Westacott, *A Century of Vivisection,* 132; *Zoophilist* 2 (1882), 194.

138. "Vivisection," *Nature* 25 (1882), 429.

139. *Zoophilist* 5 (1886), 173–175.

140. Turner, *Reckoning with the Beast,* 115.

141. French, *Antivivisection,* 285–287; Coral Lansbury has analyzed the social implications of the early twentieth-century antivivisection movement in *The Old Brown Dog: Women, Workers, and Vivisection* (Madison: University of Wisconsin Press, 1985).

142. *Zoophilist* 1 (1881), iii–iv.

143. Marie Louise de la Ramée [Ouida] and Frances Power Cobbe, quoted in M. Jeanne Peterson, *The Medical Profession in Mid-Victorian London* (Berkeley: University of California Press, 1978), 196.

144. *Zoophilist* 3 (1883), 187.

145. For example, Henry Salt; see *Animals' Rights,* 91–92.

146. Cobbe, *Life,* II, 666–667. Henry Salt dramatized the self-seeking scientist as well as the foolishly sentimental humanitarian in a one-act play entitled "A Lover of Animals," Appendix A, in Hendrick, *Henry Salt.*

147. For example, the *Field* expressed its initial disapproval as follows: "The 'home' . . . had been very justly condemned, as giving encouragement to the increase of underbred curs that infest the metropolis" (H. F., "The Home for Lost and Starving Dogs," 16, 1860, 434).

148. The *Zoophilist* of April 1, 1882, carried several articles on this contretemps.

149. "The Home for Lost Dogs," *Strand Magazine* 1 (1891), 652.

150. Antimaterialism could be broadly interpreted. In Germany antivivisection and anti-Semitism were closely connected, and even in England an antivivisection periodical could refer pointedly to "the uncongenial influences of Judaism and Materialism." *Zoophilist* 1 (1881), 27–28, quoted in French, *Antivivisection,* 347.

151. Lionel John Wallace, "Vivisection," *Westminster Review* 137 (1892), 259.

152. See, for example, "The Anti-Vivisection Movement," *Punch* 70 (1876), 105; "Address to Animals' Friends," *Punch* 70 (1876), 249; and "The Crusade against Cruelty," *Punch* 70 (1876), 265.

153. *Zoophilist* 1 (1882), 160.

154. *Zoophilist* 1 (1881), 9.

155. See, for example, *Annual Report*, 1847, 61–69; *Annual Report*, 1851, 51–70.

156. "Proceedings of the Association," *Voice of Humanity* 3 (1833), 110.

4. *Cave Canem*

1. J. R. Fisher, "The Economic Effects of Cattle Disease in Britain and Its Containment, 1850–1900," *Agricultural History* 54 (1980), 278–279.

2. Iain Pattison, *The British Veterinary Profession, 1791–1948* (London: J. A. Allen, 1984), 54, 59.

3. Pattison, *British Veterinary Profession*, ch. 7; John Fisher, "Professor Gamgee and the Farmers," *Veterinary History*, n.s., 1 (1979–80), 53–57.

4. John Broad, "Cattle Plague in Eighteenth-Century England," *Agricultural History Review* 31, pt. 2 (1983), 104–115.

5. Lise Wilkinson, "Rinderpest and Mainstream Infectious Disease Concepts in the Eighteenth Century," *Medical History* 28 (1984), 149–150.

6. In general, "rabies" referred to the disease in dogs and other animals, whereas "hydrophobia" was used to describe the disease in humans. The two diseases were in fact the same, and the term "hydrophobia" was misleading—because in the late stages of the disease some human victims manifested not a fear of water, but an aversion to liquids, caused by their inability to swallow. "Rabies" tended to displace "hydrophobia," at least in scientific usage, as the century progressed.

7. Each of these committees produced a report: Report from the Select Committee on the Bill to Prevent the Spreading of Canine Madness, *Parliamentary Papers*, 1830 no. 651, vol. X.685, will be hereafter abbreviated as *PP*, 1830; Report of a Committee Appointed by the Local Government Board to Inquire into M. Pasteur's Treatment of Hydrophobia, *Parliamentary Papers*, 1887, c. 5087, vol. LXVI.429, as *PP*, 1887, Pasteur; Report from the Select Committee of the House of Lords on Rabies in Dogs, *Parliamentary Papers*, 1887, no. 322, vol. XI.451, as *PP*, 1887, Rabies; and Report of the Departmental Committee to Inquire into and Report upon the Working of the Laws Relating to Dogs, *Parliamentary Papers*, 1897, c. 8320 and c. 8378, vol. XXXIV, as *PP*, 1897.

8. For extended discussion of differential responses to familiar killers like diptheria and tuberculosis and unfamiliar ones like cholera, see Charles Rosenberg, *The Cholera Years: The United States in 1832, 1849, and 1866* (Chicago: University of Chicago Press, 1962); R. J. Morris, *Cholera 1832: The Social Response to an Epidemic* (New York: Holmes and Meier, 1976); and John Duffy, "Social Impact of Disease in the Late Nineteenth Century," *Bulletin of the New York Academy of Medicine* 47 (1971), 797–811.

9. George Fleming, *Rabies and Hydrophobia: Their History, Nature, Causes, Symptoms, and Prevention* (London: Chapman and Hall, 1872), 1.

10. Charlotte Brontë, *Shirley, a Tale* (1849; rpt. London: Dent, 1968), 402.

11. There is no record of the pattern of outbreaks that was to characterize rabies

in nineteenth-century England until about 1735. At that time the incidence of rabies seems to have increased noticeably, especially in the domestic dog. Fairly widespread epizootics recurred every decade or so, always traceable to focuses of infection in London and, beginning in the nineteenth century, in industrial Lancashire. N. H. Hole, "Rabies and Quarantine," *Nature* 224 (1969), 244; Colin Kaplan, "The World Problem," in *Rabies: The Facts*, ed. Colin Kaplan (Oxford: Oxford University Press, 1977), 7–8; Fleming, *Rabies and Hydrophobia*, 34.

12. Fleming, *Rabies and Hydrophobia*, 34; *Times*, October 31, 1877; *PP*, 1887, Rabies, 178; Arthur Shadwell, "Rabies and Muzzling," *National Review* 15 (1890), 230–231.

13. Thomas Watson, "Rabies and Hydrophobia," *Nineteenth Century* 2 (1877), 718; Gordon Stables, *Dogs in Their Relation to the Public (Social, Sanitary and Legal)* (London: Cassell, Petter and Galpin, 1877), 18–20.

14. *PP*, 1887, Rabies, 43–48, 206; *Sherborne, Dorchester and Taunton Journal*, November 12, 1877. After 1889, when the Board of Agriculture assumed responsibility for rabies regulation, national statistics became available (*PP*, 1897, 7).

15. *Truth*, November 8, 1877; *PP*, 1887, Rabies, 206.

16. *Exeter Flying-Post*, February 26, 1773, 3.

17. Daniel Peter Layard, *An Essay on the Bite of a Mad Dog* (London: John Rivington and Thomas Payne, 1763), 120.

18. *Times*, October 31, 1877; "Toby to Punch," *Punch* 73 (1877), 237.

19. Grantley F. Berkeley, *Fact against Fiction: The Habits and Treatment of Animals Practically Considered* (London: Samuel Tinsley, 1874), I, 332; *PP*, 1887, Rabies, 64.

20. Robert Hamilton, *Remarks on the Means of Obviating the Fatal Effects of the Bite of a Mad Dog or Other Rabid Animal* (Ipswich: Shave and Jackson, 1785), 123; Layard, *Essay on the Bite of a Mad Dog*, 125–126.

21. *PP*, 1830, 13.

22. William Youatt, *On Canine Madness* (London: Longman, 1830), 16; *PP*, 1887, Rabies, 82.

23. Emmanuel Eupen Vander Borck, "On Hydrophobia," *Commercial and Agricultural Magazine* 3 (July 1800), 7.

24. Pattison, *British Veterinary Profession*, 52.

25. Youatt, *On Canine Madness*, 2–3; "Hydrophobia," *Westminster Review* 13 (1830), 415–416; George Henry Lewes, "Mad Dogs," *Blackwood's Magazine* 90 (1861), 222.

26. Morris, *Cholera 1832*, 14; Rosenberg, *Cholera Years*, 120.

27. David Johnson, *Sketches of Indian Field Sports . . . with Remarks on Hydrophobia and Rabid Animals* (London: Robert Jennings, 1827), 211; "An Old Shirkurrer: Wild Dog Spearing in India," *Field* 1 (1853), 58.

28. *PP*, 1830, 29; Rusticus, "On Hydrophobia," *Annals of Sporting and Fancy Gazette* 4 (1823), 104–105; "Case of Rabies Furor," *Veterinary Record* 3 (1847), 284–285; Lewes, "Mad Dogs," 231.

29. Rudyard Kipling, *The Jungle Books* (1894–95; rpt. New York: New American Library, 1961), 12.

30. This vocabulary was widely used. See, for example, the testimony of veterinary surgeon John Atkinson (*PP*, 1887, Rabies, 106); Fleming's learned treatise *Rabies and Hydrophobia* (394 and elsewhere), and Watson's popular article "Hydrophobia and Rabies," 717–736.

31. *The Natural History of Domestic Animals, Containing an Account of Their Habits and*

Instincts and of the Services They Render to Man (Dublin: J. Jones, 1821), 13–14; George Archdale, "Our Dogs," *Temple Bar* 78 (1886), 461; Louisa Sarah Guggenberger, "Dogs in Germany," *Nineteenth Century* 22 (1887), 195.

32. Frederick Lupton, *The Law Relating to Dogs* (London: Stevens, 1888), 2–4.

33. *PP,* 1887, Rabies, 67–70. The commissioner was as concerned with its interference with other police functions, by consuming time and arousing citizen hostility, as with its unpleasantness and danger.

34. Youatt, *On Canine Madness,* 30–31; *PP,* 1887, Rabies, 6–7; *Sixth Report and Proceedings of the Annual Meeting of the Society for the Prevention of Cruelty to Animals,* 1832, 48; *PP,* 1897, 63–64.

35. *PP,* 1897, 63–64; *Standard,* November 2, 1877; Fleming, *Rabies and Hydrophobia,* 354.

36. Quoted in Roy Porter, *English Society in the Eighteenth Century* (Harmondsworth, Middlesex: Penguin, 1981), 373; Gareth Stedman Jones, *Outcast London: A Study in the Relationship between Classes in Victorian Society* (1971; rpt. New York: Pantheon, 1984), 186.

37. W. H. R., "Street Dogs," *Illustrated London News* 20 (1852), 58.

38. *Twelfth Report and Proceedings of the Annual Meeting of the Society for the Prevention of Cruelty to Animals,* 1838, 90; *PP,* 1887, Rabies, 181; *PP,* 1830, 10; *PP,* 1887, Rabies, 201.

39. *Times,* October 30, 1877; *General Evening Post,* January 12–14, 1748. Some explanations of the fact that strays carried rabies more frequently than other animals did not smack so strongly of class prejudice. Several of the veterinarians who testified before the House of Lords Select Committee in 1887 pointed out that starving mongrels would be more vulnerable to all kinds of infection than well-cared for dogs, and that their constant presence in the streets made them more likely to be bitten by a passing mad dog (*PP,* 1887, Rabies, 38–39, 87).

40. Vander Borck, "On Hydrophobia," 5.

41. *PP,* 1887, Rabies, 146; Fleming, *Rabies and Hydrophobia,* 353; *PP,* 1887, Rabies, 164, 168.

42. Fleming, *Rabies and Hydrophobia,* 110; *PP,* 1887, Rabies, 206.

43. Anna Kingsford, *Pasteur: His Method and Its Results* (London: North London Antivivisection Society, 1886), 21; *PP,* 1887, Rabies, 226; J. Hart of Manningham, Bradford, to George R. Jesse, in "Hydrophobia" scrapbook, n.p. This is one of nine scrapbooks in the George Richard Jesse Collection at the British Library: one entitled "Hydrophobia," five entitled "Publications on Vivisection," two entitled "Pamphlets on Vivisection," and one entitled "Tracts on Vivisection, Footpaths, Rabies Canina, Muzzling Dogs, Game Laws." The contents of the scrapbooks are not as diverse as the titles might suggest.

44. *Times,* November 18, 1877; "Fox Hound Kennel at Beachborough," Brockman Papers, vol. CXXXV, pp. 25b–24b (British Library Add. Ms. 45, 202); *Annals of Sporting and Fancy Gazette* 1 (1822), 193; *Sportsman's Journal and Fancier's Guide* 1 (1878), 3; *Times,* August 31, 1876.

45. So significant were the sporting interests of many of the committee members that they were noted in the *Dictionary of National Biography.*

46. Rabies in deer, although rare, received a great deal of attention. An outbreak among the deer in London's Richmond Park prompted its own parliamentary inquiry in 1888, and Louis Pasteur himself chose to use such an episode as the dramatic beginning

of an article addressed to the English general public: "At the time of writing this paper rabies is raging in England in a herd of deer in the park of the Marquis of Bristol, at Ickworth" ("Rabies," trans. Armand Ruffer, *New Review* 1, 1889, 505).

47. Berkeley, *Fact against Fiction,* I, 338–339.

48. PP, 1886, Rabies, 101; *Standard,* November 6, 1877; letter of James Brierly to Edward Smith Stanley, thirteenth earl of Derby, January 13, 1851, in the Archive of the Liverpool Record Office; "A Herd of Rabid Deer," *Illustrated London News* 28 (1856), 395.

49. William Broderip, *Zoological Recreations* (London: H. Colburn, 1847), 188; David Low, *On the Domesticated Animals of the British Islands* (London: Longman, Brown, Green, and Longmans, n.d.), 698.

50. Fleming, *Rabies and Hydrophobia,* 194.

51. William Hiller Onslow, "Dogs in Disgrace," *National Review* 10 (1887), 336; Philip Gilbert Hamerton, *Chapters on Animals* (Boston: Roberts Brothers, 1874), 29; Fleming, *Rabies and Hydrophobia,* 194.

52. *Exeter Flying-Post,* February 26, 1773, 3; PP, 1887, Rabies, 46.

53. *The Kent Dog Owners and the New Muzzling Order* (London, 1890), 3.

54. For detailed accounts of Victorian administrative attempts to control venereal disease, see Judith R. Walkowitz, *Prostitution and Victorian Society: Women, Class, and the State* (Cambridge: Cambridge University Press, 1980), esp. chs. 3 and 4; Keith Nield, "Introduction" to *Prostitution in the Victorian Age: Debates on the Issue from Nineteenth Century Critical Journals,* ed. Keith Nield (Westmead, England: Grigg, 1973); and Margaret Hamilton, "Opposition to the Contagious Diseases Act, 1864–1886," *Albion* 10 (1978), 14–27.

55. *Times,* October 24, 1877.

56. George Fleming, *Animal Plagues: Their History, Nature, and Prevention* (London: Chapman and Hall, 1871), I, xxxiii.

57. He reasoned that if the period of confinement exceeded the incubation period, then all rabid animals would become ill and die while confined, without passing on the disease. Sherwin A. Hall, "The Bardsley Plan and the Early Nineteenth Century Controversy on Rabies," *Veterinary History* 9 (Summer 1977), 15–16, 19. Bardsley subsequently reiterated his proposal in a book, *Medical Reports of Cases and Experiments with Observations Chiefly Derived from Hospital Practice to which Are Added an Inquiry into the Origin of Canine Madness* (London: W. Stratford, 1807).

58. PP, 1887, Rabies, 206; *The Bazaar, the Exchange and Mart,* December 8, 1877; PP, 1887, Rabies, 31; Kingsford, *Pasteur,* 20.

59. PP, 1887, Rabies, 136; Youatt, *On Canine Madness,* 16; PP, 1830, 3.

60. Hamilton, *Remarks,* 159; P. B. Munsche, *Gentlemen and Poachers: The English Game Laws, 1671–1831* (Cambridge: Cambridge University Press, 1981), 82–83; PP, 1897, 149. The cost of a license varied from time to time; in 1867 the duty was 5s. per animal per year, and in 1878 it was raised to 7s. Subsequently, there was pressure to raise the dog duty as high as a guinea, but this was resisted by governments anxious not to be accused of persecuting decent working men and their dogs. John K. Walton, "Mad Dogs and Englishmen: The Conflict over Rabies in Late Victorian England," *Journal of Social History* 13 (1979), 235.

61. *Parliamentary Papers,* 1830–31, no. 139, vol. I.301.

62. PP, 1830, 21; *Sixth Report and Proceedings of the Annual Meeting of the Society for the Prevention of Cruelty to Animals,* 1832, 48; *Macclesfield Chronicle,* November 30, 1877; William

Hone, *The Every-Day and Table Book* (London: T. Tegg, 1835), I, 899.

63. Stables, *Dogs in Their Relation to the Public*, 10–11; *PP*, 1897, 4; "On Mad Dogs," *Annals of Sporting and Fancy Gazette* 6 (July 1824), 11.

64. Appendix I ("A Digest of Certain Acts of Parliament Relating to Dogs") of *PP*, 1897, 149–152.

65. *PP*, 1887, Rabies, 17, 67.

66. *PP*, 1887, Rabies, 93.

67. *Fifty-ninth Report and Proceedings of the Annual Meeting of the Royal Society for the Prevention of Cruelty to Animals*, 1885, 84.

68. Stables, *Dogs in Their Relation to the Public*, 12; Christopher Hibbett, ed., *Queen Victoria in Her Letters and Journals* (London: John Murray, 1984), 300; *PP*, 1887, Rabies, 112, 126; *Fifty-seventh Report and Proceedings of the Annual Meeting of the Royal Society for the Prevention of Cruelty to Animals*, 1883, 68.

69. "To All Cat Owners," *Ladies' Kennel Journal* 5 (1897), 208.

70. G. P. West, "Rabies: Some Glimpses into the Past," *Veterinary History* 8 (1976–77), 6; Gerald L. Geison, "Pasteur," *Dictionary of Scientific Biography*, X, 403–404.

71. *PP*, 1887, Rabies, 178, 67.

72. *PP*, 1887, Pasteur, i–iv.

73. *PP*, 1887, Pasteur, vii, 9–11.

74. *PP*, 1887, Rabies, 118–119, vii.

75. Horsley's recollections appeared in the *British Medical Journal*, which is quoted in Lise Wilkinson, "The Development of the Virus Concept as Reflected in the Corpora of Studies on Individual Pathogens, 4: Rabies—Two Millenia of Ideas and Conjectures on the Aetiology of a Virus Disease," *Medical History* 21 (1977), 30. It is interesting that none of these authorities considered the possibility that cats or wild animals would continue to harbor the disease and reinfect even a muzzled, registered, and quarantined dog population. The 1887 House of Lords Committee received evidence about both rabid cats (191) and rabid foxes (41). Nevertheless, a program focused exclusively on dogs ultimately succeeded in eradicating rabies from Britain, which is strong prima facie evidence of the absence of sylvatic infection. According to a modern veterinary scientist, however, "because of the wandering habits of rabid dogs and the extreme susceptibility of the fox to experimental infection, it seems very curious that sylvatic infection has not occurred" (Hole, "Rabies and Quarantine," 244).

76. For a brief history of English rabies control, very much from the official perspective, see Ministry of Agriculture, Fisheries and Food, *Animal Health, A Centenary, 1865–1965: A Century of Endeavour to Control Diseases of Animals* (London: HMSO, 1965), 207–208, 272.

77. *PP*, 1897, 7–8; Carruthers Gould, *Froissart's Modern Chronicles* (London: T. Fisher Unwin, 1902), 78.

78. The spokesman for the board defended its exercise of authority on principle, stating, "nothing that the members of the deputation would have said . . . would have modified in the slightest degree the policy of the Board" (*The Kent Dog Owners and the New Muzzling Order*, 37).

79. *PP*, 1887, Rabies, 102.

80. *PP*, 1887, Rabies, 111.

81. *Zoophilist* 6 (1886), 86.

82. Jesse, "Hydrophobia" scrapbook, n.p.

83. Ibid.

84. *Times*, October 10, 1877.

85. Berkeley, *Fact against Fiction*, I, 132.

86. *Worcestershire Chronicle*, December 22, 1877; *Kennel Review* 4 (1885), 191; *PP*, 1887, Rabies, 223.

87. Robert White, *Doubts of Hydrophobia as a Specific Disease to be Communicated by the Bite of a Dog* (London: Knight and Lacey, 1826), 2–3, 133; "Brighton Rabies," *Annals of Sporting and Fancy Gazette* 7 (1825), 62.

88. Kingsford, *Pasteur*, 7; Gordon Stables, *Hints about Home and Farm Favourites for Pleasure, Prizes, and Profit* (London: Frederick Warne, 1889), 33; John H. Clarke, *The Pasteur Craze* (London: Victoria Street Society United with the International Association for the Protection of Animals from Vivisection, 1886), 3.

89. Jesse, "Publications of Vivisection" scrapbook, I, n.p.; Thomas M. Dolan, *Pasteur and Rabies* (London: George Bell and Sons, 1890), 76.

90. Pasteur, "Rabies," 629; Kingsford, *Pasteur*, 24; *British Medical Journal*, November 6, 1886.

91. *Standard*, November 2, 1886; A. Lutaud, *Hydrophobia in Relation to Pasteur's Method and the Report of the English Committee* (London: Whittaker, 1887), 12.

92. Kingsford, *Pasteur*, 22–23.

5. Exotic Captives

1. E. W. Brayley, "Some Account of the Life and Writings . . . of the Late Sir Thomas Stamford Raffles . . . ," *Zoological Journal* 11 (1827), 382–406; Emily Hahn, *Raffles of Singapore: A Biography* (New York: Doubleday, 1946), 113, 414–416; Sophia Raffles, *Memoir of the Life and Public Services of Sir Thomas Stamford Raffles . . . by His Widow* (London: John Murray, 1830), 641, 568.

2. See generally Gustave Loisel, *Histoire des ménageries de l'antiquité à nos jours* (Paris: Octave Doin et Fils, 1912), vol. I, and Yi-Fu Tuan, *Dominance and Affection: The Making of Pets* (New Haven: Yale University Press, 1984), 75–80.

3. Loisel, *Histoire*, I, 210–212, and II, 13–14; Richard D. Altick, *The Shows of London* (Cambridge, Mass.: Harvard University Press, 1978), 87–89.

4. Posters and newspaper clippings in the Johnson Collection of Printed Ephemera, Bodleian Library.

5. *Catalogue of Bostock and Wombwell's Royal Menagerie* (n.d.), 12–13, item 944/177 in the Circus Collection of the Tyne and Wear County Archives.

6. William Hone, *The Every-Day Book and Table Book* (London: T. Tegg, 1835), I, 1175–78, 1191–92, 1197–99; Thomas Frost, *The Old Showmen and the Old London Fairs* (London: Chatto and Windus, 1881), 257–259, 274–284.

7. Richard Hodgkinson, "Journal of a Journey to London on Account of the Lancashire Canal, Begun 26th Feby 1794," item L15/2/1 in the Archives Department of the Manchester Central Library; Dix Harwood, *Love for Animals and How It Developed in Great Britain* (New York: Columbia University, 1928), 227; E. T. Bennett, *The Tower Menagerie: Comprising the Natural History of the Animals Contained in That Establishment; with Anecdotes of Their Characters and Histories* (London: Robert Jennings, 1829), xv–xvi.

8. Richard Hodgkinson, "Minutes of a Journey to London, Begun May 11th to Attend a Committee in the House of Commons upon the Leeds and Liverpool Canal

Extension Bill" (1819), item L15/2/12/1 in the Archives Department of the Manchester Central Library.

9. R. Ackermann, "Polito's Menagerie, Exeter Change," *Repository of Arts, Literature, Commerce, Manufactures, Fashions, and Politics* 7 (July 1812), 27–30; Terence Templeton, "The Wild Beasts' Banquet," *New Monthly Magazine* 11 (1824), 362–364.

10. Poster in the Johnson Collection of Printed Ephemera, Bodleian Library.

11. Advertisements in the *Exeter Flying-Post,* November 11, 1806, and May 14, 1812.

12. Frost, *The Old Showmen,* 241.

13. Poster, Fillinham Collection, British Library; Manchester Zoological Gardens Company, *Report of the Directors* (Manchester, 1837), 3.

14. John Bastin, "The First Prospectus of the Zoological Society of London: A New Light on the Society's Origins," *Journal of the Society for the Bibliography of Natural History* 5 (1970), 370–372.

15. John Bastin, "A Further Note on the Origins of the Zoological Society of London," *Journal of the Society for the Bibliography of Natural History* 6 (1973), 237; *Report of the Council of the Zoological Society of London,* 1829, 15.

16. "Prospectus of a Society for Introducing and Domesticating New Breeds or Varieties of Animals . . . and for Forming a General Collection in Zoology," quoted in Bastin, "The First Prospectus," 385.

17. *Guide to the Gardens of the Zoological Society* (London: Richard Taylor, 1829), 2.

18. *Report of the Council of the Zoological Society of London,* 1835, 11.

19. Zoological Society of London, "Minutes of Council," July 17, 1833, in III, 187; February 21, 1838, in V, 269; October 20, 1841, in VII, 142; February 21, 1841, in VII, 12; September 1, 1841, in VII, 130; June 16, 1847, in IX, 5.

20. "Illustrations of New or Rare Animals in the Zoological Society's Living Collection," *Nature* 23 (1880), 36.

21. A member of the University of Dublin, *A Stroll in the Gardens of the London Zoological Society* . . . (London: E. Wallis, 1828), 4–5; "The Zoological Gardens—Regent's Park," *Quarterly Review* 56 (1836), 313; E. T. Bennett, *The Gardens and Menagerie of the Zoological Society Delineated* (Chiswick: T. Tegg and N. Hailes), I, v.

22. Zoological Society of London, "Minutes of Council," February 27, 1827, and April 3, 1827, in I, 17, 20.

23. Zoological Society of London, admission tickets, n.d., Fillinham Collection, British Library; R. Ackermann, "Polito's Menagerie, Exeter Change," 30; C. H. Keeling, *Where the Lion Trod: A Study of Forgotten Zoological Gardens* (Guildford, Surrey: Clam Publications, 1984), 15.

24. Quoted in Wilfred Blunt, *The Ark in the Park: The Zoo in the Nineteenth Century* (London: Hamish Hamilton, 1976), 32.

25. William Swainson, *A Preliminary Discourse on the Study of Natural History* (London: Longman, Rees, Orme, Brown, Green and Longmans, 1834), 315; "Zoological Gardens, Regent's Park," *Punch* 6 (1844), 186.

26. "Acclimatisation of Animals," *Edinburgh Review* 111 (1860), 173; Bennett, *Gardens and Menagerie,* I, v.

27. Zoological Society of London, "Minutes of Council," June 30, 1826, in I, 9; February 18, 1829, in I, 136; December 21, 1831, in II, 332–333.

28. P. Chalmers Mitchell, *Centenary History of the Zoological Society of London* (London: Zoological Society of London, 1929), 86.

29. Lucinda Lambton, *Beastly Buildings: The National Trust Book of Architecture for Animals* (London: Jonathan Cape, 1985), 156; Robert K. Dent, *The Making of Birmingham; Being the Rise and Growth of the Midland Metropolis* (Birmingham: J. L. Allday, 1894), 427.

30. For accounts of the Zoological Society's early financial difficulties, see "Acclimatisation of Animals," 173–174; Blunt, *Ark in the Park*, 35; "The Zoological Society of London," *Nature* 36 (1887), 189.

31. *Report of the Council of the Zoological Society of London*, 1865, 6; *News of the World*, May 22, 1853; "The Zoological Gardens," *Quarterly Review* 98 (1855), 248.

32. Royal Zoological Society of Ireland, *Proceedings of the Society*, 1841 (rpt. Dublin: Council of the Society, 1908), 7.

33. Quoted in Keeling, *Where the Lion Trod*, 38.

34. Quoted in David Hancocks, *Animals and Architecture* (London: Hugh Evelyn, 1971), 121; F. T. Buckland, "The Wild-Beast Show," *Field* 12 (1858), 436.

35. *Companion to the Royal Surrey Zoological Gardens* (London: J. King, 1839), 24.

36. *Visitors' Hand Book to the Liverpool Zoological Gardens* (Liverpool: John R. Isaac, 1841); Bostock and Wombwell's Royal Menagerie, *Illustrated Catalogue* (n.d. [late nineteenth century], n.p.), item 944/177 in the Tyne and Wear County Archives.

37. Posters in the Fillinham Collection, British Library, and the Johnson Collection of Printed Ephemera, Bodleian Library.

38. D. W. Mitchell and Philip Lutley Sclater, *Guide to the Gardens of the Zoological Society of London* (London: Bradbury and Evans, 1859), 53; Zoological Society of London, "Minutes of Council," February 2, 1853, in X, 333; "The Zoological Gardens," *Quarterly Review* 98 (1855), 223.

39. "The Zoological Society of London," *Nature* 36 (1887), 189; Gwynne Vevers, comp., *London's Zoo* (London: Bodley Head, 1976).

40. *Illustrated London News* 25 (1854), 648; *Illustrated London News* 21 (1852), 312.

41. For some recent discussions of the significance of wild animal exhibits, see John Berger, "Why Look at Animals?" in *About Looking* (New York: Pantheon, 1980), 1–26 (somewhat anachronistic with regard to the nineteenth century); Tuan, *Dominance and Affection*, ch. 5; and Paul Bouissac, *Circus and Culture: A Semiotic Approach* (Bloomington: Indiana University Press, 1976), chs. 6 and 7.

42. *Gore's Liverpool Directory*, 1841, 1; *Guide to the Zoological Gardens, Belle Vue* (Manchester, 1880), 6.

43. "The Zoological Gardens," *Quarterly Review* 98 (1855), 220.

44. *Report of the Council of the Zoological Society of London*, 1855, 14.

45. *Times*, August 12, 1875; *Illustrated London News* 35 (1859), 427.

46. *Popular Zoology: Comprising Memoirs and Anecdotes of the Quadrupeds, Birds, and Reptiles in the Zoological Society's Menagerie* (London: John Sharpe, 1832), 102, 194.

47. "A Visit to the Zoological Gardens," *New Monthly Magazine and Literary Journal*, pt. 2 (1836), 480, 489–491.

48. *Popular Zoology*, xxx; W. P. Jolly, *Jumbo* (London: Constable, 1976), 81; Henry Scherren, *Walks and Talks in the Zoo* (London: Religious Tract Society, 1900), 13; Charles J. Cornish, *Sir William Henry Flower: A Personal Memoir* (London: Macmillan, 1904), 78.

49. *Punch* 60 (1871), 240; *Visitors' Hand Book to the Liverpool Zoological Gardens*, 6; "The Zoological Gardens—Regent's Park," 313; *Punch* 56 (1869), 192.

50. Frank E. Beddard, *Natural History in Zoological Gardens* (London: Archibald Constable, 1905), 55; F. G. Aflalo, *A Walk through the Zoological Gardens* (London: Sands, 1900),

14; P. Chalmers Mitchell, *Official Guide to the Gardens of the Zoological Society of London* (London: Zoological Society of London, 1904), 57.

51. Aflalo, *Walk through the Gardens,* 101, 108; *Popular Zoology,* 83.

52. William Bingley, *Animal Biography* (London: Richard Phillips, 1804), I, 59; "The Zoological Gardens," *Quarterly Review* 169 (1889), 537; Edward Wilson, *Guide to the Gardens of the Bristol, Clifton, and West of England Zoological Society* (Bristol: William F. Mach, 1886), 13.

53. "The Zoological Gardens—Regent's Park," 322.

54. Aflalo, *Walk through the Gardens,* 177.

55. For example, the *Visitors' Hand Book to the Liverpool Zoological Gardens* prefaced its listing of the animals with "VISITORS ARE REQUESTED NOT TO TEAZE THE ANIMALS" (3); in 1859 the Council of the Royal Zoological Society of Ireland decided to remove threats of penalty or prosecution from the placards in the Dublin zoo, appealing instead to the visitors' sense of propriety: "Please don't tease the animals" (Royal Zoological Society of Ireland, *Proceedings of the Society,* 1859, 107).

56. *Punch* 60 (1871),240; *Times,* September 29, 1852.

57. Royal Zoological Society of Ireland, *Proceedings of the Society,* 1864, 13; *Daily Telegraph,* May 7, 1879.

58. *Report of the Council of the Zoological Society of London,* 1843, 11; *Report of the Council of the Zoological Society of London,* 1844, 11.

59. *Visitors' Hand Book to the Liverpool Zoological Gardens,* 10–14; Wilson, *Guide to the Gardens of the Bristol, Clifton, and West of England Zoological Society,* 9; Bostock and Wombwell's Royal Menagerie, *Illustrated Catalogue,* 9–10.

60. Posters in Fillinham Collection, British Library.

61. Templeton, "The Wild Beasts' Banquet," 365, 361; poster in Fillinham Collection, British Library. In 1844 the Zoological Society's council ordered that its advertisements in "Four Morning Papers" include notices that "the carnivora are fed daily at five o'clock" ("Minutes of Council," March 20, 1844, in VIII, 85).

62. *Exeter Flying-Post,* November 6, 1806; H. Frost, "Biographical Sketch of I. A. Van Amburgh" (New York: Samuel Booth, n.d.), 15; clipping of June 4, 1870 from an unidentified newspaper in the collection of Cutting Books at the Zoological Society of London Library.

63. Miriam Rothschild, *Dear Lord Rothschild: Birds, Butterflies and History* (Philadelphia: Balaban, 1983), 103–104; *Nature* 10 (1874), 470.

64. *Glasgow Evening Post,* September 28, 1836; *Saturday Review,* May 17, 1879, 612.

65. *Carlisle Patriot,* June 22, 1836; clipping from an unidentified newspaper of April 11, 1830 in vol. VII of the Fillinham Collection, British Library.

66. Hone, *Every-Day Book,* II, 323–324; Pierce Egan, *Anecdotes . . . of the Turf, the Chase, the Ring, and the Stage* (London: Knight and Lacey, 1827), 284.

67. Hone, *Every-Day Book,* II, 325–326. Chunee's affliction and its temporary nature was widely and correctly understood, although some dissenters attributed his irritability to the pangs of toothache rather than desire ("The Zoological Gardens—Regent's Park," 323).

68. Hone, *Every-Day Book,* II, 326–334; poster in the Johnson Collection of Printed Ephemera, Bodleian Library; Abraham D. Bartlett, *Wild Animals in Captivity* (London: Chapman and Hall, 1898), 44.

69. Altick, *Shows of London,* 314–316.

70. "The Zoological Gardens—Regent's Park," 322.

71. "Acclimatisation of Animals," 174; Frederica Graham, *Visits to the Zoological Gardens* (London: George Routledge, 1853), n.p.; Francis Buckland, *Curiosities of Natural History, Third Series* (1865; rpt. London: Macmillan, 1900), 109.

72. Mitchell and Sclater, *Guide to the Gardens*, 53; unidentified clipping of 1851 in the Cutting Books of the Zoological Society of London Library; *Nature* 27 (1883), 247.

73. Beddard, *Natural History*, 24–25.

74. C. V. A. Peel, *The Zoological Gardens of Europe: Their History and Chief Features* (London: F. E. Robinson, 1903), 205–206; "In Memory of Consul," pamphlet in the Belle Vue Collection, Chetham's Library.

75. *Nature* 44 (1891), 206.

76. F. T. Buckland, "Death of a Lion," *Field* 16 (1860), 537.

77. "The Zoological Gardens," *Quarterly Review* 98 (1855), 245; Peel, *Zoological Gardens*, 181, 188.

78. Aflalo, *Walk through the Gardens*, 16; "The Zoological Gardens—Regent's Park," 316; Bennett, *Gardens and Menagerie*, I, 224.

79. Mildred Archer, *Natural History Drawings in the India Office Library* (London: HMSO, 1962), 29–31; James Forbes, *Oriental Memoirs* (London: T. Bensley, 1813), II, 171. See Lucille H. Brockway, *Science and Colonial Expansion: The Role of the British Royal Botanical Gardens* (New York: Academic Press, 1979), for an absorbing discussion of this issue as illustrated by exotic plant collections.

80. For example, in 1830 it was reported that "the Consuls at Tripoli and Tangiers are zealously exerting themselves for the Society" (*Report of the Council of the Zoological Society of London*, 1830, 15).

81. Quoted in Bastin, "The First Prospectus," 385.

82. Bennett, *Gardens and Menagerie*, I, v; John Timbs, *Curiosities of London* (London: David Bogue, 1829), 779.

83. *Nature* 43 (1891), 355.

84. *Nature* 25 (1882), 386; Phineas Taylor Barnum, *Selected Letters of P. T. Barnum*, ed. A. H. Saxon (New York: Columbia University Press, 1983), 222; Charles John Cornish, *Wild Animals in Captivity; or, Orpheus at the Zoo* (New York: Macmillan, 1894), 156–158.

85. *The Farewell of the Zoo Pet* (London, 1882); *Jumbo* (London, 1882).

86. These attempts were crippled by both lack of knowledge and lack of space, but some of them were surprisingly successful. C. H. Keeling, who prefers nineteenth-century methods of wild animal husbandry to the modern methods that have superseded them, has paid special attention to the breeding achievements of Victorian zoos (for example, with leopards, marmosets, and striped hyenas) in *Where the Lion Trod*.

87. Beddard, *Natural History*, 81; Richard Aylward Vigors to Lord Derby, January 9, 1831, item 1/179/1 in the Liverpool Record Office.

88. Bristol and Clifton Zoological Society, *Annual Report*, 1864, 6, and *Annual Report*, 1870, 6. The keeper in charge of the tigers was given a bonus of £10 because the mother had reared the cubs rather than killing or abandoning them ("Proceedings of the General Committees," January 5, 1870).

89. W. B. Tegetmeier, "On the Breeding from Wild Animals in Confinement," *Field* 24 (1864), 17.

90. Charles Darwin, *The Variation of Animals and Plants under Domestication* (1868; rpt. New York: D. Appleton, 1892), II, 131–133.

91. Zoological Society of London, "Minutes of Council," July 19, 1837, in V, 189; undated letter from Lord Derby to Sir Robert Heron, in an uncataloged file in the Archives of the Liverpool Record Office.

92. Alfred Tichborne to Frank Buckland, March 25, 1864, item 138M/F801 in the archives of the Devon Record Office; *Farrier and Naturalist* 1 (1828), 86.

93. Bristol and Clifton Zoological Society, "Minutes of the Subcommittee for Zoology," May 28, 1836; C. J. Cornish, "How to See the Zoo," *Cornhill Magazine* 74 (1896), 374; Edward Jesse, *Gleanings in Natural History, Second Series* (London: John Murray, 1834), 124; *List of the Animals in the Gardens of the Zoological Society* (London: Richard Taylor, 1833), 17; Frank Buckland, *Log Book of a Fisherman and Zoologist* (London: Chapman and Hall, 1876), 234. (From this perspective, the park deer of England can be considered at least semidomesticated.)

94. *Visitors' Hand Book to the Liverpool Zoological Gardens*, 10–11.

95. Quoted in Bastin, "The First Prospectus," 385.

96. Zoological Society of London, "Minutes of Council," July 12, 1832, in II, 474; September 4, 1833, in III, 217.

97. "Zoological Gardens," *Quarterly Review* 98 (1855), 239–240; Peter Lund Simmonds, *The Curiosities of Food; or, The Dainties and Delicacies of Different Nations Obtained from the Animal Kingdom* (London, n.p., 1859), 2–3.

98. Peter Brent, *Charles Darwin: A Man of Enlarged Curiosity* (London: Heinemann, 1981), 78; G. H. O. Burgess, *The Eccentric Ark: The Curious World of Frank Buckland* (New York: Horizon Press, 1967), 11; Blunt, *Ark in the Park*, 201; George C. Bompas, *Life of Frank Buckland* (London: Smith, Elder, 1885), 46, 128.

99. Ian Cameron, *The History of the Royal Geographical Society, 1830–1980* (London: Macdonald and James, 1980), 16.

100. Rothschild, *Dear Lord Rothschild*, 102; "New Creatures for Old Countries," *Quarterly Review* 192 (1900), 200, 204–205; Mary Russell, "A Record of the Collection of Foreign Animals Kept by the Duke of Bedford, in Woburn Park, 1892 to July 1905" (1905) copy in the British Museum (Natural History); A Circumnavigator, "The Eland Antelope and Kangaroo," *Field* 8 (1856).

101. See, for example, the printed "Naturalist's Diary" for 1794 in the Stanley collection of the Liverpool Record Office.

102. Letter dated May 30, 1830, in the steward's letter book for 1829–30, record no. DDK 1680, Stanley Collection, Lancashire Record Office.

103. *Catalogue of the Menagerie and Aviary at Knowsley* (Liverpool: Joshua Walmsley, 1851); T. J. Moore, "History of the Living Collections at Knowsley, I," *Transactions of the Biological Society of Liverpool* 5 (c. 1890), 3; Graham, *Visits to the Zoological Gardens*, n.p.; William Pollard, *The Stanleys of Knowsley: A History of that Noble Family* (London: Frederick Warne, 1869), 111.

104. Louis Fraser, *Catalogue of the Knowsley Collections* (Knowsley, 1850), iii; *Catalogue of the Menagerie and Aviary at Knowsley*.

105. Christopher Lever, *The Naturalized Animals of the British Isles* (London: Hutchinson, 1977), 29. Acclimatisation Society of Great Britain and Ornithological Society of London, *Sixth Annual Report*, 1866, 25–27, 29–35, 39; *Second Annual Report*, 1862, 7; *Third Annual Report*, 1863, 10–11.

106. Lever, *Naturalized Animals*, 34–35; Acclimatisation Society, *Sixth Annual Report*, 45–67.

107. R. Templeton to Lord Derby, August 16, 1847, item 1/168/1 in the Stanley Collection, Liverpool Record Office; items 3/1/1–3/1/5 in the same collection.

108. Acclimatisation Society of Victoria, *First Annual Report*, 1862, 8, 39, and *Sixth Annual Report*, 1868, 29–30; South Australian Zoological and Acclimatization Society, *Seventh Annual Report*, 1885, 7; Acclimatisation Society of Victoria, *Third Annual Report*, 1864, 30, and *Fifth Annual Report*, 1867, 25.

109. See Lever, *Naturalized Animals*.

110. *Nature* 36 (1887), 188.

6. The Thrill of the Chase

1. E. H. Bostock, *Menageries, Circuses and Theatres* (New York: Frederick A. Stokes, 1928), 2; Gustave Loisel, *Histoire des ménageries de l'antiquité à nos jours* (Paris: Octave Doin et Fils, 1912), II, 17.

2. Edward Braddon, "Thirty Years of Shikar," *Blackwood's Magazine* 154 (1893), 511.

3. *Sportsman's Journal and Fancier's Guide*, n.s., 1 (November 30, 1878), 3.

4. "Jamrach's," *Saturday Review*, May 17, 1879, 611.

5. Charles John Cornish, *Wild Animals in Captivity; or, Orpheus at the Zoo and Other Papers* (New York: Macmillan, 1894), 183–184; "Jamrach's," 612; Albert E. Gunther, *A Century of Zoology at the British Museum, through the Lives of Two Keepers, 1815–1914* (London: Dawson's of Pall Mall, 1975), 269.

6. Herman Reichenbach, "Carl Hagenbeck's Tierpark and Modern Zoological Gardens," *Journal of the Society for the Bibliography of Natural History* 9 (1980), 576; *Field* 49 (February 10, 1877), n.p.; Edward Tebbutt, "At the Sign of Cross's," *Sandow's Magazine*, n.d., 1–4 (the Merseyside County Record Office owns a typescript copied from the magazine).

7. Carl Hagenbeck, *Beasts and Men; Being Carl Hagenbeck's Experiences for Half a Century among Wild Animals*, abr. and trans. Hugh S. R. Elliot and A. G. Thacker (London: Longmans, Green, 1909), vi.; Loisel, *Histoire*, III, 329.

8. Alfred Russel Wallace, *My Life: A Record of Events and Opinions* (1905; rpt. Farnsborough, Hants.: Gregg International Publishers, 1969), I, 344; Edward Braddon, "Thirty Years of Shikar.—III," *Blackwood's Magazine* 155 (1894), 294; Frank C. Bostock, *The Training of Wild Animals*, ed. Ellen Velvin (New York: Century, 1903), 113; Thomas Williamson, *Oriental Field Sports; Being a Complete, Detailed, and Accurate Description of the Wild Sports of the East . . .* (London: Edward Orme, 1807), I, 176.

9. C. V. A. Peel, *Somaliland; Being an Account of Two Expeditions into the Far Interior . . .* (London: F. E. Robinson, 1900), 159–161.

10. Christopher Hibbert, *Africa Explored: Europeans in the Dark Continent, 1769–1889* (London: Allen Lane, 1982), 97; Peel, *Somaliland*, 256.

11. Samuel White Baker, *Wild Beasts and Their Ways: Reminiscences of Europe, Africa, Asia, and America* (London: Macmillan, 1891), 321; Roland Anthony Oliver, *Sir Harry Johnston and the Scramble for Africa* (London: Chatto and Windus, 1959), 314.

12. Fitzwilliam Thomas Pollok, *Sport in British Burmah, Assam, and the Cassyah and Jyntiah Hills* (London: Chapman and Hall, 1879), I, 72.

13. Peel, *Somaliland*, 6; Oliver, *Sir Harry Johnston*, 315; Williamson, *Oriental Field*

Sports, II, 32; Edward Braddon, "Thirty Years of Shikar.—Conclusion," *Blackwood's Magazine* 156 (1894), 407–409.

14. Richard Altick, *The Shows of London* (Cambridge, Mass.: Harvard University Press, 1978), 235–237; E. F. Greenwood, "A History of Liverpool Natural History Collections," *Journal of the Society for the Bibliography of Natural History* 9 (1980), 375–382; *Magazine of Natural History,* n.s., 1 (1837), 332–333; Ernst Hartert, *Guide to the Hon. Walter Rothschild's Zoological Museum at Tring* (Tring, n.p., 1898), 4, 13–15, 65.

15. See, for example, "Appeal for Skeletons of Wild Specimens of the Larger Carnivora for Our Museums," *Nature* 6 (1872), 435.

16. Ray Desmond, *The India Museum, 1801–1879* (London: HMSO, 1982), 36–38, 49–50.

17. *The Illustrated Exhibitor: A Tribute to the World's Industrial Jubilee* (London: John Cassell, 1851), 537; Francis T. Buckland, *Curiosities of Natural History, Third Series* (London: Macmillan, 1900), 252; *American Exhibition, London, 1887: Catalogue of the Hunting Trophies* (New York and London: J. J. Garnett and B. W. Dinsmore, n.d.), 20, 9.

18. Roualeyn Gordon Cumming, *Five Years of a Hunter's Life in the Far Interior of South Africa; with Notices of the Native Tribes, and Anecdotes of the Chase of the Lion, Elephant, Hippopotamus, Giraffe, Rhinoceros, &c.* (London: John Murray, 1850), I, vii–ix, II, 369.

19. Gordon Cumming, *Five Years of a Hunter's Life,* II, 370; "The Lion-Hunter," *New Monthly Magazine* 89 (1850), 505; "African Sporting," *Blackwood's Magazine* 68 (1850), 233.

20. "Mr. Gordon Cumming's South African Entertainment," *Illustrated London News* 28 (1856), 5; poster in the Johnson Collection of Printed Ephemera, Bodleian Library.

21. "The Lion-Hunter," 504, 508; "Mr. Gordon Cumming's South African Entertainment," 5.

22. "African Sporting," 243; "The Lion-Hunter," 508; "A Sporting Settler in Ceylon," *Blackwood's Magazine* 75 (1854), 228.

23. "Mr. Selous on African Adventure," *Times,* January 15, 1895, 6.

24. Ibid.; "Mr. Selous at Exeter-Hall," *Times,* March 19, 1895, 13; "Mr. Selous at the London Institution," *Times,* January 11, 1898, 6; Ray Allen Billington, *Land of Savagery, Land of Promise: The European Image of the American Frontier in the Nineteenth Century* (New York: W. W. Norton, 1981), 49; J. G. Millais, *Life of Frederick Courteney Selous, D.S.O., Capt. Twenty-Fifth Royal Fusiliers* (New York: Longmans, Green, 1919), 189.

25. Millais, *Life of Selous,* 91; J. G. Dollman, *Catalogue of the Selous Collection of Big Game in the British Museum (Natural History)* (London: British Museum, Natural History, 1921), 1–2; "Mr. Selous on African Adventure," 6; "Mr. Selous at Exeter-Hall," 13.

26. "The Gorillas in the 'Field' Window," *Field* 18 (1861), 100–101; "The Tiger in 'The Field' Window," *Field* 22 (1863), 578. For a somewhat different connection of late nineteenth-century imperialism with the values of traditional English rural life, see Martin Wiener, *English Culture and the Decline of the Industrial Spirit, 1850–1980* (Cambridge: Cambridge University Press, 1981), 56.

27. Rowland Ward, *The Sportsman's Handbook to Collecting, Preserving, and Setting-up Trophies and Specimens, Together with a Guide to the Hunting Grounds of the World* (London: Rowland Ward, 1906), 21; Henry Faulkner, *Elephant Haunts; Being a Sportsman's Narrative of the Search for Doctor Livingstone, with Scenes of Elephant, Buffalo, and Hippopotamus Hunting* (1868; rpt. Blantyre, Malawi: Society of Malawi, 1984), 166; *Handbook of Instructions for Collectors* (London: British Museum, Natural History, 1902), 7–8.

28. "Modern Taxidermy," *Cornhill Magazine* 7 (1863), 120.

29. Ward, *Sportsman's Handbook*, 19; *American Exhibition*, 12; F. C. Selous, *Travel and Adventure in South-East Africa; Being the Narrative of the Last Eleven Years Spent by the Author on the Zambesi and Its Tributaries* (1893; rpt. London: Century Publishing, 1984), 91.

30. Lynn Barber, *The Heyday of Natural History, 1820–1870* (New York: Doubleday, 1980), 276–277; *American Exhibition*, 10; Francis Buckland, "Tiger Cubs Stuffed," *Field* 22 (1863), 412. For an engaging discussion of the symbolic uses of taxidermy on the other side of the Atlantic, see Donna Haraway, "Teddy Bear Patriarchy: Taxidermy in the Garden of Eden, New York City, 1908–1936," *SocialText* 11 (1984–85), 20–64.

31. J. G. Elliott, *Field Sports in India, 1800–1947* (London: Gentry Books, 1973), 22–27; A. C. McMaster, *Vagrancy Acts* (Trimulgherry: Military Prison Press, 1875), 142.

32. McMaster, *Vagrancy Acts*, 64; Edmund Francis Burton, *Reminiscences of Sport in India* (London: W. H. Allen, 1885), 12–13.

33. Hammond Innes, "Introduction," in Selous, *Travel and Adventure in South-East Africa*, vii–viii; "African Sporting," 242; "The Big Game of South Africa," *Blackwood's Magazine* 159 (1896), 121; "Recent Sporting Adventure in the Old World," *Edinburgh Review* 189 (1899), 218.

34. "Recent Sporting Adventure in the Old World," 218; George P. Sanderson, *Thirteen Years among the Wild Beasts of India: Their Haunts and Habits from Personal Observation . . .* (Edinburgh: John Grant, 1907), 3; "Letters from a Competition Wallah, Letter VI:—A Tiger-Party in Nepaul," *Macmillan's Magazine* 9 (1893), 18; Parker Gillmore, *The Hunter's Arcadia* (London: Chapman and Hall, 1886), 1.

35. For a selection of the articles on big game hunting carried by mainstream Victorian periodicals, see the citations throughout this chapter.

36. Michael Brander, *The Perfect Victorian Hero* (Edinburgh: Mainstream, 1982), 46, 108; Reginald Gilbert, "Notes on Man-Eating Tigers," *Journal of the Bombay Natural History Society* 4 (1889), 195–196.

37. Millais, *Life of Selous*, 65.

38. Theodore Roosevelt, "Books on Big Game," *Fortnightly Review* 69 (1898), 604. Most of Roosevelt's collection has been preserved in the Library of Congress; it has been described by Frederick R. Goff in "TR's Big Game Library," *Quarterly Journal of the Library of Congress* 21 (1964), 167–171.

39. For an analysis of Barrow's work as travel writing, see Mary Louise Pratt, "Scratches on the Face of the Country; or, What Mr. Barrow Saw in the Land of the Bushmen," *Critical Inquiry* 12 (1985), 119–143.

40. William Cornwallis Harris, *The Wild Sports of Southern Africa; Being the Narrative of a Hunting Expedition from the Cape of Good Hope . . .*, 5th ed. (London: Henry G. Bohn, 1852), xv; William Cornwallis Harris, *Portraits of the Game and Wild Animals of Southern Africa, Delineated from Life in Their Native Haunts . . . with Sketches of the Field Sports* (London: W. Pickering, 1840), vi.

41. For an appreciative description of aristocratic hunting in Europe, see Erich Hobusch, *Fair Game: A History of Hunting, Shooting and Animal Conservation*, trans. Ruth Michaelis-Jena and Patrick Murray (New York: Arco, 1980), 71–164; for an analysis of the role of the chase in enforcing English social distinctions, see P. B. Munsche, *Gentlemen and Poachers: The English Game Laws, 1671–1831* (Cambridge: Cambridge University Press, 1981).

42. Richard Blome, *The Gentleman's Recreations,* 2nd ed. (London: 1710), title page; Matthew Arnold, *Culture and Anarchy: An Essay in Political and Social Criticism* (1869; rpt. New York: Macmillan, 1883), 77–78.

43. Roosevelt, "Books on Big Game," 608.

44. "A Sporting Settler in Ceylon," 228.

45. Dermot Robert Wyndham Bourke, *Sport in Abyssinia; or, The Mareb and Tackazzee* (London: John Murray, 1876), v; William Charles Baldwin, *African Hunting from Natal to the Zambesi . . . from 1852 to 1860* (New York: Harper and Brothers, 1863), 13.

46. Peel, *Somaliland,* 16; Bourke, *Sport in Abyssinia,* 48; George Francis Scott Elliot, *A Naturalist in Mid-Africa; Being an Account of a Journey to the Mountains of the Moon and Tanganyika* (London: A. D. Innes, 1896), 35.

47. "Mr. Selous on African Adventure," 6; "Boar-Hunting," *New Monthly Magazine* 56 (1839), 213; "My Tiger Watch," *Cornhill Magazine* 48 (1883), 85; Francis Arthur Dickinson, *Lake Victoria to Khartoum with Rifle and Camera* (London: John Lane, 1910), 109.

48. Gordon Cumming, *Five Years of a Hunter's Life,* I, 16–17; William Cornwallis Harris, *Narrative of an Expedition into Southern Africa, during the Years 1836 and 1837 . . .* (Bombay: American Mission Press, 1838), 340.

49. Montagu Gilbert Gerard, "The Tiger, Panther and Bear," in *The Sportsman's Book for India,* ed. F. G. Aflalo (London: Horace Marshall, 1904), 12; Samuel Howitt et al., *Foreign Field Sports, Fisheries, Sporting Anecdotes, &c.* (London: W. Gilling, 1814), 68; Williamson, *Oriental Field Sports,* I, 1; "The Prince of Wales in Nepaul," *Times,* April 3, 1876, 8.

50. F. G. Aflalo, ed., *The Cost of Sport* (London: John Murray, 1899), 50, 59–60; Gerard, "The Tiger, Panther and Bear," 6–8.

51. Alfred J. Bethell, *Notes on South African Hunting and Notes on a Ride to the Victoria Falls of the Zambesi* (York: J. Sampson and London: Whittaker, 1887), 36–40.

52. Henry Anderson Bryden, *Kloof and Karroo: Sport, Legend and Natural History in Cape Colony . . .* (London: Longmans, Green, 1889), 61. This grim testimony was corroborated by that of Baldwin (*African Hunting,* 341) and Gordon Cumming (*Five Years of a Hunter's Life,* II, 369). ·

53. Harris, *Portraits of the Game and Wild Animals,* vi.

54. "A Bear Hunt in the Himalayas," *Temple Bar* 19 (1867), 229; Isabel Savory, *A Sportswoman in India: Personal Adventures and Experiences of Travel in Known and Unknown India* (London: Hutchinson, 1900), 282–283; Edward Braddon, "Thirty Years of Shikar.—III," 289; Williamson, *Oriental Field Sports,* I, 277–278.

55. Selous, *Travel and Adventure in South-East Africa,* 221–238.

56. For example, John C. Willoughby described "a typical hunter's dinner, consisting of soup, fish, uncommonly tough rhino, roast monkey, ibis curry, *blanc-mange* and honey, native beans, and stewed bananas," in *East Africa and Its Big Game: the Narrative of a Sporting Trip from Zanzibar to the Borders of the Masai* (London: Longmans, Green, 1889), 136.

57. Savory, *A Sportswoman in India,* 259; Peel, *Somaliland,* 275.

58. Horace G. Hutchinson, ed., *Big Game Shooting* (London: "Country Life," 1905), II, 238; Gillmore, *Hunter's Arcadia,* 180; Baldwin, *African Hunting,* 239. For general discussions of these attitudes, see Christine Bolt, *Victorian Attitudes to Race* (London: Routledge and Kegan Paul, 1971), and Patrick Brantlinger, "Victorians and Africans: The Genealogy of the Myth of the Dark Continent," *Critical Inquiry* 12 (1985), 166–203.

59. Gillmore, *Hunter's Arcadia,* 180; Selous, *Travel and Adventure in South-East Africa,* 5; Baldwin, *African Hunting,* 177–178.

60. Baker, *Wild Beasts and Their Ways,* 352; Harris, *Portraits of the Game and Wild Animals,* 159.

61. Selous, *Travel and Adventure in South-East Africa,* 300.

62. Gordon Cumming, *Five Years of a Hunter's Life,* II, 321–322; "Indian Sporting," *Times,* December 22, 1845, 3.

63. James Greenwood, *Wild Sports of the World: A Boy's Book of Natural History and Adventure* (London: S. O. Beeton, 1862), 88.

64. For an account of an expedition organized on this principle, see Denis David Lyell, *Hunting Trips in Northern Rhodesia, with Accounts of Sport and Travel in Nyasaland and Portuguese East Africa* (London: Horace Cox, 1910), 24–25.

65. "Bison-Stalking," *Blackwood's Magazine* 141 (1887), 805–806.

66. Gordon Cumming, *Five Years of a Hunter's Life,* II, 100; William Henry Drummond, *The Large Game and Natural History of South and South-East Africa* (Edinburgh: Edmonston and Douglas, 1875), 91.

67. M. G. Watkins, "The Royal Bengal Tiger," *Fraser's Magazine* 95 (1876), 160–161; Selous, *Travel and Adventure in South-East Africa,* 432–434, 37–40.

68. Baldwin, *African Hunting,* 39–40; H. G. C. Swayne, *Seventeen Trips through Somaliland* (London: Rowland Ward, 1895), 162; Edward Lockwood, *Natural History, Sport, and Travel* (London: William H. Allen, 1878), 128.

69. Selous, *Travel and Adventure in South-East Africa,* 173.

70. Harris, *Narrative of an Expedition into Southern Africa,* 193; Savory, *A Sportswoman in India,* 28.

71. Swayne, *Seventeen Trips through Somaliland,* 322.

72. Gordon Cumming, *Five Years of a Hunter's Life,* I, 168; for one example, see Baker, *Wild Beasts and Their Ways,* 327–328.

73. Eva Wyndham Quin, "Sport in Nepal," *Nineteenth Century* 26 (1889), 64; "Bison-Stalking," 804.

74. "The Big Game of South Africa," 125.

75. Gordon Cumming, *Five Years of a Hunter's Life,* I, 102.

76. Savory, *A Sportswoman in India,* 28.

77. Drummond, *Large Game and Natural History of South and South-East Africa,* 216.

78. Williamson, *Oriental Field Sports,* I, 178; "Bear Hunting in India," *Fraser's Magazine* 46 (1852), 383–384.

79. Frederick Vaughan Kirby, *In Haunts of Wild Game: A Hunter-Naturalist's Wanderings from Kahlamba to Libombo* (Edinburgh: William Blackwood, 1896), 52.

80. Greenwood, *Wild Sports of the World,* 393.

81. McMaster, *Vagrancy Acts,* 224; "Review of *The Mammalia of India,*" *Journal of the Bombay Natural History Society* 7 (1892), 399.

82. Baker, *Wild Beasts and Their Ways,* 97; F. G. Aflalo, ed., *The Sportsman's Book for India* (London: Horace Marshall, 1904), 182.

83. Kirby, *In Haunts of Wild Game,* 391; William Rice, *Tiger-Shooting in India; Being an account of Hunting Experiences on Foot in Rajpootana, during the Hot Seasons, from 1850 to 1854* (London: Smith, Elder, 1857), v.

84. Pollok, *Sport in British Burmah,* I, 17; Thomas D'Ewes, *Sporting in Both Hemispheres* (London: G. Routledge, 1858), 90; Howitt et al., *Foreign Field Sports,* 75.

85. *The Book of Sports, British and Foreign* (London: Walter Spiers, 1843), 6; Lyell, *Hunting Trips in Northern Rhodesia,* 42; Savory, *A Sportswoman in India,* 202.

86. Harris, *Portraits of the Game and Wild Animals*, 41; Baldwin, *African Hunting*, 17; quoted in Christopher Hibbert, *Africa Explored*, 217.

87. Harris, *Portraits of the Game and Wild Animals*, 41; Gordon Cumming, *Five Years of a Hunter's Life*, II, 18.

88. Gordon Cumming, *Five Years of a Hunter's Life*, I, 63.

89. Alfred Wilks Drayson, *Sporting Scenes among the Kaffirs of South Africa* (London: G. Routledge, 1858), 53; Baldwin, *African Hunting*, 62.

90. H. A. Leveson, *The Hunting Grounds of the Old World* (London: Saunders, Otley, 1860), 213; "Correspondence Relating to the Preservation of Wild Animals in Africa," *Parliamentary Papers*, 1906, cd. 3189, vol. LXXIX, 38; "Bear Hunting in India," 385.

91. T. Douglas Murray and A. Silva White, *Sir Samuel White Baker: A Memoir* (London: Macmillan, 1895), 391; W. J. Stillman, "A Plea for Wild Animals," *Contemporary Review* 75 (1899), 670; Gillmore, *Hunter's Arcadia*, vi; Samuel White Baker, *The Rifle and the Hound in Ceylon* (Philadelphia: J. Lippincott, 1869), 6; Elliott, *Field Sports in India*, 27.

92. Drummond, *Large Game and Natural History of South and South-East Africa*, 201; F. C. Selous, *A Hunter's Wanderings in Africa* (London: Richard Bentley, 1895), 81.

93. Willoughby P. Lowe, *The Trail That Is Always New* (London: Gurney and Jackson, 1932), 79–80; "The Prince of Wales," *Times*, December 13, 1875, 8; Drayson, *Sporting Scenes amongst the Kaffirs*, 250–251.

94. Frank Oates, *Matabele Land and the Victoria Falls: A Naturalist's Wanderings in the Interior of South Africa . . .*, ed. Charles George Oates (London: C. Kegan Paul, 1881), xv.

95. Savory, *A Sportswoman in India*, 85; Harris, *Portraits of the Game and Wild Animals*, 93.

96. Harris, *Narrative of an Expedition into Southern Africa*, 256; Pollok, *Sport in British Burmah*, I, 18; Faulkner, *Elephant Haunts*, 169.

97. J. D. Inverarity, "The Indian Wild Buffalo," *Journal of the Bombay Natural History Society* 10 (1895–1897), 49; Lowe, *The Trail That Is Always New*, 82.

98. Selous, *Travel and Adventure in South-East Africa*, 129, 364, 450.

99. *American Exhibition*, 9.

100. Rowland Ward, *Records of Big Game . . .* (London: Rowland Ward, 1896), xi; Watkins, "The Royal Bengal Tiger," 147.

101. "Elephant-Catching," *Quarterly Review* 146 (1878), 374; H. Littledale, "Rough Notes of Travel and Sport in Kashmir and Little Thibet," *Journal of the Bombay Natural History Society* 4 (1889), 105.

102. Samuel Daniell and William Daniell, *Sketches Representing the Native Tribes, Animals, and Scenery of Southern Africa* (London: Richard and Arthur Taylor, 1820), 5; Rice, *Tiger-Shooting in India*, 213; Dollman, *Catalogue of the Selous Collection*, 2; Sanderson, *Thirteen Years among the Wild Beasts of India*, 194.

103. Edward Braddon, "Thirty Years of Shikar.—II," *Blackwood's Magazine* 154 (1893), 619.

104. Williamson, *Oriental Field Sports*, II, 156; Watkins, "The Royal Bengal Tiger," 158; Frederick Glyn Wolverton, *Five Months' Sport in Somali Land* (London: Chapman and Hall, 1894), 59.

105. C. F. Gordon Cumming, *Two Happy Years in Ceylon* (Edinburgh: William Blackwood, 1892), II, 74.

106. Harris, *Portraits of the Game and Wild Animals*, v; H. A. Bryden, "Introductory," in Hutchinson, ed., *Big Game Shooting*, II, 6; Burton, *Reminiscences of Sport in India*, 377.

107. Harris, *Narrative of an Expedition into Southern Africa*, 68; "Immense Slaughter of

Game in South Africa," *Field* 20 (1862), 105; Sanderson, *Thirteen Years among the Wild Beasts of India*, 4.

108. Drummond, *Large Game and Natural History*, 23; Reginald Gilbert, "Notes on the Indian Bear (Melursus ursinus)," *Journal of the Bombay Natural History Society* 10 (1895–1897), 689.

109. Rice, *Tiger-Shooting in India*, 103; Baldwin, *African Hunting*, 61.

110. Pollok, *Sport in British Burmah*, I, 24, II, 30; "The Game and Game Laws of India," *Quarterly Review* 167 (1888), 101.

111. P. R. Bairnsfather, "The Deer and Antelope of the Indian Plains," in Aflalo, ed., *Sportsman's Book for India*, 196; W. L., "Extermination of Large Game," *Field* 49 (1877), 423; Roosevelt, "Books on Big Game," 611.

112. Baker, *The Rifle and the Hound*, 13–14; Bryden, "Introductory," in Hutchinson, ed., *Big Game Shooting*, II, 6.

113. F. Vaughan Kirby, *Sport in East Central Africa: Being an Account of Hunting Trips in Portuguese and Other Districts of East Central Africa* (London: Rowland Ward, 1899), ix.

114. F. C. Selous, J. G. Millais, and Abel Chapman, *The Big Game of Africa and Europe* (London: London and Counties Press Association, 1914), 17; Edward Braddon, "Thirty Years of Shikar.—II," 630; Kirby, *In Haunts of Wild Game*, 275.

115. Burton, *An Indian Olio* (London: Spencer Blackett, 1888), 259; J. T. Newall, *Scottish Moors and Indian Jungles: Scenes of Sport in the Lews and India* (London: Hurst and Blackett, 1889), 282.

116. "Correspondence Relating to the Preservation of Wild Animals in Africa," 57; Bryden, *Kloof and Karroo*, 218–219; F. G. Aflalo, "Spare the Wild Game," *Times*, January 16, 1906, 15.

117. Ewart S. Grogan, "Big Game in Africa," *Times*, May 7, 1900, 6; Gillmore, *Hunter's Arcadia*, 248; Ewart S. Grogan, "Big Game in Africa," *Times*, May 1, 1900, 12.

118. *Times*, July 28, 1909, 11.

119. Florence Dixie, "The Horrors of Sport," *Westminster Review* 137 (1892), 49.

120. *Punch* 119 (1900), 129, 147; Kirby, *In Haunts of Wild Game*, x; W. L., "Extermination of Large Game," 423.

121. Kirby, *Sport in East Central Africa*, x.

122. William Swainson, *Animals in Menageries* (London: Longman, Orme, Brown, Green, and Longmans, 1820), 134; for extended discussions of the numerical consequences of the fur trade see Arthur Radclyffe Dugmore, *The Romance of the Beaver; Being the History of the Beaver in the Western Hemisphere* (London: William Heinemann, 1914), ch. 4, and Briton Cooper Busch, *The War against the Seals: A History of the North American Seal Fishery* (Kingston and Montreal: McGill-Queen's University Press, 1985).

123. Piebald, "The Neilgherry Elk," *Oriental Sporting Magazine* 2 (1831), 20; A Lover of the Sport, "A Tour through the Goruckpore Terrai," *Oriental Sporting Magazine* 1 (1835), 334. Despite their similar names, these are different periodicals.

124. John Barrow, *An Account of Travels into the Interior of Southern Africa, in the Years 1797 and 1798* (London: T. Cadell Jun. and W. Davies, 1801, 1804), I, 27; William Burchell, *Travels in the Interior of Southern Africa* (London: Longman, Hurst, Rees, Orme, and Brown, 1822, 1824), I, 259, 311; Harris, *Portraits of the Game and Wild Animals*, 11.

125. Selous, Millais, and Chapman, *Big Game of Africa and Europe*, 3.

126. Elliott, *Field Sports in India*, 23; Edward Lockwood, *Natural History, Sport, and Travel*, 237.

127. Kirby, *In Haunts of Wild Game*, 9.

128. Gordon Cumming, *Five Years of a Hunter's Life*, I, 10.

129. William H. G. Kingston and Charles Rathbone Low, *Great African Travellers from Bruce and Mungo Park to Livingstone and Stanley* (London: George Routledge, 1890), 263; Selous, *Travel and Adventure in South-East Africa*, 100; Bourke, *Sport in Abyssinia*, 13.

130. Bryden, "Introductory," in Hutchinson, ed., *Big Game Shooting*, II, 5.

131. *American Exhibition*, 41; "The Year," *Journal of the Society for the Preservation of the Wild Fauna of the Empire* 2 (1905), 7.

132. Oates, *Matabele Land and the Victoria Falls*, 82; W. H. Flower, *The Horse* (1891), 90–91, quoted in "Correspondence Relating to the Preservation of Wild Animals in Africa," 106; Bryden, *Kloof and Karroo*, 402.

133. Government of Madras Law Department, *The Madras Code*, vol. I, *1862–1918* (Madras: Royal Printing Works, 1958), 161–164; Government of Pakistan Ministry of Law, *The Unrepealed Central Acts*, vol. II, *1872–1881* (Karachi: Government of Pakistan Press, 1951), 381–383; "Correspondence Relating to the Preservation of Wild Animals in Africa," 374.

134. Charles Fitzwilliam Cadiz, *Natal Ordinances, Laws and Proclamations*, vol. I, *1845–1869* (Pietermaritzburg: William Watson, Government Printer, 1891), 569–571; Hercules Tennant, ed., *Statutes of the Cape of Good Hope, 1652–1895* (Cape Town: W. A. Richards, 1895), II, 2419–23; Richard Fitter and Peter Scott, *The Penitent Butchers: The Fauna Preservation Society, 1903–1978* (London: Fauna Preservation Society, 1978), 13, 16.

135. "Convention for the Preservation of Wild Animals, Birds and Fish in Africa, Signed at London, May 19, 1900," *Parliamentary Papers*, 1900, cd. 101, vol. XIV, 8–13.

136. See generally "Correspondence Relating to the Preservation of Wild Animals in Africa," and "Further Correspondence Relating to the Preservation of Wild Animals in Africa," *Parliamentary Papers*, 1909, cd. 4472, vol. LIX.

137. "An Enactment to Provide for the Protection of Wild Animals and Birds," *Perak Government Gazette*, December 20, 1902, 1048–53.

138. "Further Correspondence Relating to the Preservation of Wild Animals in Africa," 57.

139. "The Society for the Preservation of the Wild Fauna of the Empire," *Journal of the Society for the Preservation of the Wild Fauna of the Empire* 1 (1904), 3–4.

140. "Correspondence Relating to the Preservation of Wild Animals in Africa," 359, 369, 145; Millais, *Life of Selous*, 183–184; "Further Correspondence Relating to the Preservation of Wild Animals in Africa," 94–95.

141. Dickinson, *Lake Victoria to Khartoum*, 231; Bryden, "Introductory," in Hutchinson, ed., *Big Game Shooting*, II, 17.

142. "Big Game in India," *Times*, December 14, 1907, 16; H. Walbeeter, "In the Lion's Jaws," *Journal of the Society for the Preservation of the Wild Fauna of the Empire* 1 (1904), 48; Harry H. Johnston, *British Central Africa* (London: Methuen, 1898), 296.

Illustration Credits

page 127:   Courtesy of the Yale Center for British Art. Paul Mellon Collection.

page 151:   Courtesy of Sabin Galleries Limited, London.

page 195:   Courtesy of Harold J. Hanham.

page 208:   Courtesy of the Museum of London.

page 209:   Courtesy of the Yale Center for British Art. Paul Mellon Collection.

page 221:   Courtesy of the Bodleian Library, Oxford. John Johnson Collection (Animals on Show).

page 227:   Courtesy of the Bodleian Library, Oxford. John Johnson Collection (Animals on Show).

page 229:   Courtesy of Chetham's Library.

page 233:   Courtesy of the Harvard Theatre Collection.

page 236:   Courtesy of the Bodleian Library, Oxford. John Johnson Collection (Animals on Show).

page 251:   Courtesy of the Bodleian Library, Oxford. John Johnson Collection (Circuses).

page 265:   Courtesy of the Museum of Comparative Zoology, Harvard University.

page 269:   By permission of the Houghton Library, Harvard University.

Index

339